THE FOUNDATIONS OF INDIAN CULTURE

THE FOUNDATIONS OF INDIAN CULTURE

SRI AUROBINDO

GYAN

Published by

Gyan Publishing House
5, Ansari Road
Daryaganj, New Delhi-110002
Phone: 011-47034999, 9811692060
E-mail: books@gyanbooks.com

Distribution Network
gyanbooks.com
India, USA, Canada, UK, Australia

ISBN: 978-93-7169-132-1 (HB)

First Published, 1940

2nd Impression 2025

Printed at: Gyan Press, Delhi.

THE FOUNDATIONS OF INDIAN CULTURE
Author: SRI AUROBINDO

THE FOUNDATIONS OF INDIAN CULTURE

SRI AUROBINDO

CONTENTS

I

THE ISSUE:
IS INDIA CIVILISED?

IS INDIA CIVILISED?

CHAPTER I

A BOOK under this rather startling title was published some years ago by Sir John Woodroffe, the well-known scholar and writer on Tantric philosophy, in answer to an extravagant *jeu d'esprit* by Mr. William Archer. That well-known dramatic critic leaving his safe natural sphere for fields in which his chief claim to speak was a sublime and confident ignorance, assailed the whole life and culture of India and even lumped together all her greatest achievements, philosophy, religion, poetry, painting, sculpture, Upanishads, Mahabharata, Ramayana, in one wholesale condemnation as a repulsive mass of unspeakable barbarism. It was argued by many at the time that to reply to a critic of this kind was to break a butterfly, or it might be in this instance a bumble-bee upon the wheel. But Sir John Woodroffe insisted that even an attack of this ignorant kind ought not to be neglected; he took it as a particularly useful type in the general kind, first, because it raised the question from the rationalistic and not from the Christian and missionary standpoint and, again, because it betrayed the grosser underlying motives of all such attacks. But his book was important, not so much as an answer to a particular critic, but because it raised with great point and power the whole question of the survival of Indian civilisation and the inevitability of a war of cultures.

The question whether there has been or is a civilisation in India is not any longer debatable; for everyone whose opinion counts recognises the presence of a distinct and a great civilisation unique in its character. Sir John Woodroffe's purpose was to disclose the conflict of European and Asiatic culture and, in greater prominence, the distinct meaning and value of Indian civilisation, the peril it now runs and the calamity its destruction would be to the world. The author held its preservation to be of an immense importance to mankind and he believed it to be in great danger. In the stupendous rush of change which is coming on the human world as a result of the present tornado of upheaval, ancient India's culture, attacked by European modernism, overpowered in the material field, betrayed by the indifference of her children, may perish for ever along with the soul of the nation that holds it in its keeping. The book was an urgent invitation to us to appreciate better this sacred trust and the near peril which besets it and to stand firm and faithful in the hour of the ordeal. It will be useful to state briefly its gist as an introduction to this all-important issue.

A true happiness in this world is the right terrestrial aim of man, and true happiness lies in the finding and maintenance of a natural harmony of spirit, mind and body. A culture is to be valued to the extent to which it has discovered the right key of this harmony and organised its expressive motives and movements. And a civilisation must be judged by the manner in which all its principles, ideas, forms, ways of living work to bring that harmony out, manage its rhythmic play and secure its continuance or the development of its motives. A civilisation in pursuit of this aim may be predominantly material like modern European culture, predominantly mental and intellectual like the old Graeco-Roman or predominantly spiritual like the still persistent culture of India. India's central conception is that of the Eternal, the Spirit here incased in matter, involved and immanent in it and evolving on the material plane by rebirth of the individual up the scale of being till in mental man it enters the world of ideas and realm of conscious morality, *dharma*. This achievement, this victory over unconscious matter develops its lines, enlarges its scope, elevates its levels until the increasing manifestation of the sattwic or spiritual portion of the vehicle of mind enables the individual mental being in man to identify himself with the pure spiritual consciousness beyond Mind. India's social system is built upon this conception; her philosophy formulates it; her religion is an aspiration to the spiritual consciousness and its fruits; her art and literature have the same upward look; her whole dharma or law of being is founded upon it. Progress she admits, but this spiritual progress, not the externally self-unfolding process of an always more and more prosperous and efficient material civilisation. It is her founding of life upon this exalted conception and her urge towards the spiritual and the eternal that constitute the distinct value of her civilisation. And it is her fidelity, with whatever human shortcomings, to this highest ideal that has made her people a nation apart in the human world.

But there are other cultures led by a different conception and even an opposite motive. And by the law of struggle which is the first law of existence in the material universe, varying cultures are bound to come into conflict. A deep-seated urge in Nature compels them to attempt to extend themselves and to destroy, assimilate and replace all disparates or opposites. Conflict is not indeed the last and ideal stage; for that comes when various cultures develop freely, without hatred, misunderstanding or aggression and even with an underlying sense of unity, their separate special motives. But so long as the principle of struggle prevails, one must face the lesser law; it is fatal to disarm in the midmost of the battle. The culture which gives up its living separateness, the civilisation which neglects an active self-defence will be swallowed up and the nation which lived by it will lose its soul and perish. Each nation is a Shakti or power of the evolving spirit in humanity and lives by the principle which it embodies. India is the Bharata Shakti, the living energy of a great spiritual conception, and fidelity to it is the very principle of her existence. For by its virtue alone she has been one of the immortal nations; this alone has been the secret of her amazing persistence and perpetual force of survival and revival.

The principle of struggle has assumed the large historical aspect of an agelong clash and pressure of conflict between Asia and Europe. This clash, this mutual pressure has had its material side, but has borne also its cultural and spiritual aspect. Both materially and spiritually Europe has thrown herself repeatedly upon Asia, Asia too upon Europe, to conquer, assimilate and dominate. There has been a constant alternation, a flowing backward and forward of these two seas of power. All Asia has always had the spiritual tendency in more or less intensity, with more or less clearness; but in this essential matter India is the quintessence of the Asiatic way of being. Europe too in mediaeval times had a culture in which by the dominance of the Christian idea—but Christianity was of Asiatic origin—the spiritual motive took the lead; then there was an essential similarity as well as a certain difference. Still the differentiation of cultural temperament has on the whole been constant. Since some centuries Europe has become material, predatory, aggressive, and has lost the harmony of the inner and outer man which is the true meaning of civilisation and the efficient condition of a true progress. Material comfort, material progress, material efficiency have become the gods of her worship. The modern European civilisation which has invaded Asia and which all violent attacks on Indian ideals represent, is the effective form of this materialistic culture. India, true to her spiritual motive, has never shared in the physical attacks of Asia upon Europe; her method has always been an infiltration of the world with her ideas, such as we today see again in progress. But she has now been physically occupied by Europe and this physical conquest must necessarily be associated with an attempt at cultural conquest; that invasion too has also made some progress. On the other hand English rule has enabled India still to retain her identity and social type; it has awakened her to herself and has meanwhile, until she became conscious of her strength, guarded her against the flood which would otherwise have submerged and broken her civilisation.* It is for her now to recover herself, defend her cultural existence against the alien penetration, preserve her distinct spirit, essential principle and characteristic forms for her own salvation and the total welfare of the human race.

But many questions may arise,—and principally whether such a spirit of defence and attack is the right spirit, whether union, harmony, interchange are not our proper temperament for the coming human advance. Is not a unified world-culture the large way of the future? Can either an exaggeratedly spiritual or an excessively temporal civilisation be the sound condition of human progress or human perfection? A happy or just reconciliation would seem to be a better key to a harmony of Spirit, Mind and Body. And there is the question too whether the forms of Indian culture must be preserved intact as well as the spirit. To these queries the reply of the author is to be found in his law of graduality of the spiritual advance of humanity, its need of advancing through three successive stages.

The first stage is the period of conflict and competition which has been ever dominant in the past and still overshadows the present of mankind. For even when the crudest forms of material conflict are mitigated, the conflict itself still survives and the cultural struggle comes into greater prominence. The second step brings the stage of concert. The third and last is marked by the spirit of sacrifice in which, because all is known

* This contention cannot be accepted in an unqualified sense. English rule has by its general principle of social and religious non-interference prevented any direct and violent touch, any deliberate and purposeful social pressure; but it has undermined and deprived of living strength all the pre-existing centres and instruments of Indian social life and by a sort of unperceived rodent process left it only a rotting shell without expansive power or any better defensive force than the force of inertia.

as the one Self, each gives himself for the good of others. The second stage has hardly at all commenced for most; the third belongs to the indeterminate future. Individuals have reached the highest stage; the perfected Sannyasin, the liberated man, the soul that has become one with the Spirit, knows all being as himself and for him all self-defence and attack are needless. For strife does not belong to the law of his seeing; sacrifice and self-giving are the whole principle of his action. But no people has reached that level, and to follow a law or principle involuntarily or ignorantly or contrary to the truth of one's consciousness is a falsehood and a self-destruction. To allow oneself to be killed, like the lamb attacked by the wolf, brings no growth, farthers no development, assures no spiritual merit. Concert or unity may come in good time, but it must be an underlying unity with a free differentiation, not a swallowing up of one by another or an incongruous and inharmonious mixture. Nor can it come before the world is ready for these greater things. To lay down one's arms in a state of war is to invite destruction and it can serve no compensating spiritual purpose.

Spiritual and temporal have indeed to be perfectly harmonised, for the spirit works through mind and body. But the purely intellectual or heavily material culture of the kind that Europe now favours bears in its heart the seed of death; for the living aim of culture is the realisation on earth of the kingdom of heaven. India, though its urge is towards the Eternal, since that is always the highest, the entirely real, still contains in her own culture and her own philosophy a supreme reconciliation of the eternal and the temporal and she need not seek it from outside. On the same principle the form of the interdependence of mind, body and spirit in a harmonious culture is important as well as the pure spirit; for the form is the rhythm of the spirit. It follows that to break up the form is to injure the spirit's self-expression or at least to put it into grave peril. Change of forms there may and will be, but the novel formation must be a new self-expression or self-creation developed from within; it must be characteristic of the spirit and not servilely borrowed from the embodiments of an alien nature.

Where then does India actually stand in this critical hour of her necessity and how far can she be said to be still firmly seated on her eternal foundations? Already she has been largely affected by European culture and the peril is far from over; on the contrary it will be greater, more insistent, more imperatively violent in the immediate future. Asia is re-arising; but that very fact will intensify and is already intensifying the attempt, natural and legitimate according to the law of competition, of European civilisation to assimilate Asia. For if she is culturally transformed and conquered, then when she again counts in the material order of the world, it will not be with any menace of the invasion of Europe by the Asiatic ideal. It is a cultural quarrel complicated with a political question. Asia must become culturally a province of Europe and form politically one part of a Europeanised if not a European concert; otherwise Europe may become culturally a province of Asia, Asiaticised by the dominant influence of wealthy, enormous, powerful Asiatic peoples in the new world-system. The motive of Mr. Archer's attack is frankly a political motive. This is the burden of all his song that the reconstruction of the world must take place in the forms and follow the canons of a rationalistic and materialistic European civilisation. On his reasoning, India if she adheres to her own civilisation, if she cherishes its spiritual motive, if she clings to its spiritual principle of formation, will stand out as a living denial, a hedious "blot" upon this fair, luminous, rationalistic world. Either she must Europeanise, rationalise, materialise her whole being and deserve liberty by the change or else she must be kept in subjection and administered by her cultural superiors: her people of three hundred million religious savages must be held down firmly, taught and civilised by her noble and enlightened Christian-atheistic European warders and tutors. A grotesque statement in form, but in substance it has in it the root of the matter. As against the attack—not universal, for understanding and appreciation of Indian culture are now more common than before,—India is indeed awaking and defending herself, but not sufficiently and not with the whole-heartedness, the clear sight and the firm resolution which can alone save her from the peril. Today it is close; let her choose,—for the choice is imperatively before her, to live or to perish.

The warning cannot be neglected; recent utterances of European publicists and statesmen, recent books and writings against India and the joyful and enthusiastic welcome they have received from the public of occidental countries, point to the reality of the danger. It arises indeed as a necessity from the present political situation and cultural trend of humanity at this moment of enormous decisive change. It is not necessary to follow the writer in all the viewpoints expressed in his book. I cannot myself accept in full his eulogy of the mediaeval civilisation of Europe. Its interest, the beauty of its artistic motives, its deep and sincere spiritual urgings are marred for me by its large strain of ignorance and obscurantism, its cruel intolerance, its revolting early-Teutonic hardness, brutality, ferocity and coarseness. He seems to me to hit a little too hard at the later European culture. This predominantly economic type of civilisation has been ugly enough in its strain of utilitarian materialism, which we shall err grossly if we imitate; still it has been uplifted by some nobler ideals that have done much for the race. But even these are crude and imperfect in their form and need to be spiritualised in their meaning before they can be wholly admitted by the mind of India. I think too that the author has a little underrated the force of the Indian revival. I do not mean its outward realised strength, for that is very deficient, but the inevitability of its drive, its spiritual and potential force. And he has made a little too much of the servile type of Indian who is capable of mouthing the portentously obsequeous imagination that "European institutions are the standard by which the aspirations of India are set." That, except for the rapidly dwindling class to which this spokesman belongs, has its truth now only in a single field, the political,—a very important exception, I admit, and one which opens the door to a peril of stupendous proportions. But even there a deep change of spirit is foreshadowed although it has not yet taken definite form and has now to meet a fresh invasion of furious Europeanism inspired by the militant crudeness of proletarian Russia. Again he does not attach a sufficient importance to the increasing infiltration of India's spiritual thought into Europe and America, which is her characteristic retort to the European invasion. It is from this point of view that the whole question takes on a different aspect.

Sir John Woodroffe invites us to a vigorous self-defence. But defence by itself in the modern struggle can only end in defeat, and if battle there must be, the only sound strategy is a vigorous aggression based on a strong, living and mobile defence; for by that aggressive force alone can the defence itself be effective. Why are a certain class of Indians still hypnotised in all fields by European culture and why are we all still hypnotised by it in the field of politics? Because they constantly saw all the power, creation, activity on the side of Europe, all the immobility or weakness of a static inefficient defence on the side of India. But wherever the Indian spirit has been able to react, to attack with energy and to create with éclat, the European glamour has begun immediately to lose its hypnotic power. No one now feels the weight of the religious assault from Europe which was very powerful at the outset, because the creative activities of the Hindu revival have made Indian religion a living and evolving, a secure, triumphant and self-assertive power. But the seal was put to this work by two events, the Theosophical movement and the appearance of Swami Vivekananda at Chicago. For these two things showed the spiritual ideas for which India stands, no longer on the defence but aggressive and invading the materialised mentality of the Occident. All India had been vulgarised and anglicised in its aesthetic notions by English education and influence, until the brilliant and sudden dawn of the Bengal school of art cast its rays so far as to be seen in Tokio, London and Paris. That significant cultural event has already effected an aesthetic revolution in the country, not yet by any means complete, but irresistible and sure of the future. The same phenomenon extends to other fields. Even in the province of politics that was the internal sense of the policy of the so-called extremist party in the Swadeshi movement; for it was a movement which attempted to override the previous apparent impossibility of political creation by the Indian spirit upon other than imitative European lines. If it failed for the time being, not by any falsity in its inspiration, but by the strength of a hostile pressure and the weakness still left by a past decadence, if its incipient creations were broken or left languishing and deprived of their original significance, yet it will remain as a finger-post on the roads. The attempt is bound to be renewed as soon as a wider gate is opened under more favourable conditions. Till that attempt comes and succeeds, a serious danger besets the soul of India; for a political Europeanisation would be followed by a social turn of the same kind and bring a cultural and spiritual death in its train. Aggression must be successful and creative if the defence is to be effective.

This great question must be given its larger world-wide import if we are to see it in its true lines. The principle of struggle, conflict and competition still governs and for some time will still govern international relations; for even if war is abolished in the near future by some as yet improbable good fortune of the race, conflict will take other forms. At the same time a certain growing mutual closeness of the life of humanity is the most prominent phenomenon of the day. The war has brought it into violent relief; but the after-war is bringing out all its implications as well as the mass of its difficulties. This is as yet no real concert, still less the beginning of a true unity, but only a compelling physical oneness forced on us by scientific inventions and modern circumstances. But this physical oneness must necessarily bring its mental, cultural and psychological results. At first it will probably accentuate rather than diminish conflict in many directions, enhance political and economic struggles of many kinds and hasten too a cultural struggle. There it may bring about in the end a swallowing unification and a destruction of all other civilisations by one aggressive European type. Whether that type will be bourgeois economical or labour materialistic or a rationalistic intellectualism cannot easily be foreseen, but at present in one form or another this is the actuality that is most in the front. On the other hand, it may lead to a free concert with some underlying oneness. But the ideal of the entire separateness of the peoples each developing its sharply separatist culture with an alien exclusion law for other leading ideas and cultural forms, although it has been for some time abroad and was growing in vigour, is not likely to prevail. For that to happen the whole aim of unification preparing in Nature must fall to pieces, an improbable but not quite impossible catastrophe. Europe dominates the world and it is natural to forecast a westernised world with such petty differences as might be permissible in a European unity given up to the rigorous scientific pursuit of the development and organisation of material life. Across this possibility falls the shadow of India.

Sir John Woodroffe quotes the dictum of Professor Lowes Dickinson that the opposition is not so much between Asia and Europe as between India and the rest of the world. There is a truth behind that dictum; but the cultural opposition of Europe and Asia remains an unabolished factor. Spirituality is not the monopoly of India; however it may hide submerged in intellectualism or hid in other concealing veils, it is a necessary part of human nature. But the difference is between spirituality made the leading motive and the determining power of both the inner and the outer life and spirituality suppressed, allowed only under disguises or brought in as a minor power, its reign denied or put off in favour of the intellect or of a dominant materialistic vitalism. The former way was the type of the ancient wisdom at one time universal in all civilised countries—literally, from China to Peru. But all other nations have fallen away from it and diminished its large pervasiveness or fallen away from it altogether as in Europe. Or they are now, as in Asia, in danger of abandoning it for the invading economic, commercial, industrial, intellectually utilitarian modern type. India alone, with whatever fall or decline of light and vigour, has remained faithful to the heart of the spiritual motive. India alone is still obstinately recalcitrant; for Turkey and China and Japan, say her critics, have outgrown that foolishness, by which it is meant that they have both grown rationalistic and materialistic. India alone as a nation, whatever individuals or a small class may have done, has till now refused to give up her worshipped Godhead or bow her knee to the strong reigning idols of rationalism, commercialism and economism, the successful iron gods of the West. Affected she has been, but not yet overcome. Her surface mind rather than her deeper intelligence has been obliged to admit many Western ideas,—liberty, equality, democracy and others,—and to reconcile them with her Vedantic Truth; but she has not been altogether at ease with them in the Western form and she seeks about already in her thought to give to them an Indian which cannot fail to be a spiritualised turn. The first passion to imitate English ideas and culture has passed; but another more dangerous has recently taken its place, the passion to imitate Continental European culture at large and in particular the crude and vehement turn of revolutionary Russia. On the other hand one sees a growing revival of the ancient Hindu religion and the immense sweep of a spiritual awakening and its significant movements. And out of this ambiguous situation there can be only one out of two issues. Either India will be rationalised and industrialised out of all recognition and she will be no longer India or else she will be the leader in a new world-phase, aid by her example and cultural infiltration the new tendencies of the West and spiritualise the human race. That is the one radical and poignant question at issue. Will the spiritual motive which India represents prevail on Europe and create there new forms congenial to the West, or will European rationalism and commercialism put an end for ever to the Indian type of culture?

Not then, whether India is civilised is the query that should be put, but whether the motive which has shaped her civilisation or the old-European intellectual or the new-European materialistic motive is to lead human culture. Is the harmony of the spirit, mind and body to found itself on the gross law of our physical nature rationalised only or touched at the most by an ineffective spiritual glimmer, or is the dominant power of spirit to take the lead and force the lesser powers of the intellect, mind and body to a more exalted effort after a highest harmony, a victorious ever-developing equipoise? India must defend herself by reshaping her cultural forms to express more powerfully, intimately and perfectly her ancient ideal. Her aggression must lead the waves of the light thus liberated in triumphant self-expanding rounds all over the world which it once possessed or at least enlightened in far-off ages. An appearance of conflict must be admitted for a time, for as long as the attack of an opposite culture continues. But since it will be in effect an assistance to all the best that is emerging from the advanced thought of the Occident, it will culminate in the beginning of a concert on a higher plane and a preparation of oneness.

IS INDIA CIVILISED?

CHAPTER II

THIS question of Indian civilisation, once it has raised this greater issue, shifts from its narrow meaning and disappears into a much larger problem. Does the future of humanity lie in a culture founded solely upon reason and science? Is the progress of human life the effort of a mind, a continuous collective mind constituted by an ever changing sum of transient individuals, that has emerged from the darkness of the inconscient material universe and is stumbling about in it in search of some clear light and some sure support amid its difficulties and problems? And does civilisation consist in man's endeavour to find that light and support in a rationalised knowledge and a rationalised way of life? An ordered knowledge of the powers, forces, possibilities of physical Nature and of the psychology of man as a mental and physical being is then the only true science. An ordered use of that knowledge for a progressive social efficiency and well-being, which will make his brief existence more efficient, more tolerable, more comfortable, happier, better appointed, more luxuriously enriched with the pleasures of the mind, life and body, is the only true art of life. All our philosophy, all our religion,—supposing religion has not been outgrown and rejected,—all our science, thought, art, social structure, law and institution must found itself upon this idea of existence and must serve this one aim and endeavour. This is the formula which European civilisation has accepted and is still labouring to bring into some kind of realisation. It is the formula of an intelligently mechanised civilisation supporting a rational and utilitarian culture.

Or is not the truth of our being rather that of a Soul embodied in Nature which is seeking to know itself, to find itself, to enlarge its consciousness, to arrive at a greater way of existence, to progress in the spirit and grow into the full light of self-knowledge and some divine inner perfection? Are not religion, philosophy, science, thought, art, society, all life even means only of this growth, instruments of the spirit to be used for its service and with this spiritual aim as their dominant or at least their ultimate preoccupation? That is the idea of life and being,—the knowledge of it, as she claims,—for which India stood till yesterday and still strives to stand with all that is most persistent and powerful in her nature. It is the formula of a spiritualised civilisation striving through the perfection but also through an exceeding of mind, life and body towards a high soul-culture.

Whether the future hope of the race lies in a rational and an intelligently mechanised or in a spiritual, intuitive and religious civilisation and culture,—that, then, is the important issue. When the rationalist critic denies that India is or ever has been civilised, when he declares the Upanishads, the Vedanta, Buddhism, Hinduism, ancient Indian art and poetry a mass of barbarism, the vain production of a persistently barbaric mind, what he means is simply that civilisation is synonymous and identical with the cult and practice of the materialistic reason and that anything which falls below or goes above that standard does not deserve the name. A too metaphysical philosophy, a too religious religion,—if not indeed all philosophy and all religion,—any too idealistic and all mystic thought and art and every kind of occult knowledge, all that refines and probes beyond the limited purview of the reason dealing with the physical universe and seems therefore to it bizarre, over-subtle, excessive, unintelligible, all that responds to the sense of the Infinite, all that is obsessed with the idea of the Eternal, and a society which is too much governed by ideas born of these things and not solely by intellectual clarity and the pursuit of a material development and efficiency, are not the products of civilisation, but the offspring of a crudely subtle barbarism. But this thesis obviously proves too much; most of the great past of humanity would fall under its condemnation. Even ancient Greek culture would not escape it; much of the thought and art of modern European civilisation itself would in that case have to be damned as at least semi-barbarous. Evidently, we cannot without falling into exaggeration and absurdity narrow the sense of the word and impoverish the significance of the past strivings of the race. Indian civilisation in the past has been and must be recognised as the fruit of a great culture, quite as much as the Graeco-Roman, the Christian, the Islamic or the later Renaissance civilisation of Europe.

But the essential question remains open; the dispute is only narrowed to its central issue. A more moderate and perspicacious rationalistic critic would admit the past value of India's achievements. He would not condemn Buddhism and Vedanta and all Indian art and philosophy and social ideas as barbarous, but he would still contend that not there lies any future good for the human race. The true line of advance lies through European modernism, the mighty works of Science and the great modern adventure of humanity, its effort well founded not upon speculation and imagination but on ascertained and tangible scientific truth, its laboriously increased riches of sure and firmly tested scientific organisation. An Indian mind faithful to its ideals would contend on the contrary that while reason and science and all other auxiliaries have their place in the human effort, the real truth goes beyond them. The secret of our ultimate perfection is to be discovered deeper within us and things and Nature; it is to be sought centrally in spiritual self-knowledge and self-perfection and in the founding of life on that self-knowledge.

When the issue is so stated, we can at once see that the gulf between East and West, India and Europe is much less profound and unbridgeable now than it was thirty or forty years ago. The basic difference still remains; the life of the West is still chiefly governed by the rationalistic idea and a materialistic preoccupation. But at the summits of thought and steadily penetrating more and more downward through art and poetry and music and general literature an immense change is in progress. A reaching towards deeper things, an increasing return of seekings which had been banished, an urge towards higher experience yet unrealised, an admission of ideas long foreign to the Western mentality can be seen everywhere. Aiding this process and aided by it there has been a certain infiltration of Indian and Eastern thought and influence; even here and there we find some growing recognition of the high value or the superior greatness of the ancient spiritual ideal. This infiltration began at a very early stage of the near contact between the farther Orient and Europe of which the English occupation of India was the most direct occasion. But at first it was a slight and superficial touch, at most an intellectual influence on a few superior minds. An academic interest or an attracted turn of scholars and thinkers towards Vedanta, Sankhya, Buddhism, admiration for the subtlety and largeness of Indian philosophic idealism, the stamp left by the Upanishads and the Gita on great intellects like Schopenhauer and Emerson and on a few lesser thinkers, this was the first narrow inlet of the floods. The impression did not go very far at the best and the little effect it might have produced was counteracted and even effaced for a time by the great flood of scientific materialism which submerged the whole life-view of later nineteenth century Europe.

But now other movements have arisen and laid hold on thought and life with a triumphant success. Philosophy and thought have taken a sharp curve away from rationalistic materialism and its confident absolutisms. On the one hand, as a first consequence of the seeking for a larger thought and vision of the universe, Indian Monism has taken a subtle but powerful hold on many minds, though often in strange disguises. On the other hand new philosophies have been born, not indeed directly spiritual, vitalistic rather and pragmatic, but yet by their greater subjectivity already nearer to Indian ways of thinking. The old limits of scientific interest have begun to break down; various forms of psychical research and novel departures in psychology and even an interest in psychism and occultism, have come into increasing vogue and fasten more and more their hold inspite of the anathemas of orthodox religion and orthodox science. Theosophy with its comprehensive combinations of old and new beliefs and its appeal to ancient spiritual and psychic systems, has everywhere exercised an influence far beyond the circle of its professed adherents. Opposed for a long time with obloquy and ridicule, it has done much to spread the belief in Karma, reincarnation, other planes of existence, the evolution of the embodied soul through intellect and psyche to spirit, ideas which once accepted must change the whole attitude towards life. Even Science itself is constantly arriving at conclusions which only repeat upon the physical plane and in its language truths which ancient India had already affirmed from the standpoint of spiritual knowledge in the tongue of the Veda and Vedanta. Every one of these advances leads directly or in its intrinsic meaning towards a nearer approach between the mind of East and West and to that extent to a likelihood of a better understanding of Indian thought and ideals.

In some directions the change of attitude has gone remarkably far and seems to be constantly increasing. A Christian missionary quoted by Sir John Woodroffe is "amazed to find the extent to which Hindu Pantheism has begun to permeate the religious conceptions of Germany, of America, even of England" and he considers its cumulative effect an imminent "danger" to the next generation. Another writer cited by him goes so far as to attribute all the highest philosophical thought of Europe to the previous thinking of the Brahmins and affirms even that all modern solutions of intellectual problems will be found anticipated in the East. A distinguished French psychologist recently told an Indian visitor that India had already laid down all the large lines and main truths, the broad schema, of a genuine psychology and all that Europe can now do is to fill them in with exact details and scientific verifications. These utterances are the extreme indications of a growing change of which the drift is unmistakable.

Nor is it only in philosophy and the higher thinking that this turn is visible. European art has moved in certain directions far away from its old moorings; it is developing a new eye and opening in its own manner to motives which until now were held in honour only in the East. Eastern art and decoration have begun to be widely appreciated and have exercised a strong if subtle influence. Poetry has for some time commenced to speak uncertainly a new language,—note that the world-wide fame of Tagore would have been unthinkable thirty years ago,—and one often finds the verse even of ordinary writers teeming with thoughts and expressions which could formerly have found few parallels outside Indian, Buddhistic and Sufi poets. And there are some first preliminary signs of a similar phenomenon in general literature. More and more the seekers of new truth are finding their spiritual home in India or owe to her much of their inspiration or at least acknowledge her light and undergo her influence. If this turn continues to accentuate its drive, and there is little chance of a reversion, the spiritual and intellectual gulf between East and West if not filled up, will at least be bridged and the defence of Indian culture and ideals will stand in a stronger position.

But then, it may be said, if there is this certainty of an approximative understanding, what is the need of an aggressive defence of Indian culture or of any defence at all? Indeed, what is the need for the continuance of any distinctive Indian civilisation in the future? East and West will meet from two opposite sides and merge in each other and found in the life of a unified humanity a common world-culture. All previous or existing forms, systems, variations will fuse in this new amalgam and find their fulfilment. But the problem is not so easy, not so harmoniously simple. For, even if we could assume that in a united world-culture there would be no spiritual need and no vital utility for strong distinctive variations, we are still very far from any such oneness. The subjective and spiritual turn of the more advanced modern thought is still confined to a minority and has only very superficially coloured the general intelligence of Europe. Moreover, it is a movement of the thought only; the great life-motives of European civilisation stand as yet where they were. There is a greater pressure of certain idealistic elements in the proposed reshaping of human relations, but they have not shaken off or even loosened the yoke of the immediate materialistic past. It is precisely at this critical moment and in these conditions that the whole human world, India included, is about to be forced into the stress and travail of a swift transformation. The danger is that the pressure of dominant European ideas and motives, the temptations of the political needs of the hour, the velocity of rapid inevitable change will leave no time for the growth of sound thought and spiritual reflection and may strain to bursting-point the old Indian cultural and social system, and shatter this ancient civilisation before India has had time to readjust her mental stand and outlook or to reject, remould or replace the forms that can no longer meet her environmental national necessities, create new characteristic powers and figures and find a firm basis for a swift evolution in the sense of her own spirit and ideals. In that event a rationalised and Westernised India, a brown ape of Europe, might emerge from the chaos, keeping some elements only of her ancient thought to modify, but no longer to shape and govern her total existence. Like other countries she would have passed into the mould of occidental modernism; ancient India would have perished.

Certain minds would see in this contingency no disaster, but rather a most desirable turn and a happy event. It would mean, in their view, that India had given up her spiritual separation and undergone the much needed intellectual and moral change that would at least entitle her to enter into the comity of modern peoples. And since in the new world-comity there would enter an increasing spiritual and subjective element and much perhaps of India's own religious and philosophical thought would be appropriated by its culture, the disappearance of her antique spirit and personal self-expression need be no absolute loss. Ancient India would have passed like ancient Greece, leaving its contribution to a new and more largely progressive life of the race. But the absorption of the Graeco-Roman culture by the later European world, even though many of its elements still survive in a larger and more complex civilisation, was yet attended with serious diminutions. There was a deplorable loss of its high and clear intellectual order, a still more calamitous perdition of the ancient cult of beauty, and even now after so many centuries there has been no true recovery of the lost spirit. A much greater diminution of the world's riches would result from the disappearance of a distinctive Indian civilisation, because the difference between its standpoint and that of European modernism is deeper, its spirit unique and the rich mass and diversity of its thousand lines of inner experience a heritage that still India alone can preserve in its intricate truth and dynamic order.

The tendency of the normal Western mind is to live from below upward and from out inward. A strong foundation is taken in the vital and material nature and higher powers are invoked and admitted only to modify and partially uplift the natural terrestrial life. The inner existence is formed and governed by the external powers. India's constant aim has been on the contrary to find a basis of living in the higher spiritual truth and to live from the inner spirit outwards, to exceed the present way of mind, life and body, to command and dictate to external Nature. As the old Vedic seers put it, "Their divine foundation was above even while they stood below, let its rays be settled deep within us," *nīcīnāḥ sthur upari budhna eṣām, asme antar nihitāḥ ketavaḥ syuḥ*. Now that difference is no unimportant subtlety but of a great and penetrating practical consequence. And we can see how Europe would deal with any spiritual influence by her treatment of Christianity and its inner rule which she never really accepted as the law of her life. It was admitted but only as an ideal and emotional influence and used only to chasten and give some spiritual colouring to the vital vigour of the Teuton and the intellectual clarity and sensuous refinement of the Latins. Any new spiritual development she might accept would be taken in the same way and used to a like limited and superficial purpose, if an insistent living culture were not there in the world to challenge this lesser ideal and insist on the true life of the spirit.

It may well be that both tendencies, the mental and the vital and physical stress of Europe and the spiritual and psychic impulse of India, are needed for the completeness of the human movement. But if the spiritual ideal points the final way to a triumphant harmony of manifested life, then it is all-important for India not to lose hold of the truth, not to give up the highest she knows and barter it away for a perhaps more readily practicable but still lower ideal alien to her true and constant nature. It is important too for humanity that a great collective effort to realise this highest ideal—however imperfect it may have been, into whatever confusion and degeneration it may temporarily have fallen,—should not cease, but continue. Always it can recover its force and enlarge its expression; for the spirit is not bound to temporal forms but ever-new, immortal and infinite.

A new creation of the old Indian *svadharma*, not a transmutation to some law of the Western nature, is our best way to serve and increase the sum of human progress.

There arises the necessity of a defence and a strong, even an aggressive defence; for only an aggressive defence can be effective in the conditions of the modern struggle. But here we find ourselves brought up against an opposite turn of mind and its stark obstructive temper. For there are plenty of Indians now who are for a stubbornly static defence, and whatever aggressiveness they put into it consists in a rather vulgar and unthinking cultural Chauvinism which holds that whatever we have is good for us because it is Indian or even that whatever is in India is best, because it is the creation of the Rishis. As if all the later clumsy and chaotic developments were laid down by those much misused, much misapplied and often very much forged founders of our culture. But the question is whether a static defence is of any effective value. I hold that it is of no value, because it is inconsistent with the truth of things and doomed to failure. It amounts to an attempt to sit stubbornly still while the Shakti of the world is rapidly moving on her way, and not only the Shakti of the world but the Shakti in India also. It is a determination to live only on our past cultural capital, to eke it out, small as it has grown in our wasteful and incompetent hands, to the last anna: but to live on our capital without using it for fresh gains is to end in bankruptcy and pauperism. The past has to be used and spent as mobile and current capital for some larger profit, acquisition and development of the future: but to gain we must release, we must part with something in order to grow and live more richly,—that is the universal law of existence. Otherwise the life within us will stagnate and perish in its immobile torpor. Thus to shrink from enlargement and change is too a false confession of impotence. It is to hold that India's creative capacity in religion and in philosophy came to an end with Shankara, Ramanuja, Madhwa and Chaitanya and in social construction with Raghunandan and Vidyaranya. It is to rest in art and poetry either in a blank and uncreative void or in a vain and lifeless repetition of beautiful but spent forms and motives. It is to cling to social forms that are crumbling and will continue to crumble in spite of our efforts and risk to be crushed in their collapse.

The objection to any large change—for a large and bold change is needed and no peddling will serve our purpose—can be given a plausible turn only if we rest it on the contention that the forms of a culture are the right rhythm of its spirit and in breaking the rhythm we may expel the spirit and dissipate the harmony for ever. Yes, but though the Spirit is eternal in its essence and in the fundamental principles of its harmony immutable, the actual rhythm of its self-expression in form is ever mutable. Immutable in its being and in the powers of its being but richly mutable in life, that is the very nature of the Spirit's manifested existence. And we have to see too whether the actual rhythm of the moment is still a harmony or whether it has not become in the hands of an inferior and ignorant orchestra a discord and no longer expresses rightly or sufficiently the ancient spirit. To recognise defect in the form is not to deny the inherent spirit; it is rather the condition for moving onward to a greater future amplitude, a more perfect realisation, a happier outflow of the Truth we harbour. Whether we shall actually find a greater expression than the past gave us, depends on our own selves, on our capacity of response to the eternal Power and Wisdom and the illumination of the Shakti within us and on our skill in works, the skill that comes by unity with the eternal Spirit we are in the measure of our light labouring to express; *yogaḥ karmasu kauṣalam.*

This from the standpoint of Indian culture, and that must be always for us the first consideration and the intrinsic standpoint. But there is also the standpoint of the pressure of the Time Spirit upon us. For this too is the action of the universal

Shakti and cannot be ignored, held at arm's length or forbidden entrance. Here too the policy of new creation imposes itself as the true and only effective way. Even if to stand still and stiff within our well-defended gates were desirable, it is no longer possible. We can no longer take our single station apart in humanity, isolated like a solitary island in the desert ocean, neither going forth nor allowing to enter in,—if indeed we ever did it. For good or for ill the world is with us; the flood of modern ideas and forces are pouring in and will take no denial. There are two ways of meeting them, either to offer a forlorn and hopeless resistance or to seize and subjugate them. If we offer only an inert or stubborn passive resistance, they will still come in on us, break down our defences where they are weakest, sap them where they are stiffer, and where they can do neither, steal in unknown or ill-apprehended by underground mine and tunnel. Entering unassimilated they will act as disruptive forces, and it will be only partly by outward attack but much more by an inward explosion that this ancient Indian civilisation will be shattered to pieces. Ominous sparks are already beginning to run about which nobody knows how to extinguish, and if we could extinguish them, we should be no better off, for we should yet have to deal with the source from which they are starting. Even the most rigid defenders of the present in the name of the past show in their every word how strongly they have been affected by new ways of thinking. Many if not most are calling passionately, calling inevitably for innovations in certain fields, changes European in spirit and method which once admitted without some radical assimilation and Indianisation, will end by breaking up the whole social structure they think they are defending. That arises from confusion of thought and an incapacity of power. Because we are unable to think and create in certain fields, we are obliged to borrow without assimilation or with only an illusory pretence of assimilation. Because we cannot see the whole sense of what we are doing from a high inner and commanding point of vision, we are busy bringing together disparates without any saving reconciliation. A slow combustion and swift explosion are likely to be the end of our efforts.

Aggressive defence implies a new creation from this inner and commanding vision and while it demands a bringing of what we have to a more expressive force of form, it must allow also an effective assimilation of whatever is useful to our new life and can be made harmonious with our spirit. Battle, shock and struggle themselves are no vain destruction; they are a violent cover for Time's great interchanges. Even the most successful victor receives much from the vanquished and if sometimes he appropriates it, as often it takes him prisoner. The Western attack is not confined to a breaking down of the forms of Eastern culture; there is at the same time a large, subtle and silent appropriation of much that is valuable in the East for the enrichment of Occidental culture. Therefore to bring forward the glories of our past and scatter on Europe and America as much of its treasures as they will receive, will not save us. That liberality will enrich and strengthen our cultural assailants, but for us it will only serve to give a self-confidence which will be useless and even misleading if it is not made a force of will for a greater creation. What we have to do is to front the attack with new and more powerful formations which will not only throw it back, but even, where that is possible and helpful to the race, carry the war into the assailant's country. At the same time we must take by a strong creative assimilation whatever answers to our own needs and responds to the Indian spirit. In certain directions, as yet all too few, we have begun both these movements. In others we have simply created an unintelligent mixture or else have taken and are still taking over rash crude and undigested borrowings. Imitation, a rough and haphazard borrowing of the assailant's engines and methods may be temporarily useful, but by itself it is only another way of submitting to conquest. A stark appropriation is not sufficient; successful assimilation to the Indian spirit is the needed movement. The problem is one of great immediate difficulty and stupendous in its proportions and we have not yet approached it with wisdom and insight. All the more pressing is the need to awaken to the situation and meet it with original thinking and a conscious action wise and powerful in insight and sure in process. A mastering and helpful assimilation of new stuff into an eternal body has always been in the past a peculiar power of the genius of India.

IS INDIA CIVILISED?

CHAPTER III

But there is yet another point of view from which the challenge put in front of us ceases to be an issue crudely and provokingly phrased in a conflict of cultures. Instead it presents itself as a problem with a deep significance; it becomes a thought-provoking suggestion that affects not only ours but all civilisations still in existence.

We can reply on the cultural issue from the view-point of the past and the valuation of different cultures as acquired contributions to the growth of the human race, that Indian civilisation has been the form and expression of a culture as great as any of the historic civilisations of mankind, great in religion, great in philosophy, great in science, great in thought of many kinds, great in literature, art and poetry, great in the organisation of society and politics, great in craft and trade and commerce. There have been dark spots, positive imperfections, heavy shortcomings; what civilisation has been perfect, which has not had its deep stains and cruel abysses? There have been considerable lacunae, many blind alleys, much uncultured or ill-cultured ground; what civilisation has been without its unfilled parts, its negative aspects? But our ancient civilisation can survive the severest comparisons of either ancient or mediaeval times. More high-reaching, subtle, many-sided, curious and profound than the Greek, more noble and humane than the Roman, more large and spiritual than the old Egyptian, more vast and original than any other Asiatic civilisation, more intellectual than the European prior to the eighteenth century, possessing all that these had and more, it was the most powerful, self-possessed, stimulating and wide in influence of all past human cultures.

And if we look from the view-point of the present and the fruitful workings of the progressive Time-Spirit, we can say that even here in spite of our downfall all is not on the debit side. Many of the forms of our civilisation have become inapt and effete and others stand in need of radical change and renovation. But that can be said equally well of European culture; for all its recently acquired progressiveness and habit of more rapid self-adaptation, large parts of it are already rotten and out of date. In spite of all drawbacks and in spite of downfall the spirit of Indian culture, its central ideas, its best ideals have still their message for humanity and not for India alone. And we in India hold that they are capable of developing out of themselves by contact with new need and idea as good and better solutions of the problems before us than those which are offered to us secondhand from Western sources. But besides the comparisons of the past and the needs of the present there is too a view-point of the ideal future. There are the farther goals towards which humanity is moving, and the present is only a crude aspiration towards them and the immediate future we now see in hope and strive to bring about in form, only its crude preparatory stage. There is an unrealised standard of the ideas which to the mind of the moment are figments of Utopia, but may become to a more developed humanity the commonplaces of their daily environment, the familiar things of the present which they have to overpass. How stands Indian civilisation with regard to this yet unrealised future of the race? Are its master ideas and dominant powers guiding lights or helping forces towards it or do they end in themselves with no vistas on the evolutionary potentialities of the earth's coming ages?

The very idea of progress is an illusion to some minds; for

they imagine that the race moves constantly in a circle. Or even their view is that greatness more often than not is to be found in the past and that the line of our movement is a curve of deterioration, a downward lapse. But that is an illusion created when we look too much upon the highlights of the past and forget its shadows or concentrate too much on the dark spaces of the present and ignore its powers of light and its aspects of happier promise. It is created too by a mistaken deduction from the phenomenon of an uneven progress. For Nature effects her evolution through a rhythm of advance and relapse, day and night, waking and sleep; there is a temporary pushing of certain results at the expense of others not less desirable for perfection and to a superficial eye there may seem to be a relapse even in our advance. Progress admittedly does not march on securely in a straight line like a man sure of his familiar way or an army covering an unimpeded terrain or well-mapped unoccupied spaces. Human progress is very much an adventure through the unknown, an unknown full of surprises and baffling obstacles; it stumbles often, it misses its way at many points, it cedes here in order to gain there, it retraces its steps frequently in order to get more widely forward. The present does not always compare favourably with the past; even when it is more advanced in the mass, it may still be inferior in certain directions important to our inner or our outer welfare. But earth does move forward after all, *eppur si muove*. Even in failure there is a preparation for success: our nights carry in them the secret of a greater dawn. This is a frequent experience in our individual progress, but the human collectivity also moves in much the same manner. The question is whither are we marching or what are the true routes and harbours of our voyage.

Western civilisation is proud of its successful modernism. But there is much that it has lost in the eagerness of its gains and much which men of old strove towards that it has not even attempted to accomplish. There is much too that it has wilfully flung aside in impatience or scorn to its own great loss, to the injury of its life, to the imperfection of its culture. An ancient Greek of the time of Pericles or the philosophers suddenly transported in time to this century would be astonished by the immense gains of the intellect and the expansion of the mind, the modern many-sidedness of the reason and inexhaustible habit of inquiry, the power of endless generalisation and precise detail. He would admire without reserve the miraculous growth of science and its giant discoveries, the abundant power, richness and minuteness of its instrumentation, the wonder-working force of its inventive genius. He would be overcome and stupefied rather than surprised and charmed by the enormous stir and pulsation of modern life. But at the same time he would draw back repelled from its unashamed mass of ugliness and vulgarity, its unchastened external utilitarianism, its vitalistic riot and the morbid exaggeration and unsoundness of many of its growths. He would see in it much ill-disguised evidence of the uneliminated survival of the triumphant barbarian. If he recognised its intellectuality and the scrupulous application of thought and scientific reason to the machinery of life, he would miss in it his own later attempt at the clear and noble application of the ideal reason to the inner life of the mind and the soul. He would find that in this civilisation beauty had become an exotic and the shining ideal mind in some fields a debased and exploited slave and in others a neglected stranger.

As for the great spiritual seekers of the past, they would experience in all this huge activity of the intellect and the life the sense of an aching void. A feeling of its illusion and unreality because that which is greatest in man and raises him beyond himself had been neglected, would oppress them at every step. The discovery of the laws of physical Nature would not compensate in their eyes for the comparative decline—for a long time it was the almost absolute cessation—of a greater seeking and finding, the discovery of the freedom of the spirit.

But an unbiassed view will prefer to regard this age of civilisation as an evolutionary stage, an imperfect but important turn of the human advance. It is then possible to see that great gains have been made which are of the utmost value to an ultimate perfection, even if they have been made at a great price. There is not only a greater generalisation of knowledge and the more thorough use of intellectual power and activity in multiple fields. There is not only the advance of Science and its application to the conquest of our environment, an immense apparatus of means, vast utilisations, endless minute conveniences, an irresistible machinery, a tireless exploitation of forces. There is too a certain development of powerful if not high-pitched ideals and there is an attempt, however external and therefore imperfect, to bring them to bear upon the working of human society as a whole. Much has been diminished or lost, but it can be recovered, eventually, if not with ease. Once restored to its true movement, the inner life of man will find that it has gained in materials, in power of plasticity, in a new kind of depth and wideness. And we shall have acquired a salutory habit of many-sided thoroughness and a sincere endeavour to shape the outer collective life into an adequate image of our highest ideals. Temporary diminutions will not count before the greater inner expansion that is likely to succeed this age of external turmoil and outward-looking endeavour.

If on the other hand an ancient Indian of the time of the Upanishads, the Buddhist period or the later classical age were to be set down in modern India and note that larger part of its life which belongs to the age of decline, he would experience a much more depressing sensation, the sense of a national, a cultural debacle, a fall from the highest summits to discouragingly low levels. He might well ask himself what this degenerate posterity had done with the mighty civilisation of the past. He would wonder how with so much to inspire, to elevate, to spur them to yet greater accomplishment and self-exceeding, they could have lapsed into this impotent and inert confusion and, instead of developing the high motives of Indian culture to yet deeper and wider issues, allowed them to overload themselves with ugly accretions, to rust, to rot, almost to perish. He would see his race clinging to forms and shells and rags of the past and missing nine-tenths of its nobler values. He would compare the spiritual light and energy of the heroic ages of the Upanishads and the philosophies with the later inertia or small and broken fragmentarily derivative activity of our philosophic thought. After the intellectual curiosity, the scientific development, the creative literary and artistic greatness, the noble fecundity of the classical age he would be amazed by the extent of a later degeneracy, its mental poverty, immobility, static repetition, the comparative feebleness of the creative intuition, the long sterility of art, the cessation of science. He would deplore a prone descent to ignorance, a failing of the old powerful will and *tapasya,* almost a volitional impotence. In place of the simpler and more spiritually rational order of old times he would find a bewildering chaotic disorganised organisation of things without centre and without any large harmonising idea. He would find not a true social order but a half arrested, half hastening putrescence. In place of the great adaptable civilisation which assimilated with power and was able to return tenfold for what it received, he would meet a helplessness that bore passively or only with a few ineffectual galvanic reactions the forces of the outside world and the stress of adverse circumstance. At one time he would see that there had been even a loss of faith and self-confidence so considerable as to tempt the intellectuals of the nation to scrap the ancient spirit and ideals for an alien and imported culture. He would note indeed the beginning of a change, but might perhaps doubt how deep it had gone or whether it was powerful enough to save, forceful enough to upheave the whole nation from its cherished torpor and weakness, enlightened enough to guide a new and robust creative activity towards the building of new significant forms for the ancient spirit.

Here too a better understanding points to hope rather than to the flat despondency suggested by a too hasty surface glance. This last age of Indian history is an example of the constant local succession of night even to the most long and brilliant day in the evolution of the race. But it was a night filled at first with many and brilliant constellations and even at its thickest and worst it was the darkness of Kalidasa's *viceya-tārakā prabhāta-kalpeva śarvarī,* "night preparing for dawn, with a few just decipherable stars." Even in the decline all was not lost; there were needed developments, there were spiritual and other gains of the greatest importance for the future. And in the worst period of decline and failure the spirit was not dead in India, but only torpid, concealed and shackled; now emerging in answer to a pressure of constant awakening shocks for a strong self-liberation it finds that its sleep was a preparation of new potentialities behind the veil of that slumber. If the high spiritualised mind and stupendous force of spiritual will, *tapasya,* that characterised ancient India were less in evidence, there were new gains of spiritual emotion and sensitiveness to spiritual impulse on the lower planes of consciousness, that had been lacking before. Architecture, literature, painting, sculpture lost the grandeur, power, nobility of old, but evoked other powers and motives full of delicacy, vividness and grace. There was a descent from the heights to the lower levels, but a descent that gathered riches on its way and was needed for the fullness of spiritual discovery and experience. The decline of our past culture may even be regarded as a needed waning and dying of old forms to make way not only for a new, but, if we will that it should be so, a greater and more perfect creation.

For after all it is the will in the being that gives to circumstances their value, and often an unexpected value; the hue of apparent actuality is a misleading indicator. If the will in a race or civilisation is towards death, if it clings to the lassitude of decay and the laissez-faire of the moribund or even in strength insists blindly upon the propensities that lead to destruction or if it cherishes only the powers of dead Time and puts away from it the powers of the future, if it prefers life that was to life that will be, nothing, not even abundant strength and resources and intelligence, not even many calls to live and constantly offered opportunities will save it from an inevitable disintegration or collapse. But if there comes to it a strong faith in itself and a robust will to live, if it is open to the things that shall come, willing to seize on the future and what it offers and strong to compel it where it seems adverse, it can draw from adversity and defeat a force of invincible victory and rise from apparent helplessness and decay in a mighty flame of renovation to the light of a more splendid life. This is what Indian civilisation is now re-arising to do as it has always done in the eternal strength of its spirit.

The greatness of the ideals of the past is a promise of greater ideals for the future. A continual expansion of what stood behind past endeavour and capacity is the one abiding justification of a living culture. But it follows that civilisation and barbarism are words of a quite relative significance. For from the view of the evolutionary future European and Indian civilisations at their best have only been half achievements, infant dawns pointing to the mature sunlight that is to come. Neither Europe nor India nor any race, country or continent of mankind has ever been fully civilised from this point of view; none has grasped the whole secret of a true and perfect human living, none has applied with an entire insight or a perfectly vigilant sincerity even the little they were able to achieve. If we define civilisation as a harmony of spirit, mind and body, where has that harmony been entire or altogether real? Where have there not been glaring deficiencies and painful discords? Where has the whole secret of the harmony been altogether grasped in all its parts or the complete music of life evolved into the triumphant ease of a satisfying, durable and steadily mounting concord? Not only are there everywhere positive, ugly, even "hedious" blots on the life of man, but much that we now accept with equanimity, much in which we take pride, may well be regarded by a future humanity as barbarism or at least as semi-barbarous and immature. The achievements that we regard as ideal, will be condemned as a self-satisfied imperfection blind to its own errors; the ideas that we vaunt as enlightenment will appear as a demi-light or a darkness. Not only will many forms of our life that claim to be ancient or even eternal, as if that could be said of any form of things, fail and disappear; the subjective shapes given to our best principles and ideals will perhaps claim from the future at best an understanding indulgence. There is little that will not have to undergo expansion and mutation, change perhaps beyond recognition or accept to be modified in a new synthesis. In the end the coming ages may look on Europe and Asia of today much as we look on savage tribes or primitive peoples. And this view from the future if we can get it, is undoubtedly the most illuminating and dynamic standpoint from which we can judge our present, but it does not invalidate our comparative appreciation of past and extant cultures.

For this past and present are creating the greater steps of that future and much of it will survive even in that which supplants it. There is behind our imperfect cultural figures a permanent spirit to which we must cling and which will remain permanent even hereafter; there are certain fundamental motives or essential idea-forces which cannot be thrown aside, because they are part of the vital principle of our being and of the aim of Nature in us, our *svadharma*. But these motives, these idea-forces are, whether for nation or for humanity as a whole, few and simple in their essence, and capable of an application always varying and progressive. The rest belongs to the less internal layers of our being and must undergo the changing pressure and satisfy the forward-moving demands of the Time-Spirit. There is this permanent spirit in things and there is this persistent *svadharma* or law of our nature; but there is too a less binding system of laws of successive formulation,—rhythms of the spirit, forms, turns, habits of the nature, and these endure the mutations of the ages, *yugadharma*. The race must obey this double principle of persistence and mutation or bear the penalty of a decay and deterioration that may taint even its living centre.

Certainly we must repel with vigour every disintegrating or injurious attack; but it is much more important to form our own true and independent view of our own past achievement, present position and future possibilities,—what we were, what we are and what we may be. In our past we must distinguish all that was great, essential, elevating, vitalising, illuminating, victorious, effective. And in that again we must distinguish what was close to the permanent, essential spirit and the persistent law of our cultural being and separate from it what was temporary and transiently formulative. For all that was great in the past cannot be preserved as it was or repeated for ever; there are new needs, there are other vistas before us. But we have to distinguish too what was deficient, ill-grasped, imperfectly formulated or only suited to the limiting needs of the age or unfavourable circumstances. For it is quite idle to pretend that all in the past, even at its greatest, was entirely admirable and in its kind the highest consummate achievement of the human mind and spirit. Afterwards we have to make a comparison of this past with our present and to understand the causes of our decline and seek the remedy of our shortcomings and ailments. Our sense of the greatness of our past must not be made a fatally hypnotising lure to inertia; it should be rather an inspiration to renewed and greater achievement. But in our criticism of the present we must not be one-sided or condemn with a foolish impartiality all that we are or have done. Neither flattering or glossing over our downfall nor fouling our nest to win the applause of the stranger, we have to note our actual weakness and its roots, but to fix too our eyes with a still firmer attention on our elements of strength, our abiding potentialities, our dynamic impulses of self-renewal.

A second comparison has to be made between the West and India. In the past of Europe and the past of India we can observe with an unbiassed mind the successes of the West, the gifts it brought to humanity, but also its larger gaps, striking deficiencies, terrible and even "hideous" vices and failures. On the other balance we have to cast ancient and mediaeval India's achievements and failures. Here we shall find that there is little for which we need lower our heads before Europe and much in which we rise well and sometimes immeasurably above her. But we have to scrutinise next the present of the West in its strong success, vitality, conquering insolence. What has been great in it we shall allow, but take deep note too of its defects, stumblings and dangers. And with this dangerous greatness we must compare the present of India, her downfall and its causes, her velleities of revival, her elements that still make for superiority now and in the future. Let us see and take account of all that we must inevitably receive from the West and consider how we can assimilate it to our own spirit and ideals. But let us see too what founts of native power there are in ourselves from which we can draw deeper, more vital and fresher streams of the power of life than from anything the West can offer. For that will help us more than Occidental forms and motives, because it will be more natural to us, more stimulating to our idiosyncracy of nature, more packed with creative suggestions, more easily taken up and completely followed in power of practice.

But far more helpful than any of these necessary comparisons will be the forward look from our past and present towards our own and not any foreign ideal of the future. For it is our evolutionary push towards the future that will give to our past and present their true value and significance. India's nature, her mission, the work that she has to do, her part in the earth's destiny, the peculiar power for which she stands is written there in her past history and is the secret purpose behind her present sufferings and ordeals. A reshaping of the forms of our spirit will have to take place; but it is the spirit itself behind past forms that we have to disengage and preserve and to give to it new and powerful thought-significances, culture values, a new instrumentation, greater figures. And so long as we recognise these essential things and are faithful to their spirit, it will not hurt us to make even the most drastic mental or physical adaptations and the most extreme cultural and social changes. But these changes themselves must be cast in the spirit and mould of India and not in any other, not in the spirit of America or Europe, not in the mould of Japan or Russia. We must recognise the great gulf between what we are and what we may and ought to strive to be. But this we must do not in any spirit of discouragement or denial of ourselves and the truth of our spirit, but in order to measure the advance we have to make. For we have to find its true lines and to find in ourselves the aspiration and inspiration, the fire and the force to conceive them and to execute.

An original truth-seeking thought is needed if we are to take this stand and make this movement, a strong and courageous intuition, an unfailing spiritual and intellectual rectitude. The courage to defend our culture against ignorant Occidental criticism and to maintain it against the gigantic modern pressure comes first but with it there must be the courage to admit not from any European standpoint but from our own outlook the errors of our culture. Apart from all phenomena of decline or deterioration we should recognise without any sophistical denial those things in our creeds of life and social institutions which are in themselves mistaken and some of them indefensible, things weakening to our national life, degrading to our civilisation, dishonouring to our culture. A flagrant example can be found in the treatment of our outcastes. There are those who would excuse it as an unavoidable error in the circumstances of the past; there are others who contend that it was the best possible solution then available. There are still others who would justify it and, with whatever modifications, prolong it as necessary to our social synthesis. The excuse was there, but it is no justification for continuance. The contention is highly disputable. A solution which condemns by segregation one-sixth of the nation to permanent ignominy, continued filth, uncleanliness of the inner and outer life and a brutal animal existence instead of lifting them out of it is no solution but rather an acceptance of weakness and a constant wound to the social body and to its collective spiritual, intellectual, moral and material welfare. A social synthesis which can only live by making a permanent rule of the degradation our fellowmen and countrymen stands condemned and foredoomed to decay and disturbance. The evil effects may be kept under for a long time and work only by the subtler unobserved action of the law of Karma; but once the light of Truth is let in on these dark spots, to perpetuate them is to maintain a seed of disruption and ruin our chances of eventual survival.

Again, we have to look on our cultural ideas and our social forms and see where they have lost their ancient spirit or real significance. Many of them are now a fiction and no longer in accordance with the ideas they assume or with the facts of life. Others even if good in themselves or else beneficent in their own time, are no longer sufficient for our growth. All these must either be transformed or discarded and truer ideas and better formulations must be found in their place. The new turn we must give them will not always be a return upon their old significance. The new dynamic truths we have to discover need not be parked within the limited truth of a past ideal. On our past and present ideals we have to turn the searchlight of the spirit and see whether they have not to be surpassed or enlarged or brought into consonance with new wider ideals. All we do or create must be consistent with the abiding spirit of India, but framed to fit into a greater harmonised rhythm and plastic to the call of a more luminous future. If faith in ourselves and fidelity to the spirit of our culture are the first requisites of a continued and vigorous life, a recognition of greater possibilities is a condition not less indispensable. There cannot be a healthy and victorious survival if we make of the past a fetish instead of an inspiring impulse.

The spirit and ideals of our civilisation need no defence, for in their best parts and in their essence they were of eternal value. India's internal and individual seeking of them was earnest, powerful, effective. But the application in the collective life of society was subjected to serious reserves. Never sufficiently bold and thoroughgoing, it became more and more limited and halting when the life-force declined in her peoples. This defect, this gulf between ideal and collective practice, has pursued all human living and was not peculiar to India; but the dissonance became especially marked with the lapse of time and it put at last on our society a growing stamp of weakness and failure. There was a large effort in the beginning at some kind of synthesis between the inner ideal and the outer life; but a static regulation of society was its latter end. An underlying principle of spiritual idealism, an elusive unity and fixed helpful forms of mutuality remained always there, but also an increasing element of strict bondage and minute division and fissiparous complexity in the social mass. The great Vedantic ideals of freedom, unity and the godhead in man were left to the inner spiritual effort of individuals. The power of expansion and assimilation diminished and when powerful and aggressive forces broke in from outside, Islam, Europe, the later Hindu society was content with an imprisoned and static self-preservation, a mere permission to live. The form of living became more and more narrow and it endured a continually restricted assertion of its ancient spirit.

Duration, survival was achieved, but not in the end a really secure and vital duration, not a great, robust and victorious survival.

And now survival itself has become impossible without expansion. If we are to live at all, we must resume India's great interrupted endeavour; we must take up boldly and execute thoroughly in the individual and in the society, in the spiritual and in the mundane life, in philosophy and religion, in art and literature, in thought, in political and economic and social formulation the full and unlimited sense of her highest spirit and knowledge. And if we do that, we shall find that the best of what comes to us draped in Occidental forms, is already implied in our own ancient wisdom and has there a greater spirit behind it, a profounder truth and self-knowledge and the capacity of a will to nobler and more ideal formations. Only we need to work out thoroughly in life what we have always known in the spirit. There and nowhere else lies the secret of the needed harmony between the essential meaning of our past culture and the environmental requirements of our future.

That view opens out a prospect beyond the battle of cultures which is the immediate dangerous aspect of the meeting of East and West. The Spirit in man has one aim before it in all mankind; but different continents or peoples approach it from different sides, with different formulations and in a different spirit. Not recognising the underlying unity of the ultimate divine motive, they give battle to each other and claim that theirs alone is the way for mankind. The one real and perfect civilisation is the one in which they happen to be born, all the rest must perish or go under. But the real and perfect civilisation yet waits to be discovered; for the life of mankind is still nine-tenths of barbarism to one-tenth of culture. The European mind gives the first place to the principle of growth by struggle; it is by struggle that it arrives at some kind of concert. But this concert is itself hardly more than an organisation for growth by competition, aggression and further battle. It is a peace that is constantly breaking, even within itself, into a fresh strife of principles, ideas, interests, races, classes. It is an organisation precarious at its base and in its centre because it is founded on half-truths that deteriorate into whole falsehoods; but it is still or has been till now vigorous in constant achievement and able to grow powerfully and to devour and assimilate. Indian culture proceeded on the principle of a concert that strove to find its base in a unity and reached out again towards some greater oneness. Its aim was a lasting organisation that would minimise or even eliminate the principle of struggle. But it ended by achieving peace and stable arrangement through exclusion, fragmentation and immobility of status; it drew a magic circle of safety and shut itself up in it for good. In the end it lost its force of aggression, weakened its power of assimilation and decayed within its barriers. A static and limited concert, not always enlarging itself, not plastic becomes in our human state of imperfection a prison or a sleeping-chamber. Concert cannot be anything but imperfect and provisional in its form and can only preserve its vitality and fulfil its ultimate aim if it constantly adapts, expands, progresses. Its lesser unities must widen towards a broader and more comprehensive and above all a more real and spiritual oneness. In the larger statement of our culture and civilisation that we have now to achieve, a greater outward expression of spiritual and psychological oneness, but with a diversity which the mechanical method of Europe does not tolerate, will surely be one leading motive. A concert, a unity with the rest of mankind, in which we shall maintain our spiritual and our outer independence, will be another line of our endeavour. But what now appears as a struggle may well be the first necessary step, before we can formulate that unity of mankind which the West sees only in idea, but cannot achieve because it does not possess its spirit. Therefore Europe labours to establish unity by accommodation of conflicting interests and the force of mechanical institutions;

but so attempted, it will either not be founded at all or will be founded on sand. Meanwhile she wishes to blot out every other culture, as if hers were the only truth or all the truth of life and there were no such thing as truth of the spirit. India, the ancient possessor of the truth of the spirit, must resist that arrogant claim and aggression and affirm her own deeper truths in spite of heavy odds and against all comers. For in its preservation lies the only hope that mankind instead of marching to a new cataclysm and primitive beginning with a constant repetition of the old blind cycles will at last emerge into the light and accomplish the drive forward which will bring the terrestrial evolution to its next step of ascent in the progressive manifestation of the Spirit.

II

A NATIONALISTIC CRITIC ON INDIAN CULTURE

A RATIONALISTIC CRITIC ON INDIAN CULTURE

CHAPTER I

WHEN we try to appreciate a culture, and when that culture is the one in which we have grown up or from which we draw our governing ideals and are likely from overpartiality to minimise its deficiencies or from overfamiliarity to miss aspects or values of it which would strike an unaccustomed eye, it is always useful as well as interesting to know how others see it. It will not move us to change our view-point for theirs; but we can get fresh light from a study of this kind and help our self-introspection. But there are different ways of seeing a foreign civilisation and culture. There is the eye of sympathy and intuition and a close appreciative self-identification: that gives us work like Sister Nivedita's *Web of Indian Life* or Mr. Fielding's book on Burma or Sir John Woodroffe's studies of Tantra. These are attempts to push aside all concealing veils and reveal the soul of a people. It may well be that they do not give us all the hard outward fact, but we are enlightened of something deeper which has its greater reality; we get not the thing as it is in the deficiencies of life, but its ideal meaning. The soul, the essential spirit is one thing, the forms taken in this difficult human actuality are another and are often imperfect or perverted; neither can be neglected if we would have a total vision. Then there is the eye of the discerning and dispassionate critic who tries to see the thing as it is in its intention and actuality, apportion the light and shade, get the balance of merit and defect, success and failure, mark off that which evokes appreciative sympathy from that which calls for critical censure. We may not always agree; the standpoint is different and by its externality, by failure of intuition and self-identification it may miss things that are essential or may not get the whole meaning of that which it praises or condemns: still we profit, we can add to our sense of shade and tone or correct our own previous judgment. Finally there is the eye of the hostile critic, convinced of the inferiority of the culture in question, who gives plainly and honestly without deliberate overcharging what he conceives to be sound reason for his judgment. That too has its use for us; hostile criticism of this kind is good for the soul and the intellect, provided we do not allow ourselves to be afflicted, beaten down or shaken from the upholding centre of our living faith and action. Most things in our human world are imperfect and it is sometimes well to get a strong view of our imperfections. Or, if nothing else, we can at least learn to appreciate opposite standpoints and get at the source of the opposition; wisdom, insight and sympathy grow by such comparisons.

But hostile criticism to be of any sound value must be criticism, not slander and false witness, not vitriol-throwing: it must state the facts without distortion, preserve consistent standards of judgment, observe a certain effort at justice, sanity, measure. Mr. William Archer's well-known book on India, which on account of its very demerits I have taken as the type of the characteristic Western or anti-Indian regard on our culture, was certainly not of this character. It is not only that here we have a wholesale and unsparing condemnation, a picture all shade and no light: that is a recommendation, for Mr. Archer's professed object was to challenge the enthusiastic canonisation of Indian culture by its admirers in the character of a devil's advocate whose business is to find out and state in its strongest terms everything that can be said against the claim. And for us too it is useful to have before us an attack which covers the whole field so that we may see in one comprehensive view the entire enemy case against our culture. But there are three vitiating elements in his statement. First, it had an ulterior, a political object; it started with the underlying idea that India must be proved altogether barbarous in order to destroy or damage her case for self-government. That sort of extraneous motive at once puts his whole pleading out of court; for it means a constant deliberate distortion in order to serve a material interest, foreign altogether to the disinterested intellectual objects of cultural comparison and criticism.

In fact this book is not criticism; it is literary or rather journalistic pugilism. There too it is of a peculiar kind; it is a furious sparring at a lay figure of India which is knocked down at pleasure through a long and exuberant dance of misstatement and exaggeration in the hope of convincing an ignorant audience that the performer has prostrated a living adversary. Sanity, justice, measure are things altogether at a discount: a show-off of the appearance of staggering and irresistible blows is the object held in view, and for that anything comes in handy,—the facts are altogether misstated or clumsily caricatured, the most extraordinary and unfounded suggestions advanced with an air of obviousness, the most illogical inconsistencies permitted if an apparent point can be scored. All this is not the occasional freak of a well-informed critic suffering from a fit of mental biliousness and impelled to work it off by an extravagant intellectual exercise, an irresponsible fantasia or a hostile war-dance around a subject with which he is not in sympathy. That is a kind of extravagance, which is sometimes permissible and may be interesting and amusing. It is a sweet and pleasant thing, cries the Roman poet, to play the fool in place and right season, *dulce est desipere in loco*. But Mr. Archer's constant departures into irrational extravagance are not by any means *in loco*. We discover very soon,—in addition to his illegitimate motive and his deliberate unfairness this is a third and worst cardinal defect,—that for the most part he knew absolutely nothing about the things on which he was passing his confident damnatory judgments. What he has done is to collect together in his mind all the unfavourable comments he had read about India, eke them out with casual impressions of his own and advance this unwholesome and unsubstantial compound as his original production, although his one genuine and native contribution is the cheery cocksureness of his secondhand opinions. The book is a journalistic fake, not an honest critical production.

The writer was evidently no authority on metaphysics, which he despises as a misuse of the human mind; yet he lays down the law at length about the values of Indian philosophy. He was a rationalist to whom religion is an error, a psychological disease, a sin against reason; yet he adjudges here between the comparative claims of religions, assigning a *proxime accessit* to Christianity, mainly, it seems, because Christians do not seriously believe in their own religion,—let not the reader laugh, the book advances quite seriously this amazing reason,—and bestowing the wooden spoon on Hinduism. He admits his incompetence to speak about music, yet that has not prevented him from relegating Indian music to a position of hopeless inferiority. His judgment on art and architecture is of the narrowest kind; but he is generously liberal of his decisive depreciations. In drama and literature one would expect from him better things; but the astonishing superficiality of his standards and his arguments here leaves one wondering how in the world he got his reputation as a dramatic and literary critic: one concludes that either he must have used a very different method in dealing with European literature or else it is very easy to get a reputation of this kind in England. An ill-informed misrepresentation of facts, a light-hearted temerity of judgment on things he has not cared to study constitute this critic's title to write on Indian culture and dismiss it authoritatively as a mass of barbarism.

It is not then for a well-informed outside view or even an instructive adverse criticism of Indian civilisation that I have turned to Mr. William Archer. In the end it is only those who possess a culture who can judge the intrinsic value of its productions, because they alone can enter entirely into its spirit. To the foreign critic we can only go for help in forming a comparative judgment,—which too is indispensable. But if for any reason we had to depend on a foreign judgment for the definitive view of these things, it is evident that in each field it is to men who can speak with some authority that we must turn. It matters very little to me what Mr. Archer or Dr. Gough or Sir John Woodroffe's unnamed English professor may say about Indian philosophy; it is enough for me to know what Emerson or Schopenhauer or Nietzsche, three entirely different minds of the greatest power in this field, or what thinkers like Cousin and Schlegel have to say about it or to mark the increasing influence of some of its conceptions, the great parallel lines of thought in earlier European thinking and the confirmations of ancient Indian metaphysics and psychology which are the results of the most modern research and inquiry. For religion I shall not go to Mr. Harold Begbie or any European atheist or rationalist for a judgment on our spirituality, but see rather what are the impressions of open-minded men of religious feeling and experience who can alone be judges, a spiritual and religious thinker such as Tolstoi, for instance. Or I may study even, allowing for an inevitable bias, what the more cultured Christian missionary has to say about a religion which he can no longer dismiss as a barbarous superstition. In art I shall not turn to the opinion of the average European who knows nothing of the spirit, meaning or technique of Indian architecture, painting and sculpture. For the first I shall consult some recognised authority like Ferguson; for the others if critics like Mr. Havell are to be dismissed as partisans, I can at least learn something from Okakura or Mr. Laurence Binyon. In literature I shall be at a loss, for I cannot remember that any Western writer of genius or high reputation as a critic has had any first-hand knowledge of Sanskrit literature or of the Prakritic tongues, and a judgment founded on translations can only deal with the substance,—and even that in most translations of Indian work is only the dead substance with the whole breath of life gone out of it. Still even here Goethe's well-known epigram on the Shakuntala will be enough by itself to show me that all Indian writing is not of a barbarous inferiority to European creation. And perhaps we may find a scholar here and there with some literary taste and judgment, not a too common combination, who will be of help to us. This sort of excursion will certainly not give us an entirely reliable scheme of values, but at any rate we shall be safer than in a resort to the great lowland clan of Goughs, Archers and Begbies.

If I still find it necessary or useful to notice these lucubrations, it is for quite another purpose. Even for that purpose all that Mr. Archer writes is not of utility; much of it is so irrational, inconsequent or unscrupulous in suggestion that one can only note and pass on. When for instance he assures his readers that Indian philosophers think that sitting cross-legged and contemplating one's own navel is the best way of ascertaining the truths of the universe and that their real object is an indolent immobility and to live upon the alms of the faithful, his object in thus describing one of the postures of abstracted meditation is to stamp the meditation itself in the eyes of ignorant English readers with the character of a bovine absurdity and a selfish laziness; that is an instance of his unscrupulousness which helps us to observe the kinks of his own rationalistic mind, but is useful for nothing else. When he denies that there is any real morality in Hinduism or affirms that it has never claimed moral teaching as one of its functions, statements which are the exact contrary of the facts, when he goes so far as to say that Hinduism is the character of the people and it indicates a melancholy proclivity towards *whatever* is monstrous and unwholesome, one can only conclude that truth-speaking is not one of the ethical virtues which Mr. William Archer thought it necessary to practise or at least that it need be no part of a rationalist's criticism of religion.

But no, after all Mr. Archer does throw a grudging tribute on the altar of truth; for he admits in the same breath that Hinduism talks much of righteousness and allows that there are in the Hindu writings many admirable ethical doctrines. But that only proves that Hindu philosophy is illogical,—the morality is there indeed, but it ought not to be; its presence does not suit Mr. Archer's thesis. Admire the logic, the rational consistency of this champion of rationalism! Mark that at the same time one of his objections to the Ramayana, admitted to be one of the Bibles of the Hindu people, is that its ideal characters, Rama and Sita, the effective patterns of the highest Indian manhood and womanhood, are much too virtuous for his taste. Rama is too saintly for human nature. I do not know in fact that Rama is more saintly than Christ or St. Francis, yet I had always thought they were within the pale of human nature; but perhaps this critic will reply that, if not beyond that pale, their excessive virtues are at least like the daily practice of the Hindu cult,—shall we say for example, scrupulous physical purity and personal cleanliness and the daily turning of the mind to God in worship and meditation,—"sufficient to place them beyond the pale of civilisation." For he tells us that Sita, the type of conjugal fidelity and chastity, is so excessive in her virtue "as to verge on immorality." Meaningless smart extravagance has reached its highest point when it can thus verge on the idiotic. I am as sorry to use the epithet as Mr. Archer to harp on Indian "barbarism," but there is really no help for it; "it expresses the essence of the situation." If all were of this character,—there is too much of it and it is deplorable,—a contemptuous silence would be the only possible reply. But fortunately Apollo does not always stretch his bow thus to the breaking-point; all Mr. Archer's shafts are not of this wildgoose flight. There is much in his writing that expresses crudely, but still with sufficient accuracy the feeling of recoil of the average Occidental mind at its first view of the unique characteristics of Indian culture and that is a thing worth noting and sounding; it is necessary to understand it and find out its value.

This is the utility I wish to seize on; for it is an utility and even more. It is through the average mind that we get best at the bedrock of the psychological differences which divide from each other great blocks of our common humanity. The cultured mind tends to diminish the force of these prejudices or at least even in difference and opposition to develop points of similarity or of contact. In the average mentality we have a better chance of getting them in their crude strength and can appreciate their full force and bearing. Mr. Archer helps us here admirably. Not that we have not to clear away much rubbish to get at what we want. I should have preferred to deal with a manual of misunderstanding which had the same thoroughness of scope, but expressed itself with a more straightforward simplicity and less of vicious smartness and of superfluous ill-will; but none such is available. Let us take Mr. Archer then and dissect some of his prejudices to get at their inner psychology. We shall perhaps find that through all this unpleasant crudity we can arrive at the essence of a historic misunderstanding of continents. An exact understanding of it may even help us towards an approach to some kind of reconciliation.

A RATIONALISTIC CRITIC ON INDIAN CULTURE

CHAPTER II

It is best to start with a precise idea of the species of critic from whom we are going to draw our estimate of oppositions. What we have before us are the ideas of an average and typical Occidental mind on Indian culture, a man of sufficient education and wide reading, but no genius or exceptional capacity, rather an ordinary successful talent, no flexibility or broad sympathy of mind, but pronounced and rigid opinions which are backed up and given an appearance of weight by the habit of using to good effect a varied though not always sound information. This is in fact the mind and standpoint of an average Englishman of some ability formed in the habit of journalism. That is precisely the kind of thing we want in order to seize the nature of the antagonism which led Mr. Rudyard Kipling,—himself a super-journalist and "magnified non-natural" average man, the average lifted up, without ceasing to be itself, by the glare of a kind of crude and barbaric genius,—to affirm the eternal incompatibility of the East and the West. Let us see what strikes such a mentality as unique and abhorrent in the Indian mind and its culture: if we can put aside all sensitiveness of personal feeling and look dispassionately at this phenomenon, we shall find it an interesting and illuminative study.

A certain objection may be advanced against taking a rationalistic critic with a political bias, a mind belonging at best to the today which is already becoming yesterday, in this widely representative capacity. The misunderstanding of continents has been the result of a long-enduring and historic difference, and this book gives us only one phase of it which is of a very modern character. But it is in modern times, in an age of scientific and rationalistic enlightenment, that the difference has become most pronounced, the misunderstanding most aggressive and the sense of cultural incompatibility most conscious and self-revealing. An ancient Greek, full of disinterested intellectual curiosity and a flexible aesthetic appreciation, was in spite of his feeling of racial and cultural superiority to the barbarian much nearer to the Indian mind than a typical modern European. Not only could a Pythagoras or a philosopher of the Neo-platonist school, an Alexander or a Menander understand with a more ready sympathy the root ideas of Asiatic culture, but an average man of ability, a Megasthenes for instance, could be trusted to see and understand, though not inwardly and perfectly, yet in a sufficient measure. The mediaeval European, for all his militant Christianity and his prejudice against the infidel and paynim, yet resembled his opponent in many characteristic ways of seeing and feeling to an extent which is no longer possible to an average European mind, unless it has been imbued with the new ideas which are once more lessening the gulf between the continents. It was the rationalising of the Occidental mind, the rationalising even of its religious ideas and sentiments, which made the gulf so wide as to appear unbridgeable. Our critic represents this increased hostility in an extreme form, a shape given to it by the unthinking freethinker, the man who has not thought out originally these difficult problems, but imbibed his views from his cultural environment and the intellectual atmosphere of the period. He will exaggerate enormously the points of opposition, but by his very exaggeration he will make them more strikingly clear and intelligible. He will make up for his want of correct information and intelligent study by a certain sureness of instinct in his attack upon things alien to his own mental outlook.

It is this sureness of instinct which has led him to direct the real gravamen of his attack against Indian philosophy and religion. The culture of a people may be roughly described as the expression of a consciousness of life which formulates itself in three aspects. There is a side of thought, of ideal, of upward will and the soul's aspiration; there is a side of creative self-expression and appreciative aesthesis, intelligence and imagination; and there is a side of practical and outward formulation. A people's philosophy and higher thinking give us its mind's purest, largest and most general formulation of its consciousness of life and its dynamic view of existence. Its religion formulates the most intense form of its upward will and the soul's aspirations towards the fulfilment of its highest ideal and impulse. Its art, poetry, literature provide for us the creative expression and impression of its intuition, imagination, vital turn and creative intelligence. Its society and politics provide in their forms an outward frame in which the more external life works out what it can of its inspiring ideal and of its special character and nature under the difficulties of the environment. We can see how much it has taken of the crude material of living, what it has done with it, how it has shaped as much of it as possible into some reflection of its guiding consciousness and deeper spirit. None of them express the whole secret spirit behind, but they derive from it their main ideas and their cultural character. Together they make up its soul, mind and body. In Indian civilisation philosophy and religion, philosophy made dynamic by religion, religion enlightened by philosophy have led, the rest follow as best they can. This is indeed its first distinctive character, which it shares with the more developed Asiatic peoples, but has carried to an extraordinary degree of thoroughgoing pervasiveness. When it is spoken of as a Brahminical civilisation, that is the real significance of the phrase. The phrase cannot truly imply any domination of sacerdotalism, though in some lower aspects of the culture the sacerdotal mind has been only too prominent; for the priest as such has had no hand in shaping the great lines of the culture. But it is true that its main motives have been shaped by philosophic thinkers and religious minds, not by any means all of them of Brahmin birth. The fact that a class has been developed whose business was to preserve the spiritual traditions, knowledge and sacred law of the race,—for this and not a mere priest trade was the proper occupation of the Brahmin,—and that this class could for thousands of years maintain in the greatest part, but not monopolise, the keeping of the national mind and conscience, and the direction of social principles, forms and manners, is only a characteristic indication. The fact behind is that Indian culture has been from the beginning and has remained a spiritual, an inward-looking religio-philosophical culture. Everything else in it has derived from that one central and original peculiarity or has been in some way dependent on it or subordinate to it; even external life has been subjected to the inward look of the spirit.

Our critic has felt the importance of this central point and directed upon it his most unsparing attack; in other quarters he may make concessions, allow attenuations, here he will make none. All here must be bad and harmful, or if not deleterious, then ineffective, by the very nature of the central ideas and motives, for any real good. This is a significant attitude. Of course there is the polemical motive. That which is claimed for the Indian mind and its civilisation is a high spirituality, high on all the summits of thought and religion, permeating art and literature and religious practice and social ideas and affecting even the ordinary man's attitude to life. If the claim is conceded, as it is conceded by all sympathetic and disinterested inquirers even when they do not accept the Indian view of life, then Indian culture stands, its civilisation has a right to live. More, it has a right even to throw a challenge to rationalistic modernism and say, "Attain first my level of spirituality before you claim to destroy and supersede me or call on me to modernise myself entirely in your sense. No matter if I have myself latterly fallen from my own heights or if my present forms cannot meet all the requirements of the future mind of humanity; I can reascend, the power is there in me. I may even be able to develop a spiritual modernism which will help you in your effort to exceed yourself and arrive at a larger harmony than any you have reached in the past or can dream of in the present." The hostile critic feels that he must deny this claim at its roots. He tries to prove Indian philosophy to be unspiritual and Indian religion to be an irrational animistic cult of monstrosity. In this effort which is an attempt to stand Truth on her head and force her to see facts upside down, he lands himself in a paradoxical absurdity and inconsistency which destroy his case by sheer overstatement. Still there arise even from this farrago two quite genuine issues. First, we can ask whether the spiritual and religio-philosophical view of life and the government of civilisation by its ideas and motives or the rationalistic and external view of life and the satisfaction of the vital being governed by the intellectual and practical reason give the best lead to mankind. And granting the value and power of a spiritual conception of life, we can ask whether the expression given to it by Indian culture is the best possible and the most helpful to the growth of humanity towards its highest level. These are the real questions at issue between this Asiatic or ancient mind and the European or modern intelligence.

The typical Occidental mind, which prolongs still the mentality of the eighteenth and nineteenth centuries, has been almost entirely fashioned by the second view; it has grown into the mould of the vitalistic rational idea. Its attitude to life has never been governed by a philosophic conception of existence except during a brief period of Graeco-Roman culture and then only in a small class of thinking and highly cultivated minds; always it is dominated by environmental necessity and the practical reason. It has left behind it too the ages in which spiritual and religious conceptions which invaded it from the East, strove to impose themselves on the vitalistic and rational tendency; it has largely rejected them or thrust them into a corner. Its religion is the religion of life, a religion of earth and of terrestrial humanity, an ideal of intellectual growth, vital efficiency, physical health and enjoyment, a rational social order. This mind confronted by Indian culture is at once repelled, first by its unfamiliarity and strangeness, then by a sense of irrational abnormality and a total difference and often a diametrical opposition of standpoints and finally by an abundance and plethora of unintelligible forms. These forms appear to its eye to teem with the supranatural and therefore, as it thinks, with the false. Even the unnatural is there, a persistent departure from the common norm, from right method and sound device, a frame of things in which everything, to use Mr. Chesterton's expression, is of the wrong shape. The old orthodox Christian point of view might regard this culture as a thing of hell, an abnormal creation of demons; the modern orthodox rationalistic standpoint looks at it as a nightmare not only irrational, but antirational, a monstrosity, an out-of-date anomaly, at best a coloured fantasia of the oriental past. That is no doubt an extreme attitude,—it is Mr. Archer's,—but incomprehension and distaste are the rule. One continually finds traces of these feelings even in minds which try to understand and sympathise; but to the average Occidental content with his first raw natural impressions all is a repellent confusion. Indian philosophy is an incomprehensible, subtly unsubstantial cloud-weaving; Indian religion meets his eye as a mixture of absurd asceticism and an absurder gross, immoral and superstitious polytheism. He sees in Indian art a riot of crudely distorted or conventional forms and an impossible seeking after suggestions of the infinite—whereas all true art should be a beautiful and rational reproduction or fine imaginative representation of the natural and finite. He condemns in Indian society an anachronistic and semibarbaric survival of old-world and mediaeval ideas and institutions. This view, which has recently undergone some modification and is less loud and confident in expression, but still subsists, is the whole foundation of Mr. Archer's philippic.

This is evident from the nature of all the objections he brings against Indian civilisation. When you strip them of their journalistic rhetoric, you find that they amount simply to this natural antagonism of the rationalised vital and practical man against a culture which subordinates reason to a suprarational spirituality and life and action to a feeling after something which is greater than life and action. Philosophy and religion are the soul of Indian culture, inseparable from each other and interpenetrative. The whole objective of Indian philosophy, its entire *raison d'être,* is knowledge of the spirit, the experience of it and the right way to a spiritual existence; its single aim coincides with the highest significance of religion. Indian religion draws all its characteristic value from the spiritual philosophy which illumines its supreme aspiration and colours even most of what is drawn from an inferior range of religious experience. But what are Mr. Archer's objections, first to Indian philosophy? Well, his first objection simply comes to this that it is too philosophical. His second accusation is that even as that worthless thing, metaphysical philosophy, it is too metaphysical. His third charge, the most positive and plausible, is that it enervates and kills the personality and the will-power by false notions of pessimism, ascetiscism, Karma and reincarnation. If we take his criticism under each of these heads, we shall see that it is really not a dispassionate intellectual criticism, but the exaggerated expression of a mental dislike and a fundamental difference of temperament and standpoint.

Mr. Archer cannot deny,—the denial would go beyond even his unequalled capacity for affirming absurdities,—that the Indian mind has displayed an unparalleled activity and fruitfulness in philosophical thinking. He cannot deny that a familiarity with metaphysical conceptions and the capacity of discussing with some subtlety a metaphysical problem is much more wide-spread in India than in any other country. Even an ordinary Indian intellect can understand and deal with questions of this kind where an Occidental mind of corresponding culture and attainments would be as hopelessly out of its depth as is Mr. Archer in these pages. But he denies that this familiarity and this subtlety are any proof of great mental capacity—"necessarily," he adds, I suppose in order to escape the charge of having suggested that Plato, Spinoza or Berkeley did not show a great mental capacity. Perhaps it is not "necessarily" such a proof; but it does show in one great order of questions, in one large and especially difficult range of the mind's powers and interests a remarkable and unique general development. The European journalist's capacity for discussing with some show of acumen questions of economy and politics or, for that matter, art, literature and drama, is not "necessarily" proof of a great mental capacity; but it does show a great development of the European mind in general, a wide-spread information and normal capacity in these fields of its action. The crudity of his opinions and his treatment of his subjects may sometimes seem a little "barbaric" to an outsider; but the thing itself is a proof that there is a culture, a civilisation, a great intellectual and civic achievement and a sufficient wide-spread interest in the achievement. Mr. Archer has to avoid a similar conclusion in another subtler and more difficult range about India. He does it by denying that philosophy is of any value; this activity of the Indian mind is for him only an unequalled diligence in knowing the unknowable and thinking about the unthinkable. And why so? Well, because philosophy deals with a region where there is no possible "test of values" and in such a region thought itself, since it is simply unverifiable speculation, can be of little or no value.

There we come to a really interesting and characteristic

opposition of standpoints, more, a difference in the very grain of the mind. As stated, it is the sceptical argument of the atheist and agnostic, but after all that is only the extreme logical statement of an attitude common to the average European turn of thinking which is inherently a positivist attitude. Philosophy has been pursued in Europe with great and noble intellectual results by the highest minds, but very much as a pursuit apart from life, a thing high and splendid, but ineffective. It is remarkable that while in India and China philosophy has seized hold on life, has had an enormous practical effect on the civilisation and got into the very bones of current thought and action, it has never at all succeeded in achieving this importance in Europe. In the days of the Stoics and Epicureans it got a grip, but only among the highly cultured; at the present day, too, we have some renewed tendency of the kind. Nietzsche has had his influence, certain French thinkers also in France, the philosophies of James and Bergson have attracted some amount of public interest; but it is a mere nothing compared with the effective power of Asiatic philosophy. The average European draws his guiding views not from the philosophic, but from the positive and practical reason. He does not absolutely disdain philosophy like Mr. Archer, but he considers it, if not a "man-made illusion," yet a rather nebulous, remote and ineffective kind of occupation. He honours the philosophers, but he puts their works on the highest shelf of the library of civilisation, not to be taken down or consulted except by a few minds of an exceptional turn. He admires, but he distrusts them. Plato's idea of philosophers as the right rulers and best directors of society seems to him the most fantastic and unpractical of notions; the philosopher, precisely because he moves among ideas, must be without any hold on real life. The Indian mind holds on the contrary that the Rishi, the thinker, the seer of spiritual truth is the best guide not only of the religious and moral, but the practical life. The seer, the Rishi is the natural director of society; to the Rishis he attributes the ideals and guiding intuitions of his civilisation. Even today he is very ready to give the name to anyone who can give a spiritual truth which helps his life or a formative idea and inspiration which influences religion, ethics, society, even politics.

This is because the Indian believes that the ultimate truths are truths of the spirit and that truths of the spirit are the most fundamental and most effective truths of our existence, powerfully creative of the inner, salutarily reformative of the outer life. To the European the ultimate truths are more often truths of the ideative intellect, the pure reason; but, whether intellectual or spiritual, they belong to a sphere beyond the ordinary action of the mind, life and body where alone there are any daily verifying "tests of values." These tests can only be given by living experience of outward fact and the positive and practical reason. The rest are speculations and their proper place is in the world of ideas, not in the world of life. That brings us to a difference of standpoint which is the essence of Mr. Archer's second objection. He believes that all philosophy is speculation and guessing; the only verifiable truth, we must suppose, is that of the normal fact, the outward world and our responses to it, truth of physical science and a psychology founded on physical science. He reproaches Indian philosophy for having taken its speculations seriously, for presenting speculation in the guise of dogma, for the "unspiritual" habit which mistakes groping for seeing and guessing for knowing,—in place, I presume, of the very spiritual habit which holds the physically sensible for the only knowable and takes the knowledge of the body for the knowledge of the soul and spirit. He waxes bitterly sarcastic over the idea that philosophic meditation and Yoga are the best way to ascertain the truth of Nature and the constitution of the universe. Mr. Archer's descriptions of Indian philosophy are a grossly ignorant misrepresentation of its idea and spirit, but in their essence they represent the view inevitably taken by the normal positivist mind of the Occident.

In fact, Indian philosophy abhors mere guessing and speculation. That word is constantly applied by European critics to the thoughts and conclusions of the Upanishads, of the philosophies, of Buddhism; but Indian philosophers would reject it altogether as at all a valid description of their method. If our philosophy admits an ultimate unthinkable and unknowable, it does not concern itself with any positive description or analysis of that supreme Mystery,—the absurdity the rationalist ascribes to it; it concerns itself with whatever is thinkable and knowable to us at the highest term as well as on the lower ranges of our experience. If it has been able to make its conclusions articles of religious faith,—dogmas, as they are here called,—it is because it has been able to base them on an experience verifiable by any man who will take the necessary means and apply the only possible tests. The Indian mind does not admit that the only possible test of values or of reality is the outward scientific, the test of a scrutiny of physical Nature or the everyday normal facts of our surface psychology, which is only a small movement upon vast hidden subconscious and superconscious heights, depths and ranges. What are the tests of these more ordinary or objective values? Evidently, experience, experimental analysis and synthesis, reason, intuition,—for I believe the value of intuition is admitted nowadays by modern philosophy and science. The tests of this other subtler order of truths are the same, experience, experimental analysis and synthesis, reason, intuition. Only, since these things are truths of the soul and spirit, it must necessarily be a psychological and spiritual experience, a psychological and psycho-physical experimentation, analysis and synthesis, a larger intuition which looks into higher realms, realities, possibilities of being, a reason which admits something beyond itself, looks upward to the suprarational, tries to give as far as may be an account of it to the human intelligence. Yoga, which Mr. Archer invites us so pressingly to abandon, is itself nothing but a well-tested means of opening up these greater realms of experience.

Mr. Archer and minds of his type cannot be expected to know these things; they are beyond the little narrow range of facts and ideas which is to them the whole arc of knowledge. But even if he knew, it would make no difference to him; he would reject the very thought with scornful impatience, without any degrading of his immense rationalistic superiority by any sort of examination into the possibility of an unfamiliar truth. In this attitude he would have the average positivist mind on his side. To that mind such notions seem in their very nature absurd and incomprehensible,—much worse than Greek and Hebrew, languages which have very respectable and creditworthy professors; but these are hieroglyphs which can only be upheld as decipherable signs by Indians and Theosophists and mystical thinkers, a disreputable clan. It can understand dogma and speculation about spiritual truth, a priest, a Bible, whether disbelieving them or giving them a conventional acceptance; but profoundest verifiable spiritual truth, firmly ascertainable spiritual values! The idea is foreign to this mentality and sounds to it like jargon. It can understand, even when it dismisses, an authoritative religion, an "I believe because it is rationally impossible"; but a deepest mystery of religion, a highest truth of philosophical thinking, a farthest ultimate discovery of psychological experience, a systematic and ordered experimentation of self-search and self-analysis, a constructive inner possibility of self-perfection, all arriving at the same result, assenting to each other's conclusions, reconciling spirit and reason and the whole psychological nature and its deepest needs,—this great ancient and persistent research and triumph of Indian culture baffles and offends the average positivist mind of the West. It is bewildered by the possession of a knowledge which the West never more than fumbled after and ended by missing. Irritated, perplexed, contemptuous, it refuses to recognise the superiority of such a harmony to its own lesser self-divided culture. For it is accustomed only to a religious seeking and experience which is at war with science and philosophy or oscillates between irrational belief and a troubled or else a self-confident scepticism. In Europe philosophy has been sometimes the handmaid—not the sister—of religion; but more often it has turned its back on religious belief in hostility or in a disdainful separation. The war between religion and science has been almost the leading phenomenon of European culture. Even philosophy and science have been unable to agree; they too have quarrelled and separated. These powers still coexist in Europe, but they are not a happy family; civil war is their natural atmosphere.

No wonder that the positivist mind to which this seems the natural order of things, should turn from a way of thinking and knowing in which there is a harmony, a consensus, a union between philosophy and religion and a systematised well-tested psychological experience. It is easily moved to escape from the challenge of this alien form of knowledge by readily dismissing Indian psychology as a jungle of self-hypnotic hallucinations, Indian religion as a rank growth of antirational superstitions, Indian philosophy as a remote cloud-land of unsubstantial speculation. It is unfortunate for the peace of mind which this self-satisfied attitude brings with it and for the effect of Mr. Archer's facile and devastating method of criticism that the West too has recently got itself pushed into paths of thinking and discovery which seem dangerously likely to justify all this mass of unpleasant barbarism and to bring Europe herself nearer to so monstrous a way of thinking. It is becoming more and more clear that Indian philosophy has anticipated in its own way most of what has been or is being thought out in metaphysical speculation. One finds even scientific thought repeating very ancient Indian generalisations from the other end of the scale of research. Indian psychology which Mr. Archer dismisses along with Indian cosmology and physiology as baseless classification and ingenious guessing,—it is anything but that, for it is based rigorously on experience,—is justified more and more by all the latest psychological discoveries. The fundamental ideas of Indian religion look perilously near to a conquest by which they will become the prominent thought and sentiment of a new and universal religious mentality and spiritual seeking. Who can say that the psycho-physiology of Indian Yoga may not be justified if certain lines of "groping and guessing" in the West are pushed a little farther? And even perhaps the Indian cosmological idea that there are other planes of being than this easily sensible kingdom of Matter, may be rehabilitated in a not very distant future? But the positivist mind may yet be of good courage: for its hold is still strong and it has still the claim of intellectual orthodoxy and the prestige of the right of possession; many streams must swell and meet together before it is washed under and a tide of uniting thought sweeps humanity towards the hidden shores of the Spirit.

A RATIONALISTIC CRITIC ON INDIAN CULTURE

CHAPTER III

THIS criticism so far is not very formidable; its edge, if it has any apart from the edge of trenchant misrepresentation, turns against the assailant. To have put a high value on philosophy, sought by it the highest secrets of our being, turned an effective philosophic thought on life and called in the thinkers, the men of profoundest spiritual experience, highest ideas, largest available knowledge to govern and shape society, to have subjected creed and dogma to the test of the philosophic mind and founded religious belief upon spiritual intuition, philosophical thought and psychological experience, are signs, not of barbarism or of a mean and ignorant culture, but marks of the highest possible type of civilisation. There is nothing here that would warrant us in abasing ourselves before the idols of the positivist reason or putting the spirit and aim of Indian culture at all lower than the spirit and aim of Western civilisation whether in its high ancient period of rational enlightenment and the speculative idea or in its modern period of broad and minute scientific thought and strong applied knowledge. Different it is, inferior it is not, but has rather a distinct element of superiority in the unique height of its motive and the spiritual nobility of its endeavour.

It is useful to lay stress on this greatness of spirit and aim, not only because it is of immense importance and the first test of the value of a culture, but because the assailants take advantage of two extraneous circumstances to create a prejudice and confuse the real issues. They have the immense advantage of attacking India when she is prostrate and in the dust and, materially, Indian civilisation seems to have ended in a great defeat and downfall. Strong in this temporary advantage they can afford to show a superb and generous courage in kicking the surrounding dust and mire with their hooves upon the sick and wounded lioness caught in the nets of the hunters and try to persuade the world that she had never any strength and virtue in her. It is an easy task in this age of the noble culture of Reason and Mammon and Science doing the works of Moloch, when the brazen idol of the great goddess Success is worshipped as she was never before worshipped by cultured human beings. But they have too the yet greater advantage of representing her to the world in a period of the eclipse of her civilisation when after at least two thousand years of the most brilliant and many-sided cultural activity she had for a time lost everything except the memory of her past and her long depressed and obscured but always living and now strongly reviving religious spirit.

I have touched elsewhere on the significance of this failure and this temporary eclipse. I may have to deal with it again at closer quarters, since it has been raised as an objection to the value of Indian culture and Indian spirituality. At present it will be enough to say that culture cannot be judged by material success; still less can spirituality be brought to that touchstone. Philosophic, aesthetic, poetic, intellectual Greece failed and fell while drilled and militarist Rome triumphed and conquered, but no one dreams of crediting for that reason the victorious imperial nation with a greater civilisation and a higher culture. The religious culture of Judea is not disproved or lessened by the destruction of the Jewish State, any more than it is proved and given greater value by the commercial capacity shown by the Jewish race in their dispersion. But I admit, as ancient Indian thought admitted, that material and economic capacity and prosperity are a necessary, though not the highest or most essential part of the total effort of human civilisation. In that respect India throughout her long period of cultural activity can claim equality with any ancient or mediaeval country. No people before modern times reached a higher splendour of wealth, commercial prosperity, material appointment, social organisation. That is the record of history, of ancient documents, of contemporary witnesses; to deny it is to give evidence of a singular prepossession and obfuscation of the view, an imaginative, or is it unimaginative, misreading of present actuality into past actuality. The splendour of Asiatic and not least of Indian prosperity, the wealth of Ormuz and of Ind, the "barbaric doors rough with gold," *barbaricae postes squalentes auro,* were once stigmatised by the less opulent West as a sign of barbarism. Circumstances are now strangely reversed; the opulent barbarism and a much less artistic ostentation of wealth are to be found in London, New York and Paris, and it is the nakedness of India and the squalor of her poverty which are flung in her face as evidence of the worthlessness of her culture.

India's ancient and mediaeval political, administrative, military and economic organisation was no mean achievement; the records stand and can be left to contradict the ignorance of the uninstructed and the rhetoric of the journalistic critic or the interested politician. There was no doubt an element of failure and defect, almost unavoidable in the totality of a problem on so large a scale and in the then conditions. But to exaggerate that into a count against her civilisation would be a singular severity of criticism which few civilisations watched to their end could survive. Failure in the end, yes, because of the decline of her culture, but not as a result of its most valuable elements. A later eclipse of the more essential elements of her civilisation is not a disproof of their original value. Indian civilisation must be judged mainly by the culture and greatness of its millenniums, not by the ignorance and weakness of a few centuries. A culture must be judged, first by its essential spirit, then by its best accomplishment and, lastly, by its power of survival, renovation and adaptation to new phases of the permanent needs of the race. In the poverty, confusion and disorganisation of a period of temporary decline, the eye of the hostile witness refuses to see or to recognise the saving soul of good which still keeps this civilisation alive and promises a strong and vivid return to the greatness of its permanent ideal. Its obstinate elastic force of rebound, its old measureless adaptability are again at work; it is no longer even solely on the defense, but boldly aggressive. Not survival alone, but victory and conquest are the promise of its future.

But our critic does not merely deny the lofty aim and greatness of spirit of Indian civilisation, which stand too high to be vulnerable to an assault of this ignorant and prejudiced character. He questions its leading ideas, denies its practical life-value, disparages its fruits, efficacy, character. Has this disparagement any critical value or is it only a temperamental expression of the misunderstanding natural to a widely different view of life and to a diametrically opposite estimate of our nature's highest significances and realities? If we consider the character of the attack and its terms, we shall see that it amounts to no more than a condemnation passed by the positivist mind attached to the normal values of life upon the quite different standards of a culture which looks beyond the ordinary life of man, points to something greater behind it and makes it a passage to something eternal, permanent and infinite. India, we are told, has no spirituality,—a portentous discovery; on the contrary she has succeeded, it would seem, in killing the germs of all sane and virile spirituality. Mr. Archer evidently puts his own sense, a novel and interesting and very Occidental sense, on the word. Spirituality has meant hitherto a recognition of something greater than mind and life, the aspiration to a consciousness pure, great, divine beyond our normal mental and vital nature, a surge and rising of the soul in man out of the littleness and bondage of our lower parts towards a greater thing secret within him. That at least is the idea, the experience, which is the very core of Indian thinking. But the rationalist does not believe in the spirit in this sense; life, human will-force and reason are his highest godheads. Spirituality then,—it would have been simpler and more logical to reject the word when the thing on which it rests is denied,— has to be given another sense, some high passion and effort of the emotions, will and reason, directed towards the finite, not towards the infinite, towards things temporary, not towards the eternal, towards perishable life, not towards any greater reality which overpasses and supports the superficial phenomena of life. The thought and suffering which seam and furrow the ideal head of Homer, there, we are told, is the sane and virile spirituality. The calm and compassion of Buddha victorious over ignorance and suffering, the meditation of the thinker tranced in communion with the Eternal, lifted above the seekings of thought into identity with a supreme Light, the rapture of the saint made one by love in the pure heart with the transcendent and universal Love, the will of the Karmayogin raised above egoistic desire and passion into the impersonality of the divine and universal Will, these things on which India has set the highest value and which have been the supreme endeavour of her greatest spirits, are not sane, not virile. This, one may be allowed to say, is a very Occidental and up-to-date idea of spirituality. Homer, Shakespeare, Raphael, Spinoza, Kant, Charlemagne, Abraham Lincoln, Lenin, Mussolini, these, shall we suggest, are to figure henceforth not only as great poets and artists or heroes of thought and action, but as our typical heroes and exemplars of spirituality. Not Buddha, not Christ, Chaitanya, St. Francis, Ramakrishna; these are either semibarbaric Orientals or touched by the feminine insanity of an Oriental religion. The impression made on an Indian mind resembles the reaction that a cultured intellectual might feel if he were told that good cooking, good dressing, good engineering, good schoolmastering are the true beauty and their pursuit the right, sane, virile aesthetic cult, and literature, architecture, sculpture and painting are only a useless scribbling on paper, an insane hacking of stone and an effeminate daubing of canvas; Vauban, Pestolozzi, Dr. Parr, Vatal and Beau Brummel are then the true heroes of artistic creation and not da Vinci, Angelo, Sophocles, Dante, Shakespeare or Rodin. Whether Mr. Archer's epithets and his accusations against Indian spirituality stand in the comparison, let the judicious determine. But meanwhile we see the opposition of the standpoints and begin to understand the inwardness of the difference between the West and India.

This forms the gravamen of the charge against the effective value of Indian philosophy, that it turns away from life, nature, vital will and the effort of man upon earth. It denies all value to life; it leads not towards the study of nature, but away from it. It expels all volitional individuality; it preaches the unreality of the world, detachment from terrestrial interests, the unimportance of the life of the moment compared with the endless chain of past and future existences. It is an enervating metaphysic tangled up with false notions of pessimism, asceticism, Karma and reincarnation,—all of them ideas fatal to that supreme spiritual thing, volitional individuality. This is a grotesquely exaggerated and false notion of Indian culture and philosophy, got up by presenting one side only of the Indian mind in colours of a sombre emphasis, after a manner which I suppose Mr. Archer has learned from the modern masters of realism. But in substance and spirit it is a fairly correct statement of the notions which the European mind has formed in the past about the character of Indian thought and culture, sometimes in ignorance, sometimes in defiance of the evidence. For a time even it managed to impress some strong shadow of this error on the mind of educated India. It is best to begin by setting right the tones of the picture; that done, we can better judge the opposition of mentality which is at the bottom of the criticism.

To say that Indian philosophy has led away from the study of nature is to state a gross unfact and to ignore the magnificent history of Indian civilisation. If by nature is meant physical Nature, the plain truth is that no nation before the modern epoch carried scientific research so far and with such signal success as India of ancient times. That is a truth which lies on the face of history for all to read; it has been brought forward with great force and much wealth of detail by Indian scholars and scientists of high eminence, but it was already known and acknowledged by European savants who had taken the trouble to make a comparative study in the subject. Not only was India in the first rank in mathematics, astronomy, chemistry, medicine, surgery, all the branches of physical knowledge which were practised in ancient times, but she was, along with the Greeks, the teacher of the Arabs from whom Europe recovered the lost habit of scientific enquiry and got the basis from which modern science started. In many directions India had the priority of discovery,—to take only two striking examples among a multitude, the decimal notation in mathematics or the perception that the earth is a moving body in astronomy,—*calā pṛthvī sthirā bhāti,* the earth moves and only appears to be still, said the Indian astronomer many centuries before Galileo. This great development would hardly have been possible in a nation whose thinkers and men of learning were led by its metaphysical tendencies to turn away from the study of nature. A remarkable feature of the Indian mind was a close attention to the things of life, a disposition to observe minutely its salient facts, to systematise and to found in each department of it a science, Shastra, well-founded scheme and rule. That is at least a good beginning of the scientific tendency and not the sign of a culture capable only of unsubstantial metaphysics.

It is perfectly true that Indian science came abruptly to a

halt somewhere about the thirteenth century and a period of darkness and inactivity prevented it from proceeding forward or sharing at once in the vast modern development of scientific knowledge. But this was not due to any increase or intolerance of the metaphysical tendency calling the national mind away from physical nature. It was part of a general cessation of new intellectual activity, for philosophy too ceased to develop almost at the same time. The last great original attempts at spiritual philosophy are dated only a century or two later than the names of the last great original scientists. It is true also that Indian metaphysics did not attempt, as modern philosophy has attempted without success, to read the truth of existence principally by the light of the truths of physical Nature. This ancient wisdom founded itself rather upon an inner experimental psychology and a profound psychic science, India's special strength, —but study of mind too and of our inner forces is surely study of nature,—in which her success was greater than in physical knowledge. This she could not but do, since it was the spiritual truth of existence for which she was seeking; nor is any really great and enduring philosophy possible except on this basis. It is true also that the harmony she established in her culture between philosophical truth and truth of psychology and religion was not extended in the same degree to the truth of physical Nature; physical Science had not then arrived at the great universal generalisations which would have made and are now making that synthesis entirely possible. Nevertheless from the beginning, from as early as the thought of the Vedas, the Indian mind had recognized that the same general laws and powers hold in the spiritual, the psychological and the physical existence. It discovered too the omnipresence of life, affirmed the evolution of the soul in Nature from the vegetable and the animal to the human form, asserted on the basis of philosophic intuition and spiritual and psychological experience many of the truths which modern science is reaffirming from its own side of the approach to knowledge. These things too were not the results of a barren and empty metaphysics, not the inventions of bovine navel-gazing dreamers.

Equally is it a misrepresentation to say that Indian culture denies all value to life, detaches from terrestrial interests and insists on the unimportance of the life of the moment. To read these European comments one would imagine that in all Indian thought there was nothing but the nihilistic school of Buddhism and the monistic illusionism of Shankara and that all Indian art, literature and social thinking were nothing but the statement of their recoil from the falsehood and vanity of things. It does not follow that because these things are what the average European has heard about India or what most interests or strikes the European scholar in her thought, therefore they are, however great may have been their influence, the whole of Indian thinking. The ancient civilisation of India founded itself very expressly upon four human interests; first, desire and enjoyment, next, material, economic and other aims and needs of the mind and body, thirdly, ethical conduct and the right law of individual and social life, and, lastly spiritual liberation; *kāma, artha, dharma, mokṣa.* The business of culture and social organisation was to lead, to satisfy, to support these things in man and to build some harmony of the forms and motives. Except in very rare cases the satisfaction of the three mundane objects must run before the other; fullness of life must precede the surpassing of life. The debt to the family, the community and the gods could not be scamped; earth must have her due and the relative its play, even if beyond it there was the glory of heaven or the peace of the Absolute. There was no preaching of a general rush to the cave and the hermitage.

The symmetric character of ancient Indian life and the vivid variety of its literature were inconsistent with any exclusive other-worldly direction. The great mass of Sanskrit literature is a literature of human life; certain philosophic and religious writings are devoted to the withdrawal from it, but even these are not as a rule contemptuous of its value. If the Indian mind gave the highest importance to a spiritual release,—and whatever the positivist mood may say, a spiritual liberation of some kind is the highest possibility of the human spirit,—it was not interested in that alone. It looked equally at ethics, law, politics, society, the sciences, the arts and crafts, everything that appertains to human life. It thought on these things deeply and scrutinisingly and it wrote of them with power and knowledge. What a fine monument of political and administrative genius is the *Śukra-Nīti*, to take one example only, and what a mirror of the practical organisation of a great civilised people! Indian art was not always solely hieratic,—it seemed so only because it is in the temples and cave cathedrals that its greatest work survived; as the old literature testifies, as we see from the Rajput and Mogul paintings, it was devoted as much to the court and the city and to cultural ideas and the life of the people as to the temple and monastery and their motives. Indian education of women as well as of men was more rich and comprehensive and many-sided than any system of education before modern times. The documents which prove these things are now available to any one who cares to study. It is time that this parrot talk about the unpractical, metaphysical, quietistic, anti-vital character of Indian civilisation should cease and give place to a true and understanding estimate.

But it is perfectly true that Indian culture has always set the highest value on that in man which rises beyond the terrestrial preoccupation; it has held up the goal of a supreme and arduous self-exceeding as the summit of human endeavour. The spiritual life was to its view a nobler thing than the life of external power and enjoyment, the thinker greater than the man of action, the spiritual man greater than the thinker. The soul that lives in God is more perfect than the soul that lives only in outward mind or only for the claims and joys of thinking and living matter. It is here that the difference comes in between the typical Western and the typical Indian mentality. The West has acquired the religious mind rather than possessed it by nature and it has always worn its acquisition with a certain looseness. India has constantly believed in worlds behind of which the material world is only the antechamber. Always she has seen a self within us greater than the mental and vital self, greater than the ego. Always she has bowed her intellect and heart before a near and present Eternal in which the temporal being exists and to which in man it increasingly turns for transcendence. The sentiment of the Bengali poet, the wonderful singer and rapt devotee of the Divine Mother,—

How rich an estate man lies fallow here!
If this were tilled, a golden crop would spring,

—expresses the real Indian feeling about human life. But it is most attracted by the greater spiritual possibilities man alone of terrestrial beings possesses. The ancient Aryan culture recognised all human possibilities, but put this highest of all and graded life according to a transitional scale in its system of the four classes and the four orders. Buddhism first gave an exaggerated and enormous extension to the ascetic ideal and the monastic impulse, erased the transition and upset the balance. Its victorious system left only two orders, the householder and the ascetic, the monk and the layman, an effect which subsists to the present day. It is this upsetting of the Dharma for which we find it fiercely attacked in the Vishnu Purana under the veil of an apologue, for it weakened in the end the life of society by its tense exaggeration and its hard system of opposites. But Buddhism too had another side, a side turned towards action and creation, and gave a new light, a new meaning and a new moral and ideal power to life. Afterwards there came the lofty illusionism of Shankara at the close of the two greatest known millenniums of Indian culture. Life thenceforward was too much depreciated as an unreality or a relative phenomenon, in the end not worth living, not worth our assent to it and persistence in its motives. But this dogma was not universally accepted, nor admitted without a struggle; Shankara was even denounced by his adversaries as a masked Buddhist. The later Indian mind has been powerfully impressed by his idea of Maya; but popular thought and sentiment was never wholly shaped by it. The religions of devotion which see in life a play or Lila of God and not a half sombre, half glaring illusion defacing the white silence of eternity had a closer growing influence. If they did not counteract, they humanised the austere ideal. It is only recently that educated India accepted the ideas of English and German scholars, imagined for a time Shankara's Mayavada to be the one highest thing, if not the whole of our philosophy, and put it in a place of exclusive prominence. But against that tendency too there is now a powerful reaction, not towards replacing the spirit without life by life without the spirit, but towards a spiritual possession of mind, life and matter. Still it is true that the ascetic ideal which in the ancient vigour of our culture was the fine spire of life mounting into the eternal existence, became latterly its top-heavy dome and tended under the weight of its bare and imposing sublimity to crush the rest of the edifice.

But here also we should get the right view, away from all exaggeration and false stress. Mr. Archer drags in Karma and Reincarnation into his list of anti-vital Indian notions. But it is preposterous, it is a stupid misunderstanding to speak of reincarnation as a doctrine which preaches the unimportance of the life of the moment compared with the endless chain of past and future existences. The doctrine of reincarnation and Karma tells us that the soul has a past which shaped its present birth and existence; it has a future which our present action is shaping; our past has taken and our future will take the form of recurring terrestrial births and Karma, our own action, is the power which by its continuity and development as a subjective and objective force determines the whole nature and eventuality of these repeated existences. There is nothing here to depreciate the importance of the present life. On the contrary the doctrine gives it immense vistas and enormously enhances the value of effort and action. The nature of the present act is of an incalculable importance because it determines not only our immediate but our subsequent future. There will be found too insistently pervading Indian literature and deeply settled in the mind of the people the idea of a whole-hearted concentrated present action and energy, *tapasya,* as a miraculous all-powerful force for the acquisition of our desires, whether the material or the spiritual desires of the human will. No doubt, our present life loses the exclusive importance which we give to it when we regard it only as an ephemeral moment in Time never to be repeated, our one sole opportunity, without any after-existence beyond it. But a narrow exaggerated insistence on the present shuts up the human soul in the prison of the moment: it may give a feverish intensity to action, but it is inimical to calm and joy and greatness of the spirit. No doubt, too, the idea that our present sufferings are the results of our own past action, imparts a calm, a resignation, an acquiescence to the Indian mind which the restless Western intelligence finds it difficult to understand or tolerate. This may degenerate in a time of great national weakness, depression and misfortune, into a quietistic fatalism that may extinguish the fire of the reparative endeavour. But that is not its inevitable turn, nor is it the turn given to it in the records of the more vigorous past of our culture. The note there is of action, of *tapasya.* There is too another turn given to this belief which increased with time, the Buddhistic dogma of the succession of rebirths as a chain of Karma from which the soul must escape into the eternal silence. The notion has strongly affected Hinduism; but whatever is depressing in it, belongs not properly to the doctrine of rebirth but to other elements stigmatised as an ascetic pessimism by the vitalistic thought of Europe.

Pessimism is not peculiar to the Indian mind: it has been an element in the thought of all developed civilisations. It is the sign of a culture already old, the fruit of a mind which has lived much, experienced much, sounded life and found it full of suffering, sounded joy and achievement and found that all is vanity and vexation of spirit and there is nothing new under the sun or, if there is, its novelty is but of a day. Pessimism has been as rampant in Europe as in India and it is certainly a singular thing to find the materialist of all people bringing against Indian spirituality this accusation of lowering the values of existence. For what can be more depressing than the materialistic view of the quite physical and ephemeral nature of human life? There is nothing in the most ascetic notes of the Indian mind like the black gloom of certain kinds of European pessimism, a city of dreadful night without joy here or hope beyond, and nothing like the sad and shrinking attitude before death and the dissolution of the body which pervades Western literature. The note of ascetic pessimism often found in Christianity is a distinctly Western note; for it is absent in Christ's teachings. The mediaeval religion with its cross, its salvation by suffering, its devil-ridden and flesh-ridden world and the flames of eternal hell waiting for man beyond the grave has a character of pain and terror alien to the Indian mind, to which indeed religious terror is a stranger. The suffering of the world is there, but it fades into a bliss of spiritual peace or ecstasy beyond the sorrow line. Buddha's teaching laid heavy stress on the sorrow and impermanence of things, but the Buddhist Nirvana won by the heroic spirit of moral self-conquest and calm wisdom is a state of ineffable calm and joy, open not only to a few like the Christian heavens, but to all, and very different from the blank cessation which is the mechanical release of our pain and struggle, the sorry Nirvana of the western pessimist, the materialist's brute flat end of all things. Even illusionism preached, not a gospel of sorrow, but the final unreality of joy and grief and the whole world-existence. It admits the practical validity of life and allows its values to those who dwell in the Ignorance. And like all Indian asceticism it places before man the possibility of a great effort, a luminous concentration of knowledge, a mighty urge of the will by which he can rise to an absolute peace or an absolute bliss. A not ignoble pessimism there has been about man's normal life as it is, a profound sense of its imperfection, a disgust of its futile obscurity, smallness and ignorance; but an unconquerable optimism as regards his spiritual possibility was the other side of this mood. If it did not believe in the ideal of an immense material progress of the race or a perfection of the normal man with earth as its field, it believed in a sure spiritual progress for every individual and an ultimate perfection lifted above subjection to the shocks of life. And this pessimism with regard to life is not the sole note of the Indian religious mind; its most popular forms accept life as a game of God and see beyond our present conditions for every human being the eternal nearness to the Divine. A luminous ascent into godhead was always held to be a consummation well within man's grasp. That can hardly be called a depressing or pessimistic theory of existence.

There can be no great and complete culture without some element of asceticism in it; for asceticism means the self-denial and self-conquest by which man represses his lower impulses and rises to greater heights of his nature. Indian asceticism is not a mournful gospel of sorrow or a painful mortification of the flesh in morbid penance, but a noble effort towards a higher joy and an absolute possession of the spirit. A great joy of self-conquest, a still joy of inner peace and the forceful joy of a supreme self-exceeding are at the heart of its experience. It is only a mind besotted with the flesh or too enamoured of external life and its restless effort and inconstant satisfactions that can deny the nobility or idealistic loftiness of the ascetic endeavour.

But there are the exaggerations and deflections that all ideals undergo. Those which are the most difficult to humanity suffer from them most, and asceticism may become a fanatic self-torture, a crude repression of the nature, a tired flight from existence or an indolent avoidance of the trouble of life and a weak recoil from the effort demanded of our manhood. Practised not by the comparatively few who are called to it, but preached in its extreme form to all and adopted by unfit thousands, its values may be debased, counterfeits may abound and the vital force of the community lose its elasticity and its forward spring. It would be idle to pretend that such defects and untoward results have been absent in India. I do not accept the ascetic ideal as the final solution of the problem of human existence; but even its exaggerations have a nobler spirit behind them than the vitalistic exaggerations which are the opposite defect of Western culture.

After all asceticism and illusionism are minor issues. The point to be pressed is that Indian spirituality in its greatest eras and in its inmost significance has not been a tired quietism or a conventional monasticism, but a high effort of the human spirit to rise beyond the life of desire and vital satisfaction and arrive at an acme of spiritual calm, greatness, strength, illumination, divine realisation, settled peace and bliss. The question between the culture of India and the vehement secular activism of the modern mind is whether such an endeavour is or is not essential to man's highest perfection. And if it is, then the other question arises whether it is to be only an exceptional force confined to a few rare spirits or can be made the main inspiring motive-power of a great and complete human civilisation.

A RATIONALISTIC CRITIC ON INDIAN CULTURE

CHAPTER IV

A RIGHT JUDGMENT of the life-value of Indian philosophy is intimately bound up with a right appreciation of the life-value of Indian religion; religion and philosophy are too intimately one in this culture to be divided from each other. Indian philosophy is not a purely rational gymnastic of speculative logic in the air, an ultra-subtle process of thought-spinning and word-spinning like the greater part of philosophy in Europe; it is the organised intellectual theory or the intuitive ordering perception of all that is the soul, the thought, the dynamic truth, the heart of feeling and power of Indian religion. Indian religion is Indian spiritual philosophy put into action and experience. Whatever in the religious thought and practice of that vast, rich, thousand-sided, infinitely pliable, yet very firmly structured system we call Hinduism, does not in intention come under this description,—whatever its practice,—is either social framework or projection of ritual buttresses or survival of old supports and additions. Or else it is an excrescence and growth of corruption, a degradation of its truth and meaning in the vulgar mind, part of the debased mixtures that overtake all religious thinking and practice. Or, in some instances, it is dead habit contracted in periods of fossilisation or ill-assimilated extraneous matter gathered into this giant body. The inner principle of Hinduism, the most tolerant and receptive of religious systems, is not sharply exclusive like the religious spirit of Christianity or Islam; as far as that could be without loss of its own powerful idiosyncrasy and law of being, it has been synthetic, acquisitive, inclusive. Always it has taken in from every side and trusted to the power of assimilation that burns in its spiritual heart and in the white heat of its flaming centre to turn even the most unpromising material into forms for its spirit.

But before we turn to see what it is that so fiercely irritates and exasperates our hostile Western critic in Indian religious philosophy, it is as well to consider what he has to say about other sides of this ancient, dateless and still vigorously living, growing, all-assimilating Hinduism. For he has a great deal to say and it is unsparing and without measure. There is not the intemperate drunkenness of denunciation and vomit of false witness, hatred, uncharitableness and all things degrading and unspiritual and unclean that are the mark of a certain type of "Christian literature" on the subject,—for example the superlative specimen of this noxious compound which Sir John Woodroffe has cited from the pages of Mr. Harold Begbie, "virile" perhaps if violence is virile, but certainly not sane. But still it is a mass of unsparing condemnation, exaggerated where it has any foundation at all and serenely illogical in its blithe joy of deliberate misrepresentation. Still, even from this crude mass it is possible to disengage the salient and typical antipathies that recommend it to the uncritical and even to many critical minds, and it is these alone that it is useful to discover.

The total irrationality of Hinduism is the main theme of the attack. Mr. Archer does casually admit a philosophical, and one might therefore suppose a rational element in the religion of India, but he disparages and dismisses as false and positively harmful the governing ideas of this religious philosophy as he understands or imagines he understands them. He explains the pervading irrational character of Hindu religion by the allegation that the Indian people have always gravitated towards the form rather than the substance and towards the letter rather than the spirit. One would have supposed that this kind of gravitation is a fairly universal feature of the human mind, not only in religion, but in society, politics, art, literature, even in science. In every conceivable human activity a cult of the form and forgetfulness of the spirit, a turn towards convention, externalism, unthinking dogma has been the common drift of the human mind from China to Peru and it does not skip Europe on its way. And Europe where men have constantly fought, killed, burned, tortured, imprisoned, persecuted in every way imaginable by human stupidity and cruelty for the sake of dogmas, words, rites and forms of church government, Europe where these things have done duty for spirituality and religion, has hardly a record which would entitle it to cast this reproach in the face of the East. But, we are told, this gravitation afflicts the Indian religion more than any other creed. Higher Hinduism can be scarcely said to exist except in certain small reforming sects and current Hinduism, the popular religion, is the cult of a monstrous folk-lore oppressive and paralysing to the imagination,—although here again one would think that if anything an excess rather than a paralysis of the creative imagination might be charged against the Indian mind. Animism and magic are the prevailing characteristics. The Indian people has displayed a genius for obfuscating reason and formalising, materialising and degrading religion. If India has possessed great thinkers, she has not extracted from their thoughts a rational and ennobling religion: the devotion of the Spanish or the Russian peasant is rational and enlightened by comparison. Irrationalism, anti-rationalism,—that in this laboured and overcharged accusation is the constant cry; it is the keynote of the Archer tune.

The phenomenon that has astonished and disgusted the mind of the critic is the obstinate survival in India of the old religious spirit and large antique religious types unsubmerged by the flood of modernism and its devastating utilitarian free thought. India, he tells us, still clings to what not only the Western world, but China and Japan have outgrown for ages. The religion is a superstition full of performances of piety repulsive to the free enlightened secular mind of the modern man. Its daily practices put it far outside the pale of civilisation. Perhaps, if it had confined its practice decorously to church attendance on Sundays and to marriage and funeral services and grace before meat, it might have been admitted as human and tolerable! As it is, it is the great anachronism of the modern world; it has not been cleansed for thirty centuries; it is paganism, it is a wholly unfiltered paganism; its tendency towards pollution rather than purification marks out its place as incomparably the lowest in the scale of world religions. An ingenious remedy is proposed. Christianity destroyed Paganism in Europe; therefore, since any immediate or very rapid triumph of sceptical freethought would be too happily abrupt a transition to be quite feasible, we unenlightened, polluted, impure Hindus are advised to take up for a time with Christianity, poor irrational thing that it is, dark and deformed though it looks in the ample light of the positivist reason, because Christianity and especially Protestant Christianity will be at least a good preparatory step towards the noble freedom and stainless purities of atheism and agnosticism. But if even this little cannot be hoped for in spite of numerous famine conversions, at any rate Hinduism must somehow or other get itself filtered, and until that hygienic operation has been executed, India must be denied fellowship on equal terms with the civilised nations.

Incidentally, to support this charge of irrationalism and its companion charge of Paganism, we find a third and more damaging count brought against us and our religious culture, an alleged want of all moral worth and ethical substance. There is now an increasing perception, even in Europe, that reason is not the last word of human mind, not quite the one and only sovereign way to truth and certainly not the sole arbiter of religious and spiritual truth. The accusation of paganism too does not settle the question, since plenty of cultivated minds are well able to see that there were many great, true and beautiful things in the ancient religions that were lumped together by Christian ignorance under that inappropriate nickname. Nor has the world been entirely a gainer by losing these high ancient forms and motives. But whatever the actual practice of men,—and in this respect the normal human being is a singular mixture of the sincere but quite ineffective, the just respectable, would-be ethical man and the self-deceiving or semi-hypocritical Pharisee, one can always appeal with force to a moralistic prejudice. All religions raise high the flag of morality and, whether religious or secular-minded, all but the antinomian, the rebel and the cynic, profess to follow or at least to admit that standard in their lives. This accusation is therefore about the most prejudicial charge that can be brought against any religion. The self-constituted prosecuting judge whose diatribe we are examining brings it without scruple and without measure. He has discovered that Hinduism is not an ennobling or even a morally helpful religion; if it has talked much of righteousness, it has never claimed moral teaching as one of its functions. A religion that can talk much of righteousness without performing the function of moral teaching, sounds rather like a square which can make no claim to be a quadrilateral; but let that pass. If the Hindu is comparatively free from the grosser Western vices,—as yet, only and only until he enters "the pale of civilisation" by adopting Christianity or otherwise,—it is not because there is any ethical strain in his character; it is because these vices do not come in his way. His social system founded on the barbarous idea of the Dharma, of the divine and the human, the universal and the individual, the ethical and the social law, and supported on it at every point, has stupidly neglected to supply him with the opportunities of departing from it so liberally provided by Western civilisation! And yet the whole character of Hinduism, which is the character of the people, indicates, we are calmly told, a melancholy proclivity towards whatever is monstrous and unwholesome! On that highest note of unmeasured denunciation we may leave Mr. Archer's monstrous and unwholesome dance of disparagement and turn to disengage the temperamental sources of his dislike and anger.

Two things especially distinguish the normal European mind,—for we must leave aside some great souls and some great thinkers or some moments or epochs of abnormal religiosity and look at the dominant strain. Its two significant characters are the cult of the inquiring, defining, effective, practical reason and the cult of life. The great high tides of European civilisation, Greek culture, the Roman world before Constantine, the Renaissance, the modern age with its two colossal idols, Industrialism and physical Science, have come to the West on the strong ascending urge of this double force. Whenever the tide of these powers has ebbed, the European mind has entered into much confusion, darkness and weakness. Christianity failed to spiritualise Europe, whatever it may have done towards humanising it in certain ethical directions, because it ran counter to these two master instincts; it denied the supremacy of the reason and put its anathema on a satisfied or strenuous fullness of life. But in Asia there has been neither this predominance of reason and the life-cult nor any incompatibility of these two powers with the religious spirit. The great ages of Asia, the strong culminations of her civilisation and culture,—in India the high Vedic beginning, the grand spiritual stir of the Upanishads, the wide flood of Buddhism, Vedanta, Sankhya, the Puranic and Tantric religions, the flowering of Vaishnavism and Shaivism in the Southern kingdoms—have come in on a surge of spiritual light and a massive or intense climbing of the religious or the religio-philosophic mind to its own heights, its noblest realities, its largest riches of vision and experience. It was in such periods that intellect, thought, poetry, the arts, the material life flowered into splendour. The ebbing of spirituality brought in, always on the contrary, the weakness of these other powers, periods of fossilisation or at least depression of the power of life, tracts of decline, even beginnings of decay. This is a clue to which we have to hold if we would understand the great lines of divergence between the East and the West.

Towards the spirit if not all the way to it man must rise or he misses his upward curve of strength; but there are different ways of approach to its secret forces. Europe, it would seem, must go through the life and the reason and find spiritual truth by their means as a crown and a revelation; she cannot at once take the kingdom of heaven by violence, as the saying of Christ would have men do. The attempt confuses and obscures her reason, is combated by her life instincts and leads to revolt, negation, a return to her own law of nature. But Asia, or at any rate, India lives naturally by a spiritual influx from above; that alone brings with it a spiritual evocation of her higher powers of mind and life. The two continents are two sides of the integral orb of humanity and until they meet and fuse, each must move to whatever progress or culmination the spirit in humanity seeks, by the law of its being, its own proper Dharma. A one-sided world would have been the poorer for its uniformity and the monotone of a single culture; there is a need of divergent lines of advance until we can raise our heads into that infinity of the spirit in which there is a light broad enough to draw together and reconcile all, highest ways of thinking, feeling and living. That is a truth which the violent Indian assailant of a materialistic Europe or the contemptuous enemy or cold disparager of Asiatic or Indian culture agree to ignore. There is here no real question between barbarism and civilisation, for all masses of men are barbarians labouring to civilise themselves. There is only one of the dynamic differences necessary for the completeness of the growing orb of human culture.

Meanwhile the divergence unfortunately gives rise to a

constant warring opposition of outlooks in religion and in most other matters, and the opposition brings with it more or less of an incapacity for mutual understanding and even a positive enmity or dislike. The emphasis of the Western mind is on life, the outer life above all, the things that are grasped, visible, tangible. The inner life is taken only as an intelligent reflection of the outer world, with the reason for a firm putter of things into shape, an intelligent critic, builder, refiner of the external materials offered by Nature. The present use of living, to be wholly in this life and for this life, is all the preoccupation of Europe. The present life of the individual and the continuous physical existence and developing mind and knowledge of humanity make up her one absorbing interest. Even from religion the West is apt to demand that it shall subordinate its aim or its effect to this utility of the immediate visible world. The Greek and the Roman looked on religious cult as a sanction for the life of the "polis" or a force for the just firmness and stability of the State. The Middle Ages when the Christian idea was at its height were an interregnum; it was a period during which the Western mind was trying to assimilate in its emotion and intelligence an Oriental ideal. But it never succeeded in firmly living it and had eventually to throw it aside or keep it only for a verbal homage. The present moment is in the same way for Asia an interregnum dominated by an attempt to assimilate in its intellect and life in spite of a rebellious soul and temperament the Western outlook and its earthbound ideal. And it may be safely predicted that Asia too will not succeed in living out this alien law firmly or for a long time. But in Europe even the Christian idea, marked in its purity by the emphasis of its introspective tendency and an uncompromising other-worldliness, had to compromise with the demands of the Occidental temperament and in doing that it lost its own inner kingdom. The genuine temperament of the West triumphed and in an increasing degree rationalised, secularised and almost annihilated the religious spirit. Religion became more and more a pale and ever thinning shadow pushed aside into a small corner of the life and a still smaller corner of the nature and awaiting sentence of death or exile, while outside the doors of the vanquished Church marched on their victorious way the triumphant secular pomps of the outward life and the positive reason and materialistic science.

The tendency to secularism is a necessary consequence of the cult of life and reason divorced from their inmost inlook. Ancient Europe did not separate religion and life; but that was because it had no need for the separation. Its religion, once it got rid of the Oriental element of the mysteries, was a secular institution which did not look beyond a certain supraphysical sanction and convenient aid to the government of this life. And even then the tendency was to philosophise and reason away the relics of the original religious spirit, to exile the little shadow that remained of the brooding wings of a supraratïonal mystery and to get into the clear sunlight of the logical and practical reason. But modern Europe went farther and to the very end of this way. The more effectually to shake off the obsession of the Christian idea, which like all oriental erligious thought claims to make religion commensurate with life and, against whatever obstacles may be opposed to it by the unregenerate vital nature of the animal man, spiritualise the whole being and its action, modern Europe separated religion from life, from philosophy, from art and science, from politics, from the greater part of social action and social existence. And it secularised and rationalised too the ethical demand so that it might stand in itself on its own basis and have no need of any aid from religious sanction or mystic insistence. At the end of this turn is an antinomian tendency, constantly recurring in the life-history of Europe and now again in evidence. This force seeks to annul ethics also, not by rising above it into the absolute purity of the spirit, as mystic experience claims to do, but by breaking out of its barriers below into an exultant freedom of the vital play. In this evolution religion was left aside, an impoverished system of belief and ceremony to which one might or might not subscribe with very little difference to the march of the human mind and life. Its penetrating and colouring power had been reduced to a faint minimum; a superficial pigmentation of dogma, sentiment and emotion was all that survived this drastic process.

Even the poor little corner that was still conceded to it, intellectualism insisted on flooding as much as possible with the light of reason. The trend has been to reduce, not only the infrarational, but equally the suprarational refuges of the religious spirit. The old pagan polytheistic symbolism had clothed with its beautiful figures the ancient idea of a divine Presence and supraphysical Life and Power in all Nature and in every particle of life and matter and in all animal existence and in all the mental action of man, but this idea, which to the secularist reason is only an intellectualised animism, had already been ruthlessly swept aside. The Divinity had abandoned the earth and lived far aloof and remote in other worlds, in a celestial heaven of saints and immortal spirits. But why should there be any other worlds? I admit, cried the progressing intellect, only this material world to which our reason and senses bear witness. A vague bleak abstraction of spiritual existence without any living habitation, without any means of dynamic nearness was left to satisfy the wintry remnants of the old spiritual sense or the old fantastic illusion. A blank and tepid Theism remained or a rationalised Chrisitanity without either the name of Christ or his presence. Or why should that even be allowed by the critical light of the intelligence? A Reason or Power, called God for want of a better name, represented by the moral and physical Law in the material universe, is quite sufficient for any rational mind, and so we get to Deism, to a vacant intellectual formula. Or why should there be any God at all? The reason and the senses by themselves give no witness to God; at best they can make of

Him only a plausible hypothesis. But there is no need of an unsubstantial hypothesis, since Nature is enough and the sole thing of which we have knowledge. Thus by an inevitable process we reach the atheistic or agnostic cult of secularism, the acme of denial, the zenith of the positive intelligence. And there reason and life may henceforward take their foundation and reign well satisfied over a conquered world,—if only that inconvenient veiled ambiguous infinite Something behind will leave them alone for the future!

A temperament, an outlook of this kind must necessarily be impatient of any such thing as an earnest straining after the suprarational and the infinite. It may tolerate some moderate play of these fine hallucinations as an innocent indulgence of the speculative mind or the artistic imagination, provided it is not too serious and does not intrude upon life. But asceticism and other-worldliness are abhorrent to its temperament and fatal to its outlook. Life is a thing to be possessed and enjoyed rationally or forcefully according to our power, but this earthly life, the one thing we know, our only province. At most a moderate intellectual and ethical asceticism is permissible, the simple life, plain living, high thinking; but an ecstatic spiritual asceticism is an offence to the reason, almost a crime. Pessimism of the vitalistic kind may be allowed its mood or its hour; for it admits that life is an evil that has to be lived and does not cut at its roots. But the obvious right standpoint is to take life as it is and make the most of it, either practically for the best ordering of its mixed good and evil or ideally with some hope of a relative perfection. If spirituality is to have any meaning, it can only signify the aim or the high labour of a lofty intelligence, rational will, limited beauty and moral good which will try to make the best of this life that is, but not vainly look beyond to some unhuman, unattainable, infinite or absolute satisfaction. If religion is to survive, let its function be to serve this kind of spiritual aim, to govern conduct, to give beauty and purity to our living, but let it minister only to this sane and virile spirituality, let it keep within the bounds of the practical reason and an earthly intelligence. This description no doubt isolates the main strands and ignores departures to one side or the other; and in all human nature there must be departures, often of an extreme kind. But it would not, I think, be an unfair or exaggerated description of the persistent ground and characteristic turn of the Western temperament and its outlook and the normal poise of its intelligence. This is its self-fulfilled static poise before it proceeds to that deflection or that self-exceeding to which man is inevitably moved when he reaches the acme of his normal nature. For he harbours a power in Nature that must either grow or else stagnate and cease and disintegrate, and until he has found all himself, there is for him no static abiding and no permanent home for his spirit.

Now when this Western mind is confronted with the still surviving force of Indian religion, thought, culture, it finds that all its standards are denied, exceeded or belittled; all that it honours is given a second place, all that it has rejected is still held in honour. Here is a philosophy which founds itself on the immediate reality of the Infinite, the pressing claim of the Absolute. And this is not as a thing to speculate about, but as a real Presence and a constant Power which demands the soul of man and calls it. Here is a mentality which sees the Divine in Nature and man and animal and inanimate thing, God at the beginning, God in the middle, God at the end, God everywhere. And all this is not a permissible poetical play of the imagination that need not be taken too seriously by life, but is put forward as a thing to be lived, realised, put at the back even of outward action, turned into stuff of thought, feeling and conduct! And whole disciplines are systematised for this purpose, disciplines which men still practise! And whole lives are given up to this pursuit of the supreme Person, the universal Godhead, the One, the Absolute, the Infinite! And to pursue this immaterial aim men are still content to abandon the outward life and society and home and family and their most cherished pursuits and all that has to a rational mind a substantial and ascertainable value! Here is a country which is still heavily coloured with the ochre tint of the garb of the Sannyasin, where the Beyond is still preached as a truth and men have a living belief in other worlds and reincarnation and a whole army of antique ideas whose truth is quite unverifiable by the instruments of physical Science. Here the experiences of Yoga are held to be as true or more true than the experiments of the laboratory. Is this not a thinking of things evidently unthinkable since the rational Western mind has ceased to think about them? Is it not an attempt to know things evidently unknowable since the modern mind has abandoned all attempt to know them? There is amongst these irrational half-savages an endeavour even to make this unreal thing the highest flight of life, its very goal, and a governing force, a shaping power in art and culture and conduct. But art and culture and conduct are things which, this rational mind tells us, Indian spirituality and religion ought logically not to touch at all; for they belong to the realm of the finite and can only be founded on the intellectual reason and the practical environment and the truths and suggestions of physical Nature. There in its native form is the apparent gulf between the two mentalities and it looks unbridgeable. Or rather, the Indian mind can understand well enough, even when it does not share, the positivist turn of the Occidental intelligence; but it is itself to the latter a thing, if not damnable, at least abnormal and unintelligible.

The effects of the Indian religio-philosophical standpoint on life are to the Occidental critic still more intolerable. If his reason was already offended by this suprarational and to him antirational urge, it is the strongest instincts of his temperament that are now violently shocked by their own direct contrasts and opposites. Life, the thing on which he puts an entire and unquestioning value, is questioned here. It is belittled and discouraged by the extremest consequences of one side of the Indian outlook or inlook and is nowhere accepted as it is for its own sake. Asceticism ranges rampant, is at the head of things, casts its shadow on the vital instincts and calls man to exceed the life of the body and even the life of the mental will and intelligence. The Western mind lays an enormous stress upon force of personality, upon the individual will, upon the apparent man and the desires and demands of his nature. But here is an opposing stress on a high growth towards impersonality, on the widening of the individual into the universal will, on an increasing or breaking beyond the apparent man and his limits. The flowering of the mental and vital ego or at most its subservience to the larger ego of the community is the West's cultural ideal. But here the ego is regarded as the chief obstacle to the soul's perfection and its place is proposed to be taken not by the concrete communal ego, but by something inward, abstract, transcendental, something supramental, supraphysical, absolutely real. The Western temperament is rajasic, kinetic, pragmatic, active; thought for it turns always to action and has little value except for the sake of action or else for a fine satisfaction of the mind's play and vigour. But here the type proposed for admiration is the self-possessed sattwic man for whom calm thought, spiritual knowledge and the inner life are the things of the greatest importance and action is chiefly of consequence not for its own sake, not for its rewards and fruits, but for its effects on the growth of the inner nature. Here too is a disconcerting quietism which looks forward to the cessation or Nirvana of all thought and action in a perpetual light and peace. It is not surprising that a critic with an unreleased Occidental mind should look upon these contrasts with much dissatisfaction, a recoil of antipathy, an almost ferocious repugnance.

But at any rate these things, however remote they may seem to his understanding, contain something that is lofty and noble.

He can disparage them as false, antirational and depressing, but not denounce them as evil and ignoble. Or he can do this only on the strength of such misrepresentations as some of those we have noted in Mr. Archer's more irresponsible strictures. These things may be signs of an antique or an antiquated mind, but are certainly not the fruits of a barbaric culture. But when he surveys the forms of the religion which they enlighten and animate, it does look to him as if he was in the presence of a pure barbarism, a savage ignorant muddle. For here is an abundance of everything of which he has so long been steadily emptying religion in his own culture, well content to call that emptiness reformation, enlightenment and the rational truth of things. He sees a gigantic polytheism, a superabundance of what seems to his intelligence rank superstition, a limitless readiness of belief in things that are to him without significance or incredible. The Hindu is popularly credited with thirty crores and more of gods, as many inhabitants for all the many heavens as there are men in this single earthly peninsula India, and he has no objection to adding, if need be, to this mighty multitude. Here are temples, images, a priesthood, a mass of unintelligible rites and ceremonies, the daily repetition of Sanskrit Mantras and prayers, some of them of a prehistoric creation, a belief in all kinds of supraphysical beings and forces, saints, Gurus, holy days, vows, offerings, sacrifice, a constant reference of life to powers and influences of which there can be no physical evidence, instead of a rational scientific dependence on the material laws which alone govern the existence of mortal creatures. It is to him an unintelligible chaos; it is animism; it is a monstrous folk-lore. The meaning which Indian thought puts upon these things, their spiritual sense, escapes him altogether or it leaves him incredulous or else strikes his mind as a vain and mad symbolism, subtle, useless, futile. And not only is the cult and belief of this people antiquated and mediaeval in kind, but it is not kept in its proper place. Instead of putting religion into an unobtrusive and ineffective corner, the Indian mind has the pretension, the preposterous pretension which rational man has outgrown for ever, of filling with it the whole of life.

It would be difficult to convince the too positive average European intelligence which has "outgrown" the religious mentality or is only struggling back towards it after a not yet liquidated bankruptcy of rationalistic materialism, that there is any profound truth or meaning in these Indian religious forms. It has been well said that they are rhythms of the spirit; but one who misses the spirit must necessarily miss too the connection of the spirit and the rhythm. The gods of this worship are, as every Indian knows, potent names, divine forms, dynamic personalities, living aspects of the one Infinite. Each Godhead is a form or derivation or dependent power of the supreme Trinity, each Goddess a form of the universal Energy, Conscious-Force or Shakti. But to the logical European mind monotheism, polytheism, pantheism are irreconcilable warring dogmas; oneness, many-ness, all-ness are not and cannot be different but concordant aspects of the eternal Infinite. A belief in one Divine Being superior to cosmos who is all cosmos and who lives in many forms of godhead, is a hotch-potch, mush, confusion of ideas; for synthesis, intuitive vision, inner experience are not the forte of this strongly external, analytic and logical mind. The image to the Hindu is a physical symbol and support of the supraphysical; it is a basis for the meeting between the embodied mind and sense of man and the supraphysical power, force or presence which he worships and with which he wishes to communicate. But the average European has small faith in disembodied entities and, if they are at all, he would put them away into a category apart, another unconnected world, a separate existence. A nexus between the physical and supraphysical is to his view a meaningless subtlety admissible only in imaginative poetry and romance.

The rites, ceremonies, system of cult and worship of

Hinduism can only be understood if we remember its fundamental character. It is in the first place a non-dogmatic inclusive religion and would have taken even Islam and Christianity into itself, if they had tolerated the process. All that it has met on its way it has taken into itself, content if it could put its forms into some valid relation with the truth of the supraphysical worlds and the truth of the Infinite. Again it has always known in its heart that religion, if it is to be a reality for the mass of men and not only for a few saints and thinkers, must address its appeal to the whole of our being, not only to the suprarational and the rational parts, but to all the others. The imagination, the emotions, the aesthetic sense, even the very instincts of the half subconscient parts must be taken into the influence. Religion must lead man towards the suprarational, the spiritual truth and it must take the aid of the illumined reason on the way, but it cannot afford to neglect to call Godwards the rest of our complex nature. And it must take too each man where he stands and spiritualise him through what he can feel and not at once force on him something which he cannot yet grasp as a true and living power. That is the sense and aim of all those parts of Hinduism which are specially stigmatised as irrational or antirational by the positivist intelligence. But the European mind has failed to understand this plain necessity or has despised it. It insists on "purifying" religion, by the reason and not by the spirit, on "reforming" it, by the reason and not by the spirit. And we have seen what were the results of this kind of purification and reformation in Europe. The infallible outcome of that ignorant doctoring has been first to impoverish and then slowly to kill religion; the patient has fallen a victim to the treatment, while he might well have survived the disease.

The accusation of a want of ethical content is almost monstrously false, it is the direct opposite of the truth; but we must look for its explanation in some kind of characteristic misunderstanding; for it is not new. Hindu thought and literature might almost be accused of a tyrannously pervading ethical obsession; everywhere the ethical note recurs. The idea of the Dharma is, next to the idea of the Infinite, its major chord; Dharma, next to spirit, is its foundation of life. There is no ethical idea which it has not stressed, put in its most ideal and imperative form, enforced by teaching, injunction, parable, artistic creation, formative examples. Truth, honour, loyalty, fidelity, courage, chastity, love, longsuffering, self-sacrifice, harmlessness, forgiveness, compassion, benevolence, beneficence are its common themes, are in its view the very stuff of a right human life, the essence of man's Dharma. Buddhism with its high and noble ethics, Jainism with its austere ideal of self-conquest, Hinduism with its magnificent examples of all sides of the Dharma are not inferior in ethical teaching and practice to any religion or system, but rather take the highest rank and have had the strongest effective force. For the practice of these virtues in older times there is abundant internal and foreign evidence. A considerable stamp of them still remains in spite of much degeneracy even though there has been some depression of the manlier qualities which only flourish in their fullest power on the soil of freedom. The legend to the contrary began in the minds of English scholars with a Christian bias who were misled by the stress which Indian philosophy lays on knowledge rather than works as the means of salvation. For they did not note or could not grasp the meaning of the rule well-known to all Indian spiritual seekers that a pure sattwic mind and life are presupposed as the first step towards the divine knowledge—the doers of evil find me not, says the Gita. And they were unable to realise that knowledge of the truth means for Indian thought not intellectual assent or recognition, but a new consciousness and a life according to the truth of the Spirit. Morality is for the Western mind mostly a thing of outward conduct; but conduct for the Indian mind is only one means of expression and sign of a soul-state. Hinduism only incidentally strings together a number of commandments for observance, a table of moral laws; more deeply it enjoins a spiritual or ethical purity of the mind with action as one outward index. It says strongly enough, almost too strongly, "Thou shouldst not kill," but insists more firmly on the injunction, "Thou shalt not hate, thou shalt not yield to greed, anger or malice," for these are the roots of killing. And Hinduism admits relative standards, a wisdom too hard for the European intelligence. Non-injuring is the very highest of its laws, *ahinsā paramo rharmaḥ;* still it does not lay it down as a physical rule for the warrior, but insistently demands from him mercy, chivalry, respect for the non-belligerent, the weak, the unarmed, the vanquished, the prisoner, the wounded, the fugitive, and so escapes the unpracticality of a too absolutist rule for all life. A misunderstanding of this inwardness and this wise relativity is perhaps responsible for much misrepresentation. The Western ethicist likes to have a high standard as a counsel of perfection and is not too much concerned if it is honoured more by the breach than by the observance; Indian ethics puts up an equally high and often higher standard; but less concerned with high professions than with the truth of life, it admits stages of progress and in the lower stages is satisfied if it can moralise as much as possible those who are not yet capable of the highest ethical concepts and practice.

All these criticisms of Hinduism are therefore either false in fact or invalid in their very nature. It remains to be considered whether the farther yet more common charge is justified in full or in part,—the damaging accusation that Indian culture depresses the vital force, paralyses the will, gives no great or vigorous power, no high incentive, no fortifying and ennobling motive to human life.

A RATIONALISTIC CRITIC ON INDIAN CULTURE

CHAPTER V

THE question before us is whether Indian culture has a sufficient power for the fortifying and ennobling of our normal human existence. Apart from its transcendental aims, has it any pragmatic, non-ascetic, dynamic value, any power for expansion of life and for the right control of life? This is a question of central importance. For if it has nothing of this kind to give us, then whatever its other cultural greatness, it cannot live. It becomes an abnormal cis-Himalayan hot-house splendour which could subsist in its peninsular seclusion, but must perish in the keen and arduous air of the modern struggle of life. No anti-vital culture can survive. A too intellectual or too ethereal civilisation void of strong vital stimulus and motive must languish for want of sap and blood. A culture to be permanently and completely serviceable to man must give him something more than some kind of rare transcendental uprush towards an exceeding of all earthly life-values. It must do more even than adorn with a great curiosity of knowledge, science and philosophic enquiry or a rich light and blaze of art, poetry and architecture, the long stability and orderly well-being of an old, ripe and humane society. All this Indian culture did in the past to a noble purpose. But it must satisfy too the tests of a progressive Life-power. There must be some inspiration for the terrestrial endeavour of man, an object, a stimulus, a force for development and a will to live. Whether or not our end is silence and Nirvana, a spiritual cessation or a material death, this is certain that the world itself is a mighty labour of a vast Life-Spirit and man the present doubtful crown on earth and the struggling but still unsuccessful present hero and protagonist of its endeavour or its drama. A great human culture must see this truth in some fullness; it must impart some conscious and ideal power of self-effectuation to this upward effort. It is not enough to found a stable base for life, not enough to adorn it, not enough to shoot up sublimely to summits beyond it; the greatness and growth of the race on earth must be our equal care. To miss this great intermediate reality is a capital imperfection and in itself a seal of failure.

Our critics will have it that the whole body of Indian culture bears the stamp of just such a failure. The Western impression has been that Hinduism is an entirely metaphysical and other-worldly system dreaming of things beyond, oblivious of the now and here: a depressing sense of the unreality of life or an intoxication of the Infinite turns it away from any nobility, vitality and greatness of human aspiration and the earth's labour. Its philosophy may be sublime, its religious spirit fervent, its ancient social system strong, symmetrical and stable, its literature and its art good in their own way, but the salt of life is absent, the breath of will-power, the force of a living endeavour. This new journalistic Apollo, our Archer who is out to cleave with his arrows the python coils of Indian barbarism, abounds in outcries in this sense. But, if that is so, evidently India can have done nothing great, contributed no invigorating power to human life, produced no men of mighty will, no potent personalities, no strong significant human lives, no vital human figures in art and poetry, no significant architecture and sculpture. And that is what our devil's advocate tells us in graphic phrases. He tells us that there is in this religion and philosophy a general undervaluing of life and endeavour. Life is conceived as a shoreless expanse in which generations rise and fall as helplessly and purposelessly as waves in mid-ocean; the individual is everywhere dwarfed and depreciated; one solitary great character, Gautama Buddha, who "perhaps never existed," is India's sole contribution to the world's pantheon, or for the rest a pale featureless Asoka. The characters of drama and poetry are lifeless exaggerations or puppets of supernatural powers; the art is empty of reality; the whole history of the civilisation makes a drab, effete, melancholy picture. There is no power of life in this religion and this philosophy, there is no breath of life in this history, there is no colour of life in this art and poetry; that is the blank result of Indian culture. Whoever has seen at first hand and felt the literature, followed the history, studied the civilisation of India can see that this is a bitter misrepresentation, a violent caricature, an absurd falsehood. But it is an extreme and unscrupulous way of putting an impression often given to the European mind and, as before, we must see why different eyes see the same object in such different colours. It is the same primary misunderstanding that is at the root. India has lived and lived richly, splendidly, greatly, but with a different will in life from Europe. The idea and plan of her life have been peculiar to her temperament, original and unique. Her values are not easy to seize for an outsider and her highest things are easily open to hostile misrepresentation by the ignorant, precisely because they are too high for the normal untrained mind and apt to shoot beyond its limits.

There are three powers that we must grasp in order to judge the life-value of a culture. There is, first, the power of its original conception of life; there is, next, the power of the forms, types and rhythms it has given to life; there is, last, the inspiration, the vigour, the force of vital execution of its motives manifested in the actual lives of men and of the community that flourished under its influence. The European conception of life is a thing with which we in India are now very familiar, because our present thought and effort are obscured with its shadow when they are not filled with its presence. For we have been trying hard to assimilate something of it, even to shape ourselves, and especially our political, economic and outward conduct into some imitation of its forms and rhythms. The European idea is the conception of a Force that manifests itself in the material universe and a Life in it of which man is almost the only discoverable meaning. This anthropocentric view of things has not been altered by the recent stress of Science on the vast blank inanities of an inconscient mechanical Nature. And in man, thus unique in the inert drift of Nature, the whole effort of Life is to arrive at some light and harmony of the understanding and ordering reason, some efficient rational power, adorning beauty, strong utility, vital enjoyment, economic welfare. The free power of the individual ego, the organised will of the corporate ego, these are the great needed forces. The development of individual personality and an organised efficient national life are the two things that matter in the European ideal. These two powers have grown, striven, run riot at times, and the restless and often violent vividness of the historic stir and the literary and artistic vivacity of Europe are due to their powerful colours. The enjoyment of life and force, the gallop of egoistic passion and vital satisfaction are a loud and insistent strain, a constant high-voiced motive. Against them is another opposite effort, the endeavour to govern life by reason, science, ethics, art; a restraining and harmonising utility is here the foremost motive. At different times different powers have taken the lead. Christian religiosity too has come in and added new tones, modified some tendencies, deepened others. Each age and period has increased the wealth of contributory lines and forces and helped the complexity and largeness of the total conception. At present the sense of the corporate life dominates and it is served by the idea of a great intellectual and material progress, an ameliorated political and social state governed by science. There is an ideal of intelligent utility, liberty and equality or else an ideal of stringent organisation and efficiency and a perfectly mobilised, carefully marshalled uniting of forces in a ceaseless pull towards the general welfare. This endeavour of Europe has become terribly outward and mechanical in its appearance; but some renewed power of a more humanistic idea is trying to beat its way in again and man may perhaps before long refuse to be tied on the wheel of his own triumphant machinery and conquered by his apparatus. At any rate we need not lay too much emphasis on what may be a passing phase. The broad permanent European conception of life remains and it is in its own limits a great and invigorating conception,—imperfect, narrow at the top, shut in under a heavy lid, poor in its horizons, too much of the soil, but still with a sense in it that is strenuous and noble.

The Indian conception of life starts from a deeper centre and moves on less external lines to a very different objective. The peculiarity of the Indian eye of thought is that it looks through the form, looks even through the force, and searches for the spirit in things everywhere. The peculiarity of the Indian will in life is that it feels itself to be unfulfilled, not in touch with perfection, not permanently justified in any intermediate satisfaction if it has not found and does not live in the truth of the spirit. The Indian idea of the world, of Nature and of existence is not physical, but psychological and spiritual. Spirit, soul, consciousness are not only greater than inert matter and inconscient force, but they precede and originate these lesser things. All force is power, or means of a secret spirit; the force that sustains the world is a conscious Will, and Nature is its machinery of executive power. Matter is the body or field of a consciousness hidden within it, the material universe a form and movement of the Spirit. Man himself is not a life and mind born of Matter and eternally subject to physical Nature, but a spirit that uses life and body. It is an understanding faith in this conception of existence, it is the attempt to live it out, it is the science and practice of this high endeavour, and it is the aspiration to break out in the end from this mind bound to life and matter into a greater spiritual consciousness that is the innermost sense of Indian culture. It is this that constitutes the much talked of Indian spirituality. It is evidently very remote from the dominant European idea; it is different even from the form given by Europe to the Christian conception of life. But it does not mean at all that Indian culture concedes no reality to life, follows no material or vital aims and satisfactions, or cares to do nothing for our actual human existence. It cannot truly be contended that a conception of this kind can give no powerful and inspiring motive to the human effort of man. Certainly, in this view, matter, mind, life, reason, form are only powers of the spirit and valuable not for their own sake, but because of the Spirit within them, *Atmārtham,* they exist for the sake of the Self, says the Upanishad, and this is certainly the Indian attitude to these things. But that does not depreciate them or deprive them of their value; on the contrary it increases a hundredfold their significance. Form and body immensely increase in importance if they are felt to be instinct with the life of the Spirit and are conceived as a support for the rhythm of its workings. And human life was in ancient Indian thought no vile and unworthy existence; it is the greatest thing known to us, it is desired, the Purana boldly says, even by the gods in heaven. The deepening and raising of the richest or the most potent energies of our minds, our hearts, our life-power, our bodies are all means by which the spirit can proceed to self-discovery and the return to its own infinite freedom and power. For when mind and heart and reason heighten to their greatest lights and powers, they bring embodied life to the point where it can open to a still greater light and power beyond them; the individual mind widens into a vast universal consciousness and lifts towards a high spiritual transcendence. These are at least no sterilising and depressing ideas; they exalt the life of man and make something like godhead its logical outcome.

The dignity given to human existence by the Vedantic

thought and by the thought of the classical ages of Indian culture exceeded anything conceived by the western idea of humanity. Man in the West has always been only an ephemeral creature of Nature or a soul manufactured at birth by an arbitrary breath of the whimsical Creator and set under impossible conditions to get salvation, but far more likely to be thrown away into the burning refuse-heap of Hell as a hopeless failure. At best he is exalted by a reasoning mind and will and an effort to be better than God or Nature made him. Far more ennobling, inspiring, filled with the motive-force of a great idea is the conception placed before us by Indian culture. Man in the Indian idea is a spirit veiled in the works of energy, moving to self-discovery, capable of Godhead. He is a soul that is growing through Nature to conscious self-hood; he is a divinity and an eternal existence; he is an ever-flowing wave of the God-ocean, an inextinguishable spark of the supreme Fire. Even, he is in his uttermost reality identical with the ineffable Transcendence from which he came and greater than the godheads whom he worships. The natural half-animal creature that for a while he seems to be is not at all his whole being and is not in any way his real being. His inmost reality is the divine Self or at least one dynamic eternal portion of it, and to find that and exceed his outward, apparent, natural self is the greatness of which he alone of terrestrial beings is capable. He has the spiritual capacity to pass to a supreme and extraordinary pitch of manhood and that is the first aim which is proposed to him by Indian culture. Living no more in the first crude type of an undeveloped humanity to which most men still belong, *na yathā prākṛto janaḥ*, he can even become a free perfected semi-divine man, *mukta, siddha.* But he can do more; released into the cosmic consciousness, his spirit can become one with God, one self with the Spirit of the universe or rise into a Light and Vastness that transcends the universe; his nature can become one dynamic power with universal Nature or one Light with a transcendental Gnosis. To be shut up for ever in his ego is not his ultimate perfection; he can become a universal soul, one with the supreme Unity, one with others, one with all beings. This is the high sense and power concealed in his humanity that he can aspire to this perfection and transcendence. And he can arrive at it through any or all of his natural powers if they will accept release, through his mind and reason and thought and their illuminations, through his heart and its unlimited power of love and sympathy, through his will and its dynamic drive towards mastery and right action, through his ethical nature and its hunger for the universal Good, through his aesthetic sense and its seekings after delight and beauty or through his inner soul and its power of absolute spiritual calm, wideness, joy and peace.

This is the sense of that spiritual liberation and perfection of which Indian thought and inner discipline have been full since the earliest Vedic times. However high and arduous this aim may be, it has always seemed to it possible and even in a way near and normal, once spiritual realisation has discovered its path. The positivist Western mind finds it difficult to give this conception the rank of a living and intelligible idea. The status of the *siddha, bhāgavata, mukta* appears to it a baseless chimera. It seems to its Christian associations a blasphemy against the solitary greatness of God, before whom man is only a grovelling worm, to its fierce attachment to the normal ego a negation of personality and a repellent menace, to its earth-bound rationalism a dream, a self-hypnotic hallucination or a deluding mania. And yet in ancient Europe the Stoics, Platonists, Pythagoreans had made some approach to this aspiration, and even afterwards, a few rare souls have envisaged or pursued it through occult ways. And now it is again beginning to percolate into the Western imagination, but less as a dynamic life-motive than in poetry and in certain aspects of general thought or through movements like Theosophy that draw from ancient and oriental sources. Science and philosophy and religion still regard it with scorn as an illusion, with indifference as a dream or with condemnation as a heathen arrogance. It is the distinction of Indian culture to have seized on this great dynamic hope, to have kept it a living and practicable thing and to have searched out all the possible paths to this spiritual way of perfect existence. Indian thought has made this great thing the common highest aim and universal spiritual destiny of the soul that is in every human creature.

The value of the Indian conception for life must depend on the relations and gradations by which it connects this difficult and distant perfection with our normal living and present everyday nature. Put over against the latter without any connection or any gradations that lead up to it and make it possible, it would either be a high unattainable ideal or the detached remote passion of a few exceptional spirits. Or even it would discourage the springs of our natural life by the too great contrast between the spiritual being and our own poor imperfect nature. Something of the kind has happened in later times; the current Western impression about the exaggerated asceticism and otherworldliness of Indian religion and philosophy is founded on the growing gulf created by a later thought between man's spiritual possibilities and his terrestrial status. But we must not be misled by extreme tendencies or the overemphasis put upon them in a period of decline. If we would get at the real meaning of the Indian idea of life, we must go back to its best times. And we must not look at this or that school of philosophy or at some side of it as the whole of Indian thought; the totality of the ancient philosophical thinking, religion, literature, art, society must be our ground of enquiry. The Indian conception in its early soundness made no such mistake as to imagine that this great thing can or even ought to be done by some violent, intolerant, immediate leap from one pole of existence to its opposite. Even the most extreme philosophies do not go so far. The workings of the Spirit in the universe were a reality to one side of the Indian mind, to another only a half reality, a self-descriptive Lila or illusory Maya. To the one the world was an action of the Infinite Energy, Shakti, to the other a figment of some secondary paradoxical consciousness in the Eternal, Maya: but life as an intermediate reality was never denied by any school of Indian thinking. Indian thought recognised that the normal life of man has to be passed through with a conscientious endeavour to fulfil its purpose: its powers must be developed with knowledge; its forms must be perused, interpreted and fathomed; its values must be worked out, possessed and lived; its enjoyments must be fully taken on their own level. Only afterwards can we go on to self-existence or a supra-existence. The spiritual perfection which opens before man is the crown of a long, patient, millennial outflowering of the spirit in life and nature. This belief in a gradual spiritual progress and evolution here is indeed the secret of the almost universal Indian acceptance of the truth of reincarnation. It is only by millions of lives in inferior forms that the secret soul in the universe, conscious even in the inconscient, *cetanaḥ acetaneṣu*, has arrived at humanity: it is only by hundreds or thousands, perhaps even millions of human lives that man can grow into his divine self-existence. Every life is a step which he can take backward or forward; his action in life, his will in life, his thought and knowledge by which he governs and directs his life, determine what he is yet to be from the earliest stages to the last transcendence. *Yathā karma yathā śrutam*.

This belief in a gradual soul evolution with a final perfection or divine transcendence and human life as its first direct means and often repeated opportunity, is the pivot of the Indian conception of existence. This gives to our life the figure of an ascent in spirals or circles; and the long period of the ascent has to be filled in with human knowledge and human action and human experience. There is room within it for all terrestrial aims, activities and aspirations; there is place in the ascent for all types of human character and nature. For the spirit in the world assumes hundreds of forms and follows many tendencies and gives many shapes to his play or Lila. All are part of the total mass of our necessary experience; each has its justification, each has its natural or true law and reason of being, each has its utility in the play and the process. The claim of sense satisfaction was not ignored, it was given its just importance. The soul's need of labour and heroic action was not stifled, it was urged to its fullest action and freest scope. The hundred forms of the pursuit of knowledge were given an absolute freedom of movement; the play of the emotions was allowed, refined, trained till they were fit for the divine levels; the demand of the aesthetic faculties was encouraged in its highest rarest forms and in life's commonest details. Indian culture did not deface nor impoverish the richness of the grand game of human life; it never depressed or mutilated the activities of our nature. On the contrary, subject to a certain principle of harmony and government, it allowed them their full, often their extreme value. Man was allowed to fathom on his way all experience, to give to his character and action a large rein and heroic proportions, and to fill in life opulently with colour and beauty and enjoyment. This life side of the Indian idea is stamped in strong relief over the epic and the classical literature. It is amazing indeed that anyone with an eye or a brain could have read the Ramayana, Mahabharata, the dramas, the literary epics, the romances, and the great abundance of gnomic and lyric poetry in Sanskrit and in the later tongues (to say nothing of the massive remains of other cultural work and social and political system and speculation), and yet failed to perceive this breadth, wealth and greatness. One must have read without eyes to see or without a mind to understand; most indeed of the adverse critics have not read or studied at all, but only flung about their preconceived notions with a violent or a high-browed ignorant assurance.

But while it is the generous office of culture to enrich, enlarge and encourage human life, it must also give the vital forces a guiding law, subject them to some moral and rational government and lead them beyond their first natural formulations, until it can find for life the clue to a spiritual freedom, perfection and greatness. The pre-eminent value of the ancient Indian civilisation lay in the power with which it did this work, the profound wisdom and high and subtle skill with which it based society and ordered the individual life, and encouraged and guided the propensities of human nature and finally turned them all towards the realisation of its master idea. The mind it was training, while not called away from its immediate aims, was never allowed to lose sight of the use of life as a discipline for spiritual perfection and a passage to the Infinite.

The Indian mind whether in the government of life or in the discipline of spirituality, kept always in sight two main truths of our existence. First, our being in its growth has stages through which it must pass: if there are sometimes leaps forward, yet most of its growth is a developing progression; the swiftest race has its stadia. Then again, life is complex and the nature of man is complex; in each life man has to figure a certain sum of his complexity and put that into some kind of order. But the initial movement of life is that form of it which develops the powers of the natural ego in man; self-interest and hedonistic desire are the original human motives,—*kāma, artha.* Indian culture gave a large recognition to this primary turn of our nature. These powers have to be accepted and put in order; for the natural ego-life must be lived and the forces it evolves in the human being must be brought to fullness. But this element must be kept from making any too unbridled claim or heading furiously towards its satisfaction; only so can it get its full results without disaster and only so can it be inspired eventually to go beyond itself and turn in the end to a greater spiritual Good and Bliss. An internal or external anarchy cannot be the rule; a life governed in any absolute or excessive degree by self-will, passion, sense-attraction, self-interest and desire cannot be the natural whole of a human or a humane existence. The tempting imagination that it can and that this is the true law is a lure with which the Western mind has played in characteristic leanings or outbursts; but this turn unjustly called Paganism,—for the Greek or Pagan intelligence had a noble thought for law and harmony and self-rule,—is alien to the Indian spirit. India has felt the call of the senses not less than Greece, Rome or modern Europe; she perceived very well the possibility of a materialistic life and its attraction worked on certain minds and gave birth to the philosophy of the Charvakas: but this could not take full hold or establish even for a time any dominant empire. Even if we can see in it, when lived on a grand scale, a certain perverse greatness, still a colossal egoism indulgent of the sole life of the mind and the senses was regarded by her as the nature of the Asura and Rakshasa. It is the Titanic, gigantic or demoniac type of spirit, permitted in its own plane, but not the proper law for a human life. Another power claims man and overtops desire and self-interest and self-will, the power of the Dharma.

The Dharma, at once religious law of action and deepest law of our nature, is not, as in the Western idea, a creed, cult or ideal inspiring an ethical and social rule; it is the right law of functioning of our life in all its parts. The tendency of man to seek after a just and perfect law of his living finds its truth and its justification in the Dharma. Everything indeed has its dharma, its law of life imposed on it by its nature; but for man the dharma is the conscious imposition of a rule of ideal living on all his members. Dharma is fixed in its essence, but still it develops in our consciousness and evolves and has its stages; there are gradations of spiritual and ethical ascension in the search for the highest law of our nature. All men cannot follow in all things one common and invariable rule. Life is too complex to admit of the arbitrary ideal simplicity which the moralising theorist loves. Natures differ; the position, the work we have to do has its own claims and standards; aim and bent, the call of life, the call of the spirit within is not the same for everyone: the degree and turn of development and the capacity, *adhikāra,* are not equal. Man lives in society and by society, and every society has its own general dharma, and the individual life must be fitted into this wider law of movement. But there too the individual's part in society, and his nature and the needs of his capacity and temperament vary and have many kinds and degrees: the social law must make some room for this variety and would lose by being rigidly one for all. The man of knowledge, the man of power, the productive and acquisitive man, the priest, scholar, poet, artist, ruler, fighter, trader, tiller of the soil, craftsman, labourer, servant cannot usefully have the same training, cannot be shaped in the same pattern, cannot all follow the same way of living. All ought not to be put under the same tables of the law; for that would be a senseless geometric rigidity that would spoil the plastic truth of life. Each has his type of nature and there must be a rule for the perfection of that type; each has his own proper function and there must be a canon and ideal for the function. There must be in all things some wise and understanding standard of practice and idea of perfection and living rule,—that is the one thing needful for the Dharma. A lawless impulsion of desire and interest and propensity cannot be allowed to lead human conduct; even in the frankest following of desire and interest and propensity there must be a governing and restraining and directing line, a guidance. There must be an ethic or a science, a restraint as well as a scope arising from the truth of the thing sought, a standard of perfection, an order. Differing with the type of the man and the type of the function these special dharmas would yet rise towards the greater law and truth that contains and overtops the others and is universally effective. This then was the Dharma, special for the special person, stage of development, pursuit of life or individual field of action, but universal too in the broad lines which all ought to pursue.

The universal embracing dharma in the Indian idea is a law of ideal perfection for the developing mind and soul of man; it compels him to grow in the power and force of certain high or large universal qualities which in their harmony build a highest type of manhood. In Indian thought and life this was the ideal of the best, the law of the good or noble man, the discipline laid down for the self-perfecting individual, *ārya, śreṣṭha, sajjana, sādhu*. This ideal was not a purely moral or ethical conception, although that element might predominate; it was also intellectual, religious, social, aesthetic, the flowering of the whole ideal man, the perfection of the total human nature. The most varied qualities met in the Indian conception of the best, *śreṣṭha,* the good and noble man, *ārya*. In the heart benevolence, beneficence, love, compassion, altruism, long-suffering, liberality, kindliness, patience; in the character courage, heroism, energy, loyalty, continence, truth, honour, justice, faith, obedience and reverence where these were due, but power too to govern and direct, a fine modesty and yet a strong independence and noble pride; in the mind wisdom and intelligence and love of learning, knowledge of all the best thought, an openness to poetry, art and beauty, an educated capacity and skill in works; in the inner being a strong religious sense, piety, love of God, seeking after the Highest, the spiritual turn; in social relations and conduct a strict observance of all the social dharmas, as father, son, husband, brother, kinsman, friend, ruler or subject, master or servant, priest or warrior or worker, king or sage, member of clan or caste: this was the total ideal of the Arya, the man of high upbringing and noble nature. The ideal is clearly portrayed in the written records of ancient India during two millenniums and it is the very life-breath of Hindu ethics. It was the creation of an at once ideal and rational mind, spirit-wise and worldly-wise, deeply religious, nobly ethical, firmly yet flexibly intellectual, scientific and aesthetic, patient and tolerant of life's difficulties and human weakness, but arduous in self-discipline. This was the mind that was at the base of the Indian civilisation and gave its characteristic stamp to all the culture.

But even this was only the foundation and preparation for another highest thing which by its presence exalts human life beyond itself into something spiritual and divine. Indian culture raised the crude animal life of desire, self-interest and satisfied propensity beyond its first intention to a noble self-exceeding and shapeliness by infusing into it the order and high aims of the Dharma. But its profounder characteristic aim—and in this it was unique—was to raise this nobler life too of the self-perfecting human being beyond its own intention to a mightiest self-exceeding and freedom; it laboured to infuse into it the great aim of spiritual liberation and perfection, *mukti, mokṣa.* The Law and its observance are neither the beginning nor the end of man; there is beyond the field of the Law a larger realm of consciousness in which, climbing, he emerges into a great spiritual freedom. Not a noble but ever death-bound manhood is the highest height of man's perfection: immortality, freedom, divinity are within his grasp. Ancient Indian culture held this highest aim constantly before the inner eye of the soul and insistently inspired with its prospect and light the whole conception of existence. The entire life of the individual was ennobled by this aim, the whole ordering of society was cast into a scale of graduated ascension towards this supreme summit.

A well-governed system of the individual and communal existence must be always in the first instance an ordering of the three first powers recognised by Indian thought. The claim of the natural functionings must be recognised in it to the full; the pursuit of personal and communal interest and the satisfaction of human desires as of human needs must be amply admitted and there must be an understanding combination of knowledge and labour towards these ends. But all must be controlled, uplifted and widened to greater aims by the ideal of the Dharma. And if, as India believes, there is a higher spiritual consciousness towards which man can rise, that ascent must be kept throughout in view as the supreme goal of life. The system of Indian culture at once indulged and controlled man's nature; it fitted him for his social role; it stamped on his mind the generous ideal of an accomplished humanity refined, harmonised in all its capacities, ennobled in all its members; but it placed before him too the theory and practice of a highest change, familiarised him with the conception of a spiritual existence and sowed in him a hunger for the divine and the infinite. The symbols of his religion were filled with suggestions which led towards it; at every step he was reminded of lives behind and in front and of worlds beyond the material existence; he was brought close to the nearness, even to the call and pressure of the Spirit that is greater than the life it informs, of the final goal, of a high possible immortality, freedom, God-consciousness, divine Nature. Man was not allowed to forget that he had in him a highest self beyond his little personal ego and that always he and all things live, move and have their being in God, in the Eternal, in the Spirit. There were ways and disciplines provided in number by which he could realise this liberating truth or could at least turn and follow at a distance this highest aim according to his capacity and nature, *adhikāra*. Around him he saw and revered the powerful practicants and mighty masters of these disciplines. These men were in early times the teachers of his youth, the summits of his society, the inspirers and fountain-heads of his civilisation, the great lights of his culture. Spiritual freedom, spiritual perfection were not figured as a far off intangible ideal, but presented as the highest human aim towards which all must grow in the end and were made near and possible to his endeavour from a first practicable basis of life and the Dharma. The spiritual idea governed, enlightened and gathered towards itself all the other life-motives of a great civilised people.

A RATIONALISTIC CRITIC ON INDIAN CULTURE

CHAPTER VI

THESE are the principal lines upon which the structure of Indian civilisation was founded and they constitute the power of its conception of life. I do not think it can be said that there is here any inferiority to other human cultures or to any established conception of life that has ever held sway over the mind of man in historic times. There is nothing here that can be said to discourage life and its flowering or to deprive it of impetus and elevation and a great motive. On the contrary there is a full and frank recognition and examination of the whole of human existence in all its variety and range and power, there is a clear and wise and noble idea for its right government and there is an ideal tendency pointing it upward and a magnificent call to a highest possible perfection and greatness. These are the serious uses of culture, these are the things that raise the life of man above a crude, primitive barbarism. If a civilisation is to be judged by the power of its ideas, their power for these great uses, Indian civilisation was inferior to none. Certainly, it was not perfect or final or complete; for that can be alleged of no past or present cultural idea or system. Man is in his inmost self an infinite being, in his mind and life too he is continually growing, with whatever stumblings and long relapses, and he cannot be permanently bound in any one system of ideas or frame of living. The structures in which he lives are incomplete and provisional; even those which seem the most comprehensive lose their force to stand and are convicted by time of insufficiency and must be replaced or change. But this at least can be said of the Indian idea that it seized with a remarkable depth and comprehensiveness on the main truths and needs of the whole being, on his mind and life and body, his artistic and ethical and intellectual parts of nature, his soul and spirit, and gave them a subtle and liberal, a profoundly large and high and wise, a sympathetic and yet nobly arduous direction. More cannot be said for any past or any existing culture.

But there must be in any culture aiming at completeness, not only great and noble governing and inspiring ideas, but a harmony of forms and rhythms, a mould into which the ideas and the life can run and settle. Here we must be prepared for a lesser perfection, a greater incompleteness. And the reason is that just as the spirit is vaster than its ideas, the ideas too are larger than their forms, moulds and rhythms. Form has a certain fixity which limits; no form can exhaust or fully express the potentialities of the idea or force that gave it birth. Neither can any idea, however great, or any limited play of force or form bind the infinite spirit: that is the secret of earth's need of mutation and progress. The idea is only a partial expression of the spirit. Even within its own limits, on its own lines it ought always to become more supple, to fill itself out with other views, to rise and broaden to new applications, and often it has to lose itself in uplifting transformations of its own meaning into vaster significances or fuse itself into new and richer syntheses. In the history of all great cultures therefore we find a passage through three periods, for this passage is a necessary consequence of this truth of things. There is a first period of large and loose formation; there is a second period in which we see a fixing of forms, moulds and rhythms; and there is a closing or a critical period of superannuation, decay and disintegration. This last stage is the supreme crisis in the life of a civilisation; if it cannot transform itself, it enters into a slow lingering decline or else collapses in a death agony brought about by the rapid impact of stronger and more immediately living though not necessarily greater or truer powers or formations. But if it is able to shake itself free of limiting forms, to renovate its ideas and to give a new scope to its spirit, if it is willing to understand, master and assimilate novel growths and necessities, then there is a rebirth, a fresh lease of life and expansion, a true renascence.

Indian civilisation passed in its own large and leisurely manner through all these stages. Its first period was that of a great spiritual outflowering in which the forms were supple, flexible and freely responsive to its essential spirit. That fluid movement passed away into an age of strong intellectuality in which all was fixed into distinct, sufficiently complex, but largely treated and still supple forms and rhythms. There came as a consequence a period of richly crystallised fixity shaken by crises which were partly met by a change of ideas and a modification of forms. But the hard binding of set forms triumphed at last and there was a decline of the inspiring spirit, a stagnation of living force, a progressive decay of the outward structure. The decay was accompanied and at once arrested for a moment and hastened in the end by the impact of other cultures. Today we are in the midst of a violent and decisive crisis brought about by the inflooding of the West and of all for which it stands. An upheaval resulted that began with the threat of a total death and irretrievable destruction of the culture; but its course is now uplifted on the contrary by the strong hope of a great revival, transmutation and renascence. Each of these three stages has its special significance for the student of culture. If we would understand the essential spirit of Indian civilisation, we must go back to its first formative period, the early epoch of the Veda and the Upanishads, its heroic creative seed-time. If we would study the fixed forms of its spirit and discern the thing it eventually realised as the basic rhythm of its life, we must look with an observing eye at the later middle period of the Shastras and the classic writings, the age of philosophy and science, legislation and political and social theory and many-sided critical thought, religious fixation, art, sculpture, painting, architecture. If we would discover the limitations, the points at which it stopped short and failed to develop its whole or its true spirit, we must observe closely the unhappy disclosures of its period of decline. If, finally, we would discover the directions it is likely to follow in its transformation, we must try to fathom what lies beneath the still confused movements of its crisis of renascence. None of these can indeed be cut clean apart from each other; for what developed in one period is already forecast and begun in the preceding age: but still on a certain large and imprecise scale we can make these distinctions and they are necessary for a discerning analytic view. But at present we are only concerned with the developed forms and the principal rhythms which persisted through its greater eras.

The problem which Indian culture had to solve was that of a firm outward basis on which to found the practical development of its spirit and its idea in life. How are we to take the natural life of man and, while allowing it sufficient scope and variety and freedom, yet to subject it to a law, canon, dharma, a law of function, a law of type, a law of each actual unideal human tendency and a law too of highest ideal intention? And how again are we to point that dharma towards its exceeding by fulfilment and cessation of its disciplinary purpose in the secure freedom of the spiritual life? Indian culture from an early stage seized upon a double idea for its own guidance which it threw into a basic system of the individual life in the social frame. This was the double system of the four Varnas and the four Ashramas,—four graded classes of society and four successive stages of a developing human life.

The ancient Chaturvarnya must not be judged by its later disintegrated degeneration and gross meaningless parody, the caste system. But neither was it precisely the system of the classes which we find in other civilisations, priesthood, nobility, merchant class and serfs or labourers. It may have had outwardly the same starting point, but it was given a very different revealing significance. The ancient Indian idea was that man falls by his nature into four types. There are, first and highest, the man of learning and thought and knowledge; next, the man of power and action, ruler, warrior, leader, administrator; third in the scale, the economic man, producer and wealth-getter, the merchant, artisan, cultivator: these were the twice-born, who received the initiation, Brahmin, Kshatriya, Vaishya. Last came the more undeveloped human type, not yet fit for these steps of the scale, unintellectual, without force, incapable of creation or intelligent production, the man fit only for unskilled labour and menial service, the Shudra. The economic order of society was cast in the form and gradation of these four types. The Brahmin class was called upon to give the community its priests, thinkers, men of letters, legislators, scholars, religious leaders and guides. The Kshatriya class gave it its kings, warriors, governors and administrators. The Vaishya order supplied it with its producers, agriculturists, craftsmen, artisans, merchants and traders. The Shudra class ministered to its need of menials and servants. As far as this went, there was nothing peculiar in the system except its extraordinary durability and, perhaps, the supreme position given to religion, thought and learning, not only at the top of the scale,—for that can be parallelled from one or two other civilisations,—but as the dominant power. The Indian idea in its purity fixed the status of a man in this order not by his birth, but by his capacities and his inner nature, and, if this rule had been strictly observed, that would have been a very clear mark of distinctness, a superiority of a unique kind. But even the best society is always something of a machine and gravitates towards the material sign and standard, and to found truly the social order upon this finer psychological basis would have been in those times a difficult and vain endeavour. In practice we find that birth became the basis of the Varna. It is elsewhere that we must look for the strong distinguishing mark which has made of this social structure a thing apart and sole in its type.

At no time indeed was the adherence to the economic rule quite absolute. The early ages show a considerable flexibility which was not quite lost in the process of complex crystallisation into a fixed form. And even in the greater rigidity of the latter-day caste system there has been in practice a confusion of economic functions. The vitality of a vigorous community cannot obey at every point the indications of a pattern and tradition cut by the mechanising mind. Moreover there was always a difference between the ideal theory of the system and its rougher unideal practice. For the material side of an idea or system has always its weaknesses even in its best times, and the final defect of all systems of this kind is that they stiffen into a fixed hierarchy which cannot maintain permanently its purity or the utility it was meant to serve. It becomes a soulless form and prolongs itself in a state of corruption, degeneracy or oppressive formalism when the uses that justified it are no longer in existence. Even when its ways can no longer be made consistent with the developing needs of the growth of humanity, the formal system persists and corrupts the truth of life and blocks progress. Indian society did not escape this general law; it was overtaken by these deficiencies, lost the true sense of the thing with which it set out to embody and degenerated into a chaos of castes, developing evils which we are now much embarrassed to eliminate. But it was a well-devised and necessary scheme in its time; it gave the community the firm and nobly built stability it needed for the security of its cultural development,—a stability hardly parallelled in any other culture. And, as interpreted by the Indian genius, it became a greater thing than a mere outward economic, political and social mechanism intended to serve the needs and convenience of the collective life.

For the real greatness of the Indian system of the four Varnas did not lie in its well-ordered division of economic function; its true originality and permanent value was in the ethical and spiritual content which the thinkers and builders of the society poured into these forms. This inner content started with the idea that the intellectual, ethical and spiritual growth of the individual is the central need of the race. Society itself is only the necessary framework for this growth; it is a system of relations which provides it with its needed medium, field and conditions and with a nexus of helpful influences. A secure place had to be found in the community for the individual man from which he could at once serve these relations, helping to maintain the society and pay it his debt of duty and assistance, and proceed to his own self-development with the best possible aid from the communal life. Birth was accepted in practice as the first gross and natural indicator; for heredity to the Indian mind has always ranked as a factor of the highest importance: it was even taken in later thought as a sign of the nature and as an index to the surroundings which the individual had prepared for himself by his past soul-development in former existences. But birth is not and cannot be the sole test of Varna. The intellectual capacity of the man, the turn of his temperament, his ethical nature, his spiritual stature, these are the important factors. There was erected therefore a rule of family living, a system of individual observance and self-training, a force of upbringing and education which would bring out and formulate these essential things. The individual man was carefully trained in the capacities, habits and attainments, and habituated to the sense of honour and duty necessary for the discharge of his allotted function in life. He was scrupulously equipped with the science of the thing he had to do, the best way to succeed in it as an interest, *artha,* and to attain to the highest rule, canon and recognised perfection of its activities, economic, political, sacerdotal, literary, scholastic or whatever else they might be. Even the most despised pursuits had their education, their law and canon, their ambition of success, their sense of honour in the discharge and scruple of well-doing, their dignity of a fixed standard of perfection, and it was because they had these things that even the lowest and least attractive could be in a certain degree a means of self-finding and ordered self-satisfaction. In addition to this special function and training there were the general accomplishments, sciences, arts, graces of life, those which satisfy the intellectual, aesthetic and hedonistic powers of human nature. These in ancient India were many and various, were taught with minuteness, thoroughness and subtlety and were available to all men of culture.

But while there was provision for all these things and it was made with a vivid liberality of the life-spirit and a noble sense of order, the spirit of Indian culture did not, like other ancient cultures, stop here. It said to the individual: "This is only the substructure: it is of a pressing importance indeed, but still not the last and greatest thing. When you have paid your debt to society, filled well and admirably your place in its life, helped its maintenance and continuity and taken from it your legitimate and desired satisfactions, there still remains the greatest thing of all. There is still your own self, the inner you, the soul which is a spiritual portion of the Infinite, one in its essence with the Eternal. This self, this soul in you you have to find, you are here for that, and it is from the place I have provided for you in life and by this training that you can begin to find it. For to each Varna I have supplied its highest ideal of manhood, the highest ideal way of which your nature is capable. By directing your life and nature in its own law of being towards that perfection, you can not only grow towards the ideal and enter into harmony with universal nature but come also into nearness and contact with a greater nature of divinity and move towards transcendence. That is the real object before you. From the life-basis I give you, you can rise to the liberating knowledge which brings a spiritual release, *mokṣa*. Then you can grow out of all these limitations in which you are being trained; you can grow through the fulfilled Dharma and beyond it into the eternity of your self, into the fullness, freedom, greatness and bliss of the immortal spirit; for that is what each man is behind the veils of his nature. When you have done that you are free. Then you have gone beyond all the dharmas; you are then a universal soul, one with all existence, and you can either act in that divine liberty for the good of all living things or else turn to enjoy in solitude the bliss of eternity and transcendence." The whole system of society, founded on the four Varnas, was made a harmonious means for the elevation and progress of the soul, mind and life from the natural pursuit of interest and desire, first to the perfection of the law of our being, Dharma, and at the end to a highest spiritual freedom. For man's true end in life must be always this realisation of his own immortal self, this entry in its secret of an infinite and eternal existence.

The Indian system did not entirely leave this difficult growth to the individual's unaided inner initiative. It supplied him with a framework; it gave him a scale and gradation for his life which could be made into a kind of ladder rising in that sense. This high convenience was the object of the four Ashramas. Life was divided into four natural periods and each of them marked out a stage in the working out of this cultural idea of living. There was the period of the student, the period of the householder, the period of the recluse or forest-dweller, the period of the free super-social man, *parivrājaka*. The student life was framed to lay the groundwork of what the man had to know, do and be. It gave a thorough training in the necessary arts, sciences, branches of knowledge, but it was still more insistent on the discipline of the ethical nature and in earlier days contained as an indispensable factor a grounding in the Vedic formula of spiritual knowledge. In the earlier days this training was given in suitable surroundings far away from the life of cities and the teacher was one who had himself passed through the round of this circle of living and, very usually, even, one who had arrived at some remarkable realisation of spiritual knowledge. But subsequently education became more intellectual and mundane; it was imparted in cities and universities and aimed less at an inner preparation of character and knowledge and more at instruction and the training of the intelligence. But in the beginning the Aryan man was really prepared in some degree for the four great objects of his life, *artha, kāma, dharma, mokṣa*. Entering into the householder stage to live out his knowledge, he was able to serve there the three first human objects; he satisfied his natural being and its itnerests and desire to take the joy of life, he paid his debt to the society and its demands and by the way he discharged his life functions he prepared himself for the last greatest purpose of his existence. In the third stage he retired to the forest and worked out in a certain seclusion the truth of his spirit. He lived in a broad freedom from the stricter social bonds; but if he so willed, gathering the young around him or receiving the inquirer and seeker, he could leave his knowledge to the new rising generation as an educator or a spiritual teacher. In the last stage of life, he was free to throw off every remaining tie and to wander over the world in an extreme spiritual detachment from all the forms of social life, satisfying only the barest necessities, communing with the universal spirit, making his soul ready for eternity. This circle was not obligatory on all. The great majority never went beyond the two first stages; many passed away in the *vānaprastha* or forest stage. Only the rare few made the last extreme venture and took the life of the wandering recluse. But this profoundly conceived cycle gave a scheme which kept the full course of the human spirit in its view; it could be taken advantage of by all according to their actual growth and in its fullness by those who were sufficiently developed in their present birth to complete the circle.

On this first firm and noble basis Indian civilisation grew to its maturity and became a thing rich, splendid and unique. While it filled the view with the last mountain prospect of a supreme spiritual elevation, it did not neglect the life of the levels. It lived between the busy life of the city and village, the freedom and seclusion of the forest and the last overarching illimitable ether. Moving firmly between life and death it saw beyond both and cut out a hundred high roads to immortality. It developed the external nature and drew it into the inner self; it enriched life to raise it into the spirit. Thus founded, thus trained, the ancient Indian race grew to astonishing heights of culture and civilisation; it lived with a noble, well-based, ample and vigorous order and freedom; it developed a great literature, sciences, arts, crafts, industries; it rose to the highest possible ideals and no mean practice of knowledge and culture, of arduous greatness and heroism, of kindness, philanthropy and human sympathy and oneness; it laid the inspired basis of wonderful spiritual philosophies; it examined the secrets of external nature and discovered and lived the boundless and miraculous truths of the inner being; it fathomed self and understood and possessed the world. As the civilisation grew in richness and complexity, it lost indeed the first grand simplicity of its early order. The intellect towered and widened, but intuition waned or retreated into the hearts of the saints and adepts and mystics. A greater stress came to be laid on scientific system, accuracy and order, not only in all the things of the life and mind, but even in the things of the spirit; the free flood of intuitive knowledge was forced to run in hewn channels. Society became more artificial and complex, less free and noble; more of a bond on the individual, it was less a field for the growth of his spiritual faculties. The old fine integral harmony gave place to an exaggerated stress on one or other of its elemental factors. *Artha* and *kāma*, interest and desire were in some directions developed at the expense of the *dharma*. The lines of the dharma were filled and stamped in with so rigid a distinctness as to stand in the way of the freedom of the spirit. Spiritual liberation was pursued in hostility to life and not as its full-orbed result and high crowning. But still some strong basis of the old knowledge remained to inspire, to harmonise, to keep alive the soul of India. Even when deterioration came and a slow collapse, even when the life of the community degenerated into an uneasily petrified ignorance and confusion, the old spiritual aim and tradition remained to sweeten and humanise and save in its worst days the Indian peoples. For we see that it continually swept back on the race in new waves and high outbursts of life-giving energy or leaped up in intense kindlings of the spiritualised mind or heart, even as it now rises once more in all its strength to give the impulse of a great renascence.

III

A DEFENCE OF INDIAN CULTURE

A DEFENCE OF INDIAN CULTURE

CHAPTER I

RELIGION AND SPIRITUALITY

I HAVE DESCRIBED the framework of the Indian idea from the outlook of an intellectual criticism, because that is the standpoint of the critics who affect to disparage its value. I have shown that Indian culture must be adjudged even from this alien outlook to have been the creation of a wide and noble spirit. Inspired in the heart of its being by a lofty principle, illumined with a striking and uplifting idea of individual manhood and its powers and its possible perfection, aligned to a spacious plan of social architecture, it was enriched not only by a strong philosophic, intellectual and artistic creativeness but by a great and vivifying and fruitful life-power. But this by itself does not give an adequate account of its spirit or its greatness. One might describe Greek or Roman civilisation from this outlook and miss little that was of importance; but Indian civilisation was not only a great cultural system, but an immense religious effort of the human spirit.

The whole root of difference between Indian and European culture springs from the spiritual aim of Indian civilisation. It is the turn which this aim imposes on all the rich and luxuriant variety of its forms and rhythms that gives to it its unique character. For even what it has in common with other cultures gets from that turn a stamp of striking originality and solitary greatness. A spiritual aspiration was the governing force of this culture, its core of thought, its ruling passion. Not only did it make spirituality the highest aim of life, but it even tried, as far as that could be done in the past conditions of the human race, to turn the whole of life towards spirituality. But since religion is in the human mind the first native, if imperfect form of the spiritual impulse, the predominance of the spiritual idea, its endeavour to take hold of life, necessitated a casting of thought and action into the religious mould and a persistent filling of every circumstance of life with the religious sense; it demanded a pervading religio-philosophic culture. The highest spirituality indeed moves in a free and wide air far above that lower stage of seeking which is governed by religious form and dogma; it does not easily bear their limitations and, even when it admits, it transcends them; it lives in an experience which to the formal religious mind is unintelligible. But man does not arrive immediately at that highest inner elevation and, if it were demanded from him at once, he would never arrive there. At first he needs lower supports and stages of ascent; he asks for some scaffolding of dogma, worship, image, sign, form, symbol, some indulgence and permission of mixed half-natural motive on which he can stand while he builds up in him the temple of the spirit. Only when the temple is completed, can the supports be removed, the scaffolding disappear. The religious culture which now goes by the name of Hinduism not only fulfilled this purpose, but, unlike certain other credal religions, it knew its purpose. It gave itself no name, because it set itself no sectarian limits; it claimed no universal adhesion, asserted no sole infallible dogma, set up no single narrow path or gate of salvation; it was less a creed or cult than a continuously enlarging tradition of the Godward endeavour of the human spirit. An immense many-sided and many-staged provision for a spiritual self-building and self-finding, it had some right to speak of itself by the only name it knew, the eternal religion, *sanātana dharma*. It is only if we have a just and right appreciation of this sense and spirit of Indian religion that we can come to an understanding of the true sense and spirit of Indian culture.

Now just here is the first baffling difficulty over which the European mind stumbles; for it finds itself unable to make out what Hindu religion is. Where, it asks, is its soul? Where is its mind and fixed thought? Where is the form of its body? How can there be a religion which has no rigid dogmas demanding belief on pain of eternal damnation, no theological postulates, even no fixed theology, no credo, distinguishing it from antagonistic or rival religions? How can there be a religion which has no papal head, no governing ecclesiastic body, no church, chapel or congregational system, no binding religious form of any kind obligatory on all its adherents, no one administration and discipline? For the Hindu priests are mere ceremonial officiants without any ecclesiastical authority or disciplinary powers and the Pundits are mere interpreters of the Shastra, not the law-givers of the religion or its rulers. How again can Hinduism be called a religion when it admits all beliefs, allowing even a kind of high reaching atheism and agnosticism and permits all possible spiritual experiences, all kinds of religious adventures? The only thing fixed, rigid, positive, clear is the social law, and even that varies in different castes, regions, communities. The caste rules and not the Church; but even the caste cannot punish a man for his beliefs, ban heterodoxy or prevent his following a new revolutionary doctrine or a new spiritual leader. If it excommunicates Christian or Muslim, it is not for religious belief or practice, but because they break with the social rule and order. It has been asserted in consequence that there is no such thing as a Hindu religion, but only a Hindu social system with a bundle of the most disparate religious beliefs and institutions.

The precious dictum that Hinduism is a mass of folk-lore with an ineffective coat of metaphysical daubing is perhaps the final judgment of the superficial occidental mind on this matter.

This misunderstanding springs from the total difference of outlook on religion that divides the Indian mind and the normal western intelligence. The difference is so great that it could only be bridged by a supple philosophical training or a wide spiritual culture; but the established forms of religion and the rigid methods of philosophical thought practised in the West make no provision and even allow no opportunity for either. To the Indian mind the least important part of religion is its dogma; the religious spirit matters, not the theological credo. On the contrary to the western mind a fixed intellectual belief is the most important part of a cult; it is its core of meaning, it is the thing that distinguishes it from others. For it is its formulated beliefs that make it either a true or a false religion, according as it agrees or does not agree with the credo of its critic. This notion, however foolish and shallow, is a necessary consequence of the western idea which falsely supposes that intellectual truth is the highest verity and, even, that there is no other. The Indian religious thinker knows that all the highest eternal verities are truths of the spirit. The supreme truths are neither the rigid conclusions of logical reasoning nor the affirmations of credal statement, but fruits of the soul's inner experience. Intellectual truth is only one of the doors to the outer precincts of the temple. And since intellectual truth turned towards the Infinite must be in its very nature many-sided and not narrowly one, the most varying intellectual beliefs can be equally true because they mirror different facets of the Infinite. However separated by intellectual distance, they still form so many side-entrances which admit the mind to some faint ray from a supreme Light. There are no true and false religions, but rather all religions are true in their own way and degree. Each is one of the thousand paths to the One Eternal.

Indian religion placed four necessities before human life. First, it imposed upon the mind a belief in a highest consciousness or state of existence universal and transcendent of the universe, from which all comes, in which all lives and moves without knowing it and of which all must one day grow aware, returning towards that which is perfect, eternal and infinite. Next, it laid upon the individual life the need of self-preparation by development and experience till man is ready for an effort to grow consciously into the truth of this greater existence. Thirdly, it provided it with a well-founded, well-explored, many-branching and always enlarging way of knowledge and of spiritual or religious discipline. Lastly, for those not yet ready for these higher steps it provided an organisation of the individual and collective life, a framework of personal and social discipline and conduct, of mental and moral and vital development by which they could move each in his own limits and according to his own nature in such a way as to become eventually ready for the greater existence. The first three of these elements are the most essential to any religion, but Hinduism has always attached to the last also a great importance; it has left out no part of life as a thing secular and foreign to the religious and spiritual life. Still the Indian religious tradition is not merely the form of a religio-social system, as the ignorant critic vainly imagines. However greatly that may count at the moment of a social departure, however stubbornly the conservative religious mind may oppose all pronounced or drastic change, still the core of Hinduism is a spiritual, not a social discipline. Actually we find religions like Sikhism counted in the Vedic family although they broke down the old social tradition and invented a novel form, while the Jains and Buddhists were traditionally considered to be outside the religious fold although they observed Hindu social custom and intermarried with Hindus, because their spiritual system and teaching figured in its origin as a denial of the truth of the Veda and a departure from the continuity of the Vedic line. In all these four elements that constitute Hinduism there are major and minor differences between Hindus of various sects, schools, communities and races; but nevertheless there is also a general unity of spirit, of fundamental type and form and of spiritual temperament which creates in this vast fluidity an immense force of cohesion and a strong principle of oneness.

The fundamental idea of all Indian religion is one common to the highest human thinking everywhere. The supreme truth of all that is is a Being or an existence beyond the mental and physical appearances we contact here. Beyond mind, life and body there is a Spirit and Self containing all that is finite and infinite, surpassing all that is relative, a supreme Absolute, originating and supporting all that is transient, a one Eternal. A one transcendent, universal, original and sempiternal Divinity or divine Essence, Consciousness, Force and Bliss is the fount and continent and inhabitant of things. Soul, nature, life are only a manifestation or partial phenomenon of this self-aware Eternity and this conscious Eternal. But this Truth of being was not seized by the Indian mind only as a philosophical speculation, a theological dogma, an abstraction contemplated by the intelligence. It was not an idea to be indulged by the thinker in his study, but otherwise void of practical bearing on life. It was not a mystic sublimation which could be ignored in the dealings of man with the world and Nature. It was a living spiritual Truth, an Entity, a Power, a Presence that could be sought by all according to their degree of capacity and seized in a thousand ways through life and beyond life. This Truth was to be lived and even to be made the governing idea of thought and life and action. This recognition and pursuit of something or someone Supreme behind all forms is the one universal credo of Indian religion, and if it has taken a hundred shapes, it was precisely because it was so much alive. The Infinite alone justifies the existence of the finite and the finite by itself has no entirely separate value or independent existence. Life, if it is not an illusion, is a divine Play, a manifestation of the glory of the Infinite. Or it is a means by which the soul growing in Nature through countless forms and many lives can approach, touch, feel and unite itself through love and knowledge and faith and adoration and a Godward will in works with this transcendent Being and this infinite Existence. This Self or this self-existent Being is the one supreme reality, and all things else are either only appearances or only true by dependence upon it. It follows that self-realisation and God-realisation are the great business of the living and thinking human being. All life and thought are in the end a means of progress towards self-realisation and God-realisation.

Indian religion never considered intellectual or theological conceptions about the supreme Truth to be the one thing of central importance. To pursue that Truth under whatever conception or whatever form, to attain to it by inner experience, to live in it in consciousness, this it held to be the sole thing needful. One school or sect might consider the real self of man to be indivisibly one with the universal Self or the supreme Spirit. Another might regard man as one with the Divine in essence but different from him in Nature. A third might hold God, Nature and the individual soul in man to be three eternally different powers of being. But for all the truth of Self held with equal force; for even to the Indian dualist, God is the supreme self and reality in whom and by whom Nature and man live, move and have their being and, if you eliminate God from his view of things, Nature and man would lose for him all their meaning and importance. The Spirit, universal Nature (whether called Maya, Prakriti or Shakti) and the soul in living beings, Jiva, are the three truths which are universally admitted by all the many religious sects and conflicting religious philosophies of India. Universal also is the admission that the discovery of the inner spiritual self in man, the divine soul in him, and some kind of living and uniting contact or absolute unity of the soul in man with God or supreme Self or eternal Brahman is the condition of spiritual perfection. It is open to us to conceive and have experience of the Divine as an impersonal Absolute and Infinite or to approach and know and feel Him as a transcendent and universal sempiternal Person: but whatever be our way of reaching him, the one important truth of spiritual experience is that he is in the heart and centre of all existence and all existence is in him and to find him is the great self-finding. Differences of credal belief are to the Indian mind nothing more than various ways of seeing the one Self and Godhead in all. Self-realisation is the one thing needful; to open to the inner Spirit, to live in the Infinite, to seek after and discover the Eternal, to be in union with God, that is the common idea and aim of religion, that is the sense of spiritual salvation, that is the living Truth that fulfils and releases. This dynamic following after the highest spiritual truth and the highest spiritual aim are the uniting bond of Indian religion and, behind all its thousand forms, its one common essence.

If there were nothing else to be said in favour of the spiritual genius of the Indian people or the claim of Indian civilisation to stand in the front rank as a spiritual culture, it would be sufficiently substantiated by this single fact that not only was this greatest and widest spiritual truth seen in India with the boldest largeness, felt and expressed with a unique intensity, and approached from all possible sides, but it was made consciously the grand uplifting idea of life, the core of all thinking, the foundation of all religion, the secret sense and declared ultimate aim of human existence. The truth announced is not peculiar to Indian thinking; it has been seen and followed by the highest minds and souls everywhere. But elsewhere it has been the living guide only of a few thinkers or of some rare mystics or exceptionally gifted spiritual natures. The mass of men have had no understanding, no distinct perception, not even a reflected glimpse of this something Beyond; they have lived only in the lower sectarian side of religion, in inferior ideas of the Deity or in the outward mundane aspects of life. But Indian culture did succeed by the strenuousness of its vision, the universality of its approach, the intensity of its seeking, in doing what has been done by no other culture. It succeeded in stamping religion with the essential ideal of a real spirituality; it brought some living reflection of the very highest spiritual truth and some breath of its influence into every part of the religious field. Nothing can be more untrue than to pretend that the general religious mind of India has not at all grasped the higher spiritual or metaphysical truths of Indian religion. It is a sheer falsehood or a wilful misunderstanding to say that it has lived always in the externals only of rite and creed and shibboleth. On the contrary, the main metaphysical truths of Indian religious philosophy in their broad idea aspects or in an intensely poetic and dynamic representation have been stamped on the general mind of the people. The ideas of Maya, Lila, divine Immanence are as familiar to the man in the street and the worshipper in the temple as to the philosopher in his seclusion, the monk in his monastery and the saint in his hermitage. The spiritual reality which they reflect, the profound experience to which they point has permeated the religion, the literature, the art, even the popular religious songs of a whole people.

It is true that these things are realised by the mass of men more readily through the fervour of devotion than by a strenuous effort of thinking, but that is as it must and should be, since the heart of man is nearer to the Truth than his intelligence. It is true, too, that the tendency to put too much stress on externals has always been there and worked to overcloud the deeper spiritual motive; but that is not peculiar to India, it is a common failing of human nature, not less but rather more evident in Europe than in Asia. It has needed a constant stream of saints and religious thinkers and the teaching of illuminated Sannyasins to keep the reality vivid and resist the deadening weight of form and ceremony and ritual. But the fact remains that these messengers of the spirit have never been wanting. And the still more significant fact remains that there has never been wanting either a happy readiness in the common mind to listen to the message. The ordinary materialised souls, the external minds are the majority in India as everywhere. How easy it is for the superior European critic to forget this common fact of our humanity and treat this turn as a peculiar sign of the Indian mentality! But at least the people of India, even the "ignorant masses" have this distinction that they are by centuries of training nearer to the inner realities, are divided from them by a less thick veil of the universal ignorance and are more easily led back to a vital glimpse of God and Spirit, self and eternity than the mass of men or even the cultured elite anywhere else. Where else could the lofty, austere and difficult teaching of a Buddha have seized so rapidly on the popular mind? Where else could the songs of a Tukaram, a Ramprasad, a Kabir, the Sikh gurus and the chants of the Tamil saints with their fervid devotion but also their profound spiritual thinking have found so speedy an echo and formed a popular religious literature? This strong permeation or close nearness of the spiritual turn, this readiness of the mind of a whole nation to turn to the highest realities is the sign and fruit of an age-long, a real and a still living and supremely spiritual culture.

The endless variety of Indian philosophy and religion seems to the European mind interminable, bewildering, wearisome, useless; it is unable to see the forest because of the richness and luxuriance of its vegetation; it misses the common spiritual life in the multitude of its forms. But this infinite variety is itself, as Vivekananda pertinently pointed out, a sign of a superior religious culture. The Indian mind has always realised that the Supreme is the Infinite; it has perceived, right from its

Vedic beginnings, that to the soul in Nature the Infinite must always present itself in an endless variety of aspects. The mentality of the West has long cherished the aggressive and quite illogical idea of a single religion for all mankind, a religion universal by the very force of its narrowness, one set of dogmas, one cult, one system of ceremonies, one array of prohibitions and injunctions, one ecclesiastical ordinance. That narrow absurdity prances about as the one true religion which all must accept on peril of persecution by men here and spiritual rejection or fierce eternal punishment by God in other worlds. This grotesque creation of human unreason, the parent of so much intolerance, cruelty, obscurantism and aggressive fanaticism, has never been able to take firm hold of the free and supple mind of India. Men everywhere have common human failings, and intolerance and narrowness especially in the matter of observances there has been and is in India. There has been much violence of theological disputation, there have been querulous bickerings of sects with their pretensions to spiritual superiority and greater knowledge, and sometimes, at one time especially in southern India in a period of acute religious differences, there have been brief local outbreaks of active mutual tyranny and persecution even unto death. But these things have never taken the proportions which they assumed in Europe. Intolerance has been confined for the most part to the minor forms of polemical attack or to social obstruction or ostracism; very seldom have they transgressed across the line to the major forms of barbaric persecution which draw a long, red and hideous stain across the religious history of Europe. There has played ever in India the saving perception of a higher and purer spiritual intelligence, which has had its effect on the mass mentality. Indian religion has always felt that since the minds, the temperaments, the intellectual affinities of men are unlimited in their variety, a perfect liberty of thought and of worship must be allowed to the individual in his approach to the Infinite.

India recognised the authority of spiritual experience and knowledge, but she recognised still more the need of variety of spiritual experience and knowledge. Even in the days of decline when the claim of authority became in too many directions rigorous and excessive, she still kept the saving perception that there could not be one but must be many authorities. An alert readiness to acknowledge new light capable of enlarging the old tradition has always been characteristic of the religious mind in India. Indian civilisation did not develop to a last logical conclusion its earlier political and social liberties,—that greatness of freedom or boldness of experiment belongs to the West; but liberty of religious practice and a complete freedom of thought in religion as in every other matter have always counted among its constant traditions. The atheist and the agnostic were free from persecution in India. Buddhism and Jainism might be disparaged as unorthodox religions, but they were allowed to live freely side by side with the orthodox creeds and philosophies; in her eager thirst for truth she gave them their full chance, tested all their values, and as much of their truth as was assimilable was taken into the stock of the common and always enlarging continuity of her spiritual experience. That ageless continuity was carefully conserved, but it admitted light from all quarters. In latter times the saints who reached some fusion of the Hindu and the Islamic teaching were freely and immediately recognised as leaders of Hindu religion,—even, in some cases, when they started with a Mussulman birth and from the Mussulman standpoint. The Yogin who developed a new path of Yoga, the religious teacher who founded a new order, the thinker who built up a novel statement of the many-sided truth of spiritual existence, found no serious obstacle to their practice or their propaganda. At most they had to meet the opposition of the priest and Pundit instinctively adverse to any change; but this had only to be lived down for the new element to be received into the free and pliant body of the national religion and its ever plastic order.

The necessity of a firm spiritual order as well as an untrammelled spiritual freedom was always perceived, but it was provided for in various ways and not in any one formal, external or artificial manner. It was founded in the first place on the recognition of an ever enlarging number of authorised scriptures. Of these scriptures some like the Gita possessed a common and widespread authority, others were peculiar to sects or schools: some like the Vedas were supposed to have an absolute, others a relative binding force. But the very largest freedom of interpretation was allowed, and this prevented any of these authoritative books from being turned into an instrument of ecclesiastical tyranny or a denial of freedom to the human mind and spirit. Another instrument of order was the power of family and communal tradition, *kuladharma*, persistent but not immutable. A third was the religious authority of the Brahmins; as priests they officiated as the custodians of observance, as scholars, acting in a much more important and respected role than the officiating priesthood could claim,—for to the priesthood no great consideration was given in India,—they stood as the exponents of religious tradition and were a strong conservative power. Finally, and most characteristically, most powerfully, order was secured by the succession of Gurus or spiritual teachers, *paramparā,* who preserved the continuity of each spiritual system and handed it down from generation to generation but were empowered also, unlike the priest and the Pundit, to enrich freely its significance and develop its practice. A living and moving, not a rigid continuity, was the characteristic turn of the inner religious mind of India. The evolution of the Vaishnava religion from very early times, its succession of saints and teachers, the striking developments given to it successively by Ramanuja, Madhwa, Chaitanya, Vallabhacharya and its recent stirrings of survival after a period of langour and of some fossilisation form one notable example of this firm combination of agelong continuity and fixed tradition with latitude of powerful and vivid change. A more striking instance was the founding of the Sikh religion, its long line of Gurus and the novel direction and form given to it by Guru Govind dingh in the democratic institution of the Khalsa. The Buddhist Sangha and its councils, the creation of a sort of divided pontifical authority by Shankaracharya, an authority transmitted from generation to generation for more than a thousand years and even now not altogether effete, the Sikh Khalsa, the adoption of the congregational form called Samaj by the modern reforming sects indicate an attempt towards a compact and stringent order. But it is noteworthy that even in these attempts the freedom and plasticity and living sincerity of the religious mind of India always prevented it from initiating anything like the overblown ecclesiastical orders and despotic hierarchies which in the West have striven to impose the tyranny of their obscurantist yoke on the spiritual liberty of the human race.

The instinct for order and freedom at once in any field of human activity is always a sign of a high natural capacity in that field, and a people which could devise such a union of unlimited religious liberty with an always orderly religious evolution, must be credited with a high religious capacity, even as they cannot be denied its inevitable fruit, a great, ancient and still living spiritual culture. It is this absolute freedom of thought and experience and this provision of a framework sufficiently flexible and various to ensure liberty and yet sufficiently sure and firm to be the means of a stable and powerful evolution that have given to Indian civilisation this wonderful and seemingly eternal religion with its marvellous wealth of many-sided philosophies, of great scriptures, of profound religious works, of religions that approach the Eternal from every side of his infinite Truth, of Yoga-systems of psycho-spiritual discipline and self-finding, of suggestive forms, symbols and ceremonies, which are strong to train the mind at all stages of development towards the Godward endeavour. Its firm structure capable of supporting without peril a large tolerance and assimilative spirit, its vivacity, intensity, profundity and multitudinousness of experience, its freedom from the unnatural European divorce between mundane knowledge and science on the one side and religion on the other, its reconciliation of the claims of the intellect with the claims of the spirit, its long endurance and infinite capacity of revival make it stand out today as the most remarkable, rich and living of all religious systems. The nineteenth century has thrown on it its tremendous shock of negation and scepticism but has not been able to destroy its assured roots of spiritual knowledge. A little disturbed for a brief moment, surprised and temporarily shaken by this attack in a period of greatest depression of the nation's vital force, India revived almost at once and responded by a fresh outburst of spiritual activity, seeking, assimilation, formative effort. A great new life is visibly preparing in her, a mighty transformation and farther dynamic evolution and potent march forward into the inexhaustible infinities of spiritual experience.

The many-sided plasticity of Indian cult and spiritual experience is the native sign of its truth, its living reality, the unfettered sincerity of its search and finding; but this plasticity is a constant stumbling block to the European mind. The religious thinking of Europe is accustomed to rigid impoverishing definitions, to strict exclusions, to a constant preoccupation with the outward idea, the organisation, the form. A precise creed framed by the logical or theological intellect, a strict and definite moral code to fix the conduct, a bundle of observances and ceremonies, a firm ecclesiastical or congregational organisation, that is western religion. Once the spirit is safely imprisoned and chained up in these things, some emotional fervours and even a certain amount of mystic seeking can be tolerated—within rational limits; but, after all, it is perhaps safest to do without these dangerous spices. Trained in these conceptions, the European critic comes to India and is struck by the immense mass and intricacy of a polytheistic cult crowned at its summit by a belief in the one Infinite. This belief he erroneously supposes to be identical with the barren and abstract intellectual pantheism of the West. He applies with an obstinate prejudgment the ideas and definitions of his own thinking, and this illegitimate importation has fixed many false values on Indian spiritual conceptions,—unhappily, even in the mind of "educated" India. But where our religion eludes his fixed standards, misunderstanding, denunciation and supercilious condemnation come at once to his rescue. The Indian mind on the contrary is averse to intolerant mental exclusions; for a great force of intuition and inner experience had given it from the beginning that towards which the mind of the West is only now reaching with much fumbling and difficulty,—the cosmic consciousness, the cosmic vision. Even when it sees the One without a second, it still admits his duality of Spirit and Nature; it leaves room for his many trinities and million aspects. Even when it concentrates on a single limiting aspect of the Divinity and seems to see nothing but that, it still keeps instinctively at the back of its consciousness the sense of the All and the idea of the One. Even when it distributes its worship among many objects, it looks at the same time through the objects of its worship and sees beyond the multitude of godheads the unity of the Supreme. This synthetic turn is not peculiar to the mystics or to a small literate class or to philosophic thinkers nourished on the high sublimities of the Veda and Vedanta. It permeates the popular mind nourished on the thoughts, images, traditions and cultural symbols of the Purana and Tantra; for these things are only concrete representations or living figures of the synthetic monism, the many-sided unitarianism, the large cosmic universalism of the Vedic scriptures.

Indian religion founded itself on the conception of a timeless, nameless and formless Supreme, but it did not feel called upon like the narrower and more ignorant monotheisms of the younger races, to deny or abolish all intermediary forms and names and powers and personalities of the Eternal and Infinite. A colourless monism or a pale vague transcendental Theism was not its beginning, its middle and its end. The one Godhead is worshipped as the All, for all in the universe is he or made out of his being or his nature. But Indian religion is not therefore pantheism; for beyond this universality it recognises the supracosmic Eternal. Indian polytheism is not the popular polytheism of ancient Europe; for here the worshipper of many gods still knows that all his divinities are forms, names, personalities and powers of the One; his gods proceed from the one Purusha, his goddesses are energies of the one divine Force. Those ways of Indian cult which most resemble a popular form of Theism, are still something more; for they do not exclude, but admit the many aspects of God. Indian image-worship is not the idolatry of a barbaric or undeveloped mind, for even the most ignorant know that the image is a symbol and support and can throw it away when its use is over. The later religious forms which most felt the impress of the Islamic idea, like Nanak's worship of the timeless One, Akala, and the reforming creeds of today, born under the influence of the West, yet draw away from the limitations of western or Semitic monotheism. Irresistibly they turn from these infantile conceptions towards the fathomless truth of Vedanta. The divine Personality of God and his human relations with man are strongly stressed by Vaishnavism and Shaivism as the most dynamic Truth; but that is not the whole of these religions, and this divine Personality is not the limited magnified-human personal God of the West. Indian religion cannot be described by any of the definitions known to the occidental intelligence. In its totality it has been a free and tolerant synthesis of all spiritual worship and experience. Observing the one Truth from all its many sides, it shut out none. It gave itself no specific name and bound itself by no limiting distinction. Allowing separative designations for its constituting cults and divisions, it remained itself nameless, formless, universal, infinite, like the Brahman of its agelong seeking. Although strikingly distinguished from other creeds by its traditional scriptures, cults and symbols, it is not in its essential character a credal religion at all but a vast and many-sided, an always unifying and always progressive and self-enlarging system of spiritual culture.*

It is necessary to emphasise this synthetic character and embracing unity of the Indian religious mind, because otherwise we miss the whole meaning of Indian life and the whole sense of Indian culture. It is only by recognising this broad and plastic character that we can understand its total effect on the life of the community and the life of the individual. And if we are asked, 'But after all what is Hinduism, what does it teach, what does it practise, what are its common factors,' we can answer that Indian religion is founded upon three basic ideas or rather three fundamentals of a highest and widest spiritual experience. First comes the idea of the One Existence of the Veda to whom sages give different names, the One without a second of the Upanishads who is All that is, and beyond all that is, the Permanent of the Buddhists, the Absolute of the Illusionists, the supreme God or Purusha of the Theists who holds in his power the soul and Nature,—in a word the Eternal, the Infinite. This is the first common foundation; but it can be and is expressed in an endless variety of formulas by the human intelligence. To discover and closely approach and enter into whatever kind or degree of unity with this Permanent, this Infinite, this Eternal,

* The only religion that India has apparently rejected in the end, is Buddhism; but in fact this appearance is a historical error. Buddhism lost its separative force, because its spiritual substance, as opposed to its credal parts, was absorbed by the religious mind of Hindu India. Even so, it survived in the North and was exterminated not by Shankaracharya or another, but by the invading force of Islam.

is the highest height and last effort of its spiritual experience. That is the first universal *credo* of the religious mind of India.

Admit in whatever formula this foundation, follow this great spiritual aim by one of the thousand paths recognised in India or even any new path which branches off from them and you are at the core of the religion. For its second basic idea is the manifold way of man's approach to the Eternal and Infinite. The Infinite is full of many infinities and each of these infinities is itself the very Eternal. And here in the limitations of the cosmos God manifests himself and fulfils himself in the world in many ways, but each is the way of the Eternal. For in each finite we can discover and through all things as his forms and symbols we can approach the Infinite; all cosmic powers are manifestations, all forces are forces of the One. The gods behind the workings of Nature are to be seen and adored as powers, names and personalities of the one Godhead. An infinite Conscious-Force, executive Energy, Will or Law, Maya, Prakriti, Shakti or Karma, is behind all happenings, whether to us they seem good or bad, acceptable or unacceptable, fortunate or adverse. The Infinite creates and is Brahma; it preserves and is Vishnu; it destroys or takes to itself and is Rudra or Shiva. The supreme Energy beneficent in upholding and protection is or else formulates itself as the Mother of the worlds, Luxmi or Durga. Or beneficent even in the mask of destruction it is Chandi or it is Kali, the dark Mother. The One Godhead manifests himself in the form of his qualities in various names and godheads. The God of divine love of the Vaishnava, the God of divine power of the Shakta appear as two different godheads; but in truth they are the one infinite Deity in different figures.* One may approach the Supreme through any of these names and forms,

* This explanation of Indian polytheism is not a modern invention created to meet western reproaches; it is to be found explicitly stated in the Gita; it is, still earlier, the sense of the Upanishads; it was clearly stated in so many words in the first ancient days by the "primitive" poets (in truth the profound mystics) of the Veda.

with knowledge or in ignorance; for through them and beyond them we can proceed at last to the supreme experience.

One thing however has to be noted that while many modernised Indian religionists tend, by way of an intellectual compromise with modern materialistic rationalism, to explain away these things as symbols, the ancient Indian religious mentality saw them not only as symbols but as world-realities,—even if to the Illusionist realities only of the world of Maya. For between the highest unimaginable Existence and our material way of being the spiritual and psychic knowledge of India did not fix a gulf as between two unrelated opposites. It was aware of other psychological planes of consciousness and experience and the truths of these supraphysical planes were no less real to it than the outward truths of the material universe. Man approaches God at first according to his psychological nature and his capacity for deeper experience, *svabhāva, adhikāra.* The level of Truth, the plane of consciousness he can reach is determined by the inner evolutionary stage. Thence comes the variety of religious cult, but its data are not imaginary structures, inventions of priests or poets, but truths of a supraphysical existence intermediate between the consciousness of the physical world and the ineffable superconscience of the Absolute.

The idea of strongest consequence at the base of Indian religion is the most dynamic for the inner spiritual life. It is that while the Supreme or the Divine can be approached through a universal consciousness and by piercing through all inner and outer Nature, That or He can be met by each individual soul in itself, in its own spiritual part, because there is something in it that is intimately one or at least intimately related with the one divine Existence. The essence of Indian religion is to aim at so growing and so living that we can grow out of the Ignorance which veils this self-knowledge from our mind and life and become aware of the Divinity within us. These three things put together are the whole of Hindu religion, its essential sense and, if any credo is needed, its credo.

A DEFENCE OF INDIAN CULTURE

CHAPTER II

RELIGION AND SPIRITUALITY

THE task of religion and spirituality is to mediate between God and man, between the Eternal and Infinite and this transient, yet persistent finite, between a luminous Truth-consciousness not expressed or not yet expressed here and the Mind's ignorance. But nothing is more difficult than to bring home the greatness and uplifting power of the spiritual consciousness to the natural man forming the vast majority of the race; for his mind and senses are turned outward towards the external calls of life and its objects and never inwards to the Truth which lies behind them. This external vision and attraction are the essence of the universal blinding force which is designated in Indian philosophy the Ignorance. Ancient Indian spirituality recognised that man lives in the Ignorance and has to be led through its imperfect indications to a highest inmost knowledge. Our life moves between two worlds, the depths upon depths of our inward being and the surface field of our outward nature. The majority of men put the whole emphasis of life on the outward and live very strongly in their surface consciousness and very little in the inward existence. Even the choice spirits raised from the grossness of the common vital and physical mould by the stress of thought and culture do not usually get farther than a strong dwelling on the things of the mind. The highest flight they reach—and it is this that the West persistently mistakes for spirituality—is a preference for living in the mind and emotions more than in the gross outward life or else an attempt to subject this rebellious life-stuff to the law of intellectual truth or ethical reason and will or aesthetic beauty or of all three together. But spiritual knowledge perceives that there is a greater thing in us; our inmost self, our real being is not the intellect, not the aesthetic, ethical or thinking mind, but the divinity within, the Spirit, and these other things are only the instruments of the Spirit. A mere intellectual, ethical and aesthetic culture does not go back to the inmost truth of the spirit; it is still an Ignorance, an incomplete, outward and superficial knowledge. To have made the discovery of our deepest being and hidden spiritual nature is the first necessity and to have erected the living of an inmost spiritual life into the aim of existence is the characteristic sign of a spiritual culture.

This endeavour takes in certain religions the form of a spiritual exclusiveness which revolts from the outward existence rather than seeks to transform it. The main tendency of the Christian discipline was not only to despise the physical and vital way of living, but to disparage and imprison the intellectual and distrust and discourage the aesthetic thirsts of our nature. It emphasised against them a limited spiritual emotionalism and its intense experiences as the one thing needful; the development of the ethical sense was the sole mental necessity, its translation into act the sole indispensable condition or result of the spiritual life. Indian spirituality reposed on too wide and many-sided a culture to admit as its base this narrow movement; but on its more solitary summits, at least in its later period, it tended to a spiritual exclusiveness loftier in vision, but even more imperative and excessive. A spirituality of this intolerant high-pointed kind, to whatever elevation it may rise, however it may help to purify life or lead to a certain kind of individual salvation, cannot be a complete thing. For its exclusiveness imposes on it a certain impotence to deal effectively with the problems of human existence; it cannot lead it to its integral perfection or combine its highest heights with its broadest broadness. A wider spiritual culture must recognize that the Spirit is not only the highest and inmost thing, but all is manifestation and creation of the Spirit. It must have a wider outlook, a more embracing range of applicability and, even, a more aspiring and ambitious aim of its endeavour. Its aim must be not only to raise to inaccessible heights the few elect, but to draw all men and all life and the whole human being upward, to spiritualise life and in the end to divinise human nature. Not only must it be able to lay hold on his deepest individual being but to inspire too his communal existence. It must turn, by a spiritual change, all the members of his ignorance into members of the knowledge; it must transmute all the instruments of the human into instruments of a divine living. The total movement of Indian spirituality is towards this aim; in spite of all the difficulties, imperfections and fluctuations of its evolution, it had this character. But like other cultures it was not at all times and in all its parts and movements consciously aware of its own total significance. This large sense sometimes emerged into something like a conscious synthetic clarity, but was more often kept in the depths and on the surface dispersed in a multitude of subordinate and special stand-points. Still, it is only by an intelligence of the total drift that its manifold sides and rich variations of effort and teaching and discipline can receive their full reconciling unity and be understood in the light of its own most intrinsic purpose.

Now the spirit of Indian religion and spiritual culture has been persistently and immovably the same throughout the long time of its vigour, but its form has undergone remarkable changes. Yet if we look into them from the right centre it will be apparent that these changes are the results of a logical and inevitable evolution inherent in the very process of man's growth towards the heights. In its earliest form, its first Vedic system, it took its outward foundation on the mind of the physical man whose natural faith is in things physical, in the sensible and visible objects, presences, representations and the external pursuits and aims of the material world. The means, symbols, rites, figures, by which it sought to mediate between the spirit and the normal human mentality wert drawn from these most external physical things. Man's first and primitive idea of the Divine can only come through his vision of external Nature and the sense of a superior Power or Powers concealed behind her phenomena veiled in the heaven and earth, father and mother of our being, in the sun and moon and stars, its lights and regulators, in dawn and day and night and rain and wind and storm, the oceans and the rivers and the forests, all the circumstances and forces of her scene of action, all that vast and mysterious surrounding life of which we are a part and in which the natural heart and mind of the human creature feel instinctively through whatever bright or dark or confused figures that there is here some divine Multitude or else mighty Infinite, one, manifold and mysterious, which takes these forms and manifests itself in these motions. The Vedic religion took this natural sense and feeling of the physical man; it used the conceptions to which they gave birth, and it sought to lead him through them to the psychic and spiritual truths of his own being and the being of the cosmos. It recognised that he was right when he saw behind the manifestations of Nature great living powers and godheads, even though he knew not their inner truth, and right too in offering to them worship and propitiation and atonement. For that inevitably must be the initial way in which his active physical, vital and mental nature is allowed to approach the Godhead. He approaches it through its visible outward manifestations as something greater than his own natural self, something single or multiple that guides, sustains and directs his life, and he calls to it for help and support in the desires and difficulties and distresses and struggles of his human existence.* The Vedic religion accepted also the form in which early man everywhere expressed his sense of the relation between himself and the godheads of Nature; it adopted as its central symbol the act and ritual of a physical sacrifice. However crude the notions attached to it, this idea of the necessity of sacrifice did express obscurely a first law of being. For it was founded on that secret of constant interchange between the individual and the universal powers of the cosmos which covertly supports all the process of life and develops the action of Nature.

But even in its external and exoteric side the Vedic religion did not limit itself to this acceptance and regulation of the first religious notions of the natural physical mind of man. The Vedic Rishis gave a psychic function to the godheads worshipped by the people; they spoke to them of a higher Truth, Right, Law of which the gods were the guardians, of the necessity of a truer knowledge and a larger inner living according to this Truth and Right and of a home of Immortality to which the soul of man could ascend by the power of Truth and of right doing. The people no doubt took these ideas in their most external sense; but they were trained by them to develop their ethical nature, to turn towards some initial development of their psychic being, to conceive the idea of a knowledge and truth other than that of the physical life and to admit even a first conception of some greater spiritual Reality which was the ultimate object of human worship or aspiration. This religious and moral force was the highest reach of the external cult and the most that could be understood or followed by the mass of the people.

* The Gita recognises four kinds or degrees of worshippers and God-seekers. There are first the *arthārthī* and *ārta,* those who seek him for the fulfilment of desire and those who turn for divine help in the sorrow and suffering of existence; there is next the *jijñāsu,* the seeker of knowledge, the questioner who is moved to seek the Divine in his truth and in that to meet him; last and highest, there is the *jñānī* who has already contact with the truth and is able to live in unity with the Spirit.

The deeper truth of these things was reserved for the initiates, for those who were ready to understand and practise the inner sense, the esoteric meaning hidden in the Vedic scripture. For the Veda is full of words which, as the Rishis themselves express it, are secret words that give their inner meaning only to the seer, *kavaye nivacanāni ninyāni vacāṁsi.* This is a feature of the ancient sacred hymns which grew obscure to later ages; it became a dead tradition and has been entirely ignored by modern scholarship in its laborious attempt to read the hieroglyph of the Vedic symbols. Yet its recognition is essential to a right understanding of almost all the ancient religions; for mostly they started on their upward curve through an esoteric element of which the key was not given to all. In all or most there was a surface cult for the common physical man who was held yet unfit for the psychic and spiritual life and an inner secret of the Mysteries carefully disguised by symbols whose sense was opened only to the initiates. This was the origin of the later distinction between the Shudra, the undeveloped physical-minded man and the twice-born, those who were capable of entering into the second birth by initiation and to whom alone the Vedic education could be given without danger. This too actuated the later prohibition of any reading or teaching of the Veda by the Shudra. It was this inner meaning, it was the higher psychic and spiritual truths concealed by the outer sense, that gave to these hymns the name by which they are still known, the Veda, the Book of Knowledge. Only by penetrating into the esoteric sense of this worship can we understand the full flowering of the Vedic religion in the Upanishads and in the long later evolution of Indian spiritual seeking and experience. For it is all there in its luminous seed, preshadowed or even prefigured in the verses of the early seers. The persistent notion which through every change ascribed the foundation of all our culture to the Rishis, whatever its fabulous forms and mythical ascriptions, contains a real truth and veils a sound historic tradition. It reflects the fact of a true initiation and an unbroken continuity between this great primitive past and the riper but hardly greater spiritual development of our historic culture.

This inner Vedic religion started with an extension of the psychic significance of the godheads in the Cosmos. Its primary notion was that of a hierarchy of worlds, an ascending stair of planes of being in the universe. It saw a mounting scale of the worlds corresponding to a similar mounting scale of planes or degrees or levels of consciousness in the nature of man. A Truth, Right and Law sustains and governs all these levels of Nature; one in essence, it takes in them different but cognate forms. There is for instance the series of the outer physical light, another higher and inner light which is the vehicle of the mental, vital and psychic consciousness and a highest inmost light of spiritual illumination. Surya, the Sun-God, was the lord of the physical Sun; but he is at the same time to the Vedic seer-poet the giver of the rays of knowledge which illumine the mind and he is too the soul and energy and body of the spiritual illumination. And in all these powers he is a luminous form of the one and infinite Godhead. All the Vedic godheads have this outer and this inner and inmost function, their known and their secret Names. All are in thei rexternal character powers of physical Nature; all have in their inner meaning a psychic function and psychological ascriptions; all too are various powers of some one highest Reality, *ekam sat,* the one infinite Existence. This hardly knowable Supreme is called often in the Veda "That Truth" or "That One," *tat satyam, tad ekam.* This complex character of the Vedic godheads assumes forms which have been wholly misunderstood by those who ascribe to them only their outward physical significance. Each of these gods is in himself a complete and separate cosmic personality of the one Existence and in their combination of powers they form the complete universal power, the cosmic whole, *vaiśvadevyam.* Each again apart from his special function, is one godhead with the others;

each holds in himself the universal divinity, each god is all the other gods. This is the aspect of the Vedic teaching and worship to which a European scholar, mistaking entirely its significance because he read it in the dim and poor light of European religious experience, has given the sounding misnomer, henotheism. Beyond, in the triple Infinite, these godheads put on their highest nature and are names of the one nameless Ineffable.

But the greatest power of the Vedic teaching, that which made it the source of all later Indian philosophies, religions, systems of Yoga, lay in its application to the inner life of man. Man lives in the physical cosmos subject to death and the "much falsehood" of the mortal existence. To rise beyond this death, to become one of the immortals, he has to turn from the falsehood to the Truth; he has to turn to the Light and to battle with and to conquer the powers of the Darkness. This he does by communion with the divine Powers and their aid; the way to call down this aid was the secret of the Vedic mystics. The symbols of the outer sacrifice are given for this purpose in the manner of the Mysteries all over the world an inner meaning; they represent calling of the gods into the human being, a connecting sacrifice, an intimate interchange, a mutual aid, a communion. There is a building of the powers of the godheads within man and a formation in him of the universality of the divine nature. For the gods are the guardians and increasers of the Truth, the powers of the Immortal, the sons of the infinite Mother; the way to immortality is the upward way of the gods, the way of the Truth, a journey, an ascent by which there is a growth into the law of the Truth, *ṛtasya panthā*. Man arrives at immortality by breaking beyond the limitations not only of his physical self, but of his mental and his ordinary psychic nature into the highest plane and supreme ether of the Truth: for there is the foundation of immortality and the native seat of the triple Infinite. On these ideas the Vedic sages built up a profound psychological and psychic discipline which led beyond itself to a highest spirituality and contained the nucleus of later Indian Yoga. Already we find in their seed, though not in their full expansion, the most characteristic ideas of Indian spirituality. There is the one Existence. *Ekam Sat*, supracosmic beyond the individual and the universe. There is the one God who presents to us the many forms, names, powers, personalities of his Godhead. There is the distinction between the Knowledge and the Ignorance,* the greater truth of an immortal life opposed to the much falsehood or mixed truth and falsehood of mortal existence. There is the discipline of an inward growth of man from the physical through the psychic to the spiritual existence. There is the conquest of death, the secret of immortality, the perception of a realisable divinity of the human spirit. In an age to which in the insolence of our external knowledge we are accustomed to look back as the childhood of humanity or at best a period of vigorous barbarism, this was the inspired and intuitive psychic and spiritual teaching by which the ancient human fathers, *pūrve pitaraḥ manuṣyāḥ*, founded a great and profound civilisation in India.

This high beginning was secured in its results by a larger sublime efflorescence. The Upanishads have always been recognised in India as the crown and end of the Veda; that is indicated in their general name, Vedanta. And they are in fact a large crowning outcome of the Vedic discipline and experience. The time in which the Vedantic truth was wholly seen and the Upanishads took shape, was, as we can discern from such records as the Chhandogya and Brihadaranyaka, an epoch of immense and strenuous seeking, an intense and ardent seed-time of the Spirit. In the stress of that seeking the truths held by the initiates but kept back from ordinary men broke their barriers, swept through the higher mind of the nation and fertilised the soil of Indian culture for a constant and ever increasing growth of spir-

* *Cittim acittim cinavad vi vidvān.* "Let the knower distinguish the Knowledge and the Ignorance."

itual consciousness and spiritual experience. This turn was not as yet universal; it was chiefly men of the higher classes, Kshatriyas and Brahmins trained in the Vedic system of education, no longer content with an external truth and the works of the outer sacrifice, who began everywhere to seek for the highest word of revealing experience from the sages who possessed the knowledge of the One. But we find too among those who attained to the knowledge and became great teachers men of inferior or doubtful birth like Janashruti, the wealthy Shudra, or Satyakama Jabali, son of a servant-girl who knew not who was his father. The work that was done in this period became the firm bedrock of Indian spirituality in later ages and from it gush still the life-giving waters of a perennial never failing inspiration. This period, this activity, this grand achievement created the whole difference between the evolution of Indian civilisation and the quite different curve of other cultures.

For a time had come when the original Vedic symbols must lose their significance and pass into an obscurity that became impenetrable, as did the inner teaching of the Mysteries in other countries. The old poise of culture between two extremes with a bridge of religious cult and symbolism to unite them, the crude or half-trained naturalness of the outer physical man on one side of the line, and on the other an inner and secret psychic and spiritual life for the initiates could no longer suffice as the basis of our spiritual progress. The human race in its cycle of civilisation needed a large-lined advance; it called for a more and more generalised intellectual, ethical and aesthetic evolution to help it to grow into the light. This turn had to come in India as in other lands. But the danger was that the greater spiritual truth already gained might be lost in the lesser confident half-light of the acute but unillumined intellect or stifled within the narrow limits of the self-sufficient logical reason. That was what actually happened in the West, Greece leading the way. The old knowledge was prolonged in a less inspired, less dynamic and more intellectual form by the Pythagoreans, by the Stoics, by Plato and the Neo-Platonists; but still in spite of them and in spite of the only half-illumined spiritual wave which swept over Europe from Asia in an ill-understood Christianity, the whole real trend of Western civilisation has been intellectual, rational, secular and even materialistic, and it keeps this character to the present day. Its general aim has been a strong or a fine culture of the vital and physical man by the power of an intellectualised ethics, aesthesis and reason, not the leading up of our lower members into the supreme light and power of the spirit. The ancient spiritual knowledge and the spiritual tendency it had created were saved in India from this collapse by the immense effort of the age of the Upanishads. The Vedantic seers renewed the Vedic truth by extricating it from its cryptic symbols and casting it into a highest and most direct and powerful language of intuition and inner experience. It was not the language of the intellect, but still it wore a form which the intellect could take hold of, translate into its own more abstract terms and convert into a starting point for an ever widening and deepening philosophic speculation and the reason's long search after a Truth original, supreme and ultimate. There was in India as in the West a great upbuilding of a high wide and complex intellectual, aesthetic, ethical and social culture. But left in Europe to its own resources, combated rather than helped by an obscure religious emotion and dogma, here it was guided, uplifted and more and more penetrated and suffused by a great saving power of spirituality and a vast stimulating and tolerant light of wisdom from a highest ether of knowledge.

The second or post-Vedic age of Indian civilisation was distinguished by the rise of the great philosophies, by a copious, vivid, many-thoughted, many-sided epic literature, by the beginnings of art and science, by the evolution of vigorous and complex society, by the formation of large kingdoms and empires, by manifold formative activities of all kinds and great systems of living and thinking. Here as elsewhere, in Greece, Rome, Persia, China, this was the age of a high outburst of the intelligence working upon life and the things of the mind to discover their reason and their right way and bring out a broad and noble fullness of human existence. But in India this effort never lost sight of the spiritual motive, never missed the touch of the religious sense. It was a birth time and youth of the seeking intellect and, as in Greece, philosophy was the main instrument by which it laboured to solve the problems of life and the world. Science too developed but it came second only as an auxiliary power. It was through profound and subtle philosophies that the intellect of India attempted to analyse by the reason and logical faculty what had formerly been approached with a much more living force through intuition and the soul's experience. But the philosophic mind started from the data these mightier powers had discovered and was faithful to its parent Light; it went back always in one form or another to the profound truths of the Upanishads which kept their place as the highest authority in these matters. There was a constant admission that spiritual experience is a greater thing and its light a truer if more incalculable guide than the clarities of the reasoning intelligence.

The same governing force kept its hold on all the other activities of the Indian mind and Indian life. The epic literature is full almost to excess of a strong and free intellectual and ethical thinking; there is an incessant criticism of life by the intelligence and the ethical reason, an arresting curiosity and desire to fix the norm of truth in all possible fields. But in the background and coming constantly to the front there is too a constant religious sense and an implicit or avowed assent to the spiritual truths which remained the unshakable basis of the culture. These truths suffused with their higher light secular thought and action or stood above to remind them that they were only steps towards a goal. Art in India, contrary to a common idea, dwelt much upon life; but still its highest achievement was always in the field of the interpretation of the religio-philosophical mind and its whole tone was coloured by a suggestion of the spiritual and the infinite. Indian society developed with an unsurpassed organising ability, stable effectiveness, practical insight its communal coordination of the mundane life of interest and desire, *kāma, artha;* it governed always its action by a reference at every point to the moral and religious law, the Dharma: but it never lost sight of spiritual liberation as our highest point and the ultimate aim of the effort of Life. In later times when there was a still stronger secular tendency of intellectual culture, there came in an immense development of the mundane intelligence, an opulent political and social evolution, an emphatic stressing of aesthetic, sensuous and hedonistic experience. But this effort too always strove to keep itself within the ancient frame and not to lose the special stamp of the Indian cultural idea. The enlarged secular turn was compensated by a deepening of the intensities of psycho-religious experience. New religions or mystic forms and disciplines attempted to seize not only the soul and the intellect, but the emotions, the senses, the vital and the aesthetic nature of man and turn them into stuff of the spiritual life. And every excess of emphasis on the splendour and richness and power and pleasures of life had its recoil and was balanced by a corresponding potent stress on spiritual asceticism as the higher way. The two trends, on one side an extreme of the richness of life experience, on the other an extreme and pure rigorous intensity of the spiritual life, accompanied each othed; their interaction, whatever loss there might be of the earlier deep harmony and large synthesis, yet by their double pull preserved something still of the balance of Indian culture.

Indian religion followed this line of evolution and kept its inner continuity with its Vedic and Vedantic origins; but it changed entirely its mental contents and colour and its outward basis. It did not effectuate this change through any protestant revolt or revolution, or with any idea of an iconoclastic reformation. A continuous development of its organic life took place, a natural transformation brought out latent motives or else gave to already established motive-ideas a more predominant place or effective form. At one time indeed it seemed as if a discontinuity and a sharp new beginning were needed and would take place. Buddhism seemed to reject all spiritual continuity with the Vedic religion. But this was after all less in reality than in appearance. The Buddhist ideal of Nirvana was no more than a sharply negative and exclusive statement of the highest Vedantic spiritual experience. The ethical system of the eightfold path taken as the way to release was an austere sublimation of the Vedic notion of the Right, Truth and Law followed as the way to immortality, *ṛtasya panthā*. The strongest note of Mahayana Buddhism, its stress on universal compassion and fellow-feeling was an ethical application of the spiritual unity which is the essential idea of Vedanta.* The most characteristic tenets of the new discipline, Nirvana and Karma, could have been supported from the utterances of the Brahmanas and Upanishads. Buddhism could easily have claimed for itself a Vedic origin and the claim would have been no less valid than the Vedic ascription of the Sankhya philosophy and discipline with which it had some points of intimate alliance. But what hurt Buddhism and determined in the end its rejection, was not its denial of a Vedic origin or authority, but the exclusive trenchancy of its intellectual, ethical and spiritual positions. A result of an intense stress of the union of logical reason with the spiritualised mind,—for it was by an intense spiritual seeking supported on a clear and hard rational thinking that it was born as a separate religion,—its trenchant affirmations and still more exclusive negations could not be made sufficiently compatible

* Buddha himself does not seem to have preached his tenets as a novel revolutionary creed, but as the old Aryan way, the true form of the eternal religion.

with the native flexibility, many-sided susceptibility and rich synthetic turn of the Indian religious consciousness; it was a high creed but not plastic enough to hold the heart of the people. Indian religion absorbed all that it could of Buddhism, but rejected its exclusive positions and preserved the full line of its own continuity, casting back to the ancient Vedanta.

This lasting line of change moved forward not by any destruction of principle, but by a gradual fading out of the prominent Vedic forms and the substitution of others. There was a transformation of symbol and ritual and ceremony or a substitution of new kindred figures, an emergence of things that are only hints in the original system, a development of novel idea-forms from the seed of the original thinking. And especially there was a farther widening and fathoming of psychic and spiritual experience. The Vedic gods rapidly lost their deep original significance. At first they kept their hold by their outer cosmic sense but were overshadowed by the great Trinity, Brahma-Vishnu-Shiva, and afterwards faded altogether. A new pantheon appeared which in its outward symbolic aspects expressed a deeper truth and larger range of religious experience, an intenser feeling, a vaster idea. The Vedic sacrifice persisted only in broken and lessening fragments. The house of Fire was replaced by the temple; the karmic ritual of sacrifice was transformed into the devotional temple ritual; the vague and shifting mental images of the Vedic gods figured in the mantras yielded to more precise conceptual forms of the two great deities, Vishnu and Shiva, and of their Shaktis and their offshoots. These new concepts stabilised in physical images were made the basis both for internal adoration and for the external worship which replaced sacrifice. The psychic and spiritual mystic endeavour which was the inner sense of the Vedic hymns, disappeared into the less intensely luminous but more wide and rich and complex psycho-spiritual inner life of Puranic and Tantric religion and Yoga.

The Purano-Tantric stage of the religion was once decried by European critics and Indian reformers as a base and ignorant degradation of an earlier and purer religion. It was rather an effort, successful in a great measure, to open the general mind of the people to a higher and deeper range of inner truth and experience and feeling. Much of the adverse criticism once heard proceeded from a total ignorance of the sense and intention of this worship. Much of this criticism has been uselessly concentrated on side-paths and aberrations which could hardly be avoided in this immensely audacious experimental widening of the basis of the culture. For there was a catholic attempt to draw towards the spiritual truth minds of all qualities and people of all classes. Much was lost of the profound psychic knowledge of the Vedic seers, but much also of new knowledge was developed, untrodden ways were opened and a hundred gates discovered into the Infinite. If we try to see the essential sense and aim of this development and the intrinsic value of its forms and means and symbols, we shall find that this evolution followed upon the early Vedic form very much for the same reason as Catholic Christianity replaced the mysteries and sacrifices of the early Pagan religions. For in both cases the outward basis of the early religion spoke to the outward physical mind of the people and took that as the starting point of its appeal. But the new evolution tried to awaken a more inner mind even in the common man, to lay hold on his inner vital and emotional nature, to support all by an awakening of the soul and to lead him through these things towards a highest spiritual truth. It attempted in fact to bring the mass into the temple of the spirit rather than leave them in the outer precincts. The outward physical sense was satisfied through its aesthetic turn by a picturesque temple worship, by numerous ceremonies, by the use of physical images; but these were given a psychic-emotional sense and direction that was open to the heart and imagination of the ordinary man and not reserved for the deeper sight of the elect or the strenuous tapasya of the initiates. The secret initiation remained but was now a condition for the passage from the surface psycho-emotional and religious to a profounder psychic-spiritual truth and experience.

Nothing essential was touched in its core by this new orientation; but the instruments, atmosphere, field of religious experience underwent a considerable change. The Vedic godheads were to the mass of their worshippers divine powers who presided over the workings of the outward life of the physical cosmos; the Puranic Trinity had even for the multitude a predominant psycho-religious and spiritual significance. Its more external significance, for instance the functions of cosmic creation, preservation and destruction, were only a dependent fringe of these profundities that alone touched the heart of its mystery. The central spiritual truth remained in both systems the same, the truth of the One in many aspects. The Trinity is a triple form of the one supreme Godhead and Brahman; the Shaktis are energies of the one Energy of the highest divine Being. But this greatest religious truth was no longer reserved for the initiated few; it was now more and more brought powerfully, widely and intensely home to the general mind and feeling of the people. Even the so-called henotheism of the Vedic idea was prolonged and heightened in the larger and simpler worship of Vishnu or Shiva as the one universal and highest Godhead of whom all others are living forms and powers. The idea of the Divinity in man was popularised to an extraordinary extent, not only the occasional manifestation of the Divine in humanity which founded the worship of the Avataras, but the Presence discoverable in the heart of every creature. The systems of Yoga developed themselves on the same common basis. All led or hoped to lead through many kinds of psycho-physical, inner vital, inner mental and psycho-spiritual methods to the common aim of all Indian spirituality, a greater consciousness and a more or less complete union with the One and Divine or else an immergence of the individual soul in the Absolute. The Purano-Tantric system was a wide, assured and many-sided endeavour, unparallelled in its power, insight, amplitude, to provide the race with a basis of generalised psycho-religious experience from which man could rise through knowledge, works or love or through any other fundamental power of his nature to some established supreme experience and highest absolute status.

This great effort and achievement which covered all the time between the Vedic age and the decline of Buddhism, was still not the last possibility of religious evolution open to Indian culture. The Vedic training of the physically-minded man made the development possible. But in its turn this raising of the basis of religion to the inner mind and life and psychic nature, this training and bringing out of the psychic man ought to make possible a still larger development and support a greater spiritual movement as the leading power of life. The first stage makes possible the preparation of the natural external man for spirituality; the second takes up his outward life into a deeper mental and psychical living and brings him more directly into contact with the spirit and divinity within him; the third should render him capable of taking up his whole mental, psychical, physical living into a first beginning at least of a generalised spiritual life. This endeavour has manifested itself in the evolution of Indian spirituality and is the significance of the latest philosophies, the great spiritual movements of the saints and bhaktas and an increasing resort to various paths of Yoga. But unhappily it synchronised with a decline of Indian culture and an increasing collapse of its general power and knowledge, and in these surroundings it could not bear its natural fruit; but at the same time it has done much to prepare such a possibility in the future. If Indian culture is to survive and keep its spiritual basis and innate character, it is in this direction, and not in a mere revival or a prolongation of the Puranic system, that its evolution must turn, rising so towards the fulfilment of that which the Vedic seers saw as the aim of man and his life thousands of years ago and the Vedantic sages cast into the clear and immortal forms of their luminous revelation. Even the psychic-emotional part of man's nature is not the inmost door to religious feeling, nor is his inner mind the highest witness to spiritual experience. There is behind the first the inmost soul of man, in that deepest secret heart, *hṛdaye guhāyām*, in which the ancient seers saw the very tabernacle of the indwelling Godhead and there is above the second a luminous highest mind directly open to a truth of the Spirit to which man's normal nature has as yet only an occasional and momentary access. Religious evolution, spiritual experience can find their true native road only when they open to these hidden powers and make them their support for a lasting change, a divinisation of human life and nature. An effort of this kind was the very force behind the most luminous and vivid of the later movements of India's vast religious cycles. It is the secret of the most powerful forms of Vaishnavism and Tantra and Yoga. The labour of ascent from our half animal human nature into the fresh purity of the spiritual consciousness needed to be followed and supplemented by a descent of the light and force of the spirit into man's members and the attempt to transform human into divine nature.

But it could not find its complete way or its fruit because it synchronised with a decline of the life-force in India and a lowering of power and knowledge in her general civilisation and culture. Nevertheless here lies the destined force of her survival and renewal, this is the dynamic meaning of her future. A widest and highest spiritualising of life on earth is the last vision of all that vast and unexampled seeking and experiment in a thousand ways of the soul's outermost and innermost experience which is the unique character of her past; this in the end is the mission for which she was born and the meaning of her existence.

A DEFENCE OF INDIAN CULTURE

CHAPTER III

RELIGION AND SPIRITUALITY

It is essential, if we are to get a right view of Indian civilisation or of any civilisation, to keep to the central, living, governing things and not to be led away by the confusion of accidents and details. This is a precaution which the critics of our culture steadily refuse to take. A civilisation, a culture must be looked at first in its initiating, supporting, durable central motives, in its heart of abiding principle; otherwise we shall be likely to find ourselves, like these critics, in a maze without a clue and we shall stumble about among false and partial conclusions and miss entirely the true truth of the matter. The importance of avoiding this error is evident when we are seeking for the essential significance of Indian religious culture. But the same method must be held to when we proceed to observe its dynamic formulation and the effect of its spiritual ideal on life.

Indian culture recognises the spirit as the truth of our being and our life as a growth and evolution of the spirit. It sees the Eternal, the Infinite, the Supreme, the All; it sees this as the secret highest Self of all, this is what it calls God, the Permanent, the Real, and it sees man as a soul and power of this being of God in Nature. The progressive growth of the finite consciousness of man towards this Self, towards God, towards the universal, the eternal, the infinite, in a word his growth into spiritual consciousness by the development of his ordinary ignorant natural being into an illumined divine nature, this is for Indian thinking the significance of life and the aim of human existence. To this deeper and more spiritual idea of Nature and of existence a great deal of what is strongest and most potential of fruitful consequences in recent European thinking already turns with a growing impetus. This turn may be a relapse to "barbarism" or it may be the high natural outcome of her own increasing and ripened culture; that is a question for Europe to decide. But always to India this ideal inspiration or rather this spiritual vision of Self, God, Spirit, this nearness to a cosmic consciousness, a cosmic sense and feeling, a cosmic idea, will, love, delight into which we can release the limited, ignorant suffering ego, this drive towards the transcendental, eternal and infinite, and the moulding of man into a conscious soul and power of that greater Existence have been the engrossing motive of her philosophy, the sustaining force of her religion, the fundamental idea of her civilisation and culture.

I have suggested that the formal turn, the rhythmic lines of effort of this culture must be regarded as having passed through two complete external stages; while a third has taken its initial steps and is the destiny of her future. The early Vedic was the first stage: then religion took its outward formal stand on the natural approach of the physical mind of man to the Godhead in the universe, but the initiates guarded the sacrificial fire of a greater spiritual truth behind the form. The Purano-Tantric was the second stage: then religion took its outward formal stand on the first deeper approaches of man's inner mind and life to the Divine in the universe, but a greater initiation opened the way to a far more intimate truth and pushed towards an inner living of the spiritual life in all its profundity and in all the infinite possibilites of an uttermost sublime experience. There has been long in preparation a third stage which belongs to the future. Its inspiring idea has been often cast out in limited or large, veiled and quiet or bold and striking spiritual movements and potent new disciplines and religions, but it has not yet been successful in finding its way or imposing new lines on human life. The circumstances were adverse, the hour not yet come. This greatest movement of the Indian spiritual mind has a double impulse. Its will is to call the community of men and all men each according to his power to live in the greatest light of all and found their whole life on some fully revealed power and grand uplifting truth of the Spirit. But it has had too at times a highest vision which sees the possibility not only of an ascent towards the Eternal but of a descent of the Divine Consciousness and a change of human into divine nature. A perception of the divinity hidden in man has been its crowning force. This is a turn that cannot be rightly understood in the ideas or language of the European religious reformer or his imitators. It is not what the purist of the reason or the purist of the spirit imagines it to be and by that too hasty imagination falls short in his endeavour. Its index vision is pointed to a truth that exceeds the human mind and, if at all realised in his members, would turn human life into a divine superlife. And not until this third largest sweep of the spiritual evolution has come into its own, can Indian civilisation be said to have discharged its mission, to have spoken its last word and be *functus officio*, crowned and complete in its office of mediation between the life of man and the spirit.

The past dealings of Indian religion with life must be judged according to the stages of its progress; each age of its movement must be considered on its own basis. But throughout it consistently held to two perceptions that showed great practical wisdom and a fine spiritual tact. First, it saw that the approach to the spirit cannot be sudden, simple and immediate for all individuals or for the community of men; it must come ordinarily or at least at first through a gradual culture, training, progress.

There must be an enlarging of the natural life accompanied by an uplifting of all its motives; a growing hold upon it of the higher rational, psychic and ethical powers must prepare and lead it towards a higher spiritual law. But the Indian religious mind saw too at the same time that if its greater aim was to be fruitful and the character of its culture imperative, there must be throughout and at every moment some kind of insistence on the spiritual motive. And for the mass of men this means always some kind of religious influence. That pervasive insistence was necessary in order that from the beginning some power of the universal inner truth, some ray from the real reality of our existence might cast its light or at least its sensible if subtle influence on the natural life of man. Human life must be induced to flower, naturally in a way, but at the same time with a wise nurturing and cultivation into its own profounder spiritual significance. Indian culture has worked by two coordinated, mutually stimulating and always interblended operations of which these perceptions are the principle. First, it has laboured to lead upward and enlarge the life of the individual in the community through a natural series of life-stages till it was ready for the spiritual levels. But also it has striven to keep that highest aim before the mind at every stage and throw its influence on each circumstance and action both of man's inner and his outer existence.

In the plan of its first aim it came nearer to the highest ancient culture of mankind in other regions, but in a type and with a motive all its own. The frame of its system was constituted by a triple quartette. Its first circle was the synthesis and gradation of the fourfold object of life, vital desire and hedonistic enjoyment, personal and communal interest, moral right and law, and spiritual liberation. Its second circle was the fourfold order of society, carefully graded and equipped with its fixed economic functions and its deeper cultural, ethical and spiritual significances. Its third, the most original and indeed unique of its englobing life-patterns was the fourfold scale and succession of the successive stages of life, student, householder, forest recluse and free supersocial man. This frame, these lines of a large and noble life-training subsisted in their purity, their grand natural balance of austerity and accommodation, their fine effectiveness during the later Vedic and heroic age of the civilisation: afterwards they crumbled slowly or lost their completeness and order. But the tradition, the idea with some large effect of its force and some figure of its lines endured throughout the whole period of cultural vigour. However deflected it might have been from its true form and spirit, however mutilated and complicated for the worse, there was always left some presence of its inspiration and power. Only in the decline do we get the slow collapse, the degraded and confused mass of conventions which still labours to represent the ancient and noble Aryan system, but in spite of relics of glamour and beauty, in spite of survivals of spiritual suggestion and in spite of a residue of the old high training, is little better than a detritus or a mass of confused relics. Still even in this degradation enough of the original virtue has remained to ensure a remarkable remnant of the ancient beauty, attractiveness and power of survival.

But the turn given to the other and more direct spiritual operation of this culture is of a still greater importance. For it is that which, always surviving, has coloured permanently the Indian mind and life. It has remained the same behind every change of forms and throughout all the ages of the civilisation it has renewed its effectiveness and held its field. This second side of the cultural effort took the form of an endeavour to cast the whole of life into a religious mould; it multiplied means and devices which by their insistent suggestion and opportunity and their mass of effect would help to stamp a Godward tendency on the entire existence. Indian culture was founded on a religious conception of life and both the individual and the community drank in at every moment its influence. It was stamped on them by the training and turn of the education; the entire life atmosphere, all the social surroundings were suffused with it; it breathed its power through the whole original form and hieratic character of the culture. Always was felt the near idea of the spiritual existence and its supremacy as the ideal, highest over all others; everywhere there was the pervading pressure of the notion of the universe as a manifestation of divine Powers and a movement full of the presence of the Divine. Man himself was not a mere reasoning animal, but a soul in constant relation with God and with the divine cosmic Powers. The soul's continued existence was a cyclic or upward progress from birth to birth; human life was the summit of an evolution which terminated in the conscious Spirit, every stage of that life a step in a pilgrimage. Every single action of man had its importance of fruit whether in future lives or in the worlds beyond the material existence.

But Indian religion was not content with the general pressure of these conceptions, the training, the atmosphere, the stamp on the culture. Its persistent effort was to impress the mind at every moment and in each particular with the religious influence. And to do this more effectively by a living and practical adaptation, not asking from anyone what was too much for him or too little, it took as a guiding idea its perception of the varying natural capacity of man, *adhikāra*. It provided in its system means by which each man high or low, wise or ignorant, exceptional or average might feel in the way suitable to his nature and evolutionary stage the call, the pressure, the influence. Avoiding the error of the religions that impose a single dogmatic and inflexible rule on every man regardless of the possibilities of his nature, it tried rather to draw him gently upward and help him to grow steadily in religious and spiritual experience. Every part of human nature, every characteristic turn of its action was given a place in the system; each was suitably surrounded with the spiritual idea and a religious influence, each provided with steps by which it might rise towards its own spiritual possibility and significance. The highest spiritual meaning of life was set on the summits of each evolving power of the human nature. The intelligence was called to a supreme knowledge, the dynamic active and creative powers pointed to openness and unity with an infinite and universal Will, the heart and sense put in contact with a divine love and joy and beauty. But this highest meaning was also put everywhere indicatively or in symbols behind the whole system of living, even in its details, so that its impression might fall in whatever degree on the life, increase in pervasion and in the end take up the entire control. This was the aim and, if we consider the imperfections of our nature and the difficulty of the endeavour, we can say that it achieved an unusual measure of success. It has been said with some truth that for the Indian the whole of life is a religion. True of the ideal of Indian life, it is true to a certain degree and in a certain sense in its fact and practice. No step could be taken in the Indian's inner or outer life without his being reminded of a spiritual existence. Everywhere he felt the closeness or at least saw the sign of something beyond his natural life, beyond the moment in time, beyond his individual ego, something other than the needs and interests of his vital and physical nature. That insistence gave its tone and turn to his thought and action and feeling; it produced that subtler sensitiveness to the spiritual appeal, that greater readiness to turn to the spiritual effort which are even now distinguishing marks of the Indian temperament. It is that readiness, that sensitiveness which justifies us when we speak of the characteristic spirituality of the Indian people.

The ancient idea of the *adhikāra* has to be taken into careful account if we would understand the peculiar character of Indian religion. In most other religious systems we find a high-pitched spiritual call and a difficult and rigid ethical standard far beyond the possibilities of man's half-evolved, defective and imperfect nature. This standard, this call are announced as if imperative on all; but it is evident that only a few can give an adequate response. There are presented to our view for all our picture of life the sharp division of two extremes; the saint and the worldling, the religious and the irreligious, the good and the bad, the pious and the impious, souls accepted and souls rejected, the sheep and the goats, the saved and the damned, the believer and the infidel, are the two categories set constantly before us. All between is a confusion, a tug of war, an uncertain balance. This crude and summary classification is the foundation of the Christian system of an eternal heaven and hell; at best, the Catholic religion humanely interposes a precarious chance hung between that happy and this dread alternative, the chance of a painful purgatory for more than nine-tenths of the human race. Indian religion set up on its summits a still more high-pitched spiritual call, a standard of conduct still more perfect and absolute; but it did not go about its work with this summary and unreflecting ignorance. All beings are to the Indian mind portions of the Divine, evolving souls, and sure of an eventual salvation and release into the spirit. All must feel, as the good in them grows or, more truly, the godhead in them finds itself and becomes conscious, the ultimate touch and call of their highest self and through that call the attraction to the Eternal and the Divine. But actually in life there are infinite differences between man and man; some are more inwardly evolved, others are less mature, many if not most are infant souls incapable of great steps and difficult efforts. Each needs to be dealt with according to his nature and his soul stature. But a general distinction can be drawn between three principal types varying in their openness to the spiritual appeal or to the religious influence or impulse. This distinction amounts to a gradation of three stages in the growing human consciousness. One crude, ill-formed, still outward, still vitally and physically minded can be led only by devices suited to its ignorance. Another, more developed and capable of a much stronger and deeper psycho-spiritual experience, offers a riper make of manhood gifted with a more conscious intelligence, a larger vital or aesthetic opening, a stronger ethical power of the nature. A third, the ripest and most developed of all, is ready for the spiritual heights, fit to receive or to climb towards the loftiest ultimate truth of God and of its own being and to tread the summits of divine experience.*

It was to meet the need of the first type or level that Indian religion created that mass of suggestive ceremony and effective ritual and strict outward rule and injunction and all that pageant of attracting and compelling symbol with which the cult is so richly equipped or profusely decorated. These are for the most part forming and indicative things which work upon the mind consciently and subconsciently and prepare it for an entry into the significance of the greater permanent things that lie behind them. And for this type too, for its vital mind and will, is intended all in the religion that calls on man to turn to a divine Power or powers for the just satisfaction of his desires and his interests, just because subject to the right and the law, the Dharma. In the Vedic times the outward ritual sacrifice and at a later period all the religious forms and notions that clustered visibly around the rites and imagery of temple worship, constant festival and ceremony and daily act of outward devotion were intended to serve this type or this soul-stage. Many of these things may seem to the developed mind to belong to an ignorant or half-awakened religionism; but they have their concealed truth and their psychic value and are indispensable in this stage for the development and difficult awakening of the soul shrouded in the ignorance of material Nature.

* The Tantric distinction is between the animal man, the hero man and the divine man, *paśu, vīra, deva.* Or we may grade the difference according to the three gunas,—first, the tamasic or rajaso-tamasic man ignorant, inert or moved only in a little light by small motive forces, the rajasic or sattwo-rajasic man struggling with an awakened mind and will towards self-development or self-affirmation, and the sattwic man open in mind and heart and will to the Light, standing at the top of the scale and ready to transcend it.

The middle stage, the second type starts from these things, but gets behind them; it is capable of understanding more clearly and consciently the psychic truths, the conceptions of the intelligence, the aesthetic indications, the ethical values and all the other mediating directions which Indian religion took care to place behind its symbols. These intermediate truths vivify the outward forms of the system and those who can grasp them can go through these mental indices towards things that are beyond the mind and approach the profounder truths of the spirit. For at this stage there is already something awake that can go inward to a more deeply psycho-religious experience. Already the mind, heart and will have some strength to grapple with the difficulties of the relations between the spirit and life, some urge to satisfy more luminously or more inwardly the rational, aesthetic and ethical nature and lead them upward towards their own highest heights; one can begin to train mind and soul towards a spiritual consciousness and the opening of a spiritual existence. This ascending type of humanity claims for its use all that large and opulent middle region of philosophic, psycho-spiritual, ethical, aesthetic and emotional religious seeking which is the larger and more significant portion of the wealth of Indian culture. At this stage intervene the philosophical systems, the subtle illumining debates and inquiries of the thinkers; here are the nobler or more passionate reaches of devotion, here are held up the higher, ampler or austerer ideals of the Dharma; here break in the psychical suggestions and first definite urgings of the eternal and infinite which draw men by their appeal and promise towards the practice of Yoga.

But these things, great as they were, were not final or supreme: they were openings, steps of ascension towards the luminous grandeurs of spiritual truth and its practice was kept ready and its means of attainment provided for the third and greatest type of human being, the third loftiest stage of the spiritual evolution. The complete light of spiritual knowledge when it emerges from veil and compromise and goes beyond all symbols and middle significances, the absolute and universal divine love, the beauty of the All-beautiful, the noblest dharma of unity with all beings, universal compassion and benevolence calm and sweet in the perfect purity of the spirit, the upsurge of the psychical being into the spiritual ecstasy, these divinest things were the heritage of the human being ready for divinity and their way and call were the supreme significances of Indian religion and Yoga. He reached by them the fruits of his perfect spiritual evolution, an identity with the Self and Spirit, a dwelling in or with God, the divine law of his being, a spiritual universality, communion, transcendence.

But distinctions are lines that can always be overpassed in the infinite complexity of man's nature and there was no sharp and unbridgeable division, only a gradation, since the actuality or potentiality of the three powers coexist in all men. Both the middle and the highest significances were near and present and pervaded the whole system, and the approaches to the highest status were not absolutely denied to any man, in spite of certain prohibitions: but these prohibitions broke down in practice or left a way of escape to the man who felt the call; the call itself was a sign of election. He had only to find the way and the guide. But even in the direct approach the principle of *adhikāra,* differing capacity and varying nature, *svabhāva,* was recognised in subtle ways, which it would be beyond my present purpose to enumerate. One may note as an example the significant Indian idea of the *iṣṭa-devatā,* the special name, form, idea of the Divinity which each man may choose for worship and communion and follow after according to the attraction in his nature and his capacity of spiritual intelligence. And each of the forms has its outer initial associations and suggestions for the worshipper, its appeal to the intelligence, psychical, aesthetic, emotional power in the nature and its highest spiritual significance which leads through some one truth of the Godhead into the essence of spirituality. One may note too that in the practice of Yoga the disciple has to be led through his nature and according to his capacity and the spiritual teacher and guide is expected to perceive and take account of the necessary gradations and the individual need and power in his giving of help and guidance. Many things may be objected to in the actual working of this large and flexible system and I shall take some note of them when I have to deal with the weak points or the pejorative side of the culture against which the hostile critic directs with a misleading exaggeration his missiles. But the principle of it and the main lines of the application embody a remarkable wisdom, knowledge and careful observation of human nature and an assured insight into the things of the spirit which none can question who has considered deeply and flexibly these difficult matters or had any close experience of the obstacles and potentialities of our nature in its approach to the concealed spiritual reality.

This carefully graded and complex system of religious development and spiritual evolution was linked on by a process of pervading intimate connection to that general culture of the life of the human being and his powers which must be the first care of every civilisation worth the name. The most delicate and difficult part of this task of human development is concerned with the thinking being of man, his mind of reason and knowledge. No ancient culture of which we have knowledge, not even the Greek, attached more importance to it or spent more effort on its cultivation. The business of the ancient Rishi was not only to know God, but to know the world and life and to reduce it by knowledge to a thing well understood and mastered with which the reason and will of man could deal on assured lines and on a safe basis of wise method and order. The ripe result of this effort was the Shastra. When we speak of the Shastra nowadays, we mean too often only the religio-social system of injunctions of the middle age made sacrosanct by their mythical attribution to Manu, Parasara and other Vedic sages. But in older India Shastra meant any systematised teaching and science; each department of life, each line of activity, each subject of knowledge had its science or Shastra. The attempt was to reduce each to a theoretical and practical order founded on detailed observation, just generalisation, full experience, intuitive, logical and experimental analysis and synthesis, in order to enable man to know always with a just fruitfulness for life and to act with the security of right knowledge. The smallest and the greatest things were examined with equal care and attention and each provided with its art and science. The name was given even to the highest spiritual knowledge whenever it was stated not in a mass of intuitive experience and revelatory knowledge as in the Upanishads, but for intellectual comprehension in system and order,—and in that sense the Gita is able to call its profound spiritual teaching the most secret science, *guhyatamam śāstram.* This high scientific and philosophical spirit was carried by the ancient Indian culture into all its activities. No Indian religion is complete without its outward form of preparatory practice, its supporting philosophy and its Yoga or system of inward practice or art of spiritual living: most even of what seems irrational in it to a first glance, has its philosophical turn and significance. It is this complete understanding and philosophical character which has given religion in India its durable security and immense vitality and enabled it to resist the acid dissolvent power of modern sceptical inquiry; whatever is ill-founded in experience and reason, that power can dissolve, but not the heart and mind of these great teachings. But what we have more especially to observe is that while Indian culture made a distinction between the lower and the higher learning, the knowledge of things and the knowledge of self, it did not put a gulf between them like some religions, but considered the knowledge of the world and things as a preparatory and a leading up to the knowledge of Self and God. All Shastra was put under the sanction of the names of the Rishis, who were in the beginning the teachers not only of spiritual truth and philosophy,—and we may note that all Indian philosophy, even the logic of Nyaya and the atomic theory of the Vaisheshikas, has for its highest crowning note and eventual object spiritual knowledge and liberation,—but of the arts, the social, political and military, the physical and psychic sciences, and every instructor was in his degree respected as a *guru* or *ācārya,* a guide or preceptor of the human spirit. All knowledge was woven into one and led up by degrees to the one highest knowledge.

The whole right practice of life founded on this knowledge was in the view of Indian culture a Dharma, a living according to a just, understanding and right view of self-culture, of the knowledge of things and life and of action in that knowledge. Thus each man and class and kind and species and each activity of soul, mind, life, body has its dharma. But the largest or at least most vitally important part of the Dharma was held to be the culture and ordering of the ethical nature of man. The ethical aspect of life, contrary to the amazingly ignorant observation of a certain type of critics, attracted a quite enormous amount of attention, occupied the greater part of Indian thought and writing not devoted to the things of pure knowledge and of the spirit and was so far pushed that there is no ethical formation or ideal which does not reach in it its highest conception and a certain divine absolutism of ideal practice. Indian thought took for granted,—though there are some remarkable speculations to the contrary,—the ethical nature of man and the ethical law of the world. It considered that man was justified in satisfying his desires, since that is necessary for the satisfaction and expansion of life, but not in obeying the dictates of desire as the law of his being; for in all things there is a greater law, each has not only its side of interest and desire, but its dharma or rule of right practice, satisfaction, expansion, regulation. The Dharma, then, fixed by the wise in the Shastra is the right thing to observe, the true rule of action. First in the web of Dharma comes the social law; for man's life is only initially for his vital, personal, individual self, but much more imperatively for the community, though most imperatively of all for the greatest Self one in himself and in all beings, for God, for the Spirit. Therefore first the individual must subordinate himself to the communal self, though by no means bound altogether to efface himself in it as the extremists of the communal idea imagine. He must live according to the law of his nature harmonised with the law of his social type and class, for the nation and in a higher reach of his being—this was greatly stressed by the Buddhists—for humanity. Thus living and acting he could learn to transcend the social scale of the Dharma, practise without injuring the basis of life the ideal scale and finally grow into the liberty of the spirit, when rule and duty were not binding because he would then move and act in a highest free and immortal dharma of the divine nature. All these aspects of the Dharma were closely linked up together in a progressive unity. Thus, for an example, each of the four orders had its own social function and ethics, but also an ideal rule for the growth of the pure ethical being, and every man by observing his dharma and turning his action Godwards could grow out of it into the spiritual freedom. But behind all dharma and ethics was put, not only as a safeguard but as a light, a religious sanction, a reminder of the continuity of life and of man's long pilgrimage through many births, a reminder of the Gods and planes beyond and of the Divine, and above it all the vision of a last stage of perfect comprehension and unity and of divine transcendence.

The system of Indian ethics liberalised by the catholicity of the ancient mind did not ban or violently discourage the aesthetic or even the hedonistic being of man in spite of a growing ascetic tendency and a certain high austerity of the summits. The aesthetic satisfactions of all kinds and all grades were an important part of the culture. Poetry, the drama, song, dance, music, the greater and lesser arts were placed under the sanction of the Rishis and were made instruments of the spirit's culture. A just theory held them to be initially the means of a pure aesthetic satisfaction and each was founded on its own basic rule and law, but on that basis and with a perfect fidelity to it still raised up to minister to the intellectual, ethical and religious development of the being. It is notable that the two vast Indian epics have been considered as much as Dharma-shastras as great historico-mythic epic narratives, *itihasas.* They are, that is to say, noble, vivid and puissant pictures of life, but they utter and breathe throughout their course the law and ideal of a great and high ethical and religious spirit in life and aim in their highest intention at the idea of the Divine and the way of the mounting soul in the action of the world. Indian painting, sculpture and architecture did not refuse service to the aesthetic satisfaction and interpretation of the social, civic and individual life of the human being; these things, as all evidences show, played a great part in their motives of creation, but still their highest work was reserved for the greatest spiritual side of the culture, and throughout we see them seized and suffused with the brooding stress of the Indian mind on the soul, the Godhead, the spiritual, the Infinite. And we have to note too that the aesthetic and hedonistic being was made not only an aid to religion and spirituality and liberally used for that purpose, but even one of the main gates of man's approach to the Spirit. The Vaishnava religion especially is a religion of love and beauty and of the satisfaction of the whole delight-soul of man in God and even the desires and images of the sensuous life were turned by its vision into figures of a divine soul-experience. Few religions have gone so far as this immense catholicity or carried the whole nature so high in its large puissant and many-sided approach to the spiritual and the infinite.

Finally, there is the most outwardly vital life of man, his ordinary dynamic, political, economical and social being. This too Indian culture took strenuously in hand and subjected its whole body to the pressure of its own ideals and conceptions. Its method was to build up great Shastras of social living, duty and enjoyment, military and political rule and conduct and economical well-being. These were directed on one side to success, expansion, opulence and the right art and relation of these activities, but on those motives, demanded by the very nature of the vital man and his action, was imposed the law of the Dharma, a stringent social and ethical ideal and rule—thus the whole life of the king as the head of power and responsibility was regulated by it in its every hour and function,—and the constant reminder of religious duty. In latter times a Machiavellian principle of statecraft, that which has been always and is still pursued by governments and diplomats, encroached on this nobler system, but in the best age of Indian thought this depravation was condemned as a temporarily effective, but lesser, ignoble and inferior way of policy. The great rule of the culture was that the higher a man's position and power, the larger the scope of his function and influence of his acts and example, the greater should be the call on him of the Dharma. The whole law and custom of society was placed under the sanction of the Rishis and the gods, protected from the violence of the great and powerful, given a socio-religious character and the king himself charged to live and rule as the guardian and servant of the Dharma with only an executive power over the community which was valid so long as he observed with fidelity the Law. And as this vital aspect of life is the one which most easily draws us outward and away from the inner self and the diviner aim of living, it was the most strenuously linked up at every point with the religious idea in the way the vital man can best understand, in the Vedic times by the constant reminder of the sacrifice behind every social and civic act, at a later period by religious rites, ceremonies, worship, the calling in of the gods, the insistence on the subsequent results or a supraterrestrial aim of works. So great was this preoccupation, that while in the spiritual and intellectual and other spheres a considerable or a complete liberty was allowed to speculation, action, creation, here the tendency was to impose a rigorous law and authority, a tendency which in the end became greatly exaggerated and prevented the expansion of the society into new forms more suitable for the need of the spirit of the age, the Yugadharma. A door of liberty was opened to the community by the provision of an automatic permission to changed custom and to the individual in the adoption of the religious life with its own higher discipline or freedom outside the ordinary social weft of binding rule and injunction. A rigid observation and discipline of the social law, a larger nobler discipline and freer self-culture of the ideal side of the Dharma, a wide freedom of the religious and spiritual life became the three powers of the system. The steps of the expanding human spirit mounted through these powers to its perfection.

Thus the whole general character of the application of Indian ideals to life became throughout of this one texture, the constant, subtly graded, subtly harmonised preparation of the soul of man for its spiritual being. First, the regulated satisfaction of the primary natural being of man subjected to the law of the Dharma and the ethical idea and besieged at every moment by the suggestions of religion, a religion at first appealing to his more outward undeveloped mind, but in each of its outward symbols and circumstances opening to a profounder significance, armed with the indication of a profoundest spiritual and ideal meaning as its justification. Then, the higher steps of the developed reason and psychical, ethical and aesthetic powers closely interwoven and raised by a similar opening beyond themselves to their own heights of spiritual direction and potentiality. Finally, each of these growing powers in man was made on its own line of approach a gateway into his divine and spiritual being. Thus we may observe that there was created a Yoga of knowledge for the self-exceeding of the thinking intellectual man, a

Yoga of works for the self-exceeding of the active, dynamic and ethical man, a Yoga of love and bhakti for the self-exceeding of the emotional, aesthetic, hedonistic man, by which each arrived to perfection through a self-ward, spiritual, God-ward direction of his own special power, as too a Yoga of self-exceeding through the power of the psychical being and even through the power of the life in the body,—Yogas which could be practised in separation or with some kind of synthesis. But all these ways of self-exceeding led to a highest self-becoming. To become one with universal being and all existences, one with the self and spirit, united with God, completed the human evolution, built the final step of man's self-culture.

A DEFENCE OF INDIAN CULTURE

CHAPTER IV

RELIGION AND SPIRITUALITY

I HAVE DWELT at some length, though still very inadequately, on the principles of Indian religion, the sense of its evolution and the intention of its system, because these things are being constantly ignored and battle delivered by its defenders and assailants on details, particular consequences and side issues. Those too have their importance because they are part of the practical execution, the working out of the culture in life; but they cannot be rightly valued unless we seize hold of the intention which was behind the execution. And the first thing we see is that the principle, the essential intention of Indian culture was extraordinarily high, ambitious and noble, the highest indeed that the human spirit can conceive. For what can be a greater idea of life than that which makes it a development of the spirit in man to its most vast secret and high possibilities,—a culture that conceives of life as a movement of the Eternal in time, of the universal in the individual, of the infinite in the finite, of the Divine in man, or holds that man can become not only conscious of the eternal and the infinite, but live in its power and universalise, spiritualise and divinise himself by self-knowledge? What greater aims can be for the life of man than to grow by an inner and outer experience till he can live in God, realise his spirit, become divine in knowledge, in will and in the joy of his highest existence? And that is the whole sense of the striving of Indian culture.

It is easy to say that these ideas are fantastic, chimerical and impracticable, that there is no spirit and no eternal and nothing divine, and man would do much better not to dabble in religion and philosophy, but rather make the best he can of the ephemeral littleness of his life and body. That is a negation natural enough to the vital and physical mind, but it rests on the assumption that man can only be what he is at the moment, and there is nothing greater in him which it is his business to evolve; such a negation has no enduring value. The whole aim of a great culture is to lift man up to something which at first he is not, to lead him to knowledge though he starts from an unfathomable ignorance, to teach him to live by his reason, though actually he lives much more by his unreason, by the law of good and unity, though he is now full of evil and discord, by a law of beauty and harmony, though his actual life is a repulsive muddle of ugliness and jarring barbarisms, by some high law of his spirit, though at present he is egoistic, material, unspiritual, engrossed by the needs and desires of his physical being. If a civilisation has not any of these aims, it can hardly at all be said to have a culture and certainly in no sense a great and noble culture. But the last of these aims, as conceived by ancient India, is the highest of all because it includes and surpasses all the others. To have made this attempt is to have ennobled the life of the race; to have failed in it is better than if it had never at all been attempted; to have achieved even a partial success is a great contribution to the future possibilities of the human being.

The system of Indian culture is another thing. A system is in its very nature at once an effectuation and a limitation of the spirit; and yet we must have a science and art of life, a system of living. All that is needed is that the lines laid down should be large and noble, capable of evolution so that the spirit may more and more express itself in life, flexible even in its firmness so that it may absorb and harmonise new material and enlarge its variety and richness without losing its unity. The system of Indian culture was all these things in its principle and up to a certain point and a certain period in its practice. That a decline came upon it in the end and a kind of arrest of growth, not absolute, but still very serious and dangerous to its life and future, is perfectly true, and we shall have to ask whether that was due to the inherent character of the culture, to a deformation or to a temporary exhaustion of the force of living, and, if the last, how that exhaustion came. At present, I will only note in passing one point which has its importance. Our critic is never tired of harping on India's misfortunes and he attributes them all to the incurable badness of our civilisation, the total absence of a true and sound culture. Now misfortune is not a proof of absence of culture, nor good fortune the sign of salvation. Greece was unfortunate; she was as much torn by internal dissensions and civil wars as India, she was finally unable to arrive at unity or preserve independence; yet Europe owes half its civilisation to those squabbling inconsequent petty peoples of Greece. Italy was unfortunate enough in all conscience, yet few nations have contributed more to European culture than incompetent and unfortunate Italy. The misfortunes of India have been considerably exaggerated, at least in their incidence, but take them at their worst, admit that no nation has suffered more. If all that is due to the badness of our civilisation, to what is due then the remarkable fact of the obstinate survival of India, her culture and her civilisation under this load of misfortunes, or the power which enables her still to assert herself and her spirit at this moment, to the great wrath of her critics, against the tremendous shock of the flood from Europe which has almost submerged other peoples? If her misfortunes are due to her cultural deficiencies, must not by a parity of reasoning this extraordinary vitality be due to some great force in her, some enduring virtue of truth in her spirit? A mere lie and insanity cannot live; its persistence is a disease which must before long lead to death; it cannot be the source of an unslayable life. There must be some heart of soundness, some saving truth which has kept this people alive and still enables it to raise its head and affirm its will to be and its faith in its mission.

But, finally, we have to see not only the spirit and principle of the culture, not only the ideal idea and scope of intention in its system, but its actual working and effect in the values of life. Here we must admit great limitations, great imperfections. There is no culture, no civilisation ancient or modern which in its system has been entirely satisfactory to the need of perfection in man; there is none in which the working has not been marred by considerable limitations and imperfections. And the greater the aim of the culture, the larger the body of the civilisation, the more are these flaws likely to overbear the eye. In the first place every culture suffers by the limitations or defects of its qualities and, an almost infallible consequence, by the exaggerations too of its qualities. It tends to concentrate on certain leading ideas and to lose sight of others or unduly depress them; this want of balance gives rise to one-sided tendencies which are not properly checked, not kept in their due place, and bring about unhealthy exaggerations. But so long as the vigour of the civilisation lasts, life accommodates itself, makes the most of compensating forces and in spite of all stumblings, evils, disasters, some great thing is done; but in a time of decline the defect or the excess of particular quality gets the upper hand, becomes a disease, makes a general ravage and, if not arrested, may lead to decay and death. Again, the ideal may be great, may have even, as Indian culture had in its best times, a certain kind of provisional completeness, a first attempt at comprehensive harmony, but there is always a great gulf between the ideal and the actual practice of life. To bridge that gulf or at least to make it as narrow as possible is the most difficult part of human endeavour. Finally, the evolution of our race, surprising enough if we look across the ages, is still, when all is said, a slow and embarrassed progress. Each age, each civilisation carries the heavy burden of our deficiencies, each succeeding age throws off something of the load, but loses some virtue of the past, creates other gaps and embarrasses itself with new aberrations. We have to strike a balance, to see things in the whole, to observe whither we are tending and use a large secular vision; otherwise it would be difficult to keep an unfailing faith in the destinies of the race. For, after all, what we have accomplished so far in the main at the best of times is to bring in a modicum of reason and culture and spirituality to leaven a great mass of barbarism. Mankind is still no more than semi-civilised and it was never anything else in the recorded history of its present cycle.

And therefore every civilisation presents a mixed and anomalous appearance and can be turned by a hostile or unsympathetic observation which notes and exaggerates its defects, ignores its true spirit and its qualities, masses the shades, leaves out the lights, into a mass of barbarism, a picture of almost unrelieved gloom and failure, to the legitimate surprise and indignation of those to whom its motives appear to have a great and just value. For each has achieved something of special value for humanity in the midst of its general work of culture, brought out in a high degree some potentiality of our nature and given a first large standing-ground for its future perfection. Greece developed to a high degree the intellectual reason and the sense of form and harmonious beauty, Rome founded firmly strength and power and patriotism and law and order, modern Europe has raised to enormous proportions practical reason, science and efficiency and economic capacity, India developed the spiritual mind working on the other powers of man and exceeding them, the intuitive reason, the philosophical harmony of the Dharma informed by the religious spirit, the sense of the eternal and the infinite. The future has to go on to a greater and more perfect comprehensive development of these things and to evolve fresh powers, but we shall not do this rightly by damning the past or damning other cultures than our own in a spirit of arrogant intolerance. We need not only a spirit of calm criticism, but an eye of sympathetic intuition to extract the good from the past and present effort of humanity and make the most of it for our future progress.

This being so, if our critic insists that the past culture of India was of the nature of a semi-barbarism, I shall not object, so long as I have the liberty of passing the same criticism, equally valid or invalid, on the type of European culture which he wishes to foist on us in its place. Mr. Archer feels the openings which European civilisation gives to this kind of retort and he pleads plaintively that it ought not to be made; he takes refuge in the old tag that a *tu quoque* is no argument. Certainly the retort would be irrelevant if this were only a question of the dispassionate criticism of Indian culture without arrogant comparisons and offensive pretensions. But it becomes a perfectly valid and effective argument when the critic turns into a partisan and tries to trample underfoot all the claims of the Indian spirit and its civilisation in the name of the superiority of Europe. When he insists on our renouncing our own natural being and culture in order to follow and imitate the West as docile pupils on the ground of India's failure to achieve cultural perfection or the ideal of a sound civilisation, we have a right to point out that Europe has to its credit at least as ugly a failure, and for the same fundamental reasons. We have a right to ask whether science, practical reason and efficiency and an unbridled economic production which makes man a slave of his life and body, a wheel, spring or cog in a huge mechanism or a cell of an economic organism and translates into human terms the ideal of the ant-hill and the bee-hive, is really the whole truth of our being and a sound or complete ideal of civilisation. The ideal of this culture, though it has its obstacles and difficulties, is at any rate not an unduly exalted aim and ought to be more easy of accomplishment than the arduous spiritual ideal of ancient India. But how much of the European mind and life is really governed by reason and what does this practical reason and efficiency come to in the end? To what perfection has it brought the human mind and soul and life? The aggressive ugliness of modern European life, its paucity of philosophic reason and aesthetic beauty and religious aspiration, its constant unrest, its harsh and oppressive mechanical burden, its lack of inner freedom, its recent huge catastrophe, the fierce struggle of classes are things of which we have a right to take note. To harp in the style of the Archerian lyre on these aspects alone and to ignore the brighter side of modern ideals would certainly be an injustice. There was a time indeed many years ago, when, while admiring the past cultural achievement of Europe, the present industrial form of it seemed to me an intellectualised Titanic barbarism with Germany as its too admired type and successful protagonist. A wider view of the ways of the Spirit in the world corrects the onesidedness of this notion, but still it contains a truth which Europe recognised in the hour of her agony, though now she seems to be forgetting too easily her momentary illumination. Mr. Archer argues that at least the West is trying to struggle out of its barbarism while India has been content to stagnate in her deficiencies. That may be a truth of the immediate past; but what then? The question still remains whether Europe is taking the only, the complete or the best way open to human endeavour and whether it is not the right thing for India, not to imitate Europe, though she well may learn from western experience, but to get out of her stagnation by developing what is best and most essential in her own spirit and culture.

The right, the natural path for India lies so obviously in this direction that in order to destroy it Mr. Archer in his chosen role as devil's advocate has to juggle with the truth at every step and labour hard and vainly to re-establish the spell of hypnotic suggestion, now broken for good, which led most of us for a long space to condemn wholesale ourselves and our past and imagine that the Indian's whole duty in life was to turn an imitative ape in leading-strings and dance to the mechanic barrel-organ tunes of the British civiliser. The claim of Indian culture to survival can be met first and most radically by challenging the value of its fundamental ideas and the high things which are most native to its ideal, its temperament, its way of looking at the world. To deny the truth or the value of spirituality, of the sense of the eternal and infinite, the inner spiritual experience, the philosophic mind and spirit, the religious aim and feeling, the intuitive reason, the idea of universality and spiritual unity is one resource, and this is the real attitude of our critic which emerges constantly in his vehement philippic. But he cannot carry it through consistently, because it brings him into conflict with ideas and perceptions which are ineradicable in the human mind and which even in Europe are now after a temporary obscuration beginning to come back into favour. Therefore he hedges and tries rather to prove that we find in India, even in her magnificent past, even at her best, no spirituality, no real philosophy, no true or high religious feeling, no light of intuitive reason, nothing at all of the great things to which she has directed her most strenuous aspiration. This assertion is sufficiently absurd, self-contradictory and opposed to the express testimony of those who are eminently fitted and entitled to express an authoritative opinion on these matters. He therefore establishes a third line of attack combined of two inconsistent and opposite assertions, first, that the higher Hinduism which is made up of these greater things has had no effect on India and, secondly, that it has had on the contrary a most all-pervading, a most disastrous and paralysing, a soul-killing, life-killing effect. He attempts to make his indictment effective by massing together all these inconsistent lines of attack and leading them all to the one conclusion, that the culture of India is both in theory and practice wrong, worthless, deleterious to the true aim of human living.

The last position taken is the only one which we need now consider, since the value of the essential ideas of Indian culture cannot be destroyed and to deny them is futile. The things they stand for are there, in whatever form, vaguely or distinctly seeking for themselves in the highest and deepest movements of human being and its nature. The peculiarity of Indian culture lies only in this distinction that what is vague or confused or imperfectly brought out in most other cultures, it has laboured rather to make distinct, to sound all its possibilities, to fix its aspects and lines and hold it up as a true, precise, large and practicable ideal for the race. The formulation may not be entirely complete; it may have to be still more enlarged, bettered, put otherwise, things missed brought out, the lines and forms modified, errors of stress and direction corrected; but a firm, a large foundation has been laid down not only in theory, but in solid practice. If there has been an actual complete failure in life—and that is the one point left,—it must be due to one of two causes; either there has been some essential bungling in the application of the ideal to the facts of life as it is, or else there has been a refusal to recognise the facts of life at all. Perhaps, then, there has been, to put it otherwise, an insistence on what we may be at some hardly attainable height of our being without having first made the most of what we are. The infinite can only be reached after we have grown in the finite, the eternal grasped only by man growing in time, the spiritual perfected only by man accomplished first in body, life and mind. If that necessity has been ignored, then one may fairly contend that there has been a gross, impracticable and inexcusable error in the governing idea of Indian culture. But as a matter of fact there has been no such error. We have seen what were the aim and idea and method of Indian culture and it will be perfectly clear that the value of life and its training were amply recognised in its system and given their proper place. Even the most extreme philosophies and religions, Buddhism and Illusionism, which held life to be an impermanence or ignorance that must be transcended and cast away, yet did not lose sight of the truth that man must develop himself under the conditions of this present ignorance or impermanence before he can attain to knowledge and to that Permanent which is the denial of temporal being. Buddhism was not solely a cloudy sublimation of Nirvana, nothingness, extinction and the tyrannous futility of Karma; it gave us a great and powerful discipline for the life of man on earth. The enormous positive effects it had on society and ethics and the creative impulse it imparted to art and thought and in a less degree to literature, are a sufficient proof of the strong vitality of its method. If this positive turn was present in the most extreme philosophy of denial, it was still more largely present in the totality of Indian culture.

There has been indeed from early times in the Indian mind a certain strain, a tendency towards a lofty and austere exaggeration in the direction taken by Buddhism and Mayavada. This excess was inevitable, the human mind being what it is; it had even its necessity and value. Our mind does not arrive at the totality of truth easily and by one embracing effort; an arduous search is the condition of its finding. The mind opposes different sides of the truth to each other, follows each to its extreme possibility, treats it even for a time as the sole truth, makes imperfect compromises, arrives by various adjustments and gropings nearer to the true relations. The Indian mind followed this method; it covered, as far as it could, the whole field, tried every position, looked at the truth from every angle, attempted many extremes and many syntheses. But the European critic very ordinarily labours under the idea that this exaggeration in the direction of negating life was actually the whole of Indian thought and sentiment or the one undisputed governing idea of the culture. Nothing could be more false and inaccurate. The early Vedic religion did not deny, but laid a full emphasis on life. The Upanishads did not deny life, but held that the world is a manifestation of the Eternal, of Brahman, all here is Brahman, all is in the Spirit and the Spirit is in all, the self-existent Spirit has become all these things and creatures; life too is Brahman, the life-force is the very basis of our existence, the life-spirit, Vayu, is the manifest and evident Eternal, *pratyakṣam brahma.* But it affirmed that the present way of existence of man is not the highest or the whole; his outward mind and life are not all his being; to be fulfilled and perfect he has to grow out of his physical and mental ignorance into spiritual self-knowledge.

Buddhism arrived at a later stage and seized on one side of these ancient teachings to make a sharp spiritual and intellectual opposition between the impermanence of life and the permanence of the Eternal which brought to a head and made a gospel of the ascetic exaggeration. But the synthetic Hindu mind struggled against this negation and finally threw out Buddhism, though not without contracting an increased bias in this direction. That bias came to its height in the philosophy of Shankara, his theory of Maya, which put its powerful imprint on the Indian mind and, coinciding with a progressive decline in the full vitality of the race, did tend for a time to fix a pessimistic and negative view of terrestrial life and distort the larger Indian ideal. But his theory is not at all a necessary deduction from the great Vedantic authorities, the Upanishads, Brahmasutras and Gita, and was always combated by other Vedantic philosophies and religions which drew from them and from spiritual experience very different conclusions. At the present time, in spite of a temporary exaltation of Shankara's philosophy, the most vital movements of Indian thought and religion are moving again towards the synthesis of spirituality and life which was an essential part of the ancient Indian ideal. Therefore Mr. Archer's contention that whatever India has achieved in life and creation and action has been done in spite of the governing ideas of her culture, since logically she ought to have abandoned life and creation and action, is as unsound as it is unnatural and grotesque. To develop to the full the intellectual, the dynamic and volitional, the ethical, the aesthetic, the social and economic being of man was an important element of Indian civilisation,—if for nothing else, at least as an indispensable preliminary to spiritual perfection and freedom. India's best achievements in thought, art, literature, society were the logical outcome of her religio-philosophical culture.

But still it may be argued that whatever may have been the theory, the exaggeration was there and in practice it discouraged life and action. That, when its other falsities have been eliminated, is what Mr. Archer's criticism comes to in the end; the emphasis on the Self, the eternal, the universal, the impersonal, the infinite discouraged, he thinks, life, will, personality, human action and led to a false and life-killing asceticism. India achieved nothing of importance, produced no great personalities, was impotent in will and endeavour, her literature and art are a barbaric and monstrous nullity not equal even to the third-rate work of Europe, her life story a long and dismal record of incompetence and failure. An inconsistency more or less is nothing to this critic and in the same breath he affirms that this very India, described by him elsewhere as always effete, sterile or a mother of monstrous abortions, is one of the most interesting countries in the world, that her art casts a potent and attractive spell and has numberless beauties, that her very barbarisms are magnificent and that, most wonderful of all, in presence of some of her personalities in the abodes of her ancient fine-spun aristocratic culture a European is apt to feel like a semi-barbarian intruder! But let us leave aside these signs of grace which are only an occasional glimmering of light across the darkness and gloom of Mr. Archer's mood. We must see how far there is any foundation for the substance of this criticism. What was the real value of Indian life, will, personality, achievement, creation, those things that she regards as her glories, but her critic tells her she should shudder at as her disgrace? That is the one remaining vital question.

A DEFENCE OF INDIAN CULTURE

CHAPTER V

RELIGION AND SPIRITUALITY

THE most general charge against Indian culture in its practical effects can be dismissed without any serious difficulty. The critic with whom I have to deal has, in fact, spoiled his case by the spirit of frantic exaggeration in which he writes. To say that there has been no great or vivid activity of life in India, that she has had no great personalities with the mythical exception of Buddha and the other pale exception of Asoka, that she has never shown any will-power and never done any great thing, is so contrary to all the facts of history that only a devil's advocate in search of a case could advance it at all or put it with that crude vehemence. India has lived and lived greatly, whatever judgment one may pass on her ideas and institutions. What is meant after all by life and when is it that we most fully and greatly live? Life is surely nothing but the creation and active self-expression of man's spirit, powers, capacities, his will to be and think and create and love and do and achieve. When that is wanting or, since it cannot be absolutely wanting, depressed, held under, discouraged or inert, whether by internal or external causes, then we may say that there is a lack of life. Life in its largest sense is the great web of our internal and external action, the play of Shakti, the play of Karma; it is religion and philosophy and thought and science and poetry and art, drama and song and dance and play, politics and society, industry, commerce and trade, adventure and travel, war and peace, conflict and unity, victory and defeat and aspirations and vicissitudes, the thoughts, emotions, words, deeds, joys and sorrows which make up the existence of man. In a narrower sense life is sometimes spoken of as the more obvious and external vital action, a thing which can be depressed by a topheavy intellectuality or ascetic spirituality, sicklied over with the pale cast of thought or the paler cast of world-weariness or made flat, stale and uninteresting by a formalised, conventional or too strait-laced system of society. Again, life may be very active and full of colour for a small and privileged part of the community, but the life of the mass dull, void and miserable. Or, finally, there may be all the ordinary materials and circumstances of mere living, but if life is not uplifted by great hopes, aspirations and ideals, then we may well say that the community does not really live; it is defective in the characteristic greatness of the human spirit.

The ancient and mediaeval life of India was not wanting in any of the things that make up the vivid interesting activity of human existence. On the contrary, it was extraordinarily full of colour and interest. Mr. Archer's criticism on this point, a criticism packed full of ignorance and built up by a purely fictitious construction of what things logically ought to have been on the theory of a dominating asceticism and belief in the illusionary character of the world, is not and cannot be borne out by anyone who has come close to the facts. It is true that while many European writers who have studied the history of the land and the people, have expressed strongly their appreciation of the vividness and interesting fullness, colour and beauty of life in India before the present period,—that unhappily exists no longer except in the pages of history and literature and the broken or crumbling fragments of the past,—those who see only from a distance or fix their eyes only on one aspect, speak of it often as a land of metaphysics, philosophies, dreams and brooding imaginations, and certain artists and writers are apt to write in a strain as if it were a country of the Arabian Nights, a mere glitter of strange hues and fancies and marvels. But on the contrary India has been as much a home of serious and solid realities, of a firm grappling with the problems of thought and life, of measured and wise organisation and great action as any other considerable centre of civilisation. The widely different view these perceptions express simply show the many-sided brilliance and fullness of her life. The colour and magnificence have been its aesthetic side; she has had great dreams and high and splendid imaginations, for that too is wanted for the completeness of our living; but also deep philosophical and religious thinking, a wide and searching criticism of life, a great political and social order, a strong ethical tone and a persistent vigour of individual and communal living. That is a combination which means life in all its fullness, though deficient, it may be, except in extraordinary cases, in the more violent egoistic perversities and exaggerations which some minds seem to take for a proof of the highest vigour of existence.

In what field indeed has not India attempted, achieved, created, and in all on a large scale and yet with much attention to completeness of detail? Of her spiritual and philosophic achievement there can be no real question. They stand there as the Himalayas stand upon the earth in the phrase of Kalidasa, *pṛthivyā iva mānadaṇḍaḥ*, "as if earth's measuring rod," mediating still between earth and heaven, measuring the finite, casting their plummet far into the infinite, plunging their extremities into the upper and lower seas of the superconscient and the subliminal, the spiritual and the natural being. But if her philosophies, her religious disciplines, her long list of great spiritual personalities, thinkers, founders, saints are her greatest glory, as was natural to her temperament and governing idea, they are by no means her sole glories, nor are the others dwarfed by their eminence. It is now proved that in science she went farther than any country before the modern era, and even Europe owes the beginning of her physical science to India as much as to Greece, although not directly but through the medium of the Arabs. And, even if she had only gone as far, that would have been sufficient proof of a strong intellectual life in an ancient culture. Especially in mathematics, astronomy and chemistry, the chief elements of ancient science, she discovered and formulated much and well and anticipated by force of reasoning or experiment some of the scientific ideas and discoveries which Europe first arrived at much later, but was able to base more firmly by her new and completer method. She was well-equipped in surgery and her system of medicine survives to this day and has still its value, though it declined intermediately in knowledge and is only now recovering its vitality.

In literature, in the life of the mind, she lived and built greatly. Not only has she the Vedas, Upanishads and Gita, not to speak of less supreme but still powerful or beautiful work in that field, unequalled monuments of religious and philosophic poetry, a kind in which Europe has never been able to do anything much of any great value, but that vast national structure, the Mahabharata, gathering into its cycle the poetic literature and expressing so completely the life of a long formative age, that it is said of it in a popular saying which has the justice if also the exaggeration of a too apt epigram, "What is not in this Bharata, is not in Bharatavarsha (India)," and the Ramayana, the greatest and most remarkable poem of its kind, that most sublime and beautiful epic of ethical idealism and a heroic semi-divine human life, and the marvellous richness, fullness and colour of the poetry and romance of highly cultured thought, sensuous enjoyment, imagination, action and adventure which makes up the romantic literature of her classical epoch. Nor did this long continuous vigour of creation cease with the loss of vitality by the Sanskrit tongue, but was parallelled and carried on in a mass of great or of beautiful work in her other languages, in Pali first and Prakrit, much unfortunately lost,* and Tamil, afterwards in Hindi, Bengali, Marathi and other tongues. The long tradition of her architecture, sculpture and painting speaks for itself, even in what survives after all the ruin of stormy centuries: whatever judgment may be formed of it by the narrower school of western aesthetics,—and at least its fineness of execution and workmanship cannot be denied, nor the power with which it renders the Indian mind,—it testifies at least to a continuous creative activity. And creation is proof of life and great creation of greatness of life.

But these things are, it may be said, the things of the mind, and the intellect, imagination and aesthetic mind of India may have been creatively active, but yet her outward life depressed, dull, poor, gloomy with the hues of asceticism, void of will-power and personality, ineffective, null. That would be a hard proposition to swallow; for literature, art and science do not flourish in a void of life. But here too what are the facts? India has not only had the long roll of her great saints, sages, thinkers, religious founders, poets, creators, scientists, scholars, legists; she has had her great rulers, administrators, soldiers, conquerors, heroes, men with the strong active will, the mind that plans and the seeing force that builds. She has warred and ruled, traded and colonised and spread her civilisation, built polities and organised communities and societies, done all that makes the outward activity of great peoples. A nation tends to throw out its most vivid types in that line of action which is most congenial to its temperament and expressive of its leading idea, and it is the great saints and religious personalities that stand at the head in India and present the most striking and continuous roll-call of greatness, just as Rome lived most in her warriors and statesmen

* E.g., the once famous work in Paisachi of which the *Kathāsaritsāgara* is an inferior version.

and rulers. The Rishi in ancient India was the outstanding figure with the hero just behind, while in later times the most striking feature is the long uninterrupted chain from Buddha and Mahavira to Ramanuja, Chaitanya, Nanak, Ramdas and Tukaram and beyond them to Ramakrishna and Vivekananda and Dayananda. But there have been also the remarkable achievements of statesmen and rulers, from the first dawn of ascertainable history which comes in with the striking figures of Chandragupta, Chanakya, Asoka, the Gupta emperors and goes down through the multitude of famous Hindu and Mahomedan figures of the middle age to quite modern times. In ancient India there was the life of republics, oligarchies, democracies, small kingdoms of which no detail of history now survives, afterwards the long effort at empire-building, the colonisation of Ceylon and the Archipelago, the vivid struggles that attended the rise and decline of the Pathan and Mogul dynasties, the Hindu struggle for survival in the south, the wonderful record of Rajput heroism and the great upheaval of national life in Maharashtra penetrating to the lowest strata of society, the remarkable episode of the Sikh Khalsa. An adequate picture of that outward life still remains to be given; once given it would be the end of many fictions. All this mass of action was not accomplished by men without mind and will and vital force, by pale shadows of humanity in whom the vigorous manhood had been crushed out under the burden of a gloomy and all-effacing asceticism, nor does it look like the sign of a metaphysically minded people of dreamers averse to life and action. It was not men of straw or lifeless and will-less dummies or thin-blooded dreamers who thus acted, planned, conquered, built great systems of administration, founded kingdoms and empires, figured as great patrons of poetry and art and architecture or, later, resisted heroically imperial power and fought for the freedom of clan or people. Nor was it a nation devoid of life which maintained its existence and culture and still lived on and broke out constantly into new revivals under the ever increasing stress of continuously adverse circumstances. The modern Indian revival, religious, cultural, political, called now sometimes a renaissance, which so troubles and grieves the minds of her critics, is only a repetition under altered circumstances, in an adapted form, in a greater though as yet less vivid mass of movement, of a phenomenon which has constantly repeated itself throughout a millennium of Indian history.

And it must be remembered that by virtue of its culture and its system the whole nation shared in the common life. In all countries in the past the mass has indeed lived with a less active and vivid force than the few,—sometimes with the mere elements of life, not with even any beginning of finished richness,—nor has modern civilisation yet got rid of this disparity, though it has opened the advantages or at least the initial opportunities of a first-hand life and thought and knowledge to a greater number. But in ancient India, though the higher classes led and had the lion's share of the force and wealth of life, the people too lived and until much later times intensely though on a lesser scale and with a more diffused and less concentrated force. Their religious life was more intense than that of any other country; they drank in with remarkable facility the thoughts of the philosophers and the influence of the saints; they heard and followed Buddha and the many who came after him; they were taught by the Sannyasins and sang the songs of the Bhaktas and Bauls and thus possessed some of the most delicate and beautiful poetical literature ever produced; they contributed many of the greatest names in our religion, and from the outcasts themselves came saints revered by the whole community. In ancient Hindu times they had their share of political life and power; they were the people, the *viśaḥ* of the Veda, of whom the kings were the leaders and from them as well as from the sacred or princely families were born the Rishis; they held their villages as little self-administered republics; in the time of the great kingdoms and empires they sat in the municipalities and urban councils and the bulk of the typical royal Council described in the books of political science was composed of commoners, Vaishyas, and not of Brahmin Pundits and Kshatriya nobles; for a long time they could impose their will on their kings, without the need of a long struggle, by a single demonstration of their displeasure. So long as Hindu kingdoms existed, something of all this survived, and even the entrance into India of Central Asian forms of absolutist despotism, never an indigenous Indian growth, left some remnant of the old edifice still in being. The people had their share too in art and poetry, their means by which the essence of Indian culture was disseminated through the mass, a system of elementary education in addition to the great universities of ancient times, a type of popular dramatic representation which was in some parts of the country alive even yesterday; they gave India her artists and architects and many of the famous poets in the popular tongues; they preserved by the force of their long past culture an innate aesthetic sense and faculty of which the work of Indian craftsmen remained a constant and striking evidence until it was destroyed or degraded by the vulgarisation and loss of aesthetic sense and beauty which has been one of the results of modern civilisation. Nor was the life of India ascetic, gloomy or sad, as the too logical mind of the critic would have it be. The outward form is more quiet than in other countries, there is a certain gravity and reserve before strangers which deceives the foreign observer, and in recent times asceticism and poverty and an increase of puritanic tendency had their effect; but the life portrayed in the literature of the country is glad and vivid, and even now despite certain varieties of temperament and many forces making for pression, laughter, humour, an unobtrusive elasticity and equanimity in the vicissitudes of life are very marked features of the Indian character.

The whole theory of a want of life and will and activity in

the Indian people as a result of their culture is then a myth. The circumstances which have given some colour to it in later times will be noted in their proper place; but they are a feature of the decline and even then must be taken with considerable qualification, and the much longer history of its past greatness tells quite another story. That history has not been recorded in the European fashion; for the art of history and biography, though not entirely neglected, was never brought to perfection in India, never sufficiently practised, nor does any sustained record of the doings of kings and great men and peoples before the Mussulman dynasties survive except in the one solitary instance of Cashmere. This is certainly a defect and leaves a very serious gap. India has lived much, but has not sat down to record the history of her life. Her soul and mind have left their great monuments, but so much as we know—and after all it is not little—of the rest, the more outward things, remains or has emerged recently in spite of her neglect; such exact records as she had, she has allowed to rust forgotten or disappear. Perhaps what Mr. Archer really means when he tells us that we have had no personalities in our history, is that they do not come home to his mind because their doings and sayings are not minutely recorded in the western manner; their personality, will-power and creative force emerge only in their work or in indicative tradition and anecdote or in incomplete records. And very curiously, very fancifully this defect has been set down to an ascetic want of interest in life; it is supposed that India was so much absorbed in the eternal that she deliberately despised and neglected time, so profoundly concentrated on the pursuit of ascetic brooding and quietistic peace that she looked down on and took no interest in the memory of action. That is another myth. The same phenomenon of a lack of sustained and deliberate record appears in other ancient cultures, but nobody suggests that Egypt, Assyria or Persia have to be reconstructed for us by the archaeologists for an analogous reason. The genius of Greece developed the art of history, though only in the later period of her activity, and Europe has cherished and preserved the art; India and other ancient civilisations did not arrive at it or neglected its full development. It is a defect, but there is no reason why we should go out of our way in this one case to attribute it to a deliberate motive or to any lack of interest in life. And in spite of the defect the greatness and activity of the past life of India reveals itself and comes out in bolder relief the more the inquiry into her past unearths the vast amount of material still available.

But our critic will still have it that India lived as it were in spite of herself and that in all this teeming action there is ample evidence of the dwarfing of individual will and the absence of any great individual personality. He arrives at that result by methods which savour of the skill of the journalist or pamphleteer rather than the disinterested mind of the critic. He tells us for instance that India has contributed only one or at most two great names to the world's Pantheon. By that, of course, he means Europe's Pantheon, or the world's Pantheon as constructed by the mind of Europe, crammed with the figures of western history and achievement which are near and familiar to it and admitting only a very few of the more gigantic names from the distant east, those which it finds it most difficult to ignore. One remembers the list made by a great French poet in the field of literature in which a sounding string of French names equals or outnumbers the whole contribution of the rest of Europe! If an Indian were to set about the same task in the same spirit, he would no doubt similarly pour out an interminable list of Indian names with some great men of Europe and America, Arabia, Persia, China, Japan forming a brief tail to this large peninsular body. These exercises of the partial mentality have no value. And it is difficult to find out what measure of values Mr. Archer is using when he relegates other great Indian names, allowing for three or four only, to the second plan and even there belittles them in comparison with corresponding

European immortals. In what is Shivaji with his vivid and interesting life and character, who not only founded a kingdom but organised a nation, inferior to Cromwell, or Shankara whose great spirit in the few years of its mortal life swept triumphant through India and reconstituted the whole religious life of her peoples, inferior as a personality to Luther? Why are Chanakya and Chandragupta who laid down the form of empire-building in India and whose great administrative system survived with changes often for the worse down to modern times, lesser men than the rulers and statesmen of European history? India may not present any recorded moment of her life so crowded as the few years of Athens to which Mr. Archer makes appeal; she may have no parallel to the swarm of interesting but often disturbing, questionable or even dark and revolting figures which illuminate and stain the story of the Italian cities during the Renaissance, although she has had too her crowded moments thronged by figures of a different kind. But she has had many rulers, statesmen and encouragers of art as great in their own way as Pericles or Lorenzo di Medici; the personalities of her famed poets emerge more dimly through the mist of time, but with indications which point to a lofty spirit or a humanity as great as that of Aeschylus or Euripides or a life-story as human and interesting as that of the famous Italian poets. And if, comparing this one country with all Europe as Mr. Archer insists,—mainly on the ground that Indians themselves make the comparison when they speak of the size of the country, its many races and the difficulty so long experienced in organising Indian unity,—it may be that in the field of political and military action Europe has a long lead, but what of the unparallelled profusion of great spiritual personalities in which India is pre-eminent? Again Mr. Archer speaks with arrogant depreciation of the significant figures born of the creative Indian mind which people its literature and its drama. Here too it is difficult to follow him or to accept his measure of values. To an oriental mind at least

Rama and Ravana are as vivid and great and real characters as the personalities of Homer and Shakespeare, Sita and Draupadi certainly not less living than Helen or Cleopatra, Damayanti and Shakuntala and other feminine types not less sweet, gracious and alive than Alcestis or Desdemona. I am not here affirming any superiority, but the bottomless inequality and inferiority which this critic affirms exists, not in truth, but only in his imagination or his way of seeing.

That perhaps is the one thing of significance, the one thing which is really worth noting, the difference of mentality which is at the bottom of these comparisons. There is not any inferiority of life or force or active and reactive will but, as far as the sameness of human nature allows, a difference of type, character, personality, let us say, an emphasis in different and almost opposite directions. Will-power and personality have not been wanting in India, but the direction preferably given to them and the type most admired are of a different kind. The average European mind is prone to value or at least to be more interested in the egoistic or self-asserting will which insists upon itself with a strong or a bold, an aggressive, sometimes a fierce insistence; the Indian mind not only prizes more from the ethical standpoint,—that is found everywhere,—but is more vividly interested in the calm, self-controlling or even the self-effacing personality; for the effacement of egoism seems to it to be not an effacement, but an enhancement of value and power of the true person and its greatness. Mr. Archer finds Asoka pale and featureless; to an Indian mind he is supremely vivid and attractive. Why is Asoka to be called pale in comparison with Charlemagne or, let us say, with Constantine? Is it because he only mentions his sanguinary conquest of Kalinga in order to speak of his remorse and the turning of his spirit, a sentiment which Charlemagne massacring the Saxons in order to make good Christians of them could not in the least have understood, nor any more perhaps the Pope who anointed him? Constantine gave the victory to the Christian religion, but there is nothing Christian in his personality; Asoka not only enthroned Buddhism, but strove though not with a perfect success to follow the path laid down by Buddha. And the Indian mind would account him not only a nobler will, but a greater and more attracting personality than Constantine or Charlemagne. It is interested in Chanakya, but much more interested in Chaitanya.

And in literature also just as in acutal life it has the same turn. This European mind finds Rama and Sita uninteresting and unreal, because they are too virtuous, too ideal, too white in colour; but to the Indian mind, even apart from all religious sentiment, they are figures of an absorbing reality which appeal to the inmost fibres of our being. A European scholar criticising the Mahabharata finds the strong and violent Bhima the only real character in that great poem; the Indian mind on the contrary finds greater character and a more moving interest in the calm and collected heroism of Arjuna, in the fine ethical temperament of Yudhisthira, in the divine charioteer of Kurukshetra who works not for his own hand but for the founding of the kingdom of right and justice. Those vehement or self-asserting characters or those driven by the storm of their passions which make the chief interest of European epic and drama, would either be relegated by it to the second plan or else, if set in large proportions, so brought in in order to bring into relief the greatness of the higher type of personality, as Ravana contrasts with and sets off Rama. The admiration of the one kind of mentality in the aesthetics of life goes to the coloured, that of the other to the luminous personality. Or, to put it in the form of the distinction made by the Indian mind itself, the interest of the one centres more in the rajasic, that of the other in the sattwic will and character.

Whether this difference imposes an inferiority on the aesthetics of Indian life and creation, each must judge for himself, but surely the Indian is the more evolved and spiritual conception. The Indian mind believes that the will and personality are not diminished but heightened by moving from the rajasic or more coloured egoistic to the sattwic and more luminous level of our being. Are not after all calm, self-mastery, a high balance signs of a greater and more real force of character than mere self-assertion of strength of will or the furious driving of the passions? Their possession does not mean that one must act with an inferior or less puissant, but only with a more right, collected and balanced will. And it is a mistake to think that asceticism itself rightly understood and practised implies an effacement of will; it brings much rather its greater concentration. That is the Indian view and experience and the meaning of the old legends in the epics,—to which Mr. Archer, misunderstanding the idea behind them, violently objects,—attributing so enormous a force, even when it was misused, to the power gained by ascetic self-mastery, Tapasya. The Indian mind believed and still believes that soul power is a greater thing, works from a mightier centre of will and has greater results than a more outwardly and materially active will-force. But it will be said that India has valued most the impersonal and that must obviously discourage personality. But this too,—except for the negative ideal of losing oneself in the trance or the silence of the Eternal, which is not the true essence of the matter,—involves a misconception. However paradoxical it may sound, one finds actually that the acceptance of the eternal and impersonal behind one's being and action and the attempt at unity with it is precisely the thing that carries the person to his largest greatness and power. For this impersonality is not a nullity, but an oceanic totality of the being. The perfect man, the Siddha or the Buddha, becomes universal, embraces all being in sympathy and oneness, finds himself in others as in himself and by so doing draws into himself at the same time something of the infinite power of a universal energy. That is the positive ideal of Indian culture. And when this hostile critic finds himself forced to do homage to the superiority of certain personalities who have sprung from this "fine-spun aristocratic" culture, he is really paying a tribute to some results of this preference of the sattwic to the rajasic, the universal to the limited and egoistic man. Not to be as the common man, that is to say, as the crude natural or half-baked human being, was indeed the sense of this ancient endeavour and in that sense it may be called an aristocratic culture. But it was not a vulgar outward but a spiritual nobility which was the aim of its self-discipline. Indian life, personality, art, literature must be judged in this light and appreciated or depreciated after being seen in the real sense and with the right understanding of Indian culture.

A DEFENCE OF INDIAN CULTURE

CHAPTER VI

INDIAN ART

A GOOD deal of hostile or unsympathetic western criticism of Indian civilisation has been directed in the past against its aesthetic side and taken the form of a disdainful or violent depreciation of its fine arts, architecture, sculpture and painting. Mr. Archer would not find much support in his wholesale and undiscriminating depreciation of a great literature, but here too there has been, if not positive attack, much failure of understanding: but in the attack on Indian art, his is the last and shrillest of many hostile voices. This aesthetic side of a people's culture is of the highest importance and demands almost as much scrutiny and carefulness of appreciation as the philosophy, religion and central formative ideas which have been the foundation of Indian life and of which much of the art and literature is a conscious expression in significant aesthetic forms. Fortunately, a considerable amount of work has been already done in the clearing away of misconception about Indian sculpture and painting and, if that were all, I might be content to refer to the works of Mr. Havell and Dr. Coomaraswamy or to the sufficiently understanding though less deeply informed and penetrating criticisms of others who cannot be charged with a prepossession in favour of oriental work. But a more general and searching consideration of first principles is called for in any complete view of the essential motives of Indian culture. I am appealing mainly to that new mind of India which long misled by an alien education, view and influence is returning to a sound and true idea of its past and future; but in this field the return is far from being as pervading, complete or luminous as it should be. I shall confine myself therefore first to a consideration of the sources of misunderstanding and pass from that to the true cultural significance of Indian aesthetic creation.

Mr. Archer pursuing his policy of Thorough devotes a whole chapter to the subject. This chapter is one long torrent of sweeping denunciation. But it would be a waste of time to take his attack as serious criticism and answer all in detail. His reply to defenders and eulogists is amazing in its shallowness and triviality, made up mostly of small, feeble and sometimes irrelevant points, big glaring epithets and forcibly senseless phrases, based for the rest on a misunderstanding or a sheer inability to conceive the meaning of spiritual experiences and metaphysical ideas, which betrays an entire absence of the religious sense and the philosophic mind. Mr. Archer is of course a rationalist and contemner of philosophy and entitled to his deficiencies; but why then try to judge things into the sense of which one is unable to enter and exhibit the spectacle of a blind man discoursing on colours? I will cite one or two instances which will show the quality of his criticism and amply justify a refusal to attach any positive value to the actual points he labours to make, except for the light they throw on the psychology of the objectors.

I will give first an instance amazing in its ineptitude. The Indian ideal figure of the masculine body insists on two features among many, a characteristic width at the shoulders and slenderness in the middle. Well, an objection to broadness of girth and largeness of belly—allowed only where they are appropriate as in sculptures of Ganesha or the Yakshas—is not peculiar to the Indian aesthetic sense; an emphasis, even a pronounced emphasis on their opposites is surely intelligible enough as an aesthetic tradition, however some may prefer a more realistic and prosperous presentation of the human figure. But Indian poets and authorities on art have given in this connection the simile of the lion, and lo and behold Mr. Archer solemnly discoursing on this image as a plain proof that the Indian people were just only out of the semi-savage state! It is only too clear that they drew the ideal of heroic manhood from their native jungle, from theriolatry, that is to say, from a worship of wild beasts: I presume, on the same principle and with the same stupefying ingenuity he would find in Kamban's image of the sea for the colour and depth of Sita's eyes clear evidence of a still more primitive savagery and barbaric worship of inanimate nature, or in Valmiki's description of his heroine's "eyes like wine," *madirekṣaṇā,* evidence of a chronic inebriety and the semi-drunken inspiration of the Indian poetic mind. This is one example of Mr. Archer's most telling points. It is by no means an isolated though it is an extreme specimen, and the absurdity of that particular argument only brings out the triviality of this manner of criticism. It is on a par with the common objection to the slim hands and feet loved of the Bengal painters which one hears sometimes advanced as a solid condemnation of their work. And that can be pardoned in the average man who under the high dispensation of modern culture is not expected to have any intelligent conception about art,—the instinctive appreciation has been already safely killed and buried. But what are we to say of a professed critic who ignores the deeper motives and fastens on details in order to give them this kind of significance?

But there are more grave and important objections in this criticism; for Mr. Archer turns also to deal with philosophy in art. The whole basis of Indian artistic creation, perfectly conscious and recognised in the canons, is directly spiritual and intuitive. Mr. Havell rightly lays stress on this essential distinction and speaks in passing of the infinite superiority of the method of direct perception over intellect, an assertion naturally offensive to the rationalistic mind, though it is now increasingly affirmed by leading western thinkers. Mr. Archer at once starts out to hack at it with a very blunt tomahawk. How does he deal with this crucial matter? In a way which misses the whole real point and has nothing whatever to do with the philosophy of art. He fastens on Mr. Havell's coupling of the master intuition of Buddha with the great intuition of Newton and objects to the parallel because the two discoveries deal with two different orders of knowledge, one scientific and physical, the other mental or psychic, spiritual or philosophic in nature. He trots out from its stable the old objection that Newton's intuition was only the last step in a long intellectual process, while according to this positive psychologist and philosophic critic the intuitions of Buddha and other Indian sages had no basis in any intellectual process of any kind or any verifiable experience. It is on the contrary the simple fact, well-known to all who know anything of the subject, that the conclusions of Buddha and other Indian philosophers (I am not now speaking of the inspired thought of the Upanishads which was pure spiritual experience enlightened by intuition and gnosis,) were preceded by a very acute scrutiny of relevant psychological phenomena and a process of reasoning which, though certainly not rationalistic, was as rational as any other method of thinking. He clinches his refutation by the sage remark that these intuitions which he chooses to call fantasies contradict one another and therefore, it seems, have no sort of value except their vain metaphysical subtlety. Are we to conclude that the patient study of phenomena, the scrupulous and rigidly verifiable intellectual reasonings and conclusions of western scientists have led to no conflicting or contradictory results? One could never imagine at this rate that the science of heredity is torn by conflicting "fantasies" or that Newton's "fantasies" about space and gravitational effect on space are at this day in danger of being upset by Einstein's "fantasies" in the same field. It is a minor matter that Mr. Archer happens to be wrong in his idea of Buddha's intuition when he says that he would have rejected a certain Vedantic intuition, since Buddha neither accepted nor rejected, but simply refused at all to speculate on the supreme cause. His intuition was confined to the cause of sorrow and the impermanence of things and the release by extinction of ego, desire and *Saṁskāra,* and so far as he chose to go, his intiuition of this extinction, Nirvana, and the Vedantic intuition of the supreme unity were the seeing of one truth of spiritual experience, seen no doubt from different angles of vision and couched in different intellectual forms, but with a common intuitive substance. The rest was foreign to Buddha's rigidly practical purpose. All this leads us far afield from our subject, but our critic has a remarkably confused mind and to follow him is to be condemned to divagate.

Thus far Mr. Archer on intuition. This is the character of his excursions on first principles in art. Is it really necessary to point out that a power of mind or spirit may be the same and yet act differently in different fields? or that a certain kind of intuition may be prepared by a long intellectual training, but that does not make it a last step in an intellectual process, any more than the precedence of sense activity makes intellectual reasoning a last step of sense-perception? The reason overtops sense and admits us to other and subtler ranges of truth; the intuition similarly overtops reason and admits us to a more direct and luminous power of truth. But very obviously, in the use of the intuition the poet and artist cannot proceed precisely in the same way as the scientist or philosopher. Leonardo da Vinci's remarkable intuitions in science and his creative intuitions in art started from the same power, but the surrounding or subordinate mental operations were of a different character and colour. And in art itself there are different kinds of intuition.

Shakespeare's seeing of life differs in its character and aids from Balzac's or Ibsen's, but the essential part of the process, that which makes it intuitive, is the same. The Buddhistic, the Vedantic seeing of things may be equally powerful starting-points for artistic creation, may lead one to the calm of a Buddha or the other to the rapture dance or majestic stillness of Shiva, and it is quite indifferent to the purposes of art to which of them the metaphysician may be inclined to give a logical preference. These are elementary notions and it is not surprising that one who ignores them should misunderstand the strong and subtle artistic creations of India.

The weakness of Mr. Archer's attack, its empty noise and violence and exiguity of substance must not blind us to the very real importance of the mental outlook from which his dislike of Indian art proceeds. For the outlook and the dislike it generates are rooted in something deeper than themselves, a whole cultural training, natural or acquired temperament and fundamental attitude towards existence, and it measures, if the immeasurable can be measured, the width of the gulf which till recently separated the oriental and the western mind and most of all the European and the Indian way of seeing things. An inability to understand the motives and methods of Indian art and a contempt of or repulsion from it was almost universal till yesterday in the mind of Europe. There was little difference in this regard between the average man bound by his customary first notions and the competent critic trained to appreciate different forms of culture. The gulf was too wide for any bridge of culture then built to span. To the European mind Indian art was a thing barbarous, immature, monstrous, an arrested growth from humanity's primitive savagery and incompetent childhood. If there has been now some change, it is due to the remarkably sudden widening of the horizon and view of European culture, a partial shifting even of the standpoint from which it was accustomed to see and judge all that it saw. In matters of art the western mind was long bound up as in a prison in the Greek and Renascence tradition modified by a later mentality with only two side rooms of escape, the romantic and the realistic motives, but these were only wings of the same building; for the base was the same and a common essential canon united their variations. The conventional superstition of the imitation of Nature as the first law or the limiting rule of art governed even the freest work and gave its tone to the artistic and critical intelligence. The canons of western artistic creation were held to be the sole valid criteria and everything else was regarded as primitive and half-developed or else strange and fantastic and interesting only by its curiosity. But a remarkable change has begun to set in, even though the old ideas still largely rule. The prison, if not broken, has at least had a wide breach made in it; a more flexible vision and a more profound imagination have begun to superimpose themselves on the old ingrained attitude. As a result, and as a contributing influence towards this change, oriental or at any rate Chinese and Japanese art has begun to command something like adequate recognition.

But the change has not yet gone far enough for a thorough appreciation of the deepest and most characteristic spirit and inspiration of Indian work. An eye or an effort like Mr. Havell's is still rare. For the most part even the most sympathetic criticism stops short at a technical appreciation and imaginative sympathy which tries to understand from outside and penetrates into so much only of the artistic suggestion as can be at once seized by the new wider view of a more accomplished and flexible critical mentality. But there is little sign of the understanding of the very well-spring and spiritual fountain of Indian artistic creation. There is therefore still a utility in fathoming the depths and causes of the divergence. That is especially necessary for the Indian mind itself, for by the appreciation excited by an opposing view it will be better able to understand itself and especially to seize what is essential in Indian art and must be clung to in the future and what is an incident or a phase of growth and can be shed in the advance to a new creation. This is properly a task for those who have themselves at once the creative insight, the technical competence and the seeing critical eye. But everyone who has at all the Indian spirit and feeling, can at least give some account of the main, the central things which constitute for him the appeal of Indian painting, sculpture and architecture. This is all that I shall attempt, for it will be in itself the best defence and justification of Indian culture on its side of aesthetic significance.

The criticism of art is a vain and dead thing when it ignores the spirit, aim, essential motive from which a type of artistic creation starts and judges by the external details only in the light of a quite different spirit, aim and motive. Once we understand the essential things, enter into the characteristic way and spirit, are able to interpret the form and execution from that inner centre, we can then see how it looks in the light of other standpoints, in the light of the comparative mind. A comparative criticism has its use, but the essential understanding must precede it if it is to have any real value. But while this is comparatively easy in the wider and more flexible turn of literature, it is, I think, more difficult in the other arts, when the difference of spirit is deep, because there the absence of the mediating word, the necessity of proceeding direct from spirit to line and form brings about a special intensity and exclusive concentration of aim and stress of execution. The intensity of the thing that moves the work is brought out with a more distinct power, but by its very stress and directness allows of few accommodations and combined variations of appeal. The thing meant and the thing done strike deep home into the soul or the imaginative mind, but touch it over a smaller surface and with a lesser multitude of points of contact. But whatever the reason, it is less easy for a different kind of mind to appreciate.

The Indian mind in its natural poise finds it almost or quite as difficult really, that is to say, spiritually to understand the arts of Europe, as the ordinary European mind to enter into the spirit of Indian painting and sculpture. I have seen a comparison made between a feminine Indian figure and a Greek Aphrodite which illustrates the difficulty in an extreme form. The critic tells me that the Indian figure is full of a strong spiritual sense—here of the very breath and being of devotion, an ineffable devotion, and that is true, it is a suggestion or even a revelation which breaks through or overflows the form rather than depends on the external work,—but the Greek creation can only awaken a sublimated carnal or sensuous delight. Now having entered somewhat into the heart of meaning of Greek sculpture, I can see that this is a wrong account of the matter. The critic has got into the real spirit of the Indian, but not into the real spirit of the Greek work; his criticism from that moment, as a comparative appreciation, loses all value. The Greek figure stresses no doubt the body, but appeals through it to an imaginative seeing inspiration which aims at expressing a certain divine power of beauty and gives us therefore something which is much more than a merely sensuous aesthetic pleasure. If the artist has done this with perfection, the work has accomplished its aim and ranks as a masterpiece. The Indian sculptor stresses something behind, something more remote to the surface imagination, but nearer to the soul, and subordinates to it the physical form. If he has only partially succeeded or done it with power but with something faulty in the execution, his work is less great, even though it may have a greater spirit in the intention: but when he wholly succeeds, then his work too is a masterpiece, and we may prefer it with a good conscience, if the spiritual, the higher intuitive vision is what we most demand from art. This however need not interfere with an appreciation of both kinds in their own order.

But in viewing much of other European work of the very greatest repute, I am myself aware of a failure of spiritual sympathy. I look for instance on some of the most famed pieces of

Tintoretto,—not the portraits, for those give the soul, if only the active or character soul in the man, but say, the Adam and Eve, the St. George slaying the dragon, the Christ appearing to Venetian Senators, and I am aware of standing baffled and stopped by an irresponsive blankness somewhere in my being. I can see the magnificence and power of colouring and design, I can see the force of externalised imagination or the spirited dramatic rendering of action, but I strive in vain to get out any significance below the surface or equivalent to the greatness of the form, except perhaps an incidental minor suggestion here and there and that is not sufficient for me. When I try to analyse my failure, I find at first certain conceptions which conflict with my expectation or my own way of seeing. This muscular Adam, the sensuous beauty of this Eve do not bring home to me the mother or the father of the race, this dragon seems to me only a surly portentous beast in great danger of being killed, not a creative embodiment of monstrous evil, this Christ with his massive body and benevolent philosophic visage almost offends me, is not at any rate the Christ whom I know. But these are after all incidental things; what is really the matter is that I come to this art with a previous demand for a kind of vision, imagination, emotion, significance which it cannot give me. And not being so self-confident as to think that what commands the admiration of the greatest critics and artists is not admirable, I can see this and pause on the verge of applying Mr. Archer's criticism of certain Indian work and saying that the mere execution is beautiful or marvellous but there is no imagination, nothing beyond what is on the surface. I can understand that what is wanting is really the kind of imagination I personally demand; but though my acquired cultured mind explains this to me and may intellectually catch at the something more, my natural being will not be satisfied, I am oppressed, not uplifted by this triumph of life and the flesh and of the power and stir of life,—not that I object to these things in themselves or to the greatest emphasis on the sensuous or even the sensual, elements not at all absent from Indian creation, if I can get something at least of the deeper thing I want behind it,—and I find myself turning away from the work of one of the greatest Italian masters to satisfy myself with some "barbaric" Indian painting or statue, some calm unfathomable Buddha, bronze Shiva or eighteen-armed Durga slaying the Asuras. But the cause of my failure is there, that I am seeking for something which was not meant in the spirit of this art and which I ought not to expect from its characteristic creation. And if I had steeped myself in this Renascence mind as in the original Hellenic spirit, I could have added something to my inner experience and acquired a more catholic and universal aesthesis.

I lay stress on this psychological misunderstanding or want of understanding, because it explains the attitude of the natural European mind to the great works of Indian art and puts on it its right value. This mind catches only what is kin to European effort and regards that too as inferior, naturally and quite rightly since the same thing is more sincerely and perfectly done from a more native fountain of power in western work. That explains the amazing preference of better informed critics than Mr. Archer for the bastard Gandharan sculpture to great and sincere work original and true in its unity,—Gandharan sculpture which is an unsatisfying, almost an impotent junction of two incompatible motives, incompatible at least if one is not fused into the other as here certainly it is not fused,—or its praise otherwise incomprehensible of certain second-rate or third-rate creations and its turning away from others noble and profound but strange to its conceptions. Or else it seizes with appreciation—but is it really a total and a deeply understanding appreciation?—on work like the Indo-Saracenic which though in no way akin to western types has yet the power at certain points to get within the outskirts of its circle of aesthetic conceptions. It is even so much struck by the Taj as to try to believe that it is the work of an Italian sculptor, some astonishing genius, no doubt, who Indianised himself miraculously in this one hour of solitary achievement,—for India is a land of miracles,—and probably died of the effort, for he has left us no other work to admire. Again it admires, at least in Mr. Archer, Javanese work because of its humanity and even concludes from that that it is not Indian. Its essential unity with Indian work behind the variation of manner is invisible to this mind because the spirit and inner meaning of Indian work is a blank to its vision and it sees only a form, a notation of the meaning, which, therefore, it does not understand and dislikes. One might just as well say that the Gita written in the Devanagari is a barbaric, monstrous or meaningless thing, but put into some cursive character at once becomes not Indian, because human and intelligible!

But, ordinarily, place this mind before anything ancient, Hindu, Buddhistic or Vedantic in art and it looks at it with a blank or an angry incomprehension. It looks for the sense and does not find any, because either it has not in itself the experience and finds it difficult to have the imagination, much more the realisation of what this art does really mean and express, or because it insists on looking for what it is accustomed to see at home and, not finding that, is convinced that there is nothing to see or nothing of any value. Or else if there is something which it could have understood, it does not understand because it is expressed in the Indian form and the Indian way. It looks at the method and form and finds it unfamiliar, contrary to its own canons, is revolted, contemptuous, repelled, speaks of the thing as monstrous, barbarous, ugly or null, passes on in a high dislike or disdain. Or if it is overborne by some sense of unanalysable beauty of greatness or power it still speaks of a splendid barbarism. Do you want an illuminating instance of this blankness of comprehension? Mr. Archer sees the Dhyani Buddha with its supreme, its unfathomable, its infinite spiritual calm which every cultured oriental mind can at once feel and respond to in the depths of his being, and he denies that there is anything,—only drooped eyelids, an immobile pose and an insipid, by which I suppose he means a calm passionless face.* He turns for comfort to the Hellenic nobility of expression of the Gandharan Buddha, or to the living Rabindranath Tagore more spiritual than any Buddha from Peshawar to Kamakura, an inept misuse of comparison against which I imagine the great poet himself would be the first to protest. There we have the total incomprehension, the blind window, the blocked door in the mind, and there too the reason why the natural western mentality comes to Indian art with a demand for something other than what its characteristic spirit and motive intend to give, and, demanding that, is not prepared to enter into another kind of spiritual experience and another range of creative sight, imaginative power and mode of self-expression.

This once understood, we can turn to the difference in the spirit and method of artistic creation which has given rise to the mutual incomprehension; for that will bring us to the positive side of the matter. All great artistic work proceeds from an act of intuition, not really an intellectual idea or a splendid imagination,—these are only mental translations,—but a direct intuition of some truth of life or being, some significant form of that truth, some development of it in the mind of man. And so far there is no difference between great European and great Indian work. Where then begins the immense divergence? It is there in everything else, in the object and field of the intuitive vision, in the method of working out the sight or suggestion, in the part taken in the rendering by the external form and technique, in the whole way of the rendering to the human mind, even in the

* In a note Mr. Archer mentions and very rightly discounts an absurd apology for these Buddhas, viz., that the greatness and spirituality are not at all in the work, but in the devotion of the artist! If the artist cannot put into his work what was in him—and here it is not devotion that is expressed,—his work is a futile abortion. But if he has expressed what he has felt, the capacity to feel it must also be there in the mind that looks at his work.

centre of our being to which the work appeals. The European artist gets his intuition by a suggestion from an appearance in life and nature or, if it starts from something in his own soul, relates it at once to an external support. He brings down that intuition into his normal mind and sets the intellectual idea and the imagination in the intelligence to clothe it with a mental stuff which will render its form to the moved reason, emotion, aesthesis. Then he missions his eye and hand to execute it in terms which start from a colourable "imitation" of life and Nature—and in ordinary hands too often end there—to get at an interpretation that really changes it into the image of something not outward in our own being or in universal being which was the real thing seen. And to that in looking at the work we have to get back through colour and line and disposition or whatever else may be part of the external means, to their mental suggestions and through them to the soul of the whole matter. The appeal is not direct to the eye of the deepest self and spirit within, but to the outward soul by a strong awakening of the sensuous, the vital, the emotional, the intellectual and imaginative being, and of the spiritual we get as much or as little as can suit itself to and express itself through the outward man. Life, action, passion, emotion, idea, Nature seen for their own sake and for an aesthetic delight in them, these are the object and field of this creative intuition. The something more which the Indian mind knows to be behind these things looks out, if at all, from behind many veils. The direct and unveiled presence of the Infinite and its godheads is not evoked or thought necessary to the greater greatness and the highest perfection.

The theory of ancient Indian art at its greatest—and the greatest gives its character to the rest and throws on it something of its stamp and influence—is of another kind. Its highest business is to disclose something of the Self, the Infinite, the Divine to the regard of the soul, the Self through its expressions, the Infinite through its living finite symbols, the Divine through his powers. Or the Godheads are to be revealed, luminously interpreted or in some way suggested to the soul's understanding or to its devotion or at the very least to a spiritually or religiously aesthetic emotion. When this hieratic art comes down from these altitudes to the intermediate worlds behind ours, to the lesser godheads or genii, it still carries into them some power or some hint from above. And when it comes quite down to the material world and the life of man and the things of external Nature, it does not altogether get rid of the greater vision, the hieratic stamp, the spiritual seeing, and in most good work—except in moments of relaxation and a humorous or vivid play with the obvious—there is always something more in which the seeing presentation of life floats as in an immaterial atmosphere. Life is seen in the self or in some suggestion of the infinite or of something beyond or there is at least a touch and influence of these which helps to shape the presentation. It is not that all Indian work realises this ideal; there is plenty no doubt that falls short, is lowered, ineffective or even debased, but it is the best and the most characteristic influence and execution which gives its tone to an art and by which we must judge. Indian art in fact is identical in its spiritual aim and principle with the rest of Indian culture.

A seeing in the self accordingly becomes the characteristic method of the Indian artist and it is directly enjoined on him by the canon. He has to see first in his spiritual being the truth of the thing he must express and to create its form in his intuitive mind; he is not bound to look out first on outward life and Nature for his model, his authority, his rule, his teacher or his fountain of suggestions. Why should he when it is something quite inward he has to bring out into expression? It is not an idea in the intellect, a mental imagination, an outward emotion on which he has to depend for his stimulants, but an idea, image, emotion of the spirit, and the mental equivalents are subordinate things for help in the transmission and give only a part of the colouring and the shape. A material form, colour, line and design are his physical means of the expression, but in using them he is not bound to an imitation of Nature, but has to make the form and all else significant of his vision, and if that can only be done or can best be done by some modification, some pose, some touch or symbolic variation which is not found in physical Nature, he is at perfect liberty to use it, since truth to his vision, the unity of the thing he is seeing and expressing is his only business. The line, colour and the rest are not his first, but his last preoccupation, because they have to carry on them a world of things which have already taken spiritual form in his mind. He has not for instance to re-create for us the human face and body of the Buddha or some one passion or incident of his life, but to reveal the calm of Nirvana through a figure of the Buddha, and every detail and accessory must be turned into a means or an aid of his purpose. And even when it is some human passion or incident he has to portray, it is not usually that alone, but also or more something else in the soul to which it points or from which it starts or some power behind the action that has to enter into the spirit of his design and is often really the main thing. And through the eye that looks on his work he has to appeal not merely to an excitement of the outward soul, but to the inner self, *antarātman*. One may well say that beyond the ordinary cultivation of the aesthetic instinct necessary to all artistic appreciation there is a spiritual insight or culture needed if we are to enter into the whole meaning of Indian artistic creation, otherwise we get only at the surface external things or at the most at things only just below the surface. It is an intuitive and spiritual art and must be seen with the intuitive and spiritual eye.

This is the distinctive character of Indian art and to ignore it is to fall into total incomprehension or into much misunderstanding. Indian architecture, painting, sculpture are not only intimately one in inspiration with the central things in Indian philosophy, religion, Yoga, culture, but a specially intense expression of their significance. There is much in the literature which can be well enough appreciated without any very deep entry into these things, but it is comparatively a very small part of what is left of the other arts, Hindu or Buddhistic, of which this can be said. They have been very largely a hieratic aesthetic script of India's spiritual, contemplative and religious experience.

A DEFENCE OF INDIAN CULTURE

CHAPTER VII

INDIAN ART

ARCHITECTURE, sculpture and painting, because they are the three great arts which appeal to the spirit through the eye, are those too in which the sensible and the invisible meet with the strongest emphasis on themselves and yet the greatest necessity of each other. The form with its insistent masses, proportions, lines, colours, can here only justify them by their service for the something intangible it has to express; the spirit needs all the possible help of the material body to interpret itself to itself through the eye, yet asks of it that it shall be as transparent a veil as possible of its own greater significance. The art of the East and the art of the West,—each in its characteristic or mean, for there are always exceptions,—deal with the problem of these two interlocking powers in a quite different way. The western mind is arrested and attracted by the form, lingers on it and cannot get away from its charm, loves it for its own beauty, rests on the emotional, intellectual, aesthetic suggestions that arise directly from its most visible language, confines the soul in the body; it might almost be said that for this mind form creates the spirit, the spirit depends for its existence and for everything it has to say on the form. The Indian attitude to the matter is at the opposite pole to this view. For the Indian mind form does not exist except as a creation of the spirit and draws all its meaning and value from the spirit. Every line, arrangement of mass, colour, shape, posture, every physical suggestion, however many, crowded, opulent they may be, is first and last a suggestion, a hint, very often a symbol which is in its main function a support for a spiritual emotion, idea, image that again goes beyond itself to the less definable, but more powerfully sensible reality of the spirit which has excited these movements in the aesthetic mind and passed through them into significant shapes.

This characteristic attitude of the Indian reflective and creative mind necessitates in our view of its creations an effort to get beyond at once to the inner spirit of the reality it expresses and see from it and not from outside. And in fact to start from the physical details and their synthesis appears to me quite the wrong way to look at an Indian work of art. The orthodox style of western criticism seems to be to dwell scrutinisingly on the technique, on form, on the obvious story of the form, and then pass to some appreciation of beautiful or impressive emotion and idea. It is only in some deeper and more sensitive minds that we get beyond that depth into profounder things. A criticism of that kind applied to Indian art leaves it barren or poor of significance. Here the only right way is to get at once through a total intuitive or revelatory impression or by some meditative dwelling on the whole, *dhyāna* in the technical Indian term, to the spiritual meaning and atmosphere, make ourselves one with that as completely as possible, and then only the helpful meaning and value of all the rest comes out with a complete and revealing force. For here it is the spirit that carries the form, while in most western art it is the form that carries whatever there may be of spirit. The striking phrase of Epictetus recurs to the mind in which he describes man as a little soul carrying a corpse, *psucharion ei bastazon nekron.* The more ordinary western outlook is upon animate matter carrying in its life a modicum of soul. But the seeing of the Indian mind and of Indian art is that of a great, a limitless self and spirit, *Mahān ātmā*, which carries to us in the sea of its presence a living shape of itself, small in comparison to its own infinity, but yet sufficient by the power that informs this symbol to support some aspect of that infinite's self-expression. It is therefore essential that we should look here not solely with the physical eye informed by the reason and the aesthetic imagination, but make the physical seeing a passage to the opening of the inner spiritual eye and a moved communion in the soul. A great oriental work of art does not easily reveal its secret to one who comes to it solely in a mood of aesthetic curiosity or with a considering critical objective mind, still less as the cultivated and interested tourist passing among strange and foreign things; but it has to be seen in loneliness, in the solitude of one's self, in moments when one is capable of long and deep meditation and as little weighted as possible with the conventions of material life. That is why the Japanese with their fine sense in these things,—a sense which modern Europe with her assault of crowded art galleries and over-pictured walls seems to have quite lost, though perhaps I am wrong, and those are the right conditions for display of European art,—have put their temples and their Buddhas as often as possible away on mountains and in distant or secluded scenes of Nature and avoid living with great paintings in the crude hours of daily life, but keep them by preference in such a way that their undisputed suggestion can sink into the mind in its finer moments or apart where they can go and look at them in a treasured secrecy when the soul is at leisure from life. That is an indication of the utmost value pointing to the nature of the appeal made by eastern art and the right way and mood for looking at its creations.

Indian architecture especially demands this kind of inner study and this spiritual self-identification with its deepest meaning and will not otherwise reveal itself to us. The secular buildings of ancient India, her palaces and places of assembly and civic edifices have not outlived the ravage of time; what remains to us is mostly something of the great mountain and cave temples, something too of the temples of her ancient cities of the plains, and for the rest we have the fanes and shrines of her later times, whether situated in temple cities and places of pilgrimage like Srirangam and Rameshwaram or in her great once regal towns like Madura, when the temple was the centre of life. It is then the most hieratic side of a hieratic art that remains to us. These sacred buildings are the signs, the architectural self-expression of an ancient spiritual and religious culture. Ignore the spiritual suggestion, the religious significance, the meaning of the symbols and indications, look only with the rational and secular aesthetic mind, and it is vain to expect that we shall get to any true and discerning appreciation of this art. And it has to be remembered too that the religious spirit here is something quite different from the sense of European religions; and even mediaeval Christianity, especially as now looked at by the modern European mind which has gone through the two great crises of the Renascence and recent secularism, will not in spite of its oriental origin and affinities be of much real help. To bring in into the artistic look on an Indian temple occidental memories or a comparison with Greek Parthenon or Italian church or Duomo or Campanile or even the great Gothic cathedrals of mediaeval France, though these have in them something much nearer to the Indian mentality, is to intrude a fatally foreign and disturbing element or standard in the mind. But this consciously or else subconsciously is what almost every European mind does to a greater or less degree,—and it is here a pernicious immixture, for it subjects the work of a vision that saw the immeasurable to the tests of an eye that dwells only on measure.

Indian sacred architecture of whatever date, style or dedication goes back to something timelessly ancient and now outside India almost wholly lost, something which belongs to the past, and yet it goes forward too, though this the rationalistic mind will not easily admit, to something which will return upon us and is already beginning to return, something which belongs to the future. An Indian temple, to whatever godhead it may be built, is in its inmost reality an altar raised to the divine Self, a house of the Cosmic Spirit, an appeal and aspiration to the Infinite. As that and in the light of that seeing and conception it must in the first place be understood, and everything else must be seen in that setting and that light, and then only can there be any real understanding. No artistic eye however alert and sensible and no aesthetic mind however full and sensitive can arrive at that understanding, if it is attached to a Hellenised conception of rational beauty or shuts itself up in a materialised or intellectual interpretation and fails to open itself to the great things here meant by a kindred close response to some touch of the cosmic consciousness, some revelation of the greater spiritual self, some suggestion of the Infinite. These things, the spiritual self, the cosmic spirit, the Infinite, are not rational, but suprarational, eternal presences, but to the intellect only words, and visible, sensible, near only to an intuition and revelation in our inmost selves. An art which starts from them as a first conception can only give us what it has to give, their touch, their nearness, their self-disclosure, through some responding intuition and revelation in us, in our own soul, our own self. It is this which one must come to it to find and not demand from it the satisfaction of some quite other seeking or some very different turn of imagination and more limited superficial significance.

This is the first truth of Indian architecture and its significance which demands emphasis and it leads at once to the answer to certain very common misapprehensions and objections. All art reposes on some unity and all its details, whether few and sparing or lavish and crowded and full, must go back to that unity and help its significance; otherwise it is not art. Now we find our western critic telling us with an assurance which would be stupefying if one did not see how naturally it arose, that in Indian architecture there is no unity, which is as much as to say that there is here no great art at all, but only a skill in the execution of crowded and unrelated details. We are told even by otherwise sympathetic judges that there is an overloading of ornament and detail which, however beautiful or splendid in itself, stands in the way of unity, an attempt to load every rift with ore, an absence of calm, no unfilled spaces, no relief to the eye. Mr. Archer as usual carries up the adverse criticism to its extreme clamorous top notes; his heavily shotted phrases are all a continuous insistence on this one theme. The great temples of the South of India are, he allows, marvels of massive construction. He seems by the way to have a rooted objection to massiveness in architecture or great massed effects in sculpture, regardless of their appropriateness or need, although he admits them in literature. Still this much there is and with it a sort of titanic impressiveness, but of unity, clarity, nobility there is no trace. This observation seems to my judgment sufficiently contradictory, since I do not understand how there can be a marvel of construction, whether light or massive, without any unity,—but here is not even, it seems, a trace of it,—or a mighty impressiveness without any greatness or nobility whatever, even allowing this to be a Titanic and not an Olympian nobleness. He tells us that everything is ponderous, everything here overwrought and the most prominent features swarming, writhing with contorted semi-human figures are as senseless as anything in architecture. How, one might ask, does he know that they are senseless, when he practically admits that he has made no attempt to find what is their sense, but has simply assumed from the self-satisfied sufficiency of his own admitted ignorance and failure to understand that there cannot be any meaning? And the whole thing he characterises as a monstrosity built by Rakshasas, ogres, demons, a gigantesque barbarism. The northern buildings find a little less disfavour in his eyes, but the difference in the end is small or none. There is the same ponderousness, absence of lightness and grace, an even greater profusion of incised ornament;

these too are barbaric creations. Alone the Mahomedan architecture, called Indo-Saracenic, is exempted from this otherwise universal condemnation.

It is a little surprising after all, however natural the first blindness here, that even assailants of this extreme kind, since they must certainly know that there can be no art, no effective construction without unity, should not have paused even once to ask themselves whether after all there must not be here some principle of oneness which they had missed because they came with alien conceptions and looked at things from the wrong end, and before pronouncing this magisterial judgment should not have had patience to wait in a more detached and receptive way upon the thing under their eye and seen whether then some secret of unity did not emerge. But it is the more sympathetic and less violent critic who deserves a direct answer. Now it may readily be admitted that the failure to see at once the unity of this architecture is perfectly natural to a European eye, because unity in the sense demanded by the western conception, the Greek unity gained by much suppression and a sparing use of detail and circumstance or even the Gothic unity got by casting everything into the mould of a single spiritual aspiration, is not there. And the greater unity that really is there can never be arrived at at all, if the eye begins and ends by dwelling on form and detail and ornament, because it will then be obsessed by these things and find it difficult to go beyond to the unity which all this in its totality serves not so much to express in itself, but to fill it with that which comes out of it and relieve its oneness by multitude. An original oneness, not a combined or synthetic or an effected unity, is that from which this art begins and to which its work when finished returns or rather lives in it as in its self and natural atmosphere. Indian sacred architecture constantly represents the greatest oneness of the self, the cosmic, the infinite in the immensity of its world-design, the multitude of its features of self-expression, *lakṣaṇa,* (yet the oneness is greater than and independent of their totality and in itself indefinable), and all its starting-point of unity in conception, its mass of design and immensity of material, its crowding abundance of significant ornament and detail and its return towards oneness are only intelligible as necessary circumstances of this poem, this epic or this lyric—for there are smaller structures which are such lyrics—of the Infinite. The western mentality, except in those who are coming or returning, since Europe had once something of this cult in her own way, to this vision, may find it difficult to appreciate the truth and meaning of such an art, which tries to figure existence as a whole and not in its pieces; but I would invite those Indian minds who are troubled by these criticisms or partly or temporarily overpowered by the western way of seeing things, to look at our architecture in the light of this conception and see whether all but minor objections do not vanish as soon as the real meaning makes itself felt and gives body to the first indefinable impression and emotion which we experience before the greater constructions of the Indian builders.

To appreciate this spiritual-aesthetic truth of Indian architecture, it will be best to look first at some work where there is not the complication of surroundings now often out of harmony with the building, outside even those temple towns which still retain their dependence on the sacred motive, and rather in some place where there is room for a free background of Nature. I have before me two prints which can well serve the purpose, a temple at Kalahasti, a temple at Sinhachalam, two buildings entirely different in treatment and yet one in the ground and the universal motive. The straight way here is not to detach the temple from its surroundings, but to see it in unity with the sky and low-lying landscape or with the sky and hills around and feel the thing common to both, the construction and its environment, the reality in Nature, the reality expressed in the work of art. The oneness to which this Nature aspires in her inconscient self-creation and in which she lives, the oneness to which the soul of man uplifts itself in his conscious spiritual upbuilding, his labour of aspiration here expressed in stone, and in which so upbuilt he and his work live, are the same and the soul-motive is one. Thus seen this work of man seems to be something which has started out and detached itself against the power of the natural world, something of the one common aspiration in both to the same infinite spirit of itself,—the inconscient uplook and against it the strong single relief of the self-conscient effort and success of finding. One of these buildings climbs up bold, massive in projection, up-piled in the greatness of a forceful but sure ascent, preserving its range and line to the last, the other soars from the strength of its base, in the grace and emotion of a curving mass to a rounded summit and crowning symbol. There is in both a constant, subtle yet pronounced lessening from the base towards the top, but at each stage a repetition of the same form, the same multiplicity of insistence, the same crowded fullness and indented relief, but one maintains its multiple endeavour and indication to the last, the other ends in a single sign. To find the significance we have first to feel the oneness of the infinity in which this nature and this art live, then see this thronged expression as the sign of the infinite multiplicity which fills this oneness, see in the regular lessening ascent of the edifice the subtler and subtler return from the base on earth to the original unity and seize on the symbolic indication of its close at the top. Not absence of unity, but a tremendous unity is revealed. Reinterpret intimately what this representation means in the terms of our own spiritual self-existence and cosmic being, and we have what these great builders saw in themselves and reared in stone. All objections, once we have got at this identity in spiritual experience, fall away and show themselves to be what they really are, the utterance and cavil of an impotent misunderstanding, an insufficient apprehension or a complete failure to see. To appreciate the detail of Indian architecture is easy when the whole is thus seen and known; otherwise, it is impossible.

This method of interpretation applies, however different

the construction and the nature of the rendering, to all Dravidian architecture, not only to the mighty temples of far-spread fame, but to unknown roadside shrines in small towns, which are only a slighter execution of the same theme, a satisfied suggestion here, but the greater buildings a grandiose fulfilled aspiration. The architectural language of the north is of a different kind, there is another basic style; but here too the same spiritual, meditative, intuitive method has to be used and we get at the same result, an aesthetic interpretation or suggestion of the one spiritual experience, one in all its complexity and diversity, which founds the unity of the infinite variations of Indian spirituality and religious feeling and the realised union of the human self with the Divine. This is the unity too of all the creations of this hieratic art. The different styles and motives arrive at or express that unity in different ways. The objection that an excess of thronging detail and ornament hides, impairs or breaks up the unity, is advanced only because the eye has made the mistake of dwelling on the detail first without relation to this original spiritual oneness, which has first to be fixed in an intimate spiritual seeing and union and then all else seen in that vision and experience. When we look on the multiplicity of the world, it is only a crowded plurality that we can find and to arrive at unity we have to reduce, to suppress what we have seen or sparingly select a few indications or to be satisfied with the unity of this or that separate idea, experience or imagination; but when we have realised the self, the infinite unity and look back on the multiplicity of the world, then we find that oneness able to bear all the infinity of variation and circumstance we can crowd into it and its unity remains unabridged by even the most endless self-multiplication of its informing creation. We find the same thing in looking at this architecture. The wealth of ornament, detail, circumstance in Indian temples represents the infinite variety and repetition of the worlds,—not our world only, but all the planes,—suggests the infinite multiplicity in the infinite oneness. It is a matter of our own experience and fullness of vision how much we leave out or bring in, whether we express so much or so little or attempt as in the Dravidian style to give the impression of a teeming inexhaustible plenitude. The largeness of this unity is base and continent enough for any superstructure or content of multitude.

To condemn this abundance as barbarous is to apply a foreign standard. Where after all are we bound to draw the line? To the pure classical taste Shakespeare's art once appeared great but barbarous for a similar reason,—one remembers the Gallic description of him as a drunken barbarian of genius,—his artistic unity non-existent or spoilt by crowding tropical vegetation of incident and character, his teeming imaginations violent, exaggerated, sometimes bizarre, monstrous, without symmetry, proportion and all the other lucid unities, lightnesses, graces loved by the classic mind. That mind might say of his work in language like Mr. Archer's that here there is indeed a Titanic genius, a mass of power, but of unity, clarity, classic nobility no trace, but rather an entire absence of lucid grace and lightness and restraint, a profusion of wild ornament and an imaginative riot without law or measure, strained figures, distorted positions and gestures, no dignity, no fine, just, rationally natural and beautiful classic movement and pose. But even the strictest Latin mind has now got over its objections to the "splendid barbarism" of Shakespeare and can understand that here is a fuller, less sparing and exiguous vision of life, a greater intuitive unity than the formal unities of the classic aesthesis. But the Indian vision of the world and existence was vaster and fuller than Shakespeare's, because it embraced not merely life, but all being, not merely humanity, but all the worlds and all Nature and cosmos. The European mind not having arrived except in individuals at any close, direct, insistent realisation of the unity of the infinite self or the cosmic consciousness peopled with its infinite multiplicity, is not driven to express these things, cannot understand or put up with them when they are expressed in this oriental art, speech and style and object to it as the Latin mind once objected to Shakespeare. Perhaps the day is not distant when it will see and understand and perhaps even itself try to express the same things in another language.

The objection that the crowding detail allows no calm, gives no relief or space to the eye, falls under the same heading, springs from the same root, is urged from a different experience and has no validity for the Indian experience. For this unity on which all is upborne, carries in itself the infinite space and calm of the spiritual realisation, and there is no need for other unfilled spaces or tracts of calm of a lesser more superficial kind. The eye is here only a way of access to the soul, it is to that that there is the appeal, and if the soul living in this realisation or dwelling under the influence of this aesthetic impression needs any relief, it is not from the incidence of life and form, but from the immense incidence of that vastness of infinity and tranquil silence, and that can only be given by its opposite, by an abundance of form and detail and life. As for the objection in regard to Dravidian architecture to its massiveness and its Titanic construction, the precise spiritual effect intended could not be given otherwise; for the infinite, the cosmic seen as a whole in its vast manifestation is Titanic, is mighty in material and power. It is other and quite different things also, but none of these are absent from Indian construction. The great temples of the north have often in spite of Mr. Archer's dictum, a singular grace in their power, a luminous lightness relieving their mass and strength, a rich delicacy of beauty in their ornate fullness. It is not indeed the Greek lightness, clarity or naked nobleness, nor is it exclusive, but comes in in a fine blending of opposites which is in the very spirit of the Indian religious, philosophical and aesthetic mind. Nor are these things absent from many Dravidian buildings, though in certain styles they are boldly sacrificed or only put into minor incidents,—one instance of the kind Mr.

Archer rejoices in as an oasis in the desert of this to him unintelligible mass of might and greatness,—but in either case suppressed so that the fullness of solemn and grandiose effect may have a complete, an undiminished expression.

I need not deal with adverse strictures of a more insignificant kind,—such as the dislike of the Indian form of the arch and dome, because they are not the radiating arch and dome of other styles. That is only an intolerant refusal to admit the beauty of unaccustomed forms. It is legitimate to prefer one's own things, those to which our mind and nature have been trained, but to condemn other art and effort because it also prefers its own way of arriving at beauty, greatness, self-expression, is a narrowness which with the growth of a more catholic culture ought to disappear. But there is one comment on Dravidian temple architecture which is worth noting because it is made by others than Mr. Archer and his kind. Even a sympathetic mind like Professor Geddes is impressed by some sense of a monstrous effect of terror and gloom in these mighty buildings. Such expressions are astonishing to an Indian mind because terror and gloom are conspicuously absent from the feelings aroused in it by its religion, art or literature. In the religion they are rarely awakened and only in order to be immediately healed and, even when they come, are always sustained by the sense of a supporting and helping presence, an eternal greatness and calm or love or Delight behind; the very goddess of destruction is at the same time the compassionate and loving Mother; the austere Maheswara, Rudra, is also Shiva, the auspicious, Asutosha, the refuge of men. The Indian thinking and religious mind looks with calm, without shrinking or repulsion, with an understanding born of its agelong effort at identity and oneness, at all that meets it in the stupendous spectacle of the cosmos. And even its asceticism, its turning from the world, which begins not in terror and gloom, but in a sense of vanity and fatigue, or of something higher, truer, happier than life, soon passes beyond any element of pessimistic sadness into the rapture of the eternal peace and bliss. Indian secular poetry and drama is throughout rich, vital and joyous and there is more tragedy, terror, sorrow and gloom packed into any few pages of European work than we can find in the whole mass of Indian literature. It does not seem to me that Indian art is at all different in this respect from the religion and literature. The western mind is here thrusting in its own habitual reactions upon things in the indigenous conception in which they have no proper place. Mark the curious misreading of the dance of Shiva as a dance of Death or Destruction, whereas, as anybody ought to be able to see who looks upon the Nataraja, it expresses on the contrary the rapture of the cosmic dance with the profundities behind of the unmoved eternal and infinite bliss. So too the figure of Kali which is so terrible to European eyes is, as we know, the Mother of the universe accepting this fierce aspect of destruction in order to slay the Asuras, the powers of evil in man and the world. There are other strands in this feeling in the western mind which seem to spring from a dislike of anything uplifted far beyond the human measure and others again in which we see a subtle survival of the Greek limitation, the fear, gloom and aversion with which the sunny terrestrial Hellenic mind commonly met the idea of the beyond, the limitless, the unknown; but that reaction has no place in Indian mentality. And as for the strangeness or formidable aspect of certain unhuman figures or the conception of demons or Rakshasas, it must be remembered that the Indian aesthetic mind deals not only with the earth but with psychic planes in which these things exist and ranges freely among them without being overpowered because it carries everywhere the stamp of a large confidence in the strength and the omnipresence of the Self or the Divine.

I have dwelt on Hindu and especially on Dravidian architecture because the latter is the most fiercely attacked as the most uncompromisingly foreign to European taste. But a word too may be said about Indo-Moslem architecture. I am not concerned to defend any claim for the purely indigenous origin of its features. It seems to me that here the Indian mind has taken in much from the Arab and Persian imagination and in certain mosques and tombs I seem to find an impress of the robust and bold Afghan and Moghul temperament; but it remains clear enough that it is still on the whole a typically Indian creation with the peculiar Indian gift. The richness of decorative skill and imagination has been turned to the uses of another style, but it is the same skill which we find in the northern Hindu temples, and in the ground we see, however toned down, something sometimes of the old epic mass and power, but more often that lyric grace which we see developing before the Mahomedan advent in the indigenous sculpture,—as in the schools of the North-East and of *Java*,—and sometimes a blending of the two motives. The modification, the toning down sets the average European mind at ease and secures its suffrage. But what is it that it so much admires? Mr. Archer tells us at first that it is its rational beauty, refinement and grace, normal, fair, refreshing after the monstrous riot of Hindu Yogic hallucination and nightmare. That description which might have been written of Greek art, seems to me grotesquely inapplicable. Immediately afterwards he harps on quite another and an incompatible phrase, and calls it a fairy-land of exquisite architecture. A rational fairy-land is a wonder which may perhaps be hereafter discovered by some strange intertwining of the nineteenth and twentieth century minds, but I do not think it has yet existed on earth or in the heavens. Not rational but magical beauty satisfying and enchanting to some deeper quite suprarational aesthetic soul in us is the inexpressible charm of these creations. But still where does the magic touch our critic? He tells us in a rapt journalistic style. It is the exquisite marble traceries, the beautiful domes and minarets, the stately halls of sepulture, the marvellous loggias and arcades, the magnificent plinths and platforms, the majestic gateways, et cetera. And is this then all? Only the charm of an outward material luxury and magnificence? Yes; Mr. Archer again tells us that we must be content here with a visual sensuous beauty without any moral suggestion. And that helps him to bring in the sentence of destructive condemnation without which he could not feel happy in dealing with Indian things: this Moslem architecture suggests not only unbridled luxury, but effeminacy and decadence! But in that case, whatever its beauty, it belongs entirely to a secondary plane of artistic creation and cannot rank with the great spiritual aspirations in stone of the Hindu builders.

I do not demand "moral suggestions" from architecture, but is it true that there is nothing but a sensuous outward grace and beauty and luxury in these Indo-Moslem buildings? It is not at all true of the characteristic greater work. The Taj is not merely a sensuous reminiscence of an imperial amour or a fairy enchantment hewn from the moon's lucent quarries, but the eternal dream of a love that survives death. The great mosques embody often a religious aspiration lifted to a noble austerity which supports and is not lessened by the subordinated ornament and grace. The tombs reach beyond death to the beauty and joy of Paradise. The buildings of Fatehpur-Sikri are not monuments of an effeminate luxurious decadence,—an absurd description for the mind of the time of Akbar,—but give form to a nobility, power and beauty which lay hold upon but do not wallow on the earth. There is not here indeed the vast spiritual content of the earlier Indian mind, but it is still an Indian mind which in these delicate creations absorbs the West Asian influence, and lays stress on the sensuous as before in the poetry of Kalidasa, but uplifts it to a certain immaterial charm, rises often from the earth without quite leaving it into the magical beauty of the middle world and in the religious mood touches with a devout hand the skirts of the Divine. The all-pervading spiritual obsession is not there, but other elements of life not ignored by Indian culture and gaining on it since the classical times are here brought out under a new influence and are still penetrated with some radiant glow of a superior lustre.

A DEFENCE OF INDIAN CULTURE

CHAPTER VIII

INDIAN ART

THE sculpture and painting of ancient India have recently been rehabilitated with a surprising suddenness in the eyes of a more cultivated European criticism in the course of that rapid opening of the western mind to the value of oriental thought and creation which is one of the most significant signs of a change that is yet only in its beginning. There have even been here and there minds of a fine perception and profound originality who have seen in a return to the ancient and persistent freedom of oriental art, its refusal to be shackled or debased by an imitative realism, its fidelity to the true theory of art as an inspired interpretation of the deeper soul values of existence lifted beyond servitude to the outsides of Nature, the right way to the regeneration and liberation of the aesthetic and creative mind of Europe. And actually, although much of western art runs still along the old grooves, much too of its most original recent creation has elements or a guiding direction which brings it nearer to the eastern mentality and understanding. It might then be possible for us to leave it at that and wait for time to deepen this new vision and vindicate more fully the truth and greatness of the art of India.

But we are concerned not only with the critical estimation

of our art by Europe, but much more nearly with the evil effect of the earlier depreciation on the Indian mind which has been for a long time side-tracked off its true road by a foreign, an anglicised education and, as a result, vulgarised and falsified by the loss of its own true centre, because this hampers and retards a sound and living revival of artistic taste and culture and stands in the way of a new age of creation. It was only a few years ago that the mind of educated India—"educated" without an atom of real culture—accepted contentedly the vulgar English estimate of our sculpture and painting as undeveloped inferior art or even a mass of monstrous and abortive miscreation, and though that has passed and there is a great change, there is still very common a heavy weight of secondhand occidental notions, a bluntness or absolute lacking of aesthetic taste,* a failure to appreciate, and one still comes sometimes across a strain of blatantly anglicised criticism which depreciates all that is in the Indian manner and praises only what is consistent with western canons. And the old style of European criticism continues to have some weight with us, because the lack of aesthetic or indeed of any real cultural training in our present system of education makes us ignorant and undiscriminating receptacles, so that we are ready to take the considered opinions of competent critics like Okakura or Mr. Laurence Binyon and the rash scribblings of journalists of the type of Mr. Archer, who write without authority because in these things they have neither taste nor knowledge, as of equal importance and the latter even attract a greater attention. It is still necessary therefore to reiterate things which, however obvious to a trained or sensitive aesthetic intelligence, are not yet familiar to the average mind still untutored or habituated to a system of false weights and values. The work of recovering a true and inward understanding of

* For example, one still reads with a sense of despairing stupefaction "criticism" that speaks of Ravi Varma and Abanindranath Tagore as artistic creators of different styles, but an equal power and genius!

ourselves—our past and our present self and from that our future—is only in its commencement for the majority of our people.

To appreciate our own artistic past at its right value we have to free ourselves from all subjection to a foreign outlook and see our sculpture and painting, as I have already suggested about our architecture, in the light of its own profound intention and greatness of spirit. When we so look at it, we shall be able to see that the sculpture of ancient and mediaeval India claims its place on the very highest levels of artistic achievement. I do not know where we shall find a sculptural art of a more profound intention, a greater spirit, a more consistent skill of achievement. Inferior work there is, work that fails or succeeds only partially, but take it in its whole, in the long persistence of its excellence, in the number of its masterpieces, in the power with which it renders the soul and the mind of a people, and we shall be tempted to go further and claim for it a first place. The art of sculpture has indeed flourished supremely only in ancient countries where it was conceived against its natural background and support, a great architecture. Egypt, Greece, India take the premier rank in this kind of creation. Mediaeval and modern Europe produced nothing of the same mastery, abundance and amplitude, while on the contrary in painting later Europe has done much and richly and with a prolonged and constantly renewed inspiration. The difference arises from the different kind of mentality required by the two arts. The material in which we work makes its own peculiar demand on the creative spirit, lays down its own natural conditions, as Ruskin has pointed out in a different connection, and the art of making in stone or bronze calls for a cast of mind which the ancients had and the moderns have not or have had only in rare individuals, an artistic mind not too rapidly mobile and self-indulgent, not too much mastered by its own personality and emotion and the touches that excite and pass, but founded rather on some great basis of assured thought and vision, stable in temperament, fixed in its imagination on things that are firm and enduring. One cannot trifle with ease in this sterner material, one cannot even for long or with safety indulge in them in mere grace and external beauty or the more superficial, mobile and lightly attractive motives. The aesthetic self-indulgence which the soul of colour permits and even invites, the attraction of the mobile play of life to which line of brush, pen or pencil gives latitude, are here forbidden or, if to some extent achieved, only within a line of restraint to cross which is perilous and soon fatal. Here grand or profound motives are called for, a more or less penetrating spiritual vision or some sense of things eternal to base the creation. The sculptural art is static, self-contained, necessarily firm, noble or severe and demands an aesthetic spirit capable of these qualities. A certain mobility of life and mastering grace of line can come in upon this basis, but if it entirely replaces the original dharma of the material, that means that the spirit of the statuette has come into the statue and we may be sure of an approaching decadence. Hellenic sculpture following this line passed from the greatness of Phidias through the soft self-indulgence of Praxiteles to its decline. A later Europe has failed for the most part in sculpture, in spite of some great work by individuals, an Angelo or a Rodin, because it played externally with stone and bronze, took them as a medium for the representation of life and could not find a sufficient basis of profound vision or spiritual motive. In Egypt and in India, on the contrary, sculpture preserved its power of successful creation through several great ages. The earliest recently discovered work in India dates back to the fifth century B.C. and is already fully evolved with an evident history of consummate previous creation behind it, and the latest work of some high value comes down to within a few centuries from our own time. An assured history of two millenniums of accomplished sculptural creation is a rare and significant fact in the life of a people.

This greatness and continuity of Indian sculpture is due to

the close connection between the religious and philosophical and the aesthetic mind of the people. Its survival into times not far from us was possible because of the survival of the cast of the antique mind in that philosophy and religion, a mind familiar with eternal things, capable of cosmic vision, having its roots of thought and seeing in the profundities of the soul, in the most intimate, pregnant and abiding experiences of the human spirit. The spirit of this greatness is indeed at the opposite pole to the perfection within limits, the lucid nobility or the vital fineness and physical grace of Hellenic creation in stone. And since the favourite trick of Mr. Archer and his kind is to throw the Hellenic ideal constantly in our face, as if sculpture must be either governed by the Greek standard or worthless, it is as well to take note of the meaning of the difference. The earlier and more archaic Greek style had indeed something in it which looks like a reminiscent touch of a first creative origin from Egypt and the Orient, but there is already there the governing conception which determined the Greek aesthesis and has dominated the later mind of Europe, the will to combine some kind of expression of an inner truth with an idealising imitation of external Nature. The brilliance, beauty and nobility of the work which was accomplished, was a very great and perfect thing, but it is idle to maintain that that is the sole possible method or the one permanent and natural law of artistic creation. Its highest greatness subsisted only so long—and it was not for very long—as a certain satisfying balance was struck and constantly maintained between a fine, but not very subtle, opulent or profound spiritual suggestion and an outward physical harmony of nobility and grace. A later work achieved a brief miracle of vital suggestion and sensuous physical grace with a certain power of expressing the spirit of beauty in the mould of the senses; but this once done, there was no more to see or create. For the curious turn which impels at the present day the modern mind to return to spiritual vision through a fiction of exaggerated realism which is really a pressure upon the form of things to yield the secret of the spirit in life and matter, was not open to the classic temperament and intelligence. And it is surely time for us to see, as is now by many admitted, that an acknowledgment of the greatness of Greek art in its own province ought not to prevent the plain perception of the rather strait and narrow bounds of that province. What Greek sculpture expressed was fine, gracious and noble, but what it did not express and could not by the limitations of its canon hope to attempt, was considerable, was immense in possibility, was that spiritual depth and extension which the human mind needs for its larger and deeper self-experience. And just this is the greatness of Indian sculpture that it expresses in stone and bronze what the Greek aesthetic mind could not conceive or express and embodies it with a profound understanding of its right conditions and a native perfection.

The more ancient sculptural art of India embodies in visible form what the Upanishads threw out into inspired thought and the Mahabharata and Ramayana portrayed by the word in life. This sculpture like the architecture springs from spiritual realisation, and what it creates and expresses at its greatest is the spirit in form, the soul in body, this or that living soul power in the divine or the human, the universal and cosmic individualised in suggestion but not lost in individuality, the impersonal supporting a not too insistent play of personality, the abiding moments of the eternal, the presence, the idea, the power, the calm or potent delight of the spirit in its actions and creations. And over all the art something of this intention broods and persists and is suggested even where it does not dominate the mind of the sculptor. And therefore as in the architecture so in the sculpture, we have to bring a different mind to this work, a different capacity of vision and response, we have to go deeper into ourselves to see than in the more outwardly imaginative art of Europe. The Olympian gods of Phidias are magnified and uplifted human beings saved from a too human limitation by a certain divine calm of impersonality or universalised quality, divine type, *guṇa;* in other work we see heroes, athletes, feminine incarnations of beauty, calm and restrained embodiments of idea, action or emotion in the idealised beauty of the human figure. The gods of Indian sculpture are cosmic beings, embodiments of some great spiritual power, spiritual idea and action, inmost psychic significance, the human form a vehicle of this soul meaning, its outward means of self-expression; everything in the figure, every opportunity it gives, the face, the hands, the posture of the limbs, the poise and turn of the body, every accessory, has to be made instinct with the inner meaning, help it to emerge, carry out the rhythm of the total suggestion, and on the other hand everything is suppressed which would defeat this end, especially all that would mean an insistence on the merely vital or physical, outward or obvious suggestions of the human figure. Not the ideal physical or emotional beauty, but the utmost spiritual beauty or significance of which the human form is capable, is the aim of this kind of creation. The divine self in us is its theme, the body made a form of the soul is its idea and its secret. And therefore in front of this art it is not enough to look at it and respond with the aesthetic eye and the imagination, but we must look also into the form for what it carries and even through and behind it to pursue the profound suggestion it gives into its own infinite. The religious or hieratic side of Indian sculpture is intimately connected with the spiritual experiences of Indian meditation and adoration,—those deep things of our self-discovery which our critic calls contemptuously Yogic hallucinations,—soul realisation is its method of creation and soul realisation must be the way of our response and understanding. And even with the figures of human beings or groups it is still a like inner aim and vision which governs the labour of the sculptor. The statue of a king or a saint is not meant merely to give the idea of a king or saint or to portray some dramatic action or to be a character portrait in stone, but to embody rather a soul state or experience or deeper soul quality, as for instance, not the outward emotion, but the inner soul-side of rapt ecstasy of adoration and God-vision in the saint or the devotee before the presence of the worshipped deity. This is the character of the task the Indian sculptor set before his effort and it is according to his success in that and not by the absence of something else, some quality or some intention foreign to his mind and contrary to his design, that we have to judge of his achievement and his labour.

Once we admit this standard, it is impossible to speak too highly of the profound intelligence of its conditions which was developed in Indian sculpture, of the skill with which its task was treated or of the consummate grandeur and beauty of its masterpieces. Take the great Buddhas—not the Gandharan, but the divine figures or groups in cave cathedral or temple, the best of the later southern bronzes of which there is a remarkable collection of plates in Mr. Gangoly's book on that subject, the Kalasanhara image, the Natarajas. No greater or finer work, whether in conception or execution, has been done by the human hand and its greatness is increased by obeying a spiritualised aesthetic vision. The figure of the Buddha achieves the expression of the infinite in a finite image, and that is surely no mean or barbaric achievement, to embody the illimitable calm of Nirvana in a human form and visage. The Kalasanhara Shiva is supreme not only by the majesty, power, calmly forceful control, dignity and kingship of existence which the whole spirit and pose of the figure visibly incarnates,—that is only half or less than half its achievement,—but much more by the concentrated divine passion of the spiritual overcoming of time and existence which the artist has succeeded in putting into eye and brow and mouth and every feature and has subtly supported by the contained suggestion, not emotional, but spiritual, of every part of the body of the godhead and the rhythm of his meaning which he has poured through the whole unity of this creation. Or what of the marvellous genius and skill in the treatment of the cosmic movement and delight of the dance of Shiva, the success with which the posture of every limb is made to bring out the rhythm of the significance, the rapturous intensity and abandon of the movement itself and yet the just restraint in the intensity of motion, the subtle variation of each element of the single theme in the seizing idea of these master sculptors? Image after image in the great temples or saved from the wreck of time shows the same grand traditional art and the genius which worked in that tradition and its many styles, the profound and firmly grasped spiritual idea, the consistent expression of it in every curve, line and mass, in hand and limb, in suggestive pose, in expressive rhythm,—it is an art which, understood in its own spirit, need fear no comparison with any other, ancient or modern, Hellenic or Egyptian, of the near or the far East or of the West in any of its creative ages. This sculpture passed through many changes, a more ancient art of extraordinary grandeur and epic power uplifted by the same spirit as reigned in the Vedic and Vedantic seers and in the epic poets, a later Puranic turn towards grace and beauty and rapture and an outburst of lyric ecstasy and movement, and last a rapid and vacant decadence; but throughout all the second period too the depth and greatness of sculptural motive supports and vivifies the work and in the very turn towards decadence something of it often remains to redeem from complete debasement, emptiness or insignificance.

Let us see then what is the value of the objections made to the spirit and style of Indian sculpture. This is the burden of the objurgations of the devil's advocate that his self-bound European mind finds the whole thing barbaric, meaningless, uncouth, strange, bizarre, the work of a distorted imagination labouring mid a nightmare of unlovely unrealities. Now there is in the total of what survives to us work that is less inspired or even work that is bad, exaggerated, forced or clumsy, the production of mechanic artificers mingled with the creation of great nameless artists, and an eye that does not understand the sense, the first conditions of the work, the mind of the race or its type of aesthesis, may well fail to distinguish between good and inferior execution, decadent work and the work of the great hands and the great eras. But applied as a general description the criticism is itself grotesque and distorted and it means only that here are conceptions and a figuring imagination strange to the western intelligence. The line and run and turn demanded by the Indian aesthetic sense are not the same as those demanded by the European. It would take too long to examine the detail of the difference which we find not only in sculpture, but in the other plastic arts and in music and even to a certain extent in literature, but on the whole we may say that the Indian mind moves on the spur of a spiritual sensitiveness and psychic curiosity, while the aesthetic curiosity of the European temperament is intellectual, vital, emotional and imaginative in that sense, and almost the whole strangeness of the Indian use of line and mass, ornament and proportion and rhythm arises from this difference. The two minds live almost in different worlds, are either not looking at the same things or, even where they meet in the object, see it from a different level or surrounded by a different atmosphere, and we know what power the point of view or the medium of vision has to transform the object. And undoubtedly there is very ample ground for Mr. Archer's complaint of the want of naturalism in most Indian sculpture. The inspiration, the way of seeing is frankly not naturalistic, not, that is to say, the vivid, convincing and accurate, the graceful, beautiful or strong, or even the idealised or imaginative imitation of surface or terrestrial nature. The Indian sculptor is concerned with embodying spiritual experiences and impressions, not with recording or glorifying what is received by the physical senses. He may start with suggestions from earthly and physical things, but he produces his work only after he has closed his eyes to the insistence of the physical circumstances, seen them in the psychic memory and transformed them within himself so as to bring out something other than their physical reality or their vital and intellectual significance. His eye sees the psychic line and turn of things and he replaces by them the material contours. It is not surprising that such a method should produce results which are strange to the average western mind and eye when these are not liberated by a broad and sympathetic culture. And what is strange to us is naturally repugnant to our habitual mind and uncouth to our habitual sense, bizarre to our imaginative tradition and aesthetic training. We want what is familiar to the eye and obvious to the imagination and will not readily admit that there may be here another and perhaps greater beauty than that in the circle of which we are accustomed to live and take pleasure.

It seems to be especially the application of this psychic vision to the human form which offends these critics of Indian sculpture. There is the familiar objection to such features as the multiplication of the arms in the figures of gods and goddesses, the four, six, eight or ten arms of Shiva, the eighteen arms of Durga, because they are a monstrosity, a thing not in nature. Now certainly a play of imagination of this kind would be out of place in the representation of a man or woman, because it would have no artistic or other meaning, but I cannot see why this freedom should be denied in the representation of cosmic beings like the Indian godheads. The whole question is, first, whether it is an appropriate means of conveying a significance not otherwise to be represented with an equal power and force and, secondly, whether it is capable of artistic representation, a rhythm of artistic truth and unity which need not be that of physical nature. If not, then it is an ugliness and violence, but if these conditions are satisfied, the means are justified and I do not see that we have any right, faced with the perfection of the work, to raise a discordant clamour. Mr. Archer himself is struck with the perfection of skill and mastery with which these to him superfluous limbs are disposed in the figures of the dancing Shiva, and indeed it would need an eye of impossible blindness not to see that much, but what is still more important is the artistic significance which this skill is used to serve, and, if that is understood, we can at once see that the spiritual emotion and suggestions of the cosmic dance are brought out by this device in a way which would not be as possible with a two-armed figure. The same truth holds as to the Durga with her eighteen arms slaying the Asuras or the Shivas of the great Pallava creations where the lyrical beauty of the Natarajas is absent, but there is instead a great epical rhythm and grandeur. Art justifies its own means and here it does it with a supreme perfection. And as for the "contorted" postures of some figures, the same law holds. There is often a departure in this respect from the anatomical norm of the physical body or else—and that is a rather different thing—an emphasis more or less pronounced on an unusual pose of limbs or body, and the question then is whether it is done without sense or purpose, a mere clumsiness or an ugly exaggeration, or whether it rather serves some significance and establishes in the place of the normal physical metric of Nature another purposeful and successful artistic rhythm. Art after all is not forbidden to deal with the unusual or to alter and overpass Nature, and it might almost be said that it has been doing little else since it began to serve the human imagination from its first grand epic exaggerations to the violences of modern romanticism and realism, from the high ages of Valmiki and Homer to the day of Hugo and Ibsen. The means matter, but less than the significance and the thing done and the power and beauty with which it expresses the dreams and truths of the human spirit.

The whole question of the Indian artistic treatment of the human figure has to be understood in the light of its aesthetic purpose. It works with a certain intention and ideal, a general norm and standard which permits of a good many variations and from which too there are appropriate departures. The epithets with which Mr. Archer tries to damn its features are absurd, captious, exaggerated, the forced phrases of a journalist trying to depreciate a perfectly sensible, beautiful and aesthetic norm with which he does not sympathise. There are other things here than a repetition of hawk faces, wasp waists, thin legs and the rest of the ill-tempered caricature. He doubts Mr. Havell's suggestion that these old Indian artists knew the anatomy of the body well enough, as Indian science knew it, but chose to depart from it for their own purpose. It does not seem to me to matter much, since art is not anatomy, nor an artistic masterpiece necessarily a reproduction of physical fact or a lesson in natural science. I see no reason to regret the absence of telling studies in muscles, torsos, etc., for I cannot regard these things as having in themselves any essential artistic value. The one important point is that the Indian artist had a perfect idea of proportion and rhythm and used them in certain styles with nobility and power, in others like the Javan, the Gauda or the southern bronzes with that or with a perfect grace added and often an intense and a lyrical sweetness. The dignity and beauty of the human figure in the best Indian statues cannot be excelled, but what was sought and what was achieved was not an outward naturalistic, but a spiritual and a psychic beauty, and to achieve it the sculptor suppressed, and was entirely right in suppressing, the obtrusive material detail and aimed instead at purity of outline and fineness of feature. And into that outline, into that purity and fineness he was able to work whatever he chose, mass of force or delicacy of grace, a static dignity or a mighty strength or a restrained violence of movement or whatever served or helped his meaning. A divine and subtle body was his ideal; and to a taste and imagination too blunt or realistic to conceive the truth and beauty of his idea, the ideal itself may well be a stumbling-block, a thing of offence. But the triumphs of art are not to be limited by the narrow prejudices of the natural realistic man; that triumphs and endures which appeals to the best, *sādhu-sammatam,* that is deepest and greatest which satisfies the profoundest souls and the most sensitive psychic imaginations.

Each manner of art has its own ideals, traditions, agreed conventions; for the ideas and forms of the creative spirit are many, though there is one ultimate basis. The perspective, the psychic vision of the Chinese and Japanese painters are not the same as those of European artists; but who can ignore the beauty and the wonder of their work? I dare say Mr. Archer would set a Constable or a Turner above the whole mass of Far Eastern work, as I myself, if I had to make a choice, would take a Chinese or Japanese landscape or other magic transmutation of Nature in preference to all others; but these are matters of individual, national or continental temperament and preference. The essence of the question lies in the rendering of the truth and beauty seized by the spirit. Indian sculpture, Indian art in general follows its own ideal and traditions and these are unique in their character and quality. It is the expression, great as a whole through many centuries and ages of creation, supreme at its best, whether in rare early pre-Asokan, in Asokan or later work of the first heroic age or in the magnificent statues of the cave-cathedrals and Pallava and other southern temples or the noble, accomplished or gracious imaginations of Bengal, Nepal and Java through the after centuries or in the singular skill and delicacy of the bronze work of the southern religions, a self-expression of the spirit and ideals of a great nation and a great culture which stands apart in the cast of its mind and qualities among the earth's peoples, famed for its spiritual achievement, its deep philosophies and its religious spirit, its artistic taste, the richness of its poetic imagination, and not inferior once in its dealings with life and its social endeavour and political institutions. This sculpture is a singularly powerful, a seizing and profound interpretation in stone and bronze of the inner soul of that people. The nation, the culture failed for a time in life after a long greatness, as others failed before it and others will yet fail that now flourish; the creations of its mind have been arrested, this art like others has ceased or fallen into decay, but the thing from which it rose, the spiritual fire within still burns and in the renascence that is coming it may be that this great art too will revive, not saddled with the grave limitations of modern western work in the kind, but vivified by the nobility of a new impulse and power of the ancient spiritual motive. Let it recover, not limited by old forms, but undeterred by the cavillings of an alien mind, the sense of the grandeur and beauty and the inner significance of its past achievement; for in the continuity of its spiritual endeavour lies its best hope for the future.

CHAPTER IX

INDIAN ART

THE art of painting in ancient and later India, owing to the comparative scantiness of its surviving creations, does not create quite so great an impression as her architecture and sculpture and it has even been supposed that this art flourished only at intervals, finally ceased for a period of several centuries and was revived later on by the Moghuls and by Hindu artists who underwent the Moghul influence. This however is a hasty view that does not outlast a more careful research and consideration of the available evidence. It appears, on the contrary, that Indian culture was able to arrive at a well developed and an understanding aesthetic use of colour and line from very early times and, allowing for the successive fluctuations, periods of decline and fresh outbursts of originality and vigour, which the collective human mind undergoes in all countries, used this form of self-expression very persistently through the long centuries of its growth and greatness. And especially it is apparent now that there was a persistent tradition, a fundamental spirit and turn of the aesthetic sense native to the mind of India which links even the latest Rajput art to the earliest surviving work still preserved at its highest summit of achievement in the rock-cut retreats of Ajanta.

The materials of the art of painting are unfortunately more perishable than those of any other of the greater means of creative aesthetic self-expression and of the ancient masterpieces only a little survives, but that little still indicates the immensity of the amount of work of which it is the fading remnant. It is said that of the twenty-nine caves at Ajanta almost all once bore signs of decoration by frescoes; only so long ago as forty years sixteen still contained something of the original paintings, but now six alone still bear their witness to the greatness of this ancient art, though rapidly perishing and deprived of something of the original warmth and beauty and glory of colour. The rest of all that vivid contemporaneous creation which must at one time have covered the whole country in the temples and viharas and the houses of the cultured and the courts and pleasure-houses of nobles and kings, has perished, and we have only, more or less similar to the work at Ajanta, some crumbling fragments of rich and profuse decoration in the caves of Bagh and a few paintings of female figures in two rock-cut chambers at Sigiriya.* These remnants represent the work of some six or seven centuries, but they leave gaps, and nothing now remains of any paintings earlier than the first century of the Christian era, except some frescoes, spoilt by unskilful restoration, from the first century before it, while after the seventh there is a blank which might at first sight argue a total decline of the art, a cessation and disappearance. But there are fortunately evidences which carry back the tradition of the art at one end many centuries earlier and other remains more recently discovered and of another kind outside India and in the Himalayan countries carry it forward at the other end as late as the twelfth century and help us to link it on to the later schools of Rajput painting. The history of the self-expression of the Indian mind in painting covers a period of as much as two millenniums of more or less intense artistic creation and stands on a par in this respect with the architecture and sculpture.

* Since then more paintings of high quality have been found in some southern temples, akin in their spirit and style to the work at Ajanta.

The paintings that remain to us from ancient times are the work of Buddhist painters, but the art itself in India was of pre-Buddhistic origin. The Tibetan historian ascribes a remote antiquity to all the crafts, prior to the Buddha, and this is a conclusion increasingly pointed to by a constant accumulation of evidence. Already in the third century before the Christian era we find the theory of the art well founded from previous times, the six essential elements, *ṣaḍaṅga,* recognized and enumerated, like the more or less corresponding six Chinese canons which are first mentioned nearly a thousand years later, and in a very ancient work on the art pointing back to pre-Buddhistic times a number of careful and very well-defined rules and traditions are laid down which were developed into an elaborate science of technique and traditional rule in the later Shilpasutras. The frequent references in the ancient literature also are of a character which would have been impossible without a widespread practice and appreciation of the art by both men and women of the cultured classes, and these allusions and incidents evidencing a moved delight in the painted form and beauty of colour and the appeal both to the decorative sense and to the aesthetic emotion occur not only in the later poetry of Kalidasa, Bhavabhuti and other classical dramatists, but in the early popular drama of Bhasa and earlier still in the epics and in the sacred books of the Buddhists. The absence of any actual creations of this earlier art makes it indeed impossible to say with absolute certainty what was its fundamental character and intimate source of inspiration or whether it was religious and hieratic or secular in its origin. The theory has been advanced rather too positively that it was in the courts of kings that the art began and with a purely secular motive and inspiration, and it is true that while the surviving work of Buddhist artists is mainly religious in subject or at least links on common scenes of life to Buddhist ceremony and legend, the references in the epic and dramatic literature are usually to painting of a more purely aesthetic character, personal, domestic or civic, portrait painting, the representation of scenes and incidents in the lives of kings and other great personalities or mural decoration of palaces and private or public buildings. On the other hand, there are similar elements in Buddhist painting, as, for example, the portraits of the queens of King Kashyapa at Sigiriya, the historic representation of a Persian embassy or the landing of Vijaya in Ceylon. And we may fairly assume that all along Indian painting, both Buddhist and Hindu, covered much the same kind of ground as the later Rajput work in a more ample fashion and with a more antique greatness of spirit and was in its ensemble an interpretation of the whole religion, culture and life of the Indian people. The one important and significant thing that emerges is the constant oneness and continuity of all Indian art in its essential spirit and tradition. Thus the earlier work at Ajanta has been found to be akin to the earlier sculptural work of the Buddhists, while the later paintings have a similar close kinship to the sculptural reliefs at Java. And we find that the spirit and tradition which reigns through all changes of style and manner at Ajanta, is present too at Bagh and Sigiriya, in the Khotan frescoes, in the illuminations of Buddhist manuscripts of a much later time and in spite of the change of form and manner is still spiritually the same in the Rajput paintings. This unity and continuity enable us to distinguish and arrive at a clear understanding of what is the essential aim, inner turn and motive, spiritual method which differentiate Indian painting first from occidental work and then from the nearer and more kindred art of other countries of Asia.

The spirit and motive of Indian painting are in their centre of conception and shaping force of sight identical with the inspiring vision of Indian sculpture. All Indian art is a throwing out of a certain profound self-vision formed by a going within to find out the secret significance of form and appearance, a discovery of the subject in one's deeper self, the giving of soul-form to that vision and a remoulding of the material and natural shape to express the psychic truth of it with the greatest possible purity and power of outline and the greatest possible concentrated rhythmic unity of significance in all the parts of an indivisible artistic whole. Take whatever masterpiece of Indian painting and we shall find these conditions aimed at and brought out into a triumphant beauty of suggestion and execution. The only difference from the other arts comes from the turn natural and inevitable to its own kind of aesthesis, from the moved and indulgent dwelling on what one might call the mobilities of the soul rather than on its static eternities, on the casting out of self into the grace and movement of psychic and vital life (subject always to the reserve and restraint necessary to all art) rather than on the holding back of life in the stabilities of the self and its eternal qualities and principles, *guṇa* and *tattva*. This distinction is of the very essence of the difference between the work given to the sculptor and the painter, a difference imposed on them by the natural scope, turn, possibility of their instrument and medium. The sculptor must express always in static form; the idea of the spirit is cut out for him in mass and line, significant in the stability of its insistence, and he can lighten the weight of this insistence but not get rid of it or away from it; for him eternity seizes hold of time in its shapes and arrests it in the monumental spirit of stone or bronze. The painter on the contrary lavishes his soul in colour and there is a liquidity in the form, a fluent grace of subtlety in the line he uses which imposes on him a more mobile and emotional way of self-expression. The more he gives us of the colour and changing form and emotion of the life of the soul, the more his work glows with beauty, masters the inner aesthetic sense and opens it to the thing his art better gives us than any other, the delight of the motion of the self out into a spiritually sensuous joy of beautiful shapes and the coloured radiances of existence. Painting is naturally the most sensuous of the arts, and the highest greatness open to the painter is to spiritualise this sensuous appeal by making the most vivid outward beauty a revelation of subtle spiritual emotion so that the soul and the sense are at harmony in the deepest and finest richness of both and united in their satisfied consonant expression of the inner significances of things and life. There is less of the austerity of Tapasya in his way of working, a less severely restrained expression of eternal things and of the fundamental truths behind the forms of things, but there is in compensation a moved wealth of psychic or warmth of vital suggestion, a lavish delight of the beauty of the play of the eternal in the moments of time and there the artist arrests it for us and makes moments of the life of the soul reflected in form of man or creature or incident or scene or Nature full of a permanent and opulent significance to our spiritual vision. The art of the painter justifies visually to the spirit the search of the sense for delight by making it its own search for the pure intensities of meaning of the universal beauty it has revealed or hidden in creation; the indulgence of the eye's desire in perfection of form and colour becomes an enlightenment of the inner being through the power of a certain spiritually aesthetic Ananda.

The Indian artist lived in the light of an inspiration which imposed this greater aim on his art and his method sprang from its fountains and served it to the exclusion of any more earthly sensuous or outwardly imaginative aesthetic impulse. The six limbs of his art, the *ṣaḍaṅga,* are common to all work in line and colour: they are the necessary elements and in their elements the great arts are the same everywhere; the distinction of forms, *rūpabheda,* proportion, arrangement of line and mass, design, harmony, perspective, *pramāṇa,* the emotion or aesthetic feeling expressed by the form, *bhāva,* the seeking for beauty and charm for the satisfaction of the aesthetic spirit, *lāvaṇya,* truth of the form and its suggestion, *sādṛśya,* the turn, combination, harmony of colours, *varṇikābhaṅga,* are the first constituents to which every successful work of art reduces itself in analysis. But it is the turn given to each of the constituents which makes all the difference in the aim and effect of the technique and the source and character of the inner vision guiding the creative hand in their combination which makes all the difference in the spiritual value of the achievement, and the unique character of Indian painting, the peculiar appeal of the art of Ajanta springs from the remarkably inward, spiritual and psychic turn which was given to the artistic conception and method by the pervading genius of Indian culture. Indian painting no more than Indian architecture and sculpture could escape from its absorbing motive, its transmuting atmosphere, the direct or subtle obsession of the mind that has been subtly and strangely changed, the eye that has been trained to see, not as others with only the external eye but by a constant communing of the mental parts and the inner vision with the self beyond mind and the spirit to which forms are only a transparent veil or a slight index of its own greater splendour. The outward beauty and power, the grandeur of drawing, the richness of colour, the aesthetic grace of this painting is too obvious and insistent to be denied, the psychical appeal usually carries something in it to which there is a response in every cultivated and sensitive human mind and the departures from the outward physical norm are less vehement and intense, less disdainful of the more external beauty and grace,—as is only right in the nature of this art,—than in the sculpture: therefore we find it more easily appreciated up to a certain point by the western critical mind, and even when not well appreciated, it is exposed to milder objections. There is not the same blank incomprehension or violence of misunderstanding and repulsion. And yet we find at the same time that there is something which seems to escape the appreciation or is only imperfectly understood, and this something is precisely that profounder spiritual intention of which the things the eye and aesthetic sense immediately seize are only the intermediaries.

This explains the remark often made about Indian work of the less visibly potent and quieter kind that it lacks inspiration or imagination or is a conventional art: the spirit is missed where it does not strongly impose itself, and is not fully caught even where the power which is put into the expression is too great and direct to allow of denial. Indian painting like Indian architecture and sculpture appeals through the physical and psychical to another spiritual vision from which the artist worked and it is only when this is no less awakened in us than the aesthetic sense that it can be appreciated in all the depth of its significance.

The orthodox western artist works by a severely conscientious reproduction of the forms of outward Nature; the external world is his model, and he has to keep it before his eye and repress any tendency towards a substantial departure from it or any motion to yield his first allegiance to a subtler spirit. His imagination submits itself to physical Nature even when he brings in conceptions which are more properly of another kingdom, the stress of the physical world is always with him, and the Seer of the subtle, the creator of mental forms, the inner Artist, the wide-eyed voyager in the vaster psychical realms, is obliged to subdue his inspirations to the law of the Seer of the outward, the spirit that has embodied itself in the creations of the terrestrial life, the material universe. An idealised imaginative realism is as far as he can ordinarily go in the method of his work when he would fill the outward with the subtler inner seeing. And when, dissatisfied with this confining law, he would break quite out of the circle, he is exposed to a temptation to stray into intellectual or imaginative extravagances which violate the universal rule of the right distinction of forms, *rūpabheda,* and belong to the vision of some intermediate world of sheer fantasia. His art has discovered the rule of proportion, arrangement and perspective which preserves the illusion of physical Nature and he relates his whole design to her design in a spirit of conscientious obedience and faithful dependence. His imagination is a servant or interpreter of her imaginations, he finds in the observation of her universal law of beauty his secret of unity and harmony, and his subjectivity tries to discover itself in hers by a close dwelling on the objective shapes she has given to her creative spirit. The farthest he has got in the direction of a more intimately subjective spirit is an impressionism which still waits upon her models but seeks to get at some first inward or original effect of them on the inner sense, and through that he arrives at some more strongly psychical rendering, but he does not work altogether from within outward in the freer manner of the oriental artist. His emotion and artistic feeling move in this form and are limited by this artistic convention and are not a pure spiritual or psychic emotion but usually an imaginative exaltation derived from the suggestions of life and outward things with a psychic element or an evocation of spiritual feeling initiated and dominated by the touch of the outward. The charm that he gives is a sublimation of the beauty that appeals to the outward senses by the power of the idea and the imagination working on the outward sense appeal and other beauty is only brought in by association into that frame. The truth of correspondence he depends upon is a likeness to the creations of physical Nature and their intellectual, emotional and aesthetic significances, and his work of line and wave of colour are meant to embody the flow of this vision. The method of this art is always a transcript from the visible world with such necessary transmutation as the aesthetic mind imposes on its materials. At the lowest to illustrate, at the highest to interpret life and Nature to the mind by identifying it with deeper things through some derivative touch of the spirit that has entered into and subdued itself to their shapes, *praviśya yaḥ pratirūpo babhūva*, is the governing principle.*

* All this is no longer true of European art in much of its more prominent recent developments.

The Indian artist sets out from the other end of the scale of values of experience which connect life and the spirit. The whole creative force comes here from a spiritual and psychic vision, the emphasis of the physical is secondary and always deliberately lightened so as to give an overwhelmingly spiritual and psychic impression and everything is suppressed which does not serve this purpose or would distract the mind from the purity of this intention. This painting expresses the soul through life, but life is only a means of the spiritual self-expression, and its outward representation is not the first object or the direct motive. There is a real and a very vivid and vital representation, but it is more of an inner psychical than of the outward physical life. A critic of high repute speaking of the Indian influence in a famous Japanese painting fixes on the grand strongly outlined figures and the feeling for life and character recalling the Ajanta frescoes as the signs of its Indian character: but we have to mark carefully the nature of this feeling for life and the origin and intention of this strong outlining of the figures. The feeling for life and character here is a very different thing from the splendid and abundant vitality and the power and force of character which we find in an Italian painting, a fresco from Michael Angelo's hand or a portrait by Titian or Tintoretto. The first primitive object of the art of painting is to illustrate life and Nature and at the lowest this becomes a more or less vigorous and original or conventionally faithful reproduction, but it rises in great hands to a revelation of the glory and beauty of the sensuous appeal of life or of the dramatic power and moving interest of character and emotion and action. That is a common form of aesthetic work in Europe: but in Indian art it is never the governing motive. The sensuous appeal is there, but it is refined into only one and not the chief element of the richness of a soul of psychic grace and beauty which is for the Indian artist the true beauty, *lāvaṇya:* the dramatic motive is subordinated and made only a purely secondary element, only so much is given of character and action as will help to bring out the deeper spiritual or psychic feeling, *bhāva,* and all insistence or too prominent force of these more outwardly dynamic things is shunned, because that would externalise too much the spiritual emotion and take away from its intense purity by the interference of the grosser intensity which emotion puts on in the stress of the active outward nature. The life depicted is the life of the soul and not, except as a form and a helping suggestion, the life of the vital being and the body. For the second more elevated aim of art is the interpretation or intuitive revelation of existence through the forms of life and Nature and it is this that is the starting-point of the Indian motive. But the interpretation may proceed on the basis of the forms already given us by physical Nature and try to evoke by the form an idea, a truth of the spirit which starts from it as a suggestion and returns upon it for support, and the effort is then to correlate the form as it is to the physical eye with the truth which it evokes without overpassing the limits imposed by the appearance. This is the common method of occidental art always zealous for the immediate fidelity to Nature which is its idea of true correspondence, *sādṛśya,* but it is rejected by the Indian artist. He begins from within, sees in his soul the thing he wishes to express or interpret and tries to discover the right line, colour and design of his intuition which, when it appears on the physical ground, is not a just and reminding reproduction of the line, colour and design of physical nature, but much rather what seems to us a psychical transmutation of the natural figure. In reality the shapes he paints are the forms of things as he has seen them in the psychical plane of experience: these are the soul-figures of which physical things are a gross representation and their purity and subtlety reveals at once what the physical masks by the thickness of its casings. The lines and colours sought here are the psychic lines and the psychic hues proper to the vision which the artist has gone into himself to discover.

This is the whole governing principle of the art which gives its stamp to every detail of an Indian painting and transforms the artist's use of the six limbs of the canon. The distinction of forms is faithfully observed, but not in the sense of an exact naturalistic fidelity to the physical appearance with the object of a faithful reproduction of the outward shapes of the world in which we live. To recall with fidelity something our eyes have seen or could have seen on the spot, a scene, an interior, a living and breathing person, and give the aesthetic sense and emotion of it to the mind is not the motive. There is here an extraordinary vividness, naturalness, reality, but it is a more than physical reality, a reality which the soul at once recognises as of its own sphere, a vivid naturalness of psychic truth, the convincing spirit of the form to which the soul, not the outward naturalness of the form to which the physical eye bears witness. The truth, the exact likeness is there, the correspondence, *sādṛśya,* but it is the truth of the essence of the form, it is the likeness of the soul to itself, the reproduction of the subtle embodiment which is the basis of the physical embodiment, the purer and finer subtle body of an object which is the very expression of its own essential nature, *svabhāva.* The means by which this effect is produced is characteristic of the inward vision of the Indian mind. It is done by a bold and firm insistence on the pure and strong outline and a total suppression of everything that would interfere with its boldness, strength and purity or would blur over and dilute the intense significance of the line. In the treatment of the human figure all corporeal filling in of the outline by insistence on the flesh, the muscle, the anatomical detail is minimised or disregarded: the strong subtle lines and pure shapes which make the humanity of the human form are alone brought into relief; the whole essential human being is there, the divinity that has taken this garb of the spirit to the eye, but not the superfluous physicality which he carries with him as his burden. It is the ideal psychical figure and body of man and woman that is before us in its charm and beauty. The filling in of the line is done in another way; it is effected by a disposition of pure masses, a design and coloured wave-flow of the body, *bhanga*, a simplicity of content that enables the artist to flood the whole with the significance of the one spiritual emotion, feeling, suggestion which he intends to convey, his intuition of the moment of the soul, its living self-experience. All is disposed so as to express that and that alone. The almost miraculously subtle and meaningful use of the hands to express the psychic suggestion is a common and well-marked feature of Indian paintings and the way in which the suggestion of the face and the eyes is subtly repeated or supplemented by this expression of the hands is always one of the first things that strikes the regard, but as we continue to look, we see that every turn of the body, the pose of each limb, the relation and design of all the masses are filled with the same psychical feeling. The more important accessories help it by a kindred suggestion or bring it out by a support or variation or extension or relief of the motive. The same law of significant line and suppression of distracting detail is applied to animal forms, buildings, trees, objects. There is in all the art an inspired harmony of conception, method and expression. Colour too is used as a means for the spiritual and psychic intention, and we can see this well enough if we study the suggestive significance of the hues in a Buddhist miniature. This power of line and subtlety of psychic suggestion in the filling in of the expressive outlines is the source of that remarkable union of greatness and moving grace which is the stamp of the whole work of Ajanta and continues in Rajput painting, though there the grandeur of the earlier work is lost in the grace and replaced by a delicately intense but still bold and decisive power of vivid and suggestive line. It is this common spirit and tradition which is the mark of all the truly indigenous work of India.

These things have to be carefully understood and held in mind when we look at an Indian painting and the real spirit of it first grasped before we condemn or praise. To dwell on that in it which is common to all art is well enough, but it is what is peculiar to India that is its real essence. And there again to appreciate the technique and the fervour of religious feeling is not sufficient; the spiritual intention served by the technique, the psychic significance of line and colour, the greater thing of which the religious emotion is the result has to be felt if we would identify ourself with the whole purpose of the artist. If we look long, for an example, at the adoration group of the mother and child before the Buddha, one of the most profound, tender and noble of the Ajanta masterpieces, we shall find that the impression of intense religious feeling of adoration there is only the most outward general touch in the ensemble of the emotion. That which it deepens to is the turning of the soul of humanity in love to the benignant and calm Ineffable which has made itself sensible and human to us in the universal compassion of the Buddha, and the motive of the soul moment the painting interprets is the dedication of the awakening mind of the child, the coming younger humanity, to that in which already the soul of the mother has learned to find and fix its spiritual joy. The eyes, brows, lips, face, poise of the the head of the woman are filled with this spiritual emotion which is a continued memory and possession of the psychical release, the steady settled calm of the heart's experience filled with an ineffable tenderness, the familiar depths which are yet moved with the wonder and always farther appeal of something that is infinite, the body and other limbs are grave masses of this emotion and in their poise a basic embodiment of it, while the hands prolong it in the dedicative putting forward of her child to meet the Eternal. This contact of the human and eternal is repeated in the smaller figure with a subtly and strongly indicated variation, the glad and childlike smile of awakening which promises but not yet possesses the depths that are to come, the hands disposed to receive and keep, the body in its looser curves and waves harmonising with that significance. The two have forgotten themselves and seem almost to forget or confound each other in that which they adore and contemplate, and yet the dedicating hands unite mother and child in the common act and feeling by their simultaneous gesture of maternal possession and spiritual giving. The two figures have at each point the same rhythm, but with a significant difference. The simplicity in the greatness and power, the fullness of expression gained by reserve and suppression and concentration which we find here is the perfect method of the classical art of India. And by this perfection Buddhist art became not merely an illustration of the religion and an expression of its thought and its religious feeling, history and legend, but a revealing interpretation of the spiritual sense of Buddhism and its profounder meaning to the soul of India.

To understand that—we must always seek first and foremost this kind of deeper intention—is to understand the reason of the differences between the occidental and the Indian treatment of the life motives. Thus a portrait by a great European painter will express with sovereign power the soul through character, through the active qualities, the ruling powers and passions, the master feeling and temperament, the active mental and vital man: the Indian artist tones down the outward-going dynamic indices and gives only so much of them as will serve to bring out or to modulate something that is more of the grain of the subtle soul, something more static and impersonal of which our personality is at once the mask and the index. A moment of the spirit expressing with purity the permanence of a very subtle soul quality is the highest type of the Indian portrait. And more generally the feeling for character which has been noted as a feature of the Ajanta work is of a similar kind. An Indian painting expressing, let us say, a religious feeling centred on some significant incident will show the expression in each figure varied in such a way as to bring out the universal spiritual essence of the emotion modified by the essential soul type, different waves of the one sea, all complexity of dramatic insistence is avoided, and so much stress only is laid on character in the individual feeling as to give the variation without diminishing the unity of the fundamental emotion. The vividness of life in these paintings must not obscure for us the more profound purpose for which it is the setting, and this has especially to be kept in mind in our view of the later art which has not the greatness of the classic work and runs to a less grave and highly sustained kind, to lyric emotion, minute vividness of life movement, the more naïve feelings of the people. One sometimes finds inspiration, decisive power of thought and feeling, originality of creative imagination denied to this later art; but its real difference from that of Ajanta is only that the intermediate psychic transmission between the life movement and the inmost motive has been given with less power and distinctness: the psychic thought and feeling are there more thrown outward in movement, less contained in the soul, but still the soul motive is not only present but makes the true atmosphere and if we miss it, we miss the real sense of the picture. This is more evident where the inspiration is religious, but it is not absent from the secular subject. Here too spiritual intention or psychic suggestion are the things of the first importance. In Ajanta work they are all-important and to ignore them at all is to open the way to serious errors of interpretation. Thus a highly competent and very sympathetic critic speaking of the painting of the Great Renunciation says truly that this great work excels in its expression of sorrow and feeling of profound pity, but then, looking for what a western imagination would naturally put into such a subject, he goes on to speak of the weight of a tragic decision, the bitterness of renouncing a life of bliss blended with a yearning sense of hope in the happiness of the future, and that is singularly to misunderstand the spirit in which the Indian mind turns from the transient to the eternal, to mistake the Indian art motive and to put a vital into the place of a spiritual emotion. It is not at all his own personal sorrow but the sorrow of all others, not an emotional self-pity but a poignant pity for the world, not the regret for a life of domestic bliss but the afflicting sense of the unreality of human happiness that is concentrated in the eyes and lips of the Buddha, and the yearning there is not, certainly, for earthly happiness in the future but for the spiritual way out, the anguished seeking which found its release, already foreseen by the spirit behind and hence the immense calm and restraint that support the sorrow, in the true bliss of Nirvana. There is illustrated the whole difference between two kinds of imagination, the mental, vital and physical stress of the art of Europe and the subtle, less forcefully tangible spiritual stress of the art of India.

It is the indigenous art of which this is the constant spirit and tradition, and it has been doubted whether the Moghul paintings deserve that name, have anything to do with that tradition and are not rather an exotic importation from Persia. Almost all oriental art is akin in this respect that the psychic enters into and for the most part lays its subtler law on the physical vision and the psychic line and significance give the characteristic turn, are the secret of the decorative skill, direct the higher art in its principal motive. But there is a difference between the Persian psychicality which is redolent of the magic of the middle worlds and the Indian which is only a means of transmission of the spiritual vision. And obviously the Indo-Persian style is of the former kind and not indigenous to India. But the Moghul school is not an exotic; there is rather a blending of two mentalities: on the one side there is a leaning to some kind of externalism which is not the same thing as western naturalism, a secular spirit and certain prominent elements that are more strongly illustrative than interpretative, but the central thing is still the domination of a transforming touch which shows that there as in the architecture the Indian mind has taken hold of another invading mentality and made it a help to a more outward-going self-expression that comes in as a new side strain in the spiritual continuity of achievement which began in prehistoric times and ended only with the general decline of Indian culture. Painting, the last of the arts in that decline to touch the bottom, has also been the first to rise again and lift the dawn fires of an era of new creation.

It is not necessary to dilate on the decorative arts and crafts of India, for their excellence has always been beyond dispute. The generalised sense of beauty which they imply is one of the greatest proofs that there can be of the value and soundness of a national culture. Indian culture in this respect need not fear any comparison: if it is less predominantly artistic than that of Japan, it is because it has put first the spiritual need and made all other things subservient to and a means for the spiritual growth of the people. Its civilisation, standing in the first rank in the three great arts as in all things of the mind, has proved that the spiritual urge is not, as has been vainly supposed, sterilising to the other activities, but a most powerful force for the many-sided development of the human whole.

A DEFENCE OF INDIAN CULTURE

CHAPTER X

INDIAN LITERATURE

THE arts which appeal to the soul through the eye are able to arrive at a peculiarly concentrated expression of the spirit, the aesthesis and the creative mind of a people, but it is in its literature that we must seek for its most flexible and many-sided self-expression, for it is the word used in all its power of clear figure or its threads of suggestion that carries to us most subtly and variably the shades and turns and teeming significances of the inner self in its manifestation. The greatness of a literature lies first in the greatness and worth of its substance, the value of its thought and the beauty of its forms, but also in the degree to which, satisfying the highest conditions of the art of speech, it avails to bring out and raise the soul and life or the living and the ideal mind of a people, an age, a culture, through the genius of some of its greatest or most sensitive representative spirits. And if we ask what in both these respects is the achievement of the Indian mind as it has come down to us in the Sanskrit and other literatures, we might surely say that here at least there is little room for any just depreciation and denial even by a mind the most disposed to quarrel with the effect on life and the character of the culture. The ancient and classical creations of the Sanskrit tongue both in quality and in body and abundance of excellence, in their potent originality and force and beauty, in their substance and art and structure, in grandeur and justice and charm of speech and in the height and width of the reach of their spirit stand very evidently in the front rank among the world's great literatures. The language itself, as has been universally recognised by those competent to form a judgment, is one of the most magnificent, the most perfect and wonderfully sufficient literary instruments developed by the human mind, at once majestic and sweet and flexible, strong and clearly-formed and full and vibrant and subtle, and its quality and character would be of itself a sufficient evidence of the character and quality of the race whose mind it expressed and the culture of which it was the reflecting medium. The great and noble use made of it by poet and thinker did not fall below the splendour of its capacities. Nor is it in the Sanskrit tongue alone that the Indian mind has done high and beautiful and perfect things, though it couched in that language the larger part of its most prominent and formative and grandest creations. It would be necessary for a complete estimate to take into account as well the Buddhistic literature in Pali and the poetic literatures, here opulent, there more scanty in production, of about a dozen Sanskritic and Dravidian tongues. The whole has almost a continental effect and does not fall so far short in the quantity of its really lasting things and equals in its things of best excellence the work of ancient and mediaeval and modern Europe. The people and the civilisation that count among their great works and their great names the Veda and the Upanishads, the mighty structures of the Mahabharata and the Ramayana, Kalidasa and Bhavabhuti and Bhartrihari and Jayadeva and the other rich creations of classical Indian drama and poetry and romance, the Dhammapada and the Jatakas, the Panchatantra, Tulsidas, Vidyapati and Chandidas and Ramprasad, Ramdas and Tukaram, Tiruvalluvar and Kamban and the songs of Nanak and Kabir and Mirabai and the southern Shaiva saints and the Alwars,—to name only the best-known writers and most characteristic productions, though there is a very large body of other work in the different tongues of both the first and the second excellence,—must surely be counted among the greatest civilisations and the world's most developed and creative peoples. A mental activity so great and of so fine a quality commencing more than three thousand years ago and still not exhausted is unique and the best and most undeniable witness to something extraordinarily sound and vital in the culture.

A criticism that ignores or belittles the significance of this unsurpassed record and this splendour of the self-expressing spirit and the creative intelligence, stands convicted at once of a blind malignity or an invincible prejudice and does not merit refutation. It would be a sheer waste of time and energy to review the objections raised by our devil's advocate: for nothing vital to the greatness of a literature is really in dispute and there is only to the credit of the attack a general distortion and denunciation and a laborious and exaggerated cavilling at details and idiosyncracies which at most show a difference between the idealising mind and abundant imagination of India and the more realistically observant mind and less rich and exuberant imagination of Europe. The fit parallel to this motive and style of criticism would be if an Indian critic who had read European literature only in bad or ineffective Indian translations, were to pass it under a hostile and disparaging review, dismiss the Iliad as a crude and empty semi-savage and primitive epos, Dante's great work as the nightmare of a cruel and superstitious religious fantasy, Shakespeare as a drunken barbarian of considerable genius with an epileptic imagination, the whole drama of Greece and Spain and England as a mass of bad ethics and violent horrors, French poetry as a succession of bald or tawdry rhetorical exercises and French fiction as a tainted and immoral thing, a long sacrifice on the altar of the goddess Lubricity, admit here and there a minor merit, but make no attempt at all to understand the central spirit or aesthetic quality or principle of structure and conclude on the strength of his own absurd method that the ideals of both Pagan and Christian Europe were altogether false and bad and its imagination afflicted with a "habitual and ancestral" earthiness, morbidity, poverty and disorder. No criticism would be worth making on such a mass of absurdities, and in this equally ridiculous philippic only a stray observation or two less inconsequent and opaque than the others perhaps demands a passing notice. But although these futilities do not at all represent the genuine view of the general European mind on the subject of Indian poetry and literature, still one finds a frequent inability to appreciate the spirit or the form or the aesthetic value of Indian writing and especially its perfection and power as an expression of the cultural mind of the people. One meets such criticisms even from sympathetic critics as an admission of the vigour, colour and splendour of Indian poetry followed by a conclusion that for all that it does not satisfy, and this means that the intellectual and temperamental misunderstanding extends to some degree even to this field of creation where different minds meet more readily than in painting and sculpture, that there is a rift between the two mentalities and what is delightful and packed with meaning and power to the one has no substance, but only a form, of aesthetic or intellectual pleasure for the other. This difficulty is partly due to an inability to enter into the living spirit and feel the vital touch of the language, but partly to a spiritual difference in similarity which is even more baffling than a complete dissimilarity and otherness. Chinese poetry for example is altogether of its own kind and it is more possible for a western mentality, when it does not altogether pass it by as an alien world, to develop an undisturbed appreciation because the receptivity of the mind is not checked or hampered by any disturbing memories or comparisons. Indian poetry on the contrary, like the poetry of Europe, is the creation of an Aryan or Aryanised national mind, starts apparently from similar motives, moves on the same plane, uses cognate forms, and yet has something quite different in its spirit which creates a pronounced and separating divergence in its aesthetic tones, type of imagination, turn of self-expression, ideative mind, method, form, structure. The mind accustomed to the European idea and technique expects the same kind of satisfaction here and does not meet it, feels a baffling difference to whose secret it is a stranger, and the subtly pursuing comparison and vain expectation stand in the way of a full receptivity and intimate understanding. At bottom it is an insufficient comprehension of the quite different spirit behind, the different heart of this culture that produces the mingled attraction and dissatisfaction. The subject is too large to be dealt with adequately in small limits: I shall only attempt to bring out certain points by a consideration of some of the most representative master works of creative intuition and imagination taken as a record of the soul and mind of the Indian people.

The early mind of India in the magnificent youth of the nation, when a fathomless spiritual insight was at work, a subtle intuitive vision and a deep, clear and greatly outlined intellectual and ethical thinking and heroic action and creation which founded and traced the plan and made the permanent structure of her unique culture and civilisation, is represented by four of the supreme productions of her genius, the Veda, the Upanishads and the two vast epics, and each of them is of a kind, a form and an intention not easily parallelled in any other literature. The two first are the visible foundation of her spiritual and religious being, the others a large creative interpretation of her greatest period of life, of the ideas that informed and the ideals that governed it and the figures in which she saw man and Nature and God and the powers of the universe. The Veda gave us the first types and figures of these things as seen and formed by an imaged spiritual intuition and psychological and religious experience; the Upanishads constantly breaking through and beyond form and symbol and image without entirely abandoning them, since always they come in as accompaniment or undertone, reveal in a unique kind of poetry the ultimate and unsurpassable truths of self and God and man and the world and its principles and powers in their most essential, their profoundest and most intimate and their most ample realities,—highest mysteries and clarities vividly seen in an irresistible, an unwalled perception that has got through the intuitive and psychological to the sheer spiritual vision. And after that we have powerful and beautiful developments of the intellect and the life and of ideal, ethical, aesthetic, psychic, emotional and sensuous and physical knowledge and idea and vision and experience of which the epics are the early record and the rest of the literature the continuation; but the foundation remains the same throughout, and whatever new and often larger types and significant figures replace the old or intervene to add and modify and alter the whole ensemble, are in their essential build and character transmutations and extensions of the original vision and first spiritual experience and never an unconnected departure. There is a persistence, a continuity of the Indian mind in its literary creation in spite of great changes as consistent as that which we find in painting and sculpture.

The Veda is the creation of an early intuitive and symbolical mentality to which the later mind of man strongly intellectualised and governed on the one side by reasoning idea and abstract conception, on the other hand by the facts of life and matter accepted as they present themselves to the senses and positive intelligence without seeking in them for any divine or mystic significance, indulging the imagination as a play of the aesthetic fancy rather than as an opener of the doors of truth and only trusting to its suggestions when they are confirmed by the logical reason or by physical experience, aware only of carefully intellectualised intuitions and recalcitrant for the most part to any others, has grown a total stranger. It is not surprising therefore that the Veda should have become unintelligible to our minds except in its most outward shell of language, and that even very imperfectly known owing to the obstacle of an antique and ill understood diction, and that the most inadequate interpretations should be made which reduce this great creation of the young and splendid mind of humanity to a botched and defaced scrawl, an incoherent hotch-potch of the absurdities of a primitive imagination perplexing what would be otherwise the quite plain, flat and common record of a naturalistic religion which mirrored only and could only minister to the crude and materialistic desires of a barbaric life mind. The Veda became to the later scholastic and ritualistic idea of Indian priests and pundits nothing better than a book of mythology and sacrificial ceremonies; European scholars seeking in it for what was alone to them of any rational interest, the history, myths and popular religious notions of a primitive people, have done yet worse wrong to the Veda and by insisting on a wholly external rendering still farther stripped it of its spiritual interest and its poetic greatness and beauty.

But this was not what it was to the Vedic Rishis themselves or to the great seers and thinkers who came after them and developed out of their pregnant and luminous intuitions their own wonderful structures of thought and speech built upon an unexampled spiritual revelation and experience. The Veda was to these early seers the Word discovering the Truth and clothing in image and symbol the mystic significances of life. It was a divine discovery and unveiling of the potencies of the word, of its mysterious revealing and creative capacity, not the word of the logical and reasoning or the aesthetic intelligence, but the intuitive and inspired rhythmic utterance, the *mantra*. Image and myth were freely used, not as an imaginative indulgence, but as living parables and symbols of things that were very real to their speakers and could not otherwise find their own intimate and native shape in utterance, and the imagination itself was a priest of greater realities than those that meet and hold the eye and mind limited by the external suggestions of life and the physical existence. This was their idea of the sacred poet,—a mind visited by some highest light and its forms of idea and word, a seer and hearer of the Truth, *kavayah satyaśrutayaḥ*. The poets of the Vedic verse certainly did not regard their function as it is represented by modern scholars, they did not look on themselves as a sort of superior medicine-men and makers of hymn and incantation to a robust and barbarous tribe, but as seers and thinkers, *ṛṣi, dhīra*. These singers believed that they were in possession of a high, mystic and hidden truth, claimed to be the bearers of a speech acceptable to a divine knowledge, and expressly so speak of their utterances, as secret words which declare their whole significance only to the seer, *kavaye nivacanāni ninyā vacāṁsi*. And to those who came after them the Veda was a book of knowledge, and even of the supreme knowledge, a revelation, a great utterance of eternal and impersonal truth as it had been seen and heard in the inner experience of inspired and semi-divine thinkers. The smallest circumstances of the sacrifice around which the hymns were written were intended to carry a symbolic and psychological power of significance, as was well known to the writers of the ancient Brahmanas. The sacred verses, each by itself held to be full of a divine meaning, were taken by the thinkers of the Upanishads as the profound and pregnant seed-words of the truth they sought and the highest authority they could give for their own sublime utterances was a supporting citation from their predecessors with the formula *tad eṣā ṛicābhyuktā*, "This is that word which was spoken by the Rig Veda.' Western scholars choose to imagine that the successors of the Vedic Rishis were in error, that, except for some later hymns, they put a false and non-existent meaning into the old verses and that they themselves divided from the Rishis not only by ages of time but by many gulfs and separating seas of an intellectualised mentality know infinitely better. But mere common sense ought to tell us that those who were so much nearer in both ways to the original poets had a better chance of holding at least the essential truth of the matter and suggests at least the strong probability that the Veda was really what it professes to be, the seeking for a mystic knowledge, the first form of the constant attempt of the Indian mind, to which it has always been faithful, to look beyond the appearances of the physical world and through its own inner experiences to the godheads, powers, self-existence of the One of whom the sages speak variously—the famous phrase in which the Veda utters its own central secret, *ekam sad viprā bahudhā vadanti.*

The real character of the Veda can best be understood by taking it anywhere and rendering it straightforwardly according to its own phrases and images. A famous German scholar rating from his high pedestal of superior intelligence the silly persons who find sublimity in the Veda, tells us that it is full of childish, silly, even monstrous conceptions, that it is tedious, low, commonplace, that it represents human nature on a low level of selfishness and worldliness and that only here and there are a few rare sentiments that come from the depths of the soul. It may be made so if we put our own mental conceptions into the words of the Rishis, but if we read them as they are without any such false translation into what we think early barbarians ought to have said and thought, we shall find instead a sacred poetry sublime and powerful in its words and images, though with another kind of language and imagination than we now prefer and appreciate, deep and subtle in its psychological experience and stirred by a moved soul of vision and utterance. Hear rather the word itself of the Veda:

"States upon states are born, covering over covering* awakens to knowledge: in the lap of the mother he wholly sees. They have called to him, getting a wide knowledge, they guard sleeplessly the strength,

* Or, "the coverer of the coverer."

they have entered into the strong city. The peoples born on earth increase the luminous (force) of the son of the White Mother; he has gold on his neck, he is large of speech, he is as if by (the power of) this honey wine a seeker of plenty. He is like pleasant and desirable milk, he is a thing uncompanioned and is with the two who are companions and is as a heat that is the belly of plenty and is invincible and an overcomer of many. Play, O Ray, and manifest thyself." * (Rig Veda V. 19.)

Or again in the succeeding hymn,—

"Those (flames) of thee, the forceful (godhead), that move not and are increased and puissant, uncling the hostility and crookedness of one who has another law. O Fire, we choose thee for our priest and the means of effectuation of our strength and in the sacrifices bringing the food of thy pleasure we call thee by the word . . . O god of perfect works, may we be for the felicity, for the truth, revelling with the rays, revelling with the heroes."

And finally let us take the bulk of the third hymn that follows couched in the ordinary symbols of the sacrifice,—

"As the Manu we set thee in thy place, as the Manu we kindle thee: O Fire, O Angiras, as the Manu sacrifice to the gods for him who desires the godheads. O Fire, well pleased thou art kindled in the human being and the ladles go to thee continually . . . Thee all the gods with one pleasure (in thee) made their messenger and serving thee, O seer, (men) in the sacrifices adore the god. Let the mortal adore the divine Fire with sacrifice to the godheads. Kindled, flame forth, O Bright One. Sit in the seat of Truth, sit in the seat of peace." †

* Literally, "become towards us."

† I have translated these passages with as close a literalness as the English language will admit. Let the reader compare the original and judge whether this is not the sense of the verses.

That, whatever interpretation we choose to put on its images, is a mystic and symbolic poetry and that is the real Veda.

The character of Vedic poetry apparent from these typical verses need not surprise or baffle us when we see what will be evident from a comparative study of Asiatic literature, that though distinguished by its theory and treatment of the Word, its peculiar system of images and the complexity of its thought and symbolised experience, it is in fact the beginning of a form of symbolic or figurative imagery for the poetic expression of spiritual experience which reappears constantly in later Indian writing, the figures of the Tantras and Puranas, the figures of the Vaishnava poets,—one might add even a certain element in the modern poetry of Tagore,—and has its kindred movements in certain Chinese poets and in the images of the Sufis. The poet has to express a spiritual and psychical knowledge and experience and he cannot do it altogether or mainly in the more abstract language of the philosophical thinker, for he has to bring out, not the naked idea of it, but as vividly as possible its very life and most intimate touches. He has to reveal in one way or another a whole world within him and the quite inner and spiritual significances of the world around him and also, it may well be, godheads, powers, visions and experiences of planes of consciousness other than the one with which our normal minds are familiar. He uses or starts with the images taken from his own normal and outward life and that of humanity and from visible Nature, and though they do not of themselves actually express, yet obliges them to express by implication or to figure the spiritual and psychic idea and experience. He takes them selecting freely his notation of images according to his insight or imagination and transmutes them into instruments of another significance and at the same time pours a direct spiritual meaning into the Nature and life to which they belong, applies outward figures to inner things and brings out their latent and inner spiritual or psychic significance into life's outward figures and circumstances. Or an outward figure nearest to the inward experience, its material counterpart, is taken throughout and used with such realism and consistency that while it indicates to those who possess it the spiritual experience, it means only the external thing to others,—just as the Vaishnava poetry of Bengal makes to the devout mind a physical and emotional image or suggestion of the love of the human soul for God, but to the profane is nothing but a sensuous and passionate love poetry hung conventionally round the traditional human-divine personalities of Krishna and Radha. The two methods may meet together, the fixed system of outward images be used as the body of the poetry, while freedom is often taken to pass their first limits, to treat them only as initial suggestions and transmute subtly or even cast them aside or subdue into a secondary strain or carry them out of themselves so that the translucent veil they offer to our minds lifts from or passes into the open revelation. The last is the method of the Veda and it varies according to the passion and stress of the sight in the poet or the exaltation of his utterance.

The poets of the Veda had another mentality than ours, their use of their images is of a peculiar kind and an antique cast of vision gives a strange outline to their substance. The physical and the psychical worlds were to their eyes a manifestation and a twofold and diverse and yet connected and similar figure of cosmic godheads, the inner and outer life of man a divine commerce with the gods, and behind was the one Spirit or Being of which the gods were names and personalities and powers. These godheads were at once masters of physical Nature and its principles and forms, their godheads and their bodies and inward divine powers with their corresponding states and energies born in our psychic being because they are the soul powers of the cosmos, the guardians of truth and immortality, the children of the Infinite, and each of them too is in his origin and his last reality the supreme Spirit putting in front one of his aspects. The life of man was to these seers a thing of mixed truth and falsehood, a movement from mortality to immortality, from mixed light and darkness to the splendour of a divine Truth whose home is above in the Infinite but which can be built up here in man's soul and life, a battle between the children of Light and the sons of Night, a getting of treasure, of the wealth, the booty given by the gods to the human warrior, and a journey and a sacrifice; and of these things they spoke in a fixed system of images taken from Nature and from the surrounding life of the war like, pastoral and agricultural Aryan peoples and centred round the cult of Fire and the worship of the powers of living Nature and the institution of sacrifice. The details of outward existence and of the sacrifice were in their life and practice symbols, and in their poetry not dead symbols or artificial metaphors, but living and powerful suggestions and counterparts of inner things. And they used too for their expression a fixed and yet variable body of other images and a glowing web of myth and parable, images that became parables, parables that became myths and myths that remained always images, and yet all these things were to them, in a way that can only be understood by those who have entered into a certain order of psychic experience, actual realities. The physical melted its shades into the lustres of the psychic, the psychic deepened into the light of the spiritual and there was no sharp dividing line in the transition, but a natural blending and intershading of their suggestions and colours. It is evident that a poetry of this kind, written by men with this kind of vision or imagination, cannot either be interpreted or judged by the standards of a reason and taste observant only of the canons of the physical existence. The invocation "Play, O Ray, and become towards us" is at once a suggestion of the leaping up and radiant play of the potent sacrificial flame on the physical altar and of a similar psychical phenomenon, the manifestation of the saving flame of a divine power and light within us. The western critic sneers at the bold and reckless and to him monstrous image in which Indra son of earth and heaven is said to create his own father and mother; but if we remember that Indra is the supreme spirit in one of its eternal and constant aspects, creator of earth and heaven, born as a cosmic godhead between the mental and physical worlds and recreating their powers in man, we shall see that the image is not only a powerful but in fact a true and revealing figure, and in the Vedic technique it does not matter that it outrages the physical imagination since it expresses a greater actuality as no other figure could have done with the same awakening aptness and vivid poetical force. The Bull and Cow of the Veda, the shining herds of the Sun lying hidden in the cave are strange enough creatures to the physical mind, but they do not belong to the earth and in their own plane they are at once images and actual things and full of life and significance. It is in this way that throughout we must interpret and receive the Vedic poetry according to its own spirit and vision and the psychically natural, even if to us strange and supranatural, truth of its ideas and figures.

The Veda thus understood stands out, apart from its interest as the world's first yet extant Scripture, its earliest interpretation of man and the Divine and the universe, as a remarkable, a sublime and powerful poetic creation. It is in its form and speech no barbaric production. The Vedic poets are masters of a consummate technique, their rhythms are carved like chariots of the gods and borne on divine and ample wings of sound, and are at once concentrated and wide-waved, great in movement and subtle in modulation, their speech lyric by intensity and epic by elevation an utterance of great power, pure and bold and grand in outline, a speech direct and brief in impact, full to overflowing in sense and suggestion so that each verse exists at once as a strong and sufficient thing in itself and takes its place as a large step between what came before and what comes after. A sacred and hieratic tradition faithfully followed gave them both their form and substance, but this substance consisted of the deepest psychic and spiritual experiences of which the human soul is capable and the forms seldom or never degenerate into a convention, because what they are intended to convey was lived in himself by each poet and made new to his own mind in expression by the subtleties or sublimities of his individual vision. The utterances of the greatest seers, Viswamitra, Vamadeva, Dirghatamas and many others, touch the most extraordinary heights and amplitudes of a sublime and mystic poetry and there are poems like the Hymn of Creation that move in a powerful clarity on the summits of thought on which the Upanishads lived constantly with a more sustained breathing. The mind of ancient India did not err when it traced back all its philosophy, religion and essential things of its culture to these seer-poets, for all the future spirituality of her people is contained there in seed or in first expression.

It is one great importance of a right understanding of the Vedic hymns as a form of sacred literature that it helps us to see the original shaping not only of the master ideas that governed the mind of India, but of its characteristic types of spiritual experience, its turn of imagination, its creative temperament and the kind of significant forms in which it persistently interpreted its sight of self and things and life and the universe. It is in a great part of the literature the same turn of inspiration and self-expression that we see in the architecture, painting and sculpture. Its first character is a constant sense of the infinite, the cosmic, and of things as seen in or affected by the cosmic vision, set in or against the amplitude of the one and infinite; its second peculiarity is a tendency to see and render its spiritual experience in a great richness of images taken from the inner psychic plane or in physical images transmuted by the stress of a psychic significance and impression and line and idea colour; and its third tendency is to image the terrestrial life often magnified, as in the Mahabharata and Ramayana, or else subtilised in the transparencies of a larger atmosphere, attended by a greater than the terrestrial meaning or at any rate presented against the background of the spiritual and psychic worlds and not alone in its own separate figure. The spiritual, the infinite is near and real and the gods are real and the worlds beyond not so much beyond as immanent in our own existence. That which to the western mind is myth and imagination is here an actuality and a strand of the life of our inner being, what is there beautiful poetic idea and philosophic speculation is here a thing constantly realised and present to the experience. It is this turn of the Indian mind, its spiritual sincerity and psychic positivism, that makes the Veda and Upanishads and the later religious and religio-philosophic poetry so powerful in inspiration and intimate and living in expression and image, and it has its less absorbing but still very sensible effect on the working of the poetic idea and imagination even in the more secular literature.

A DEFENCE OF INDIAN CULTURE

CHAPTER XI

INDIAN LITERATURE

THE Upanishads are the supreme work of the Indian mind, and that it should be so, that the highest self-expression of its genius, its sublimest poetry, its greatest creation of the thought and word should be not a literary or poetical masterpiece of the ordinary kind, but a large flood of spiritual revelation of this direct and profound character, is a significant fact, evidence of a unique mentality and unusual turn of spirit. The Upanishads are at once profound religious scriptures,—for they are a record of the deepest spiritual experiences,—documents of revelatory and intuitive philosophy of an inexhaustible light, power and largeness and, whether written in verse or cadenced prose, spiritual poems of an absolute, an unfailing inspiration inevitable in phrase, wonderful in rhythm and expression. It is the expression of a mind in which philosophy and religion and poetry are made one, because this religion does not end with a cult nor is limited to a religio-ethical aspiration, but rises to an infinite discovery of God, of Self, of our highest and whole reality of spirit and being and speaks out of an ecstasy of luminous knowledge and an ecstasy of moved and fulfilled experience, this philosophy is not an abstract intellectual speculation about Truth or a structure of the logical intelligence, but Truth seen, felt, lived, held by the inmost mind and soul in the joy of utterance of an assured discovery and possession, and this poetry is the work of the aesthetic mind lifted up beyond its ordinary field to express the wonder and beauty of the rarest spiritual self-vision and the profoundest illumined truth of self and God and universe. Here the intuitive mind and intimate psychological experience of the Vedic seers passes into a supreme culmination in which the Spirit, as is said in a phrase of the Katha Upanishad, discloses its own very body, reveals the very word of its self-expression and discovers to the mind the vibration of rhythms which repeating themselves within in the spiritual hearing seem to build up the soul and set it satisfied and complete on the heights of self-knowledge.

This character of the Upanishads needs to be insisted upon with a strong emphasis, because it is ignored by foreign translators who seek to bring out the intellectual sense without feeling the life of thought vision and the ecstasy of spiritual experience which made the ancient verses appear then and still make them to those who can enter into the element in which these utterances move, a revelation not to the intellect alone, but to the soul and the whole being, make of them in the old expressive word not intellectual thought and phrase, but *Sruti*, spiritual audience, an inspired Scripture. The philosophical substance of the Upanishads demands at this day no farther stress of appreciation of its value; for even if the amplest acknowledgement by the greatest minds were wanting, the whole history of philosophy would be there to offer its evidence. The Upanishads have been the acknowledged source of numerous profound philosophies and religions that flowed from it in India like her great rivers from their Himalayan cradle fertilising the mind and life of the people and kept its soul alive through the long procession of the centuries, constantly returned to for light, never failing to give fresh illumination, a fountain of inexhaustible life-giving waters. Buddhism with all its developments was only a restatement, although from a new standpoint and with fresh terms of intellectual definition and reasoning, of one side of its experience and it carried it thus changed in form but hardly in substance over all Asia and westward towards Europe. The ideas of the Upanishads can be rediscovered in much of the thought of Pythagoras and Plato and form the profoundest part of Neo-platonism and Gnosticism with all their considerable consequences to the philosophical thinking of the West, and Sufism only repeats them in another religious language. The larger part of German metaphysics is little more in substance than an intellectual development of great realities more spiritually seen in this ancient teaching, and modern thought is rapidly absorbing them with a closer, more living and intense receptiveness which promises a revolution both in philosophical and in religious thinking; here they are filtering in through many indirect influences, there slowly pouring through direct and open channels. There is hardly a main philosophical idea which cannot find an authority or a seed or indication in these antique writings—the speculations, according to a certain view, of thinkers who had no better past or background to their thought than a crude, barbaric, naturalistic and animistic ignorance. And even the larger generalisations of Science are constantly found to apply to the truth of physical Nature formulas already discovered by the Indian sages in their original, their largest meaning in the deeper truth of the spirit.

And yet these works are not philosophical speculations of the intellectual kind, a metaphysical analysis which labours to define notions, to select ideas and discriminate those that are true, to logicise truth or else to support the mind in its intellectual preferences by dialectical reasoning and is content to put forward an exclusive solution of existence in the light of this or that idea of the reason and see all things from that viewpoint, in that focus and determining perspective. The Upanishads could not have had so undying a vitality, exercised so unfailing an influence, produced such results or seen now their affirmations independently justified in other spheres of inquiry and by quite opposite methods, if they had been of that character. It is because these seers saw Truth rather than merely thought it, clothed it indeed with a strong body of intuitive idea and disclosing image, but a body of ideal transparency through which we look into the illimitable, because they fathomed things in the light of self-existence and saw them with the eye of the Infinite, that their words remain always alive and immortal, of an inexhaustible significance, an inevitable authenticity, a satisfying finality that is at the same time an infinite commencement of truth, to which all our lines of investigation when they go through to their end arrive again and to which humanity constantly returns in its minds and its ages of greatest vision. The Upanishads are Vedanta, a book of knowledge in a higher degree even than the Vedas, but knowledge in the profounder Indian sense of the word, *Jñāna.* Not a mere thinking and considering by the intelligence, the pursuit and grasping of a mental form of truth by the intellectual mind, but a seeing of it with the soul and a total living in it with the power of the inner being, a spir itual seizing by a kind of identification with the object of know edge is *Jñāna.* And because it is only by an integral knowing o the self that this kind of direct knowledge can be made com plete, it was the self that the Vedantic sages sought to know, live in and to be one with it by identity. And through this e deavour they came easily to see that the self in us is one with t universal self of all things and that this self again is the same God and Brahman, a transcendent Being or Existence, and th beheld, felt, lived in the inmost truth of all things in the u verse and the inmost truth of man's inner and outer existence the light of this one and unifying vision. The Upanishads epic hymns of self-knowledge and world-knowledge and G knowledge. The great formulations of philosophic truth which they abound are not abstract intellectual generalisat things that may shine and enlighten the mind, but do not live and move the soul to ascension, but are ardours as well as lights of an intuitive and revelatory illumination, reachings as well as seeings of the one Existence, the transcendent Godhead, the divine and universal Self and discoveries of his relation with things and creatures in this great cosmic manifestation. Chants of inspired knowledge, they breathe like all hymns a tone of religious aspiration and ecstasy, not of the narrowly intense kind, proper to a lesser religious feeling but raised beyond cult and special forms of devotion to the universal Ananda of the Divine which comes to us by approach to and oneness with the self-existent and universal spirit. And though mainly concerned with an inner vision and not directly with outward human action, all the highest ethics of Buddhism and later Hinduism are still emergences of the very life and significance of the truths to which they give expressive form and force,—and there is something greater than any ethical precept and mental rule of virtue, the supreme ideal of a spiritual action founded on oneness with God and all living beings. Therefore even when the life of the forms of the Vedic cult had passed away, the Upanishads still remained alive and creative and could generate the great devotional religions and motive the persistent Indian idea of the Dharma.

The Upanishads are the creation of a revelatory and intuitive mind and its illumined experience, and all their substance, structure, phrase, imagery, movement are determined by and stamped with this original character. These supreme and all-embracing truths, these visions of oneness and self and a universal divine being are cast into brief and monumental phrases which bring them at once before the soul's eye and make them real and imperative to its aspiration and experience or are couched in poetic sentences full of revealing power and suggestive thought-colour that discover a whole infinite through a finite image. The One is there revealed, but also disclosed the many aspects, and each is given its whole significance by the amplitude of the expression and finds as if in a spontaneous self-discovery its place and its connection by the illumining justness of each word and all the phrase. The largest metaphysical truths and the subtlest subtleties of psychological experience are taken up into the inspired movement and made at once precise to the seeing mind and loaded with unending suggestion to the discovering spirit. There are separate phrases, single couplets, brief passages which contain each in itself the substance of a vast philosophy and yet each is only thrown out as a side, an aspect, a portion of the infinite self-knowledge. All here is a packed and pregnant and yet perfectly lucid and luminous brevity and an immeasurable completeness. A thought of this kind cannot follow the tardy, careful and diffuse development of the logical intelligence. The passage, the sentence, the couplet, the line, even the half line follows the one that precedes with a certain interval full of an unexpressed thought, an echoing silence between them, a thought which is carried in the total suggestion and implied in the step itself, but which the mind is left to work out for its own profit, and these intervals of pregnant silence are large, the steps of this thought are like the paces of a Titan striding from rock to distant rock across infinite waters. There is a perfect totality, a comprehensive connection of harmonious parts in the structure of each Upanishad; but it is done in the way of a mind that sees masses of truth at a time and stops to bring only the needed word out of a filled silence. The rhythm in verse or cadenced prose corresponds to the sculpture of the thought and the phrase. The metrical forms of the Upanishads are made up of four half lines each clearly cut, the lines mostly complete in themselves and integral in sense, the half lines presenting two thoughts or distinct parts of a thought that are wedded to and complete each other, and the sound movement follows a corresponding principle, each step brief and marked off by the distinctness of its pause, full of echoing cadences that remain long vibrating in the inner hearing: each is as if a wave of the infinite that carries in it the whole voice and rumour of the ocean. It is a kind of poetry,—word of vision, rhythm of the spirit,—that has not been written before or after.

The imagery of the Upanishads is in large part developed from the type of imagery of the Veda and though very ordinarily it prefers an unveiled clarity of directly illuminative image, not unoften also it uses the same symbols in a way that is closely akin to the spirit and to the less technical part of the method of the older symbolism. It is to a great extent this element no longer seizable by our way of thinking that has baffled certain western scholars and made them cry out that these scriptures are a mixture of the sublimest philosophical speculations with the first awkward stammerings of the child mind of humanity. The Upanishads are not a revolutionary departure from the Vedic mind and its temperament and fundamental ideas, but a continuation and development and to a certain extent an enlarging transformation in the sense of bringing out into open expression all that was held covered in the symbolic Vedic speech as a mystery and a secret. It begins by taking up the imagery and the ritual symbols of the Veda and the Brahmanas and turning them in such a way as to bring out an inner and a mystic sense which will serve as a sort of psychical starting-point for its own more highly evolved and more purely spiritual philosophy. There are a number of passages especially in the prose Upanishads which are entirely of this kind and deal, in a manner recondite, obscure and even unintelligible to the modern understanding, with the psychic sense of ideas then current in the Vedic religious mind, the distinction between the three kinds of Veda, the three worlds and other similar subjects; but, leading as they do in the thought of the Upanishads to deepest spiritual truths, these passages cannot be dismissed as childish aberrations of the intelligence void of sense or of any discoverable bearing on the higher thought in which they culminate. On the contrary we find that they have a deep enough significance once we can get inside their symbolic meaning. That appears in a psycho-physical passing upward into a psycho-spiritual knowledge for which we would now use more intellectual, less concrete and imaged terms, but which is still valid for those who practise Yoga and rediscover the secrets of our psycho-physical and psycho-spiritual being. Typical passages of this kind of peculiar expression of psychic truths are Ajatashatru's explanation of sleep and dream or the passages of the Prasna Upanishad on the vital principle and its motions, or those in which the Vedic idea of the struggle between the Gods and the demons is taken up and given its spiritual significance and the Vedic godheads more openly than in Rik and Saman characterised and invoked in their inner function and spiritual power.

I may cite as an example of this development of Vedic idea and image a passage of the Taittiriya in which Indra plainly appears as the power and godhead of the divine mind:

> "He who is the Bull of the Vedas of the universal form, he who was born in the sacred rhythms from the Immortal,—may Indra satisfy me through the intelligence. O God, may I become a vessel of the Immortal. May my body be full of vision and my tongue of sweetness, may I hear the much and vast with my ears. For thou art the sheath of Brahman covered over and hidden by the intelligence."

And a kindred passage may also be cited from the Isha in which Surya the Sun-God is invoked as the godhead of knowledge whose supreme form of effulgence is the oneness of the Spirit and his rays dispersed here on the mental level are the shining diffusion of the thought mind and conceal his own infinite supramental truth, the body and self of this Sun, the truth of the spirit and the Eternal:

> "The face of the Truth is covered with a golden lid: O fostering Sun, that uncover for the law of the truth, for sight. O fosterer, O

sole Rishi, O controlling Yama, O Surya, O son of the Father of creatures, marshal and mass thy rays: the Lustre that is thy most blessed form of all, that I see, He who is this, this Purusha, He am I."

The kinship in difference of these passages with the imagery and style of the Veda is evident and the last indeed paraphrases or translates into a later and more open style a Vedic verse of the Atris:

"Hidden by your truth is the Truth that is constant for ever where they unyoke the horses of the Sun. There the ten thousands stand together, That is the One: I have seen the supreme Godhead of the embodied gods."

This Vedic and Vedantic imagery is foreign to our present mentality which does not believe in the living truth of the symbol, because the revealing imagination intimidated by the intellect has no longer the courage to accept, identify itself with and boldly embody a psychic and spiritual vision; but it is certainly very far from being a childish or a primitive and barbarous mysticism; this vivid, living, luminously poetic intuitive language is rather the natural expression of a highly evolved spiritual culture.

The intuitive thought of the Upanishads starts from this concrete imagery and these symbols, first to the Vedic Rishis secret seer words wholly expressive to the mind of the seer but veils of their deepest sense to the ordinary intelligence, link them to a less covertly expressive language and pass beyond them to another magnificently open and sublime imagery and diction which at once reveals the spiritual truth in all its splendour. The prose Upanishads show us this process of the early mind of India at its work using the symbol and then passing beyond it to the overt expression of the spiritual significance. A passage of the Prasna Upanishad on the power and significance of the mystic syllable AUM illustrates the earlier stage of the process:

"This syllable OM, O Satyakama, it is the supreme and it is the lower Brahman. Therefore the man of knowledge passes by this house of the Brahman to the one or the other. And if one meditates on the single letter, he gets by it knowledge and soon he attains on the earth. And him the Riks lead to the world of men and there perfected in Tapas and Brahmacharya and faith he experiences the greatness of the spirit. Now if by the double letter he is accomplished in the mind, then is he led up by the Yajus to the middle world, to the moon-world of Soma. He in the world of Soma experiences the majesty of the spirit and returns again. And he who by the triple letter again, even this syllable OM, shall meditate on the highest Purusha, is perfected in the light that is the Sun. As a snake puts off its skin, even so is he released from sin and evil and is led by the Samans to the world of Brahman. He from this dense of living souls sees the higher than the highest Purusha who lies in this mansion. The three letters are afflicted by death, but now they are used undivided and united to each other, then are the inner and the outer and the middle action of the spirit made whole in their perfect using and the spirit knows and is not shaken. This world by the Riks, the middle world by the Yajus and by the Samans that which the seers make known to us. The man of knowledge passes to Him by OM, his house, even to the supreme spirit that is calm and ageless and fearless and immortal."

The symbols here are still obscure to our intelligence, but indications are given which show beyond doubt that they are representations of a psychical experience leading to different states of spiritual realisation and we can see that these are three outward, mental and supramental, and as the result of the last a supreme perfection, a complete and integral action of the whole being in the tranquil eternity of the immortal Spirit. And later in the Mandukya Upanishad the other symbols are cast aside and we are admitted to the unveiled significance. Then there emerges a knowledge to which modern thought is returning through its own very different intellectual, rational and scientific method, the knowledge that behind the operations of our outward physical consciousness are working the operations of another, subliminal,—another and yet the same,—of which our waking mind is a surface action, and above—perhaps, we still say—is a spiritual superconscience in which can be found, it may well be, the highest state and the whole secret of our being. We shall see, when we look closely at the passage of the Prasna Upanishad, that this knowledge is already there, and I think we can very rationally conclude that these and similar utterances of the ancient sages, however perplexing their form to the rational mind, cannot be dismissed as a childish mysticism, but are the imaged expression, natural to the mentality of the time, of what the reason itself by its own processes is now showing us to be true and a very profound truth and real reality of knowledge.

The metrical Upanishads continue this highly charged symbolism but carry it more lightly and in the bulk of their verses pass beyond this kind of image to the overt expression. The Self, the Spirit, the Godhead in man and creatures and Nature and all this world and in other worlds and beyond all cosmos, the Immortal, the One, the Infinite is hymned without veils in the splendour of his eternal transcendence and his manifold self-revelation. A few passages from the teachings of Yama, lord of the Law and of Death, to Nachiketas, will be enough to illustrate something of their character:

"Om is this syllable. This syllable is the Brahman, this syllable is the Supreme. He who knows the imperishable Om, whatso he wills, it is his. This support is the best, this support is the highest; and when a man knows it, he is greatened in the world of Brahman. The omniscient is not born, nor dies, nor has he come into being from anywhere, nor is he anyone. He is unborn, he is constant and eternal, he is the Ancient of Days who is not slain in the slaying of the body . . .

He is seated and journeys far, and lying still he goes to every side. Who other than I should know this ecstatic Godhead? The wise man comes to know the great Lord and Self established and bodiless in these bodies that pass and has grief no longer. This self is not to be won by teaching nor by brain-power nor by much learning: he whom the Spirit chooses, by him alone it can be won, and to him this Spirit discloses its own very body. One who has not ceased from ill-doing, one who is not concentrated and calm, one whose mind is not tranquil, shall not get him by the brain's wisdom. He of whom warriors and sages are the food and death is the spice of his banquet, who knows where is He? . . .

The Self-born has cloven his doors outward, therefore man sees outward and not in the inner self: only a wise man here and there turns his eyes inward, desiring immortality, and looks on the Self face to face. The child minds follow after surface desires and fall into the net of death which is spread wide for us; but the wise know of immortality and ask not from things inconstant that which is constant. One knows by this Self form and taste and odour and touch and its pleasures and what then is here left over? The wise man comes to know the great Lord and Self by whom one sees all that is in the soul that wakes and all that is in the soul that dreams and has grief no longer. He who knows the Self, the eater of sweetness close to the living being, the lord of what was and what will be, shrinks thereafter from nothing that is. He knows him who is that which was born of old from Tapas and who was born of old from the waters and has entered in and stands in the secret cavern of being with all these creatures. He knows her who is born by the life force, the infinite Mother with all the gods in her, her who has entered in and stands in the secret cavern of being with all these creatures. This is the Fire that has the knowledge and it is hidden in the two tinders as the embryo is borne in pregnant women; this is the Fire that must be adored by men watching sleeplessly and bringing to him the offering. He is that from which the Sun rises and that in which it sets: and in him all the gods are founded and none can pass beyond him. What is here, even that is in other worlds, and what is there, even according to that is all that is here. He goes from death to death who sees here only difference. A Purusha no bigger than a thumb stands in man's central self and is the lord of what was and what shall be, and knowing him thenceforth one shrinks from nothing that is. A Purusha no bigger than a man's thumb and he is like a light without smoke; he is the Lord of what was and what shall be; it is he that is today and it is he that shall be tomorrow."

The Upanishads abound with passages which are at once poetry and spiritual philosophy, of an absolute clarity and beauty, but no translation empty of the suggestions and the grave and subtle and luminous sense echoes of the original words and rhythms can give any idea of their power and perfection. There are others in which the subtlest psychological and philosophical truths are expressed with an entire sufficiency without falling short of a perfect beauty of poetical expression and always so as to live to the mind and soul and not merely be presented to the understanding intelligence. There is in some of the prose Upanishads another element of vivid narrative and tradition which restores for us though only in brief glimpses the picture of that extraordinary stir and movement of spiritual enquiry and passion for the highest knowledge which made the Upanishads possible. The scenes of the old world live before us in a few pages, the sages sitting in their groves ready to test and teach the comer, princes and learned Brahmins and great landed nobles going about in search of knowledge, the king's son in his chariot and the illegitimate son of the servant-girl, seeking any man who might carry in himself the thought of light and the word of revelation, the typical figures and personalities, Janaka and the subtle mind of Ajatashatru, Raikwa of the cart, Yajnavalkya militant for truth, calm and ironic, taking to himself with both hands without attachment worldly possessions and spiritual riches and casting at last all his wealth behind to wander forth as a houseless ascetic, Krishna son of Devaki who heard a single word of the Rishi Ghora and knew at once the Eternal, the Ashramas, the courts of kings who were also spiritual discoverers and thinkers, the great sacrificial assemblies where the sages met and compared their knowledge. And we see how the soul of India was born and how arose this great birth-song in which it soared from its earth into the supreme empyrean of the spirit. The Vedas and the Upanishads are not only the sufficient fountain-head of Indian philosophy and religion, but of all Indian art, poetry and literature. It was the soul, the temperament, the ideal mind formed and expressed in them which later carved out the great philosophies, built the structure of the Dharma, recorded its heroic youth in the Mahabharata and Ramayana, intellectualised indefatigably in the classical times of the ripeness of its manhood, threw out so many original intuitions in science, created so rich a glow of aesthetic and vital and sensuous experience, renewed its spiritual and psychic experience in Tantra and Purana, flung itself into grandeur and beauty of line and colour, hewed and cast its thought and vision in stone and bronze, poured itself into new channels of self-expression in the later tongues and now after eclipse re-emerges always the same in difference and ready for a new life and a new creation.

A DEFENCE OF INDIAN CULTURE

CHAPTER XII

INDIAN LITERATURE

THE Veda is thus the spiritual and psychological seed of Indian culture and the Upanishads the expression of the truth of highest spiritual knowledge and experience that has always been the supreme idea of that culture and the ultimate objective to which it directed the life of the individual and the aspiration of the soul of the people: and these two great bodies of sacred writing, its first great efforts of poetic and creative self-expression, coming into being at a time preceding the later strong and ample and afterwards rich and curious intellectual development, are conceived and couched in the language of a purely psychic and spiritual mentality. An evolution so begun had to proceed by a sort of enriching descent from the spirit to matter and to pass on first to an intellectual endeavour to see life and the world and the self in all their relations as they present themselves to the reasoning and the practical intelligence. The earlier movement of this intellectual effort was naturally accompanied by a practical development and organisation of life consciously expressive of the mind and spirit of the people, the erection of a strong and successful structure of society shaped so as to fulfil the mundane objects of human existence under the control of a careful religious, ethical and social order and discipline, but also so as to provide for the evolution of the soul of man through these things to a spiritual freedom and perfection. It is this stage of which we get a remarkably ample and effective representation in the immediately succeeding period of Indian literary creation.

This movement of the Indian mind is represented in its more critical effort on one side by a strenuous philosophical thinking crystallised into the great philosophic systems, on the other by an equally insistent endeavour to formulate in a clear body and with a strict cogency an ethical, social and political ideal and practice in a consistent and organised system of individual and communal life and that endeavour resulted in the authoritative social treatises or Shastras of which the greatest and the most authoritative is the famous Laws of Manu. The work of the philosophers was to systematise and justify to the reasoning intelligence the truths of the self and man and the world already discovered by intuition, revelation and spiritual experience and embodied in the Veda and the Upanishads, and at the same time to indicate and systematise methods of discipline founded upon this knowledge by which man might effectuate the highest aim of his existence. The characteristic form in which this was done shows the action of the intuitive passing into that of the intellectual mentality and preserves the stamp and form expressive of its transitional character. The terse and pregnant phrase of the sacred literature abounding in intuitive substance is replaced by a still more compact and crowded brief expression, no longer intuitive and poetic, but severely intellectual,—the expression of a principle, a whole development of philosophic thought or a logical step burdened with considerable consequences in a few words, sometimes one or two, a shortest decisive formula often almost enigmatic in its concentrated fullness. These Sutras or aphorisms became the basis of ratiocinative commentaries developing by metaphysical and logical method and with a considerable variety of interpretation all that was contained at first in the series of aphoristic formulas. Their concern is solely with original and ultimate truth and the method of spiritual liberation, *mokṣa.*

The work of the social thinkers and legislators was on the contrary concerned with normal action and practice. It attempted to take up the ordinary life of man and of the community and the life of human desire and aim and interest and ordered rule and custom and to interpret and formulate it in the same complete and decisive manner and at the same time to throw the whole into an ordered relation to the ruling ideas of the national culture and frame and perpetuate a social system intelligently fashioned so as to provide a basis, a structure, a gradation by which there could be a secure evolution of the life from the vital and mental to the spiritual motive. The leading idea was the government of human interest and desire by the social and ethical law, the Dharma, so that it might be made,—all vital, economic, aesthetic, hedonistic, intellectual and other needs being satisfied duly and according to the right law of the nature,—a preparation for the spiritual existence. Here too we have as an initial form the aphoristic method of the Vedic Grihya-Sutras, afterwards the diffuser, fuller method of the Dharma Shastras,—the first satisfied with brief indications of simple and essential socio-religious principle and practice, the later work attempting to cover the whole life of the individual, the class and the people. The very character of the effort and its thoroughness and the constant unity of idea that reigns through the whole of it are a remarkable evidence of a very developed intellectual, aesthetic and ethical consciousness and a high turn and capacity for a noble and ordered civilisation and culture. The intelligence at work, the understanding and formative power manifested is not inferior to that of any ancient or modern people, and there is a gravity, a unified clarity and nobility of conception which balances at least in any true idea of culture the greater suppleness, more well-informed experience and science and eager flexibility of experimental hardihood which are the gains that distinguish our later humanity. At any rate it was no barbaric mind that was thus intently careful for a fine and well unified order of society, a high and clear thought to govern it and at the end of life a great spiritual perfection and release.

The pure literature of the period is represented by the two great epics, the Mahabharata, which gathered into its vast structure the greater part of the poetic activity of the Indian mind during several centuries, and the Ramayana. These two poems are epical in their motive and spirit, but they are not like any other two epics in the world, but are entirely of their own kind and subtly different from others in their principle. It is not only that although they contain an early heroic story and a transmutation of many primitive elements, their form belongs to a period of highly developed intellectual, ethical and social culture, is enriched with a body of mature thought and uplifted by a ripe nobility and refined gravity of ethical tone and therefore these poems are quite different from primitive edda and saga and greater in breadth of view and substance and height of motive—I do not speak now of aesthetic quality and poetic perfection—than the Homeric poems, while at the same time there is still an early breath, a direct and straightforward vigour, a freshness and greatness and pulse of life, a simplicity of strength and beauty that makes of them quite another kind than the elaborately constructed literary epics of Virgil or Milton, Firdausi or Kalidasa. This peculiar blending of the natural breath of an early, heroic, swift and vigorous force of life with a strong development and activity of the ethical, the intellectual, even the philosophic mind is indeed a remarkable feature; these poems are the voice of the youth of a people, but a youth not only fresh and fine and buoyant, but also great and accomplished, wise and noble. This however is only a temperamental distinction: there is another that is more far-reaching, a difference in the whole conception, function and structure.

One of the elements of the old Vedic education was a knowledge of significant tradition, *itihāsa,* and it is this word that was used by the ancient critics to distinguish the Mahabharata and the Ramayana from the later literary epics. The Itihasa was an ancient historical or legendary tradition turned to creative use as a significant mythus or tale expressive of some spiritual or religious or ethical or ideal meaning and thus formative of the mind of the people. The Mahabharata and Ramayana are Itihasas of this kind on a large scale and with a massive purpose. The poets who wrote and those who added to these great bodies of poetic writing did not intend merely to tell an ancient tale in a beautiful or noble manner or even to fashion a poem pregnant with much richness of interest and meaning, though they did both these things with a high success; they wrote with a sense of their function as architects and sculptors of life, creative exponents, fashioners of significant forms of the national thought and religion and ethics and culture. A profound stress of thought on life, a large and vital view of religion and society, a certain strain of philosophic idea runs through these poems and the whole ancient culture of India is embodied in them with a great force of intellectual conception and living presentation. The Mahabharata has been spoken of as a fifth Veda, it has been said of both these poems that they are not only great poems but dharmashastras, the body of a large religious and ethical and social and political teaching, and their effect and hold on the mind and life of the people have been so great that they have been described as the bible of the Indian people. That is not quite an accurate analogy, for the bible of the Indian people contains also the Veda and Upanishads, the Purana and Tantras and the Dharmashastras, not to speak of a large bulk of the religious poetry in the regional languages. The work of these epics was to popularise high philosophic and ethical idea and cultural practice; it was to throw out prominently and with a seizing relief and effect in a frame of great poetry and on a background of poetic story and around significant personalities that became to the people abiding national memories and representative figures all that was best in the soul and thought or true to the life or real to the creative imagination and ideal mind or characteristic and illuminative of the social, ethical, political and religious culture of India. All these things were brought together and disposed with artistic power and a telling effect in a poetic body given to traditions half legendary, half historic but cherished henceforth as deepest and most living truth and as a part of their religion by the people. Thus framed the Mahabharata and Ramayana, whether in the original Sanskrit or rewritten in the regional tongues, brought to the masses by Kathakas,—rhapsodists, reciters and exegetes,—became and remained one of the chief instruments of popular education and culture, moulded the thought, character, aesthetic and religious mind of the people and gave even to the illiterate some sufficient tincture of philosophy, ethics, social and political ideas, aesthetic emotion, poetry, fiction and romance. That which was for the cultured classes contained in Veda and Upanishad, shut into profound philosophical aphorism and treatise or inculcated in Dharma-shastra and Artha-shastra, was put here into creative and living figures, associated with familiar story and legend, fused into a vivid representation of life and thus made a near and living power that all could readily assimilate through the poetic word appealing at once to the soul and the imagination and the intelligence.

The Mahabharata especially is not only the story of the Bharatas, the epic of an early event which had become a national tradition but on a vast scale the epic of the soul and religious and ethical mind and social and political ideals and culture and life of India. It is said popularly of it and with a certain measure of truth that whatever is in India is in the Mahabharata. The Mahabharata is the creation and expression not of a single individual mind, but of the mind of a nation; it is the poem of itself written by a whole people. It would be vain to apply to it the canons of a poetical art applicable to an epic poem with a smaller and more restricted purpose, but still a great and quite conscious art has been expended both on its detail and its total structure. The whole poem has been built like a vast national temple unrolling slowly its immense and complex idea from chamber to chamber, crowded with significant groups and sculptures and inscriptions, the grouped figures carved in divine or semi-divine proportions, a humanity aggrandised and half uplifted to superhumanity and yet always true to the human motive and idea and feeling, the strain of the real constantly raised by the tones of the ideal, the life of this world amply portrayed but subjected to the conscious influence and presence of the powers of the worlds behind it, and the whole unified by the long embodied procession of a consistent idea worked out in the wide steps of the poetic story. As is needed in an epic narrative, the conduct of the story is the main interest of the poem and it is carried through with an at once large and minute movement, wide and bold in the mass, striking and effective in detail, always simple, strong and epic in its style and pace. At the same time though supremely interesting in substance and vivid in the manner of the telling as a poetic story, it is something more, —a significant tale, Itihasa, representative throughout of the central ideas and ideals of Indian life and culture. The leading motive is the Indian idea of the Dharma. Here the Vedic notion of the struggle between the godheads of truth and light and unity and the powers of darkness and division and falsehood is brought out from the spiritual and religious and internal into the outer intellectual, ethical and vital plane. It takes there in the figure of the story a double form of a personal and a political struggle, the personal a conflict between typical and representative personalities embodying the greater ethical ideals of the Indian Dharma and others who are embodiments of Asuric egoism and self-will and misuse of the Dharma, the political a battle in which the personal struggle culminates, an international clash ending in the establishment of a new rule of righteousness and justice, a kingdom or rather an empire of the Dharma uniting warring races and substituting for the ambitious arrogance of kings and aristocratic clans the supremacy, the calm and peace of a just and humane empire. It is the old struggle of Deva and Asura, God and Titan, but represented in the terms of human life.

The way in which this double form is worked out and the presentation of the movement of individual lives and of the national life first as their background and then as coming into the front in a movement of kingdoms and armies and nations show a high architectonic faculty akin in the sphere of poetry to that which laboured in Indian architecture, and the whole has been conducted with a large poetic art and vision. There is the same power to embrace great spaces in a total view and the same tendency to fill them with an abundance of minute, effective, vivid and significant detail. There is brought too into the frame of the narrative a very considerable element of other tales, legends, episodes, most of them of a significant character suitable to the method of Itihasa, and an extraordinary amount of philosophical, religious, ethical, social and political thinking sometimes direct, sometimes cast into the form of the legend and episode. The ideas of the Upanishads and of the great philosophies are brought in continually and sometimes given new developments, as in the Gita; religious myth and tale and idea and teaching are made part of the tissue; the ethical ideals of the race are expressed or are transmuted into the shape of tale and episode as well as embodied in the figures of the story, political and social ideals and institutions are similarly developed or illustrated with a high vividness and clearness and space is found too for aesthetic and other suggestions connected with the life of the people. All these things are interwoven into the epic narrative with a remarkable skill and closeness. The irregularities inevitable in so combined and difficult a plan and in a work to which many poets of an unequal power have contributed fall into their place in the general massive complexity of the scheme and assist rather than break the total impression. The whole is a poetic expression unique in its power and fullness of the entire soul and thought and life of a people.

The Ramayana is a work of the same essential kind as the Mahabharata; it differs only by a greater simplicity of plan, a more delicate ideal temperament and a finer glow of poetic warmth and colour. The main bulk of the poem in spite of much accretion is evidently by a single hand and has a less complex and more obvious unity of structure. There is less of the philosophic, more of the purely poetic mind, more of the artist, less of the builder. The whole story is from beginning to end of one piece and there is no deviation from the stream of the narrative. At the same time there is a like vastness of vision, an even more wide-winged flight of epic sublimity in the conception and sustained richness of minute execution in the detail. The structural power, strong workmanship and method of disposition of the Mahabharata remind one of the art of the Indian builders, the grandeur and boldness of outline and wealth of colour and minute decorative execution of the Ramayana suggest rather a transcript into literature of the spirit and style of Indian painting. The epic poet has taken here also as his subject an Itihasa, an ancient tale or legend associated with an old Indian dynasty and filled it in with detail from myth and folklore, but has exalted all into a scale of grandiose epic figure that it may bear more worthily the high intention and significance. The subject is the same as in the Mahabharata, the strife of the divine with the titanic forces in the life of the earth, but in more purely ideal forms, in frankly supernatural dimensions and an imaginative heightening of both the good and the evil in human character. On one side is portrayed an ideal manhood, a divine beauty of virtue and ethical order, a civilisation founded on the Dharma and realising an exaltation of the moral ideal which is presented with a singularly strong appeal of aesthetic grace and harmony and sweetness; on the other are wild and anarchic and almost amorphous forces of superhuman egoism and self-will and exultant violence, and the two ideas and powers of mental nature living and embodied are brought into conflict and led to a decisive issue of the victory of the divine man over the Rakshasa. All shade and complexity are omitted which would diminish the single purity of the idea, the representative force in the outline of the figures, the significance of the temperamental colour and only so much admitted as is sufficient to humanise the appeal and the significance. The poet makes us conscious of the immense forces that are behind our life and sets his action in a magnificent epic scenery, the great imperial city, the mountains and the ocean, the forest and wilderness, described with such a largeness as to make us feel as if the whole world were the scene of his poem and its subject the whole divine and titanic possibility of man imaged in a few great or monstrous figures. The ethical and the aesthetic mind of India have here fused themselves into a harmonious unity and reached an unexampled pure wideness and beauty of self-expression. The Ramayana embodied for the Indian imagination its highest and tenderest human ideals of character, made strength and courage and gentleness and purity and fidelity and self-sacrifice familiar to it in the suavest and most harmonious forms coloured so as to attract the emotion and the aesthetic sense, stripped morals of all repellent austerity on one side or on the other of mere commonness and lent a certain high divineness to the ordinary things of life, conjugal and filial and maternal and fraternal feeling, the duty of the prince and leader and the loyalty of follower and subject, the greatness of the great and the truth and worth of the simple, toning things ethical to the beauty of a more psychical meaning by the glow of its ideal hues. The work of Valmiki has been an agent of almost incalculable power in the moulding of the cultural mind of India: it has presented to it to be loved and imitated in figures like Rama and Sita, made so divinely and with such a revelation of reality as to become objects of enduring cult and worship, or like Hanuman, Lakshmana, Bharata the living human image of its ethical ideals; it has fashioned much of what is best and sweetest in the national character, and it has evoked and fixed in it those finer and exquisite yet firm soul tones and that more delicate humanity of temperament which are a more valuable thing than the formal outsides of virtue and conduct.

The poetical manner of these epics is not inferior to the greatness of their substance. The style and the verse in which they are written have always a noble epic quality, a lucid classical simplicity and directness rich in expression but stripped of superfluous ornament, a swift, vigorous, flexible and fluid verse constantly sure of the epic cadence. There is a difference in the temperament of the language. The characteristic diction of the Mahabharata is almost austerely masculine, trusting to force of sense and inspired accuracy of turn, almost ascetic in its simplicity and directness and a frequent fine and happy bareness; it is the speech of a strong and rapid poetical intelligence and a great and straightforward vital force, brief and telling in phrase but by virtue of a single-minded sincerity and, except in some knotted passages or episodes, without any rhetorical labour of compactness, a style like the light and strong body of a runner nude and pure and healthily lustrous and clear without superfluity of flesh or exaggeration of muscle, agile and swift and untired in the race. There is inevitably much in this vast poem that is in an inferior manner, but little or nothing that falls below a certain sustained level in which there is always something of this virtue. The diction of the Ramayana is shaped in a more attractive mould, a marvel of sweetness and strength, lucidity and warmth and grace; its phrase has not only poetic truth and epic force and diction but a constant intimate vibration of the feeling of the idea, emotion or object: there is an element of fine ideal delicacy in its sustained strength and breath of power. In both poems it is a high poetic soul and inspired intelligence that is at work; the directly intuitive mind of the Veda and Upanishads has retired behind the veil of the intellectual and outwardly psychical imagination.

This is the character of the epics and the qualities which have made them immortal, cherished among India's greatest literary and cultural treasures, and given them their enduring power over the national mind. Apart from minor defects and inequalities such as we find in all works set at this pitch and involving a considerable length of labour, the objections made by western criticism are simply expressions of a difference of mentality and aesthetic taste. The vastness of the plan and the leisurely minuteness of detail are baffling and tiring to a Western mind accustomed to smaller limits, a more easily fatigued eye and imagination and a hastier pace of life, but they are congenial to the spaciousness of vision and intent curiosity of circumstances, characteristic of the Indian mind, that spring as I have pointed out in relation to architecture from the habit of the cosmic consciousness and its sight and imagination and activity of experience. Another difference is that the terrestrial life is not seen realistically just as it is to the physical mind but constantly in relation to the much that is behind it, the human action is surrounded and influenced by great powers and forces, Daivic, Asuric and Rakshasic, and the greater human figures are a kind of incarnation of these more cosmic personalities and powers. The objection that the individual thereby loses his individual interest and becomes a puppet of impersonal forces is not true either in reality or actually in the imaginative figures of this literature, for there we see that the personages gain by it in greatness and force of action and are only ennobled by an impersonality that raises and heightens the play of their personality. The mingling of terrestrial nature and supernature, not as a mere imagination but with an entire sincerity and naturalness, is due to the same conception of a greater reality in life, and it is as significant figures of this greater reality that we must regard much to which the realistic critic objects with an absurdly misplaced violence, such as the powers gained by Tapasya, the use of divine weapons, the frequent indications of psychic action and influence. The complaint of exaggeration is equally invalid where the whole action is that of men raised beyond the usual human level, since we can only ask for proportions consonant with the truth of the stature of life conceived in the imagination of the poet and cannot insist on an unimaginative fidelity to the ordinary measures which would here be false because wholly out of place. The complaint of lifelessness and want of personality in the epic characters is equally unfounded: Rama and Sita, Arjuna and Yudhisthira, Bhishma and Duryodhana and Karna are intensely real and human and alive to the Indian mind. Only the main insistence, here as in Indian art, is not on the outward saliences of character, for these are only used secondarily as aids to the presentation, but on the soul life and the inner soul quality presented with as absolute a vividness and strength and purity of outline as possible. The idealism of characters like Rama and Sita is no pale and vapid unreality; they are vivid with the truth of the ideal life, of the greatness that man may be and does become when he gives his soul a chance and it is no sound objection that there is only a small allowance of the broken littleness of our ordinary nature.

These epics are therefore not a mere mass of untransmuted legend and folklore, as is ignorantly objected, but a highly artistic representation of intimate significances of life, the living presentment of a strong and noble thinking, a developed ethical and aesthetic mind and a high social and political ideal, the ensouled image of a great culture. As rich in freshness of life but immeasurably more profound and evolved in thought and substance than the Greek, as advanced in maturity of culture but more vigorous and vital and young in strength than the Latin epic poetry, the Indian epic poems were fashioned to serve a greater and completer national and cultural function and that they should have been received and absorbed by both the high and the low, the cultured and the masses and remained through twenty centuries an intimate and formative part of the life of the whole nation is of itself the strongest possible evidence of the greatness and fineness of this ancient Indian culture.

A DEFENCE OF INDIAN CULTURE

CHAPTER XIII

INDIAN LITERATURE

THE classical age of the ancient literature, the best known and appraised of all, covers a period of some ten centuries and possibly more, and it is marked off from the earlier writings by a considerable difference, not so much in substance, as in the moulding and the colour of its thought, temperament and language. The divine childhood, the heroic youth, the bright and strong early manhood of the people and its culture are over and there is instead a long and opulent maturity and as its sequence an equally opulent and richly coloured decline. The decline is not to death, for it is followed by a certain rejuvenescence, a fresh start and repeated beginning, of which the medium is no longer Sanskrit but the derived languages, the daughters of the dialects raised into literary instruments and developing as the grand and ancient tongue loses its last forces and inspiring life. The difference in spirit and mould between the epics and the speech of Bhartrihari and Kalidasa is already enormous and may possibly be explained by the early centuries of Buddhism when Sanskrit ceased to be the sole literary tongue understood and spoken by all educated men and Pali came up as its successful rival and the means of expression for at least a great part of the current of the national thought and life. The language and movement of the epics have all the vigour, freedom, spontaneous force and appeal of a speech that leaps straight from the founts of life; the speech of Kalidasa is an accomplished art, an intellectual and aesthetic creation consummate, deliberate, finely ornate, carved like a statue, coloured like a painting, not yet artificial, though there is a masterly artifice and device, but still a careful work of art laboured by the intelligence. It is carefully natural, not with the spontaneous ease of a first, but the accomplished air of ease of a habitual second nature. The elements of artifice and device increase and predominate in the later writers, their language is a laborious and deliberate though a powerful and beautiful construction and appeals only to an erudite audience, a learned elite. The religious writings, Purana and Tantra, moving from a deeper, still intensely living source, aiming by their simplicity at a wider appeal, prolong for a time the tradition of the epics, but the simplicity and directness is willed rather than the earlier natural ease. In the end Sanskrit becomes the language of the Pundits and except for certain philosophical, religious and learned purposes no longer a first-hand expression of the life and mind of the people.

The alteration in the literary speech corresponds however, apart from all inducing circumstances, to a great change in the centre of mentality of the culture. It is still and always spiritual, philosophical, religious, ethical, but the inner austerer things seem to draw back a little and to stand in the background, acknowledged indeed and overshadowing the rest, but nevertheless a little detaching themselves from them and allowing them to act for their own enlargement and profit. The exterior powers that stand out in front are the curious intellect, the vital urge, the aesthetic, urbanely active and hedonistic sense life. It is the great period of logical philosophy, of science, of art and the developed crafts, law, politics, trade, colonisation, the great kingdoms and empires with their ordered and elaborate administrations, the minute rule of the Shastras in all departments of thought and life, an enjoyment of all that is brilliant, sensuous, agreeable, a discussion of all that could be thought and known, a fixing and systemising of all that could be brought into the compass of intelligence and practice,—the most splendid, sumptuous and imposing millennium of Indian culture.

The intellectuality that predominates is not in any way restless, sceptical or negative, but it is enormously inquiring and active, accepting the great lines of spiritual, religious, philosophical and social truth that had been discovered and laid down by the past, but eager too to develop, to complete, to know minutely and thoroughly and fix in perfectly established system and detail, to work out all possible branches and ramifications, to fill the intelligence, the sense and the life. The grand basic principles and lines of Indian religion, philosophy, society have already been found and built and the steps of the culture move now in the magnitude and satisfying security of a great tradition; but there is still ample room for creation and discovery within these fields and a much wider province, great beginnings, strong developments of science and art and literature, the freedom of the purely intellectual and aesthetic activities, much scope too for the hedonisms of the vital and the refinements of the emotional being, a cultivation of the art and rhythmic practice of life. There is a highly intellectualised vital stress and a many-sided interest in living, an indulgence of an at once intellectual and vital and sensuous satisfaction extending even to a frankness of physical and sensual experience, but in the manner of the oriental mind with a certain decorousness and order, an element of aesthetic restraint and the observance of rule and measure even in indulgence that saves always from the unbridled license to which less disciplined races are liable. The characteristic, the central action is the play of the intellectual mind and everywhere that predominates. In the earlier age the many strands of the Indian mind and life principle are unified and inseparable, a single wide movement set to a strong and abundant but simple music; here they seem to stand side by side related and harmonised, curious and complex, multiply one. The spontaneous unity of the intuitive mind is replaced by the artificial unity of the analysing and synthetising intelligence. Art and religion still continue the predominance of the spiritual and intuitive motive, but it is less to the front in literature. A divison has been settled between religious and secular writing that did not exist to any appreciable extent in the previous ages. The great poets and writers are secular creators and their works have no chance of forming part of the intimate religious and ethical mind of the people as did the Ramayana and Mahabharata. The stream of religious poetry flows separately in Purana and Tantra.

The great representative poet of this age is Kalidasa. He establishes a type which was preparing before and endured after him with more or less of additional decoration, but substantially unchanged through the centuries. His poems are the perfect and harmoniously designed model of a kind and substance that others cast always into similar forms but with a genius inferior in power or less rhythmically balanced, faultless and whole. The art of poetic speech in Kalidasa's period reaches an extraordinary perfection. Poetry itself had become a high craft, conscious of its means, meticulously conscientious in the use of its instruments, as alert and exact in its technique as architecture, painting and sculpture, vigilant to equate beauty and power of the form with nobility and richness of the conception, aim and spirit and the scrupulous completeness of its execution with fullness of aesthetic vision or of the emotional or sensuous appeal. There was established here as in the other arts and indeed during all this era in all human activities a Shastra, a well recognised and carefully practised science and art of poetics, critical and formulative of all that makes perfection of method and prescriptive of things to be avoided, curious of essentials and possibilities but under a regime of standards and limits conceived with the aim of excluding all fault of excess or of defect and therefore in practice as unfavourable to any creative lawlessness, even though the poet's native right of fantasy and freedom is theoretically admitted, as to any least tendency towards bad or careless, hasty or irregular workmanship. The poet is expected to be thoroughly conscious of his art, as minutely acquainted with its conditions and its fixed and certain standard and method as the painter and sculptor and to govern by his critical sense and knowledge the flight of his genius. This careful art of poetry became in the end too much of a rigid tradition, too appreciative of rhetorical device and artifice and even permitted and admired the most extraordinary contortions of the learned intelligence, as in the Alexandrian decline of Greek poetry, but the earlier work is usually free from these shortcomings or they are only occasional and rare.

The classical Sanskrit is perhaps the most remarkably finished and capable instrument of thought yet fashioned, at any rate by either the Aryan or the Semitic mind, lucid with the utmost possible clarity, precise to the farthest limit of precision, always compact and at its best sparing in its formation of phrase, but yet with all this never poor or bare: there is no sacrifice of depth to lucidity, but rather a pregnant opulence of meaning, a capacity of high richness and beauty, a natural grandeur of sound and diction inherited from the ancient days. The abuse of the faculty of compound structure proved fatal later on to the prose, but in the earlier prose and poetry where it is limited, there is an air of continent abundance strengthened by restraint and all the more capable of making the most of its resources. The great and subtle and musical rhythms of the classical poetry with their imaginative, attractive and beautiful names, manifold in capacity, careful in structure, are of themselves a mould that insists on perfection and hardly admits the possibility of a mean or slovenly workmanship or a defective movement. The unit of this poetical art is the *śloka,* the sufficient verse of four quarters or *pāda,* and each sloka is expected to be a work of perfect art in itself, a harmonious vivid and convincing expression of an object, scene, detail, thought, sentiment, state of mind or emotion that can stand by itself as an independent figure; the succession of slokas must be a constant development by addition of completeness to completeness and the whole poem or canto of a long poem an artistic and satisfying structure in this manner, the succession of cantos a progression of definite movements building a total harmony. It is this carefully artistic and highly cultured type of poetic creation that reached its acme of perfection in the poetry of Kalidasa.

This pre-eminence proceeds from two qualities possessed in a degree only to be parallelled in the work of the greatest world-poets and not always combined in them in so equable a harmony and with so adequate a combination of execution and substance. Kalidasa ranks among the supreme poetic artists with Milton and Virgil and he has a more subtle and delicate spirit and touch in his art than the English, a greater breath of native power informing and vivifying his execution than the Latin poet. There is no more perfect and harmonious style in literature, no more inspired and careful master of the absolutely harmonious and sufficient phrase combining the minimum of word expenditure with the fullest sense of an accomplished ease and a divine elegance and not excluding a fine excess that is not excessive, an utmost possible refined opulence of aesthetic value. More perfectly than any other he realises the artistic combination of a harmonious economy of expression, not a word, syllable, sound in superfluity, and a total sense of wise and lavish opulence that was the aim of the earlier classical poets. None so divinely skilful as he in imparting without any overdoing the richest colour, charm, appeal and value, greatness or nobility or power or suavity and always some kind and the right kind and the fullest degree of beauty to each line and each phrase. The felicity of selection is equalled by the felicity of combination. One of the most splendidly sensuous of poets in the higher sense of that epithet because he has a vivid vision and feeling of his object, his sensuousness is neither lax nor overpowering, but always satisfying and just, because it is united with a plenary force of the intelligence, a gravity and strength sometimes apparent, sometimes disguised in beauty but appreciable within the broidered and coloured robe, a royal restraint in the heart of a regal indulgence. And Kalidasa's sovereign mastery of rhythm is as great as his sovereign mastery of phrase. Here we meet in each metrical kind with the most perfect discoveries of verbal harmony in the Sanskrit language (pure lyrical melody comes only afterwards at the end in one or two poets like Jayadeva), harmonies founded on a constant subtle complexity of the fine assonances of sound and an unobtrusive use of significant cadence that never breaks the fluent unity of tone of the music. And the other quality of Kalidasa's poetry is the unfailing adequacy of the substance. Careful always to get the full aesthetic value of the word and sound clothing his thought and substance, he is equally careful that the thought and the substance itself should be of a high, strong or rich intellectual, descriptive or emotional value. His conception is large in its view though it has not the cosmic breadth of the earlier poets and it is sustained at every step in its execution. The hand of the artist never fails in the management of its material,—exception being made of a fault of composition marring one, the least considerable of his works,—and his imagination is always as equal to its task as his touch is great and subtle.

The work to which these supreme poetic qualities were brought was very much the same at bottom, though differing in its form and method, as that achieved by the earlier epics; it was to interpret in poetic speech and represent in significant images and figures the mind, the life, the culture of India in his age. Kalidasa's seven extant poems, each in its own way and within its limits and on its level a masterpiece, are a brilliant and delicately ornate roll of pictures and inscriptions with that as their single real subject. His was a richly stored mind, the mind at once of a scholar and observer possessed of all the learning of his time, versed in the politics, law, social idea, system and detail, religion, mythology, philosophy, art of his time, intimate with the life of courts and familiar with the life of the people, widely and very minutely observant of the life of Nature, of bird and beast, season and tree and flower, all the lore of the mind and all the lore of the eye; and this mind was at the same time always that of a great poet and artist. There is not in his work the touch of pedantry or excessive learning that mars the art of some other Sanskrit poets, he knows how to subdue all his matter to the spirit of his art and to make the scholar and observer no more than a gatherer of materials for the poet, but the richness of documentation is there ready and available and constantly brought in as part of incident and description and surrounding idea and forms or intervenes in the brilliant series of images that pass before us in the long succession of magnificent couplets and stanzas. India, her great mountains and forests and plains and their peoples, her men and women and the circumstances of their life, her animals, her cities and villages, her hermitages, rivers, gardens and tilled lands are the background of narrative and drama and love poem. He has seen it all and filled his mind with it and never fails to bring it before us vivid with all the wealth of description of which he is capable. Her ethical and domestic ideals, the life of the ascetic in the forest or engaged in meditation and austerity upon the mountains and the life of the householder, her familiar customs and social standards and observances, her religious notions, cult, symbols give the rest of the surroundings and the atmosphere. The high actions of gods and kings, the nobler or the more delicate human sentiments, the charm and beauty of women, the sensuous passion of lovers, the procession of the seasons and the scenes of Nature, these are his favourite subjects.

He is a true son of his age in his dwelling on the artistic, hedonistic, sensuous sides of experience and pre-eminently a poet of love and beauty and the joy of life. He represents it also in his intellectual passion for higher things, his intense appreciation of knowledge, culture, the religious idea, the ethical ideal, the greatness of ascetic self-mastery, and these too he makes a part of the beauty and interest of life and sees as admirable elements of its complete and splendid picture. All his work is of this tissue. His great literary epic, the "House of Raghu," treats the story of a line of ancient kings as representative of the highest religious and ethical culture and ideals of the race and brings out its significances environed with a splendid decoration of almost pictorially depicted sentiment and action, noble or beautiful thought and speech and vivid incident and scene and surrounding. Another unfinished epic, a great fragment but by the virtue of his method of work complete in itself so far as the tale proceeds, is in subject a legend of the gods, the ancient subject of a strife of Gods and Titans, the solution prepared here by a union of the supreme God and the Goddess, but in treatment it is a description of Nature and the human life of India raised to a divine magnitude on the sacred mountain and in the homes of the high deities. His three dramas move around the passion of love, but with the same insistence on the detail and picture of life. One poem unrolls the hued series of the seasons of the Indian year. Another leads the messenger cloud across northern India viewing as it passes the panorama of her scenes and closes on a vivid and delicately sensuous and emotional portrayal of the passion of love. In these varied settings we get a singularly complete impression of the mind, the tradition, the sentiment, the rich, beautiful and ordered life of the India of the times, not in its very deepest things, for these have to be sought elsewhere, but in what was for the time most characteristic, the intellectual, vital and artistic turn of that period of her culture.

The rest of the poetry of the times is of one fundamental type with Kalidasa's; for it has with individual variations the same thought mind, temperament, general materials, poetic method, and much of it has a high genius or an unusual quality and distinction though not the same perfection, beauty and felicity. The literary epics of Bharavi and Magha reveal the beginning of the decline marked by the progressive encroachment of a rhetorical and laborious standard of form, method and manner that heavily burdens and is bound eventually to stifle the poetic spirit, an increasing artificiality of tradition and convention and gross faults of taste that bear evidence of the approaching transmission of the language out of the hands of the literary creator into the control of the Pundit and pedant. Magha's poem is more constructed by rule of rhetoric than created and he displays as merits the very worst puerilities of melodious jingle, intricate acrostic and laborious double meaning. Bharavi is less attainted by the decadence, but not immune, and he suffers himself to be betrayed by its influence to much that is neither suitable to his temperament and genius nor in itself beautiful or true. Nevertheless Bharavi has high qualities of grave poetic thinking and epic sublimity of description and Magha poetic gifts that would have secured for him a more considerable place in literature if the poet had not been crossed with a pedant. In this mixture of genius with defect of taste and manner the later classical poets resemble the Elizabethans with the difference that in one case the incoherence is the result of a crude and still unripe, in the other of an overripe and decadent culture. At the same time they bring out very prominently the character of this age of Sanskrit literature, its qualities but also its limitations that escape the eye in Kalidasa and are hidden in the splendour of his genius.

This poetry is pre-eminently a ripe and deliberate poetic representation and criticism of thought and life and the things that traditionally interested an aristocratic and cultured class in a very advanced and intellectual period of civilisation. The intellect predominates everywhere and, even when it seems to stand aside and leave room for pure objective presentation, it puts on that too the stamp of its image. In the earlier epics the thought, religion, ethics, life movements are all strongly lived; the poetic intelligence is at work but always absorbed in its work, self-forgetful and identified with its object, and it is this that is the secret of their great creative force and living poetic sincerity and power. The later poets are interested in the same things but with an intensely reflective experience and critical intelligence that always observes more than it lives with its objects. In the literary epics there is no real movement of life, but only a close brilliant description of life. The poet makes to pass before us a series of pictured incidents, scenes, details, figures, attitudes richly coloured, exact, vivid, convincing to the eye and attractive, but in spite of the charm and interest we speedily perceive that these are only animated pictures. Things are indeed seen vividly but with the more outer eye of the imagination, observed by the intellect, reproduced by the sensuous imagination of the poet, but they have not been deeply lived in the spirit. Kalidasa alone is immune from this deficiency of the method because there is in him a great thinking, imaginative, sensuous poetic soul that has lived and creates what he pictures and does not merely fabricate brilliant scenes and figures. The rest only occasionally rise above the deficiency and do then great and not only brilliant or effective work. Their ordinary work is so well done as to deserve great and unstinted praise for what it possesses, but not the highest praise. It is in the end more decorative than creative. There ensues from the character of this poetic method a spiritual consequence, that we see here very vividly the current thought, ethics, aesthetic culture, active and sense life of contemporary India, but not the deeper soul of these things so much as their outer character and body. There is much ethical and religious thought of a sufficiently high ideal kind, and it is quite sincere but only intellectually sincere, and therefore there is no impression of the deeper religious feeling or the living ethical power that we get in the Mahabharata and Ramayana and in most of the art and literature of India. The ascetic life is depicted, but only in its ideas and outward figure: the sensuous life is depicted in the same scrupulous manner—it is intensely observed and appreciated and well reproduced to the eye and the intelligence, but not intensely felt and created in the soul of the poet. The intellect has become too detached and too critically observant to live things with the natural force of the life or with the intuitive identity. This is the quality and also the malady of an overdeveloped intellectualism and it has always been the forerunner of a decadence.

The predominantly intellectual turn appears in the abundance of another kind of writing, the gnomic verse, *subhāsita*. This is the use of the independent completeness of the sloka to be the body in its single sufficiency of the concentrated essence and expression of a thought, an aperçu or significant incident of life, a sentiment so expressed as to convey its essential idea to the intelligence. There is a great plenty of this kind of work admirably done; for it was congenial to the keen intellect and the wide, mature and well-stored experience of the age: but in the work of Bhartrihari it assumes the proportions of genius, because he writes not only with the thought but with emotion, with what might be called a moved intellectuality of the feeling and an intimate experience that gives great potency and sometimes poignancy to his utterance. There are three centuries or *śatakas* of his sentences, the first expressing high ethical thought or worldly wisdom or brief criticisms of aspects of life, the second concerned with erotic passion, much less effective because it is the fruit of curiosity and the environment rather than the poet's own temperament and genius, and the third proclaiming an ascetic weariness and recoil from the world. Bhartrihari's triple work is significant of the three leading motives of the mind of the age, its reflective interest in life and turn for high and strong and minute thinking, its preoccupation with the enjoyment of the senses, and its ascetic spiritual turn—the end of the one and the ransom of the other. It is significant too by the character of this spirituality; it is no longer the great natural flight of the spirit to the fullness of its own high domain, but rather a turning away of the intellect and the senses wearied of themselves and life, unable to find there the satisfaction they sought, to find peace in a spiritual passivity in which the tired thought and sense could find their absolute rest and cessation.

The drama however is the most attractive though not therefore the greatest product of the poetical mind of the age. There its excessive intellectuality was compelled by the necessities of dramatic poetry to be more closely and creatively identified with the very mould and movement of life. The Sanskrit drama type is a beautiful form and it has been used in most of the plays that have come down to us with an accomplished art and a true creative faculty. At the same time it is true that it does not rise to the greatnesses of the Greek or the Shakespearian drama. This is not due to the elimination of tragedy,—for there can be dramatic creation of the greatest kind without a solution in death, sorrow, overwhelming calamity or the tragic return of Karma, a note that is yet not altogether absent from the Indian mind,—for it is there in the Mahabharata and was added later on to the earlier triumphant and victorious close of the Ramayana; but a closing air of peace and calm was more congenial to the sattwic turn of the Indian temperament and imagination. It is due to the absence of any bold dramatic treatment of the great issues and problems of life. These dramas are mostly romantic plays reproducing the images and settled paces of the most cultured life of the time cast into the frame of old myth and legend, but a few are more realistic and represent the type of the citizen householder or other scenes of the times or a historical subject. The magnificent courts of kings or the beauty of the surroundings of Nature are their more common scene.

But whatever their subject or kind, they are only brilliant transcripts or imaginative transmutations of life, and something more is needed for the very greatest or most moving dramatic creation. But their type still admits of a high or a strong or delicate poetry and a representation, if not any very profound interpretation of human action and motive and they do not fall short in this kind. A great charm of poetic beauty and subtle feeling and atmosphere,—reaching its most accomplished type in the Shakuntala of Kalidasa, the most perfect and captivating romantic drama in all literature,—or an interesting turn of sentiment and action, a skilful unobtrusive development according to the recognised principle and carefully observed formula of the art, in temperate measure without violent noise of incident or emphatic stress on situation or crowded figures, the movement subdued to a key of suavity and calm, a delicate psychology, not a strongly marked characterisation such as is commonly demanded in the dramatic art of Europe, but a subtle indication by slight touches in the dialogue and action, these are the usual characteristics. It is an art that was produced by and appealed to a highly cultured class, refined, and intellectual and subtle, loving best a tranquil aesthetic charm, suavity and beauty, and it has the limitations of the kind but also its qualities. There is a constant grace and fineness of work in the best period, a plainer and more direct but still fine vigour in Bhasa and the writers who prolong him, a breath of largeness and power in the dramas of Bhavabhuti, a high and consummate beauty in the perfection of Kalidasa.

This drama, this poetry, the prose romances crowded with descriptive detail, monographs like Bana's biography of Harsha or Jonaraja's history of Cashmere, the collections of religious or romantic or realistic tales, the Jatakas, the Kathasaritsagara with its opulence and inexhaustible abundance of narrative in verse, the Panchatantra and the more concise Hitopadesha which develop the form of the animal fable to make a piquant setting for a mass of acute worldly wisdom and policy and statecraft, and a great body of other less known work are only the surviving remnants of what, as many indications show, must have been an immense literary activity, but they are sufficiently abundant and representative to create a crowded and splendid impression, a many-toned picture of a high culture, a rich intellectuality, a great and ordered society with an opulent religious, aesthetic, ethical, economic, political and vital activity, a many-sided development, a plentiful life-movement. As completely as the earlier epics they belie the legend of an India lost in metaphysics and religious dreamings and incapable of the great things of life. The other element which has given rise to this conception, an intense strain of philosophic thinking and religious experience, follows in fact at this time an almost separate movement and develops gradually behind the pomp and motion of this outward action the thought, the influences, the temperament and tendencies that were to govern another millennium of the life of the Indian people.

A DEFENCE OF INDIAN CULTURE

CHAPTER XIV

INDIAN LITERATURE

THE dominant note in the Indian mind, the temperament that has been at the foundation of all its culture and originated and supported the greater part of its creative action in philosophy, religion, art and life has been, I have insisted, spiritual, intuitive and psychic: but this fundamental tendency has not excluded but rather powerfully supported a strong and rich intellectual, practical and vital activity. In the secular classical literature this activity comes very much to the front, is the prominent characteristic and puts the original spirit a little in the background. That does not mean that the spirit is changed or lost or that there is nothing psychic or intuitive in the secular poetry of the time. On the contrary all the type of the mind reflected there is of the familiar Indian character constant through every change, religio-philosophic, religio-ethical, religio-social, with all the past spiritual experience behind it and supporting it though not prominently in the front; the imagination is of the same kind that we have found in the art of the time; the frames of significant image, symbol and myth are those which have come down from the past subjected to the modifications and new developments that get their full body in the Puranas, and they have a strong psychic suggestion. The difference is that they take in the hands of these poets more of the form of a tradition well understood and worked upon by the intellect than of an original spiritual creation, and it is the intelligence that is prominent, accepting and observing established ideas and things in this frame and type and making its critical or reproductive observation and assent vivid with the strong lines and rich colours of artistic presentation and embellishing image. The original force, the intuitive vision work most strongly now in the outward, in the sensuous, the objective, the vital aspects of existence, and it is these that in this age are being more fully taken up, brought out and made in the religious field a support for an extension of spiritual experience.

The sense of this evolution of the culture appears more clearly outside the range of pure literature in the philosophic writings of the time and in the religious poetry of the Puranas and Tantras. It was these two strains which mixing together and soon becoming a single whole proved to be the most living and enduring movement of the classical age, had the most abiding result in the mind of the people, were the creating force and made the most conspicuous part of the later popular literatures. It is a remarkable proof of the native disposition, capacity and profound spiritual intelligence and feeling of the national mind that the philosophic thinking of this period should have left behind it this immense influence; for it was of the highest and severest intellectual character. The tendency that had begun in earlier times and created Buddhism, Jainism and the great schools of philosophy, the labour of the metaphysical intellect to formulate to the reason the truths discovered by the intuitive spiritual experience, to subject them to the close test of a logical and severely dialectical ratiocination and to elicit from them all that the thought could discover, reaches its greatest power of elaborate and careful reasoning, minute criticism and analysis and forceful logical construction and systematisation in the abundant philosophical writing of the period between the sixth and thirteenth centuries marked especially by the work of the great southern thinkers, Shankara, Ramanuja and Madhwa. It did not cease even then, but survived its greatest days and continued even up to our own times throwing up sometimes great creative thinking and often new and subtle philosophical ideas in the midst of an incessant stream of commentary and criticism on established lines. Here there was no decline but a continued vigour of the metaphysical turn in the mind of the race. The work it did was to complete the diffusion of the philosophic intelligence with the result that even an average Indian mentality, once awakened, responds with a surprising quickness to the most subtle and profound ideas. It is notable that no Hindu religion old or new has been able to come into existence without developing as its support a clear philosophic content and suggestion.

The philosophical writings in prose make no pretension to rank as literature; it is in these that the critical side is prominent, and they have no well-built creative shape, but there are other productions in which a more structural presentation of the complete thought is attempted and here the literary form adopted is ordinarily the philosophical poem. The preference for this form is a direct continuation of the tradition of the Upanishads and the Gita. These works cannot be given a very high place as poetry: they are too overweighted with thought and the preoccupation of an intellectual as distinguished from an intuitive adequacy in the phrase to have the breath of life and impetus of inspiration that are the indispensable attributes of the creative poetic mind. It is the critical and affirmative intelligence that is most active and not the vision seeing and interpretative. The epic greatness of the soul that sees and chants the self-vision and God-vision and supreme world-vision, the blaze of light that makes the power of the Upanishads, is absent, and absent too the direct thought springing straight from the soul's life and experience, the perfect, strong and suggestive phrase and the living beauty of the rhythmic pace that make the poetic greatness of the Gita. At the same time some of these poems are, if certainly not great poetry, yet admirable literature combining a supreme philosophical genius with a remarkable literary talent, not indeed creations, but noble and skilful constructions, embodying the highest possible thought, using well all the weighty, compact and sparing phrase of the classical Sanskrit speech, achieving the harmony and noble elegance of its rhythms. These merits are seen at their best in poems like the *Vivekacūḍāmani* attributed to Shankara, and there we hear even, in spite of its too abstract turn, an intellectual echo of the voice of the Upanishads and the manner of the Gita. These poems, if inferior to the grandeur and beauty of earlier Indian work, are at least equal in poetic style and superior in height of thought to the same kind anywhere else and deservedly survive to fulfil the aim intended by their writers. And one must not omit to mention a few snatches of philosophic song here and there that are a quintessence at once of philosophic thought and poetic beauty, or the abundant literature of hymns, many of them consummate in their power and fervour and their charm of rhythm and expression which prepare us for the similar but larger work in the later regional literature.

The philosophical creations of India differ in this respect from the bulk of the metaphysical thinking of Europe that even when they most adopt the intellectual form and method, yet their real substance is not intellectual, but is rather the result of a subtle and very profound intelligence working on the stuff of sight and spiritual experience. This is the result of the constant unity India has preserved between philosophy, religion and Yoga. The philosophy is the intuitive or intellectual presentation of the truth that was sought for first through the religious mind and its experiences and it is never satisfied by discovering truth to the idea and justifying it to the logical intelligence, although that is admirably done, but has its eye always turned to realisation in the soul's life, the object of Yoga. The thinking of this age, even in giving so much prominence to the intellectual side, does not depart from this constant need of the Indian temperament. It works out from spiritual experience through the exact and laborious inspection and introspection of the intellect and works backward and in again from the intellectual perceptions to new gains of spiritual experience. There is indeed a tendency of fragmentation and exclusiveness; the great integral truth of the Upanishads has already been broken into divergent schools of thought and these are now farther subdividing into still less comprehensive systems; but still in each of these lessened provinces there is a gain of minute or intensive searching and on the whole, if a loss of breadth on the heights, in recompense some extension of assimilable spiritual knowledge. And this rhythm of exchange between the spirit and the intelligence, the spirit illumining, the intelligence searching and arriving and helping the lower life to absorb the intuitions of the spirit, did its part in giving Indian spirituality a wonderful intensity, security and persistence not exampled in any other people. It is indeed largely the work of these philosophers who were at the same time Yogins that saved the soul of India alive through the gathering night of her decadence.

This however could not have been done without the aid of a great body of more easily seizable ideas, forms, images, appealing to the imagination, emotions, ethical and aesthetic sense of the people, that had to be partly an expression of the higher spiritual truth and partly a bridge of transition between the normal religious and the spiritual mentality. The need was met by the Tantras and Puranas. The Puranas are the religious poetry peculiar to this period: for although the form probably existed in ancient times, it is only now that it was entirely developed and became the characteristic and the principal literary expression of the religious spirit, and it is to this period that we must attribute, not indeed all the substance, but the main bulk and the existing shape of the Puranic writings. The Puranas have been much discredited and depreciated in recent times, since the coming in of modern ideas coloured by western rationalism and the turning of the intelligence under new impulses back towards the earlier fundamental ideas of the ancient culture. Much however of this depreciation is due to an entire misunderstanding of the purpose, method and sense of the mediaeval religious writings. It is only in an understanding of the turn of the Indian religious imagination and of the place of these writings in the evolution of the culture that we can seize their sense.

In fact the better comprehension that is now returning to us of our own self and past shows that the Puranic religions are only a new form and extension of the truth of the ancient spirituality and philosophy and socio-religious culture. In their avowed intention they are popular summaries of the cosmogony, symbolic myth and image, tradition, cult, social rule of the Indian people continued, as the name Purana signifies, from ancient times. There is no essential change, but only a change of forms. The psychic symbols or true images of truth belonging to the Vedic age disappear or are relegated to a subordinate plan with a changed and diminished sense: others take their place more visibly large in aim, cosmic, comprehensive, not starting with conceptions drawn from the physical universe, but supplied entirely from the psychic universe within us. The Vedic gods and goddesses conceal from the profane by their physical aspect their psychic and spiritual significance. The Puranic trinity and the forms of its female energies have on the contrary no meaning to the physical mind or imagination, but are philosophic and psychic conceptions and embodiments of the unity and multiplicity of the all-manifesting Godhead. The Puranic cults have been characterised as a degradation of the Vedic religion, but they might conceivably be described, not in the essence, for that remains always the same, but in the outward movement, as an extension and advance. Image worship and temple cult and profuse ceremony, to whatever superstition or externalism their misuse may lead, are not necessarily a degradation. The Vedic religion had no need of images, for the physical signs of its godheads were the forms of physical Nature and the outward universe was their visible house. The Puranic religion worshipped the psychical forms of the Godhead within us and had to express it outwardly in symbolic figures and house it in temples that were an architectural sign of cosmic significances. And the very inwardness it intended necessitated a profusion of outward symbol to embody the complexity of these inward things to the physical imagination and vision. The religious aesthesis has changed, but the meaning of the religion has been altered only in temperament and fashion, not in essence. The real difference is this that the early religion was made by men of the highest mystic and spiritual experience living among a mass still impressed mostly by the life of the physical universe: the Upanishads casting off the physical veil created a free transcendent and cosmic vision and experience and this was expressed by a later age to the mass in images containing a large philosophical and intellectual meaning of which the Trinity and the Shaktis of Vishnu and Shiva are the central figures: the Puranas carried forward this appeal to the intellect and imagination and made it living to the psychic experience, the emotions, the aesthetic feeling and the senses. A constant attempt to make the spiritual truths discovered by the Yogin and the Rishi integrally expressive, appealing, effective to the whole nature of man and to provide outward means by which the ordinary mind, the mind of a whole people might be drawn to a first approach to them is the sense of the religio-philosophic evolution of Indian culture.

It is to be observed that the Puranas and Tantras contain in themselves the highest spiritual and philosophical truths, not broken up and expressed in opposition to each other as in the debates of the thinkers, but synthetised by a fusion, relation or grouping in the way most congenial to the catholicity of the Indian mind and spirit. This is done sometimes expressly, but most often in a form which might carry something of it to the popular imagination and feeling by legend, tale, symbol, apologue, miracle and parable. An immense and complex body of psycho-spiritual experience is embodied in the Tantras, supported by visual images and systematised in forms of Yogic practice. This element is also found in the Puranas, but more loosely and cast out in a less strenuous sequence. This method is after all simply a prolongation, in another form and with a temperamental change, of the method of the Vedas. The Puranas construct a system of physical images and observances each with its psychical significance. Thus the sacredness of the confluence of the three rivers, Ganga, Yamuna and Saraswati, is a figure of an inner confluence and points to a crucial experience in a psycho-physical process of Yoga and it has too other significances, as is common in the economy of this kind of symbolism. The so-called fantastic geography of the Puranas, as we are expressly told in the Puranas themselves, are a rich poetic figure, a symbolic geography of the inner psychical universe. The cosmogony expressed sometimes in terms proper to the physical universe has, as in the Veda, a spiritual and psychological meaning and basis. It is easy to see how in the increasing ignorance of later times the more technical parts of the Puranic symbology inevitably lent themselves to much superstition and to crude physical ideas about spiritual and psychic things. But that danger attends all attempts to bring them to the comprehension of the mass of men and this disadvantage should not blind us to the enormous effect produced in training the mass mind to respond to a psycho-religious and psycho-spiritual appeal that prepares a capacity for higher things. That effect endures even though the Puranic system may have to be superseded by a finer appeal and the awakening to more directly subtle significances, and if such a supersession becomes possible, it will itself be due very largely to the work done by the Puranas.

The Puranas are essentially a true religious poetry, an art of aesthetic presentation of religious truth. All the bulk of the eighteen Puranas does not indeed take a high rank in this kind: there is much waste substance and not a little of dull and dreary matter, but on the whole the poetic method employed is justified by the richness and power of the creation. The earliest work is the best—with one exception at the end in a new style which stands by itself and is unique. The Vishnu Purana for instance in spite of one or two desert spaces is a remarkable literary creation of a very considerable quality maintaining much of the direct force and height of the old epic style. There is in it a varied movement, much vigorous and some sublime epic writing, an occasional lyrical element of a lucid sweetness and beauty, a number of narratives of the finest verve and skilful simplicity of poetic workmanship. The Bhagavat coming at the end and departing to a great extent from the more popular style and manner, for it is strongly affected by the learned and more ornately literary form of speech, is a still more remarkable production full of subtlety, rich and deep thought and beauty. It is here that we get the culmination of the movement which had the most important effects on the future, the evolution of the emotional and ecstatic religions of Bhakti. The tendency that underlay this development was contained in the earlier forms of the religious mind of India and was slowly gaining ground, but it had hitherto been overshadowed and kept from its perfect formation by the dominant tendency towards the austerities of knowledge and action and the seeking of the spiritual ecstasy only on the highest planes of being. The turn of the classical age outward to the exterior life and the satisfaction of the senses brought in a new inward turn of which the later ecstatic forms of the Vaishnava religion were the most complete manifestation. Confined to the secular and outward this fathoming of vital and sensuous experience might have led only to a relaxation of nerve and vigour, and ethical degeneracy or license; but the Indian mind is always compelled by its master impulse to reduce all its experience of life to the corresponding spiritual term and factor and the result was a transfiguring of even these most external things into a basis for new spiritual experience. The emotional, the sensuous, even the sensual motions of the being, before they could draw the soul farther outward, were taken and transmuted into a psychical form and, so changed, they became the elements of a mystic capture of the Divine through the heart and the senses and a religion of the joy of God's love, delight and beauty. In the Tantra the new elements are taken up and assigned their place in a complete psycho-spiritual and psycho-physical science of Yoga. Its popular form in the Vaishnava religion centres round the mystic apologue of the pastoral life of the child Krishna. In the Vishnu Purana the tale of Krishna is a heroic saga of the divine Avatar: in later Puranas we see the aesthetic and erotic symbol developing and in the Bhagavat it is given its full power and prepared to manifest its entire spiritual and philosophic as well as its psychic sense and to remould into its own lines by a shifting of the centre of synthesis from knowledge to spiritual love and delight the earlier significance of Vedanta. The perfect outcome of this evolution is to be found in the philosophy and religion of divine love promulgated by Chaitanya.

It is the later developments of Vedantic philosophy, the Puranic ideas and images and the poetic and aesthetic spirituality of the religions of devotion that inspired from their birth the regional literatures. The literature of the Sanskrit tongue does not come to any abrupt end. Poetry of the classical type continues to be written especially in the South down to a comparatively late period and Sanskrit remains still the language of philosophy and of all kinds of scholarship: all prose work, all the work of the critical mind is written in the ancient tongue.

But the genius rapidly fades out from it, it becomes stiff, heavy and artificial and only a scholastic talent remains to keep it in continuance. In every province the local tongues arise here earlier, there a little later to the dignity of literature and become the vehicle of poetic creation and the instrument of popular culture. Sanskrit, although not devoid of popular elements, is essentially and in the best sense an aristocratic speech developing and holding to the necessity of a noble aspiration and the great manner a high spiritual, intellectual, ethical and aesthetic culture, then possible in this manner only to the higher classes, and handing it down by various channels of impression and transfusion and especially by religion, art and social and ethical rule to the mass of the people. Pali in the hands of the Buddhists becomes a direct means of this transmission. The poetry of the regional tongues on the contrary creates, in every sense of the word, a popular literature. The Sanskrit writers were men of the three highest castes, mostly Brahmins and Kshatriyas, and later they were learned men writing for a highly cultured elite; the Buddhist writers too were for the most part philosophers, monks, kings, preachers writing sometimes for themselves, sometimes in a more popular form for the mass of the people; but the poetry of the regional tongues sprang straight from the heart of the people and its writers came from all classes from the Brahmin to the lowest Shudra and the outcaste. It is only in Urdu and to a less degree in the Southern tongues, as in Tamil whose great period is contemporaneous with the classical Sanskrit, its later production continuing during the survival of independent or semi-independent courts and kingdoms in the South, that there is a strong influence of the learned or classical temperament and habit; but even here there is a very considerable popular element as in the songs of the Shaiva saints and Vaishnava Alwars. The field here is too large to be easily known in its totality or to permit of a rapid survey, but something must be said of the character and value of this later literature that we may see how vital and persistently creative Indian culture remained even in a period which compared with its greater times might be regarded as a period of restriction and decadence.

As the Sanskrit literature begins with the Vedas and Upanishads, these later literatures begin with the inspired poetry of saints and devotees: for in India it is always a spiritual movement that is the source or at least imparts the impulse of formation to new ideas and possibilities and initiates the changes of the national life. It is this kind that predominated almost throughout the creative activity of most of these tongues before modern times, because it was always poetry of this type that was nearest to the heart and mind of the people; and even where the work is of a more secular spirit, the religious turn enters into it and provides the framework, a part of the tone or the apparent motive. In abundance, in poetic excellence, in the union of spontaneous beauty of motive and lyrical skill this poetry has no parallel in its own field in any other literature. A sincerity of devotional feeling is not enough to produce work of this high turn of beauty, as is shown by the sterility of Christian Europe in this kind; it needs a rich and profound spiritual culture. Another part of the literature is devoted to the bringing of something of the essence of the old culture into the popular tongues through new poetic versions of the story of the Mahabharata and the Ramayana or in romantic narrative founded on the ancient legends; and here again we have work of the very greatest genius as well as much of a lesser but still high order. A third type presents vividly the religious beliefs and feelings of the people, the life of court and city and village and hamlet, of landholder and trader and artisan and peasant. The bulk of the work done in the regional tongues falls under one or other of these heads, but there are variations such as the religio-ethical and political poems of Ramdas in Maharashtra or the gnomic poetry, the greatest in plan, conception and force of execution ever written in this kind, of the Tamil saint, Tiruvalluvar.

There is too in one or two of these languages a later erotic poetry not without considerable lyrical beauty of an entirely mundane inspiration. The same culture reigns amid many variations of form in all this work of the regional peoples, but each creates on the lines of its own peculiar character and temperament and this gives a different stamp, the source of a rich variety in the unity, to each of these beautiful and vigorous literatures.

Thus under the stress of temperamental variation the poetry of the Vaishnavas puts on very different artistic forms in different provinces. There is first the use of the psychical symbol created by the Puranas, and this assumes its most complete and artistic shape in Bengal and becomes there a long continued tradition. The desire of the soul for God is there thrown into symbolic figure in the lyrical love cycle of Radha and Krishna, the Nature soul in man seeking for the Divine Soul through love, seized and mastered by his beauty, attracted by his magical flute, abandoning human cares and duties for this one overpowering passion and in the cadence of its phases passing through first desire to the bliss of union, the pangs of separation, the eternal longing and reunion, the *līlā* of the love of the human spirit for God. There is a settled frame and sequence, a subtly simple lyrical rhythm, a traditional diction of appealing directness and often of intense beauty. This accomplished lyrical form springs at once to perfect birth from the genius of the first two poets who used the Bengali tongue, Bidyapati, a consummate artist of word and line, and the inspired singer Chandidas in whose name stand some of the sweetest and most poignant and exquisite love-lyrics in any tongue. The symbol here is sustained in its most external figure of human passion and so consistently that it is now supposed by many to mean nothing else, but this is quite negatived by the use of the same figures by the devout poets of the religion of Chaitanya. All the spiritual experience that lay behind the symbol was embodied in that inspired prophet and incarnation of the ecstasy of divine love and its spiritual philosophy put into clear form in his teaching. His followers continued the poetic tradition of the earlier singers and though they fall below them in genius, yet left behind a great mass of this kind of poetry always beautiful in form and often deep and moving in substance. Another type is created in the perfect lyrics of the Rajput queen Mirabai, in which the images of the Krishna symbol are more directly turned into a song of the love and pursuit of the divine Lover by the soul of the singer. In the Bengal poetry the expression preferred is the symbolic figure impersonal to the poet: here a personal note gives the peculiar intensity to the emotion. This is given a still more direct turn by a southern poetess in the image of herself as the bride of Krishna. The peculiar power of this kind of Vaishnava religion and poetry is in the turning of all the human emotions Godward, the passion of love being preferred as the intensest and most absorbing of them all, and though the idea recurs wherever there has been a strong development of devotional religion, it has nowhere been used with so much power and sincerity as in the work of the Indian poets.

Other Vaishnava poetry does not use the Krishna symbol, but is rather addressed in language of a more direct devotion to Vishnu or centres sometimes around the Rama avatar. The songs of Tukaram are the best known of this kind. The Vaishnava poetry of Bengal avoids except very rarely any element of intellectualising thought and relies purely on emotional description, a sensuous figure of passion and intensity of feeling: Maratha poetry on the contrary has from the beginning a strong intellectual strain. The first Marathi poet is at once a devotee, a Yogin and a thinker; the poetry of the saint Ramdas, associated with the birth and awakening of a nation, is almost entirely a stream of religious ethical thinking raised to the lyrical pitch; and it is the penetrating truth and fervour of a thought arising from the heart of devotion that makes the charm and power of Tukaram's songs. A long strain of devotee poets keeps sounding the note that he struck and their work fills the greater space of Marathi poetry. The same type takes a lighter and more high-pitched turn in the poetry of Kabir. In Bengal again at the end of the Mahomedan period there is the same blending of fervent devotion with many depths and turns of religious thought in the songs of Ramprasad to the divine Mother, combined here with a vivid play of imagination turning all familiar things into apt and pregnant images and an intense spontaneity of feeling. In the South a profounder philosophic utterance is often fused into the devotional note, especially in the Shaiva poets, and, as in the early Sanskrit poetry, vivified by a great power of living phrase and image, and farther north the high Vedantic spirituality renews itself in the Hindi poetry of Surdas and inspires Nanak and the Sikh gurus. The spiritual culture prepared and perfected by two millenniums of the ancient civilisation has flooded the mind of all these peoples and given birth to great new literatures and its voice is heard continually through all their course.

The narrative poetry of this age is less striking and original except for a certain number of great or famous works. Most of these tongues have felt the cultural necessity of transferring into the popular speech the whole central story of the Mahabharata or certain of its episodes and, still more universally, the story of the Ramayana. In Bengal there is the Mahabharata of Kashiram, the gist of the old epic simply retold in a lucid classical style, and the Ramayana of Krittibas, more near to the vigour of the soil, neither of them attaining to the epic manner but still written with a simple poetic skill and a swift narrative force. Only two however of these later poets arrived at a vividly living recreation of the ancient story and succeeded in producing a supreme masterpiece, Kamban, the Tamil poet who makes of his subject a great original epic, and Tulsidas whose famed Hindi Ramayana combines with a singular mastery lyric intensity, romantic richness and the sublimity of the epic imagination and is at once a story of the divine Avatar and a long chant of religious devotion. An English historian of the literature has even claimed for Tulsidas's poem superiority to the epic of Valmiki: that is an exaggeration and, whatever the merits, there cannot be a greater than the greatest, but that such claims can be made for Tulsidas and Kamban is evidence at least of the power of the poets and a proof that the creative genius of the Indian mind has not declined even in the narrowing of the range of its culture and knowledge. All this poetry indeed shows a gain in intensity that compensates to some extent for the loss of the ancient height and amplitude.

While this kind of narrative writing goes back to the epics, another seems to derive its first shaping and motive from the classical poems of Kalidasa, Bharavi and Magha. A certain number take for their subject, like that earlier poetry, episodes of the Mahabharata or other ancient or Puranic legends, but the classical and epic manner has disappeared, the inspiration resembles more that of the Puranas and there is the tone and the looser and easier development of the popular romance. This kind is commoner in western India and excellence in it is the title to fame of Premananda, the most considerable of the Gujerati poets. In Bengal we find another type of half romantic half realistic narrative which develops a poetic picture of the religious mind and life and scenes of contemporary times and has a strong resemblance in its motive to the more outward element in the aim of Rajput painting. The life of Chaitanya written in a simple and naïve romance verse, appealing by its directness and sincerity but inadequate in poetic form, is a unique contemporary presentation of the birth and foundation of a religious movement. Two other poems that have become classics, celebrate the greatness of Durga or Chandi, the goddess who is the Energy of Shiva,—the "Chandi" of Mukundaram, a pure romance of great poetic beauty which presents in its frame of popular legend a very living picture of the life of the people, and the "Annadamangal" of Bharatchandra repeating in its first part the Puranic tales of the gods as they might be imagined by the Bengali villager in the type of his own human life, telling in the second a romantic love story and in the third a historical incident of the time of Jehangir, all these disparate elements forming the development of the one central motive and presented without any imaginative elevation but with an unsurpassable vividness of description and power of vital and convincing phrase. All this poetry, the epic and the romance, the didactic poem, of which Ramdas and the famous Kural of Tiruvalluvar are the chief representatives, and the philosophic and devotional lyrics are not the creation or meant for the appreciation of a cultivated class, but with few exceptions the expression of a popular culture. The Ramayana of Tulsidas, the songs of Ramprasad and of the Bauls, the wandering Vaishnava devotees, the poetry of Ramdas and Tukaram, the sentences of Tiruvalluvar and the poetess Avvai and the inspired lyrics of the Southern saints and Alwars were known to all classes and their thought or their emotion entered deeply into the life of the people.

I have dwelt at this length on the literature because it is, not indeed the complete, but still the most varied and ample record of the culture of a people. Three millenniums at least of a creation of this kind and greatness are surely the evidence of a real and very remarkable culture. The last period shows no doubt a gradual decline, but one may note the splendour even of the decline and especially the continued vitality of religious, literary and artistic creation. At the moment when it seemed to be drawing to a close it has revived at the first chance and begins again another cycle, at first precisely in the three things that lasted the longest, spiritual and religious activity, literature and painting, but already the renewal promises to extend itself to all the many activities of life and culture in which India was once a great and leading people.

A DEFENCE OF INDIAN CULTURE

CHAPTER XV

INDIAN POLITY

I HAVE spoken hitherto of the greatness of Indian civilisation in the things most important to human culture, those activities that raise man to his noblest potentialities as a mental, a spiritual, religious, intellectual, ethical, aesthetic being, and in all these matters the cavillings of the critics break down before the height and largeness and profundity revealed when we look at the whole and all its parts in the light of a true understanding of the spirit and intention and a close discerning regard on the actual achievement of the culture. There is revealed not only a great civilisation, but one of the half dozen greatest of which we have a still existing record. But there are many who would admit the greatness of the achievement of India in the things of the mind and the spirit, but would still point out that she has failed in life, her culture has not resulted in a strong, successful or progressive organisation of life such as Europe shows to us, and that in the end at least the highest part of her mind turned away from life to asceticism and an inactive and world-shunning pursuit by the individual of his personal spiritual salvation. Or at most she has come only to a certain point and then there has been an arrest and decadence.

This charge weighs with an especial heaviness in the balance today because the modern man, even the modern cultured man, is or tends to be to a degree quite unprecedented, *politicon zoon,* a political, economic and social being valuing above all things the efficiency of the outward existence and the things of the mind and spirit mainly, when not exclusively, for their aid to humanity's vital and mechanical progress: he has not that regard of the ancients which looked up towards the highest heights and regarded an achievement in the things of the mind and the spirit with an unquestioning admiration or a deep veneration for its own sake as the greatest possible contribution to human culture and progress. And although this modern tendency is exaggerated and ugly and degrading in its exaggeration, inimical to humanity's spiritual evolution, it has this much of truth behind it that while the first value of a culture is its power to raise and enlarge the internal man, the mind, the soul, the spirit, its soundness is not complete unless it has shaped also his external existence and made of it a rhythm of advance towards high and great ideals. This is the true sense of progress and there must be as part of it a sound political, economic and social life, a power and efficiency enabling a people to survive, to grow and to move securely towards a collective perfection, and a vital elasticity and responsiveness that will give room for a constant advance in the outward expression of the mind and the spirit. If a culture does not serve these ends, then there is evidently a defect somewhere either in its essential conceptions or its wholeness or in its application that will seriously detract from its claims to a complete and integral value.

The ideals that governed the spirit and body of Indian society were of the highest kind, its social order secured an inexpugnable basic stability, the strong life force that worked in it was creative of an extraordinary energy, richness and interest, and the life organised remarkable in its opulence, variety in unity, beauty, productiveness, movement. All the records of Indian history, art and literature bear evidence to a cultural life of this character and even in decline and dissolution there survives some stamp of it to remind however faintly and distantly of the past greatness. To what then does the charge brought against Indian culture as an agent of the life power amount and what is its justification? In its exaggerated form it is founded upon the characteristics of the decline and dissolution, the features of the decadence read backward into the time of greatness, and it amounts to this that India has always shown an incompetence for any free or sound political organisation and has been constantly a divided and for the most part of her long history a subject nation, that her economic system whatever its bygone merits, if it had any, remained an inelastic and static order that led in modern conditions to poverty and failure and her society an unprogressive hierarchy, caste-ridden, full of semi-barbaric abuses, only fit to be thrown on the scrap-heap among the broken rubbish of the past and replaced by the freedom, soundness and perfection or at least the progressive perfectibility of the European social order. It is necessary to re-establish the real facts and their meaning and afterwards it will be time to pass judgment on the political, the economic and the social aspects of Indian culture.

The legend of Indian political incompetence has arisen from a false view of the historical development and an insufficient knowledge of the ancient past of the country. It has long been currently supposed that she passed at once from the freer type of the primitive Aryan or Vedic social and political organisation to a system socially marked by the despotism of the Brahmin theocracy and politically by an absolute monarchy of the oriental, by which is meant the Western Asiatic, type and has remained fixed in these two things for ever after. That summary reading of Indian history has been destroyed by a more careful and enlightened scholarship and the facts are of a quite different nature. It is true that India never evolved either the scrambling and burdensome industrialism or the parliamentary organisation of freedom and self-styled democracy characteristic of the bourgeois or Vaishya period of the cycle of European progress. But the time is passing when the uncritical praise of these things as the ideal state and the last word of social and political progress was fashionable, their defects are now visible and the greatness of an oriental civilisation need not be judged by the standard of these western developments. Indian scholars have attempted to read the modern ideas and types of democracy and even a parliamentary system into the past of India, but this seems to me an ill-judged endeavour. There was a strong democratic element, if we must use the western terms, in Indian polity and even institutions that present a certain analogy to the parliamentary form, but in reality these features were of India's own kind and not at all the same thing as modern parliaments and modern democracy. And so considered they are a much more remarkable evidence of the political capacity of the Indian people in their living adaptation to the ensemble of the social mind and body of the nation than when we judge them by the very different standard of western society and the peculiar needs of its cultural cycle.

The Indian system began with a variation of the type generally associated with the early history of the Aryan peoples; but certain features have a more general character and belong to a still earlier stage in the social development of the human race. It was a clan or tribal system, *kula,* founded upon the equality of all the freemen of the clan or race; this was not at first firmly founded upon the territorial basis, the migratory tendency was still in evidence or recurred under pressure and the land was known by the name of the people who occupied it, the Kuru country or simply the Kurus, the Malava country or the Malavas. After the fixed settlement within determined boundaries the system of the clan or tribe continued, but found a basic unit or constituent atom in the settled village community. The meeting of the people, *viśaḥ,* assembling for communal deliberation, for sacrifice and worship or as the host for war, remained for a long time the power-sign of the mass body and the agent of the active common life with the king as the head and representative, but long depending even after his position became hereditary on the assent of the people for his formal election or confirmation. The religious institution of the sacrifice developed in time a class of priests and inspired singers, men trained in the ritual or in possession of the mystic knowledge which lay behind the symbols of the sacrifice, the seed of the great Brahminic institution. These were not at first hereditary, but exercised other professions and belonged in their ordinary life to the general body of the people. This free and simple natural constitution of the society seems to have been general at first throughout Aryan India.

The later development out of this primitive form followed up to a certain point the ordinary line of evolution as we see it in other communities, but at the same time threw up certain very striking peculiarities that owing to the unique mentality of the race fixed themselves, became prominent characteristics and gave a different stamp to the political, economic and social factors of Indian civilisation. The hereditary principle emerged at an early stage and increased constantly its power and hold on the society until it became everywhere the basis of the whole organisation of its activities. A hereditary kingship was established, a powerful princely and warrior class appeared, the rest of the people were marked off as the caste of traders, artisans and agriculturalists and a subject or menial caste was added, perhaps sometimes as the result of conquest but more probably or more commonly from economic necessity, of servants and labourers. The predominance from early times of the religious and spiritual tendency in the mind of the Indian people brought about at the top of the social system the growth of the Brahmin order, priests, scholars, legists, repositories of the sacred lore of the Vedas, a development parallelled elsewhere but here given an unequalled permanence and definiteness and supreme importance. In other countries with a less complex mentality this predominance might have resulted in a theocracy: but the Brahmins in spite of their ever-increasing and finally predominant authority did not and could not usurp in India the political power. As sacrosanct priests and legists and spiritual preceptors of the monarch and the people they exercised a very considerable influence, but the real or active political power remained with the king, the Kshatriya aristocracy and the commons.

A peculiar figure for some time was the Rishi, the man of a higher spiritual experience and knowledge, born in any of the classes, but exercising an authority by his spiritual personality over all, revered and consulted by the king of whom he was sometimes the religious preceptor and in the then fluid state of social evolution able alone to exercise an important role in evolving new basic ideas and effecting direct and immediate changes of the socio-religious ideas and customs of the people. It was a marked feature of the Indian mind that it sought to attach a spiritual meaning and a religious sanction to all, even to the most external social and political circumstances of its life, imposing on all classes and functions an ideal, not except incidentally of rights and powers, but of duties, a rule of their action and an ideal way and temperament, character, spirit in the action, a dharma with a spiritual significance. It was the work of the Rishi to put this stamp enduringly on the national mind, to prolong and perpetuate it, to discover and interpret the ideal law and its practical meaning, to cast the life of the people into the well-shaped ideals and significant forms of a civilisation founded on the spiritual and religious sense. And in later ages we find the Brahminic schools of legists attributing their codes, though in themselves only formulations of existing rule and custom, to the ancient Rishis. Whatever the developments of the Indian socio-political body in later days, this original character still exercised its influence, even when all tended at last to become traditionalised and conventionalised instead of moving forward constantly in the steps of a free and living practice.

The political evolution of this early system varied in different parts of India. The ordinary development, as in most other countries, was in the direction of an increasing emphasis on the control of the king as the centre, head and unifying factor of a more and more complex system of rule and administration and this prevailed eventually and became the universal type. But for a long time it was combated and held in check by a contrary tendency that resulted in the appearance and the strong and enduring vitality of city or regional or confederated republics. The king became either a hereditary or elected executive head of the republic or an archon administering for a brief and fixed period or else he altogether disappeared from the polity of the state. This turn must have come about in many cases by a natural evolution of the power of the assemblies, but in others it seems to have been secured by some kind of revolution and there appear to have been vicissitudes, alternations between periods of monarchical and periods of republican government. Among a certain number of the Indian peoples the republican form finally asserted its hold and proved itself capable of a strong and settled organisation and a long duration lasting over many centuries. In some cases they were governed by a democratic assembly, in more by an oligarchical senate. It is unfortunate that we know little of the details of the constitution and nothing of the inner history of these Indian republics, but the evidence is clear of the high reputation they enjoyed throughout India for the excellence of their civil and the formidable efficiency of their military organisation. There is an interesting dictum of Buddha that so long as the republican institutions were maintained in their purity and vigour, a small state of this kind would remain invincible even by the arms of the powerful and ambitious Magadhan monarchy, and this opinion is amply confirmed by the political writers who consider the alliance of the republics the most solid and valuable political and military support a king could have and advise their reduction not so much by the force of arms, as that would have a very precarious chance of success, but by Machiavellian means,–similar to those actually employed in Greece by Philip of Macedon,–aimed at undermining their internal unity and the efficiency of their constitution.

These republican states were already long established and in vigorous functioning in the sixth century before Christ, contemporary therefore with the brilliant but ephemeral and troubled Greek city commonwealths, but this form of political liberty in India long outlasted the period of Greek republican freedom. The ancient Indian mind, not less fertile in political invention, must be considered superior to that of the mercurial and restless Mediterranean people in the capacity for a firm organisation and settled constitutional order. Some of these states appear to have enjoyed a longer and a more settled history of vigorous freedom than republican Rome, for they persisted even against the mighty empire of Chandragupta and Asoka and were still in existence in the early centuries of the Christian era. But none of them developed the aggressive spirit and the conquering and widely organising capacity of the Roman republic; they were content to preserve their own free inner life and their independence. India especially after the invasion of Alexander felt the need of a movement of unification and the republics were factors of division: strong for themselves, they could do nothing for the organisation of the peninsula, too vast indeed for any system of confederation of small states to be possible–and indeed in the ancient world that endeavour nowhere succeeded, always it broke down in the effort of expansion beyond certain narrow limits and could not endure against the movement towards a more centralised government. In India as elsewhere it was the monarchical state that grew and finally held the field replacing all other forms of political organisation. The republican organisation disappeared from her history and is known to us only by the evidence of coins, scattered references and the testimony of Greek observers and of the contemporary political writers and theorists who supported and helped to confirm and develop the monarchical state throughout India.

But Indian monarchy previous to the Mahomedan invasion was not, in spite of a certain sanctity and great authority conceded to the regal position and the personality of the king as the representative of the divine Power and the guardian of the Dharma, in any way a personal despotism or an absolutist autocracy: it had no resemblance to the ancient Persian monarchy or the monarchies of western and central Asia or the Roman imperial government or later European autocracies: it was of an altogether different type from the system of the Pathan or the Moghul emperors. The Indian king exercised supreme administrative and judicial power, was in possession of all the military forces of the kingdom and with his Council alone responsible for peace and war and he had too a general supervision and control over the good order and welfare of the life of the community, but his power was not personal and it was besides hedged in by safeguards against abuse and encroachment and limited by the liberties and powers of other public authorities and interests who were, so to speak, lesser copartners with him in the exercise of sovereignty and administrative legislation and control. He was in fact a limited or constitutional monarch, although the machinery by which the constitution was maintained and the limitation effected differed from the kind familiar in European history; and even the continuance of his rule was far more dependent than that of mediaeval European kings on the continued will and assent of the people.

A greater sovereign than the king was the Dharma, the religious, ethical, social, political, juridic and customary law organically governing the life of the people. This impersonal authority was considered sacred and eternal in its spirit and the totality of its body, always characteristically the same, the changes organically and spontaneously brought about in its actual form by the evolution of the society being constantly incorporated in it, regional, family and other customs forming a sort of attendant and subordinate body capable of change only from within,–and with the Dharma no secular authority had any right of autocratic interference. The Brahmins themselves were recorders and exponents of the Dharma, not its creators nor authorised to make at will any changes, although it is evident that by an authoritative expression of opinion they could and did favour or oppose this or that tendency to change of principle or detail. The king was only the guardian, executor and servant of the Dharma, charged to see to its observance and to prevent offences, serious irregularities and breaches. He himself was bound the first to obey it and observe the rigorous rule it laid on his personal life and action and on the province, powers and duties of his regal authority and office.

This subjection of the sovereign power to the Dharma was not an ideal theory inoperative in practice; for the rule of the socio-religious law actively conditioned the whole life of the people and was therefore a living reality, and it had in the political field very large practical consequences. It meant first that the king had not the power of direct legislation and was limited to the issue of administrative decrees that had to be in consonance with the religious, social, political, economic constitution of the comunity,–and even here there were other powers than that of the king who shared with him the right of promulgating and seeing to the execution of administrative decrees independently issued,–neither could he disregard in the general tenor and character and the effective result of his administration the express or tacit will of the people.

The religious liberties of the commons were assured and could not normally be infringed by any secular authority; each religious community, each new or long-standing religion could shape its own way of life and institutions and had its own authorities or governing bodies exercising in their proper field an entire independence. There was no exclusive State religion and the monarch was not the religious head of the people. Asoka in this respect seems to have attempted an extension of the royal control or influence and similar velleities were occasionally shown on a minor scale by other powerful sovereigns. But Asoka's so-called edicts of this kind had a recommendatory rather than an imperative character, and the sovereign who wished to bring about a change in religious belief or institutions had always in accordance with the Indian principle of communal freedom and the obligation of a respect for and a previous consultation of the wishes of those concerned to secure the assent of the recognised authorities or to refer the matter to a consultative assembly for deliberation, as was done in the famous Buddhist councils, or to arrange a discussion between the exponents of the different religions and abide by the issue. The monarch might personally favour a particular sect or creed and his active preference might evidently have a considerable propagandist influence, but at the same time he was bound to respect and support in his public office all the recognised religions of the people with a certain measure of impartiality, a rule that explains the support extended by Buddhist and Brahmin emperors to both the rival religions. At times there were, mainly in the South, instances of petty or violent State persecutions, but these outbreaks were a violation of the Dharma due to momentary passion at a time of acute religious ferment and were always local and of a brief duration. Normally there was no place in the Indian political system for religious oppression and intolerance and a settled State policy of that kind was unthinkable.

The social life of the people was similarly free from autocratic interference. Instances of royal legislation in this province are rare and here too, when it occurred, there had to be a consultation of the will of those concerned, as in the rearrangement or the reconstitution of the caste system by the Sena kings in Bengal after its disorganisation during a long period of Buddhist predominance. Change in the society was brought about not artificially from above but automatically from within and principally by the freedom allowed to families or particular communities to develop or alter automatically their own rule of life, *ācāra.*

In the sphere of administration the power of the king was similarly hedged in by the standing constitution of the Dharma. His right of taxation was limited in the most important sources of revenue to a fixed percentage as a maximum and in other directions often by the right of the bodies representing the various elements of the community to a voice in the matter and always by the general rule that his right to govern was subject to the satisfaction and good-will of the people. This as we shall see, was not merely a pious wish or opinion of the Brahmin custodians of the Dharma. The king was in person the supreme court and the highest control in the execution of the civil and criminal law, but here too his role was that of the executor: he was bound to administer the law faithfully as it stood through his judges or with the aid of the Brahmin legists learned in these matters. He had the complete and unfettered control in his Council only of foreign policy, military administration and war and peace and of a great number of directive activities. He was free to make efficient arrangements for all that part of the administration that served to secure and promote the welfare of the community, good order, public morals, and all such matters as could best be supervised or regulated by the sovereign authority. He had a right of patronage and punishment consistent with the law and was expected to exercise it with a strict regard to an effect of general beneficence and promotion of the public welfare.

There could therefore be ordinarily little or no room in the ancient Indian system for autocratic freak or monarchical violence and oppression, much less for the savage cruelty and tyranny of so common an occurrence in the history of some other countries. Nevertheless such happenings were possible by the sovereign's disregard of the Dharma or by a misuse of his power of administrative decree; instances occurred of the kind,—though the worst recorded is that of a tyrant belonging to a foreign dynasty; in other cases any prolonged outbreak of autocratic caprice, violence or injustice seems to have led before long to an effective protest or revolt on the part of the people. The legists provided for the possibility of oppression. In spite of the sanctity and prestige attaching to the sovereign it was laid down that obedience ceased to be binding if the king ceased to be faithful executor of the Dharma. Incompetence and violation of the obligation to rule to the satisfaction of the people were in theory and effect sufficient causes for his removal. Manu even lays it down that an unjust and oppressive king should be killed by his own subjects like a mad dog, and this justification by the highest authority of the right or even the duty of insurrection and regicide in extreme cases is sufficient to show that absolutism or the unconditional divine right of kings was no part of the intention of the Indian political system. As a matter of fact the right was actually exercised as we find both from history and literature. Another more peaceful and more commonly exercised remedy was a threat of secession or exodus which in most cases was sufficient to bring the delinquent ruler to reason. It is interesting to find the threat of secession employed against an unpopular monarch in the South as late as the seventeenth century, as well as a declaration by a popular assembly denouncing any assistance given to the king as an act of treason. A more common remedy was deposition by the council of ministers or by the public assemblies. The kingship thus constituted proved to be in effect moderate, efficient and beneficent, served well the purposes assigned to it and secured an abiding hold on the affections of the people. The monarchical institution was however only one, an approved and very important, but not, as we see from the existence of the ancient republics, an indispensable element of the Indian socio-political system, and we shall understand nothing of the real principle of the system and its working if we stop short with a view of the regal façade and fail to see what lay behind it. It is there that we shall find the clue to the essential character of the whole construction.

A DEFENCE OF INDIAN CULTURE

CHAPTER XVI

INDIAN POLITY

THE true nature of the Indian polity can only be realised if we look at it not as a separate thing, a machinery independent of the rest of the mind and life of the people, but as a part of and in its relation to the organic totality of the social existence.

A people, a great human collectivity, is in fact an organic living being with a collective or rather—for the word collective is too mechanical to be true to the inner reality—a common or communal soul, mind and body. The life of the society like the physical life of the individual human being passes through a cycle of birth, growth, youth, ripeness and decline, and if this last stage goes far enough without any arrest of its course towards decadence, it may perish,—even so all the older peoples and nations except India and China perished,—as a man dies of old age. But the collective being has too the capacity of renewing itself, of a recovery and a new cycle. For in each people there is a soul idea or life idea at work, less mortal than its body, and if this idea is itself sufficiently powerful, large and force-giving and the people sufficiently strong, vital and plastic in mind and temperament to combine stability with a constant enlargement or new application of the power of the soul idea or life idea in its being, it may pass through many such cycles before it comes to a final exhaustion. Moreover, the idea is itself only the principle of soul manifestation of the communal being and each communal soul again a manifestation and vehicle of the greater eternal spirit that expresses itself in Time and on earth is seeking, as it were, its own fullness in humanity through the vicissitudes of the human cycles. A people then which learns to live consciously not solely in its physical and outward life, not even only in that and the power of the life idea or soul idea that governs the changes of its development and is the key to its psychology and temperament, but in the soul and spirit behind, may not at all exhaust itself, may not end by disappearance or a dissolution or a fusion into others or have to give place to a new race and people, but having itself fused into its life many original smaller societies and attained to its maximum natural growth pass without death through many renascences. And even if at any time it appears to be on the point of absolute exhaustion and dissolution, it may recover by the force of the spirit and begin another and perhaps a more glorious cycle. The history of India has been that of the life of such a people.

The master idea that has governed the life, culture, social ideals of the Indian people has been the seeking of man for his true spiritual self and the use of life—subject to a necessary evolution first of his lower physical, vital and mental nature—as a frame and means for that discovery and for man's ascent from the ignorant natural into the spiritual existence. This dominant idea India has never quite forgotten even under the stress and material exigences and the externalities of political and social construction. But the difficulty of making the social life an expression of man's true self and some highest realisation of the spirit within him is immensely greater than that which attends a spiritual self-expression through the things of the mind, religion, thought, art, literature, and while in these India reached extraordinary heights and largenesses, she could not in the outward life go beyond certain very partial realisations and very imperfect tentatives,—a general spiritualising symbolism, an infiltration of the greater aspiration, a certain cast given to the communal life, the creation of institutions favourable to the spiritual idea. Politics, society, economics are the natural field of the two first and grosser parts of human aim and conduct recognised in the Indian system, interest and hedonistic desire: *Dharma,* the higher law, has nowhere been brought more than partially into this outer side of life, and in politics to a very minimum extent; for the effort at governing political action by ethics is usually little more than a pretence. The coordination or true union of the collective outward life with *mokṣa,* the liberated spiritual existence, has hardly even been conceived or attempted, much less anywhere succeeded in the past history of the yet hardly adult human race. Accordingly, we find that the governance by the Dharma of India's social, economic and even, though here the attempt broke down earlier than in other spheres, her political rule of life, system, turn of existence, with the adumbration of a spiritual significance behind,—the full attainment of the spiritual life being left as a supreme aim to the effort of the individual,—was as far as her ancient system could advance. This much endeavour, however, she did make with persistence and patience and it gave a peculiar type to her social polity. It is perhaps for a future India, taking up and enlarging with a more complete aim, a more comprehensive experience, a more certain knowledge that shall reconcile life and the spirit, her ancient mission, to found the status and action of the collective being of man on the realisation of the deeper spiritual truth, the yet unrealised spiritual potentialities of our existence and so ensoul the life of her people as to make it the Lila of the greater Self in humanity, a conscious communal soul and body of Virat, the universal spirit.

Another point must be noted which creates a difference between the ancient polity of India and that of the European peoples and makes the standards of the West as inapplicable here as in the things of the mind and the inner culture. Human society has in its growth to pass through three stages of evolution before it can arrive at the completeness of its possibilities. The first is a condition in which the forms and activities of the communal existence are those of the spontaneous play of the powers and principles of its life. All its growth, all its formations, customs, institutions are then a natural organic development,—the motive and constructive power coming mostly from the subconscient principle of the life within it,—expressing, but without deliberate intention, the communal psychology, temperament, vital and physical need, and persisting or altering partly under the pressure of an internal impulse, partly under that of the environment acting on the communal mind and temper. In this stage the people is not yet intelligently self-conscious in the way of the reason, is not yet a thinking collective being, and it does not try to govern its whole communal existence by the reasoning will, but lives according to its vital intuitions or their first mental renderings. The early framework of Indian society and polity grew up in such a period as in most ancient and mediaeval communities, but also in the later age of a growing social self-consciousness they were not rejected but only farther shaped, developed, systematised so as to be always, not a construction of politicians, legislators and social and political thinkers, but a strongly stable vital order natural to the mind, instincts and life intuitions of the Indian people.

A second stage of the society is that in which the communal mind becomes more and more intellectually self-conscious, first in its more cultured minds, then more generally, first broadly, then more and more minutely and in all the parts of its life. It learns to review and deal with its own life, communal ideas, needs, institutions in the light of the developed intelligence and finally by the power of the critical and constructive reason. This is a stage which is full of great possibilities but attended too by serious characteristic dangers. Its first advantages are those which go always with the increase of a clear and understanding and finally an exact and scientific knowledge and the culminating stage is the strict and armoured efficiency which the critical and constructive, the scientific reason used to the fullest degree offers as its reward and consequence. Another and greater outcome of this stage of social evolution is the emergence of high and luminous ideals which promise to raise man beyond the limits of the vital being, beyond his first social, economic and political needs and desires and out of their customary moulds and inspire an impulse of bold experiment with the communal life which opens a field of possibility for the realisation of a more and more ideal society. This application of the scientific mind to life with the strict, well-finished, armoured efficiency which is its normal highest result, this pursuit of great consciously proposed social and political ideals and the progress which is the index of the ground covered in the endeavour, have been, with whatever limits and drawbacks, the distinguishing advantages of the political and social effort of Europe.

On the other hand the tendency of the reason when it pretends to deal with the materials of life as its absolute governor, is to look too far away from the reality of the society as a living growth and to treat it as a mechanism which can be manipulated at will and constructed like so much dead wood or iron according to the arbitrary dictates of the intelligence. The sophisticating, labouring, constructing, efficient, mechanising reason loses hold of the simple principles of a people's vitality; it cuts it away from the secret roots of its life. The result is an exaggerated dependence on system and institution, on legislation and administration and the deadly tendency to develop, in place of a living people, a mechanical State. An instrument of the communal life tries to take the place of the life itself and there is created a powerful but mechanical and artificial organisation; but, as the price of this exterior gain, there is lost the truth of life of an organically self-developing communal soul in the body of a free and living people. It is this error of the scientific reason stifling the work of the vital and the spiritual intuition under the dead weight of its mechanical method which is the weakness of Europe and has deceived her aspiration and prevented her from arriving at the true realisation of her own higher ideals.

It is only by reaching a third stage of the evolution of the collective social as of the individual human being that the ideals first seized and cherished by the thought of man can discover their own real source and character and their true means and conditions of effectuation or the perfect society be anything more than a vision on a shining cloud constantly run after in a circle and constantly deceiving the hope and escaping the embrace. That will be when man in the collectivity begins to live more deeply and to govern his collective life neither primarily by the needs, instincts, intuitions welling up out of the vital self, nor secondarily by the constructions of the reasoning mind, but first, foremost and always by the power of unity, sympathy, spontaneous liberty, supple and living order of his discovered greater self and spirit in which the individual and the communal existence have their law of freedom, perfection and oneness. That is a rule that has not yet anywhere found its right conditions for even beginning its effort, for it can only come when man's attempt to reach and abide by the law of the spiritual existence is no longer an exceptional aim for individuals or else degraded in its more general aspiration to the form of a popular religion, but is recognised and followed out as the imperative need of his being and its true and right attainment the necessity of the next step in the evolution of the race.

The small early Indian communities developed like others through the first stage of a vigorous and spontaneous vitality, finding naturally and freely its own norm and line, casting up form of life and social and political institution out of the vital intuition and temperament of the communal being. As they fused with each other into an increasing cultural and social unity and formed larger and larger political bodies, they developed a common spirit and a common basis and general structure allowing of a great freedom of variation in minor line and figure. There was no need of a rigid uniformity; the common spirit and life impulse were enough to impose on this plasticity a law of general oneness. And even when there grew up the great kingdoms and empires, still the characteristic institutions of the smaller kingdoms, republics, peoples were as much as possible incorporated rather than destroyed or thrown aside in the new cast of the socio-political structure. Whatever could not survive in the natural evolution of the people or was no longer needed, fell away of itself and passed into desuetude: whatever could last by modifying itself to new circumstance and environment, was allowed to survive: whatever was in intimate consonance with the psychical and the vital law of being and temperament of the Indian people became universalised and took its place in the enduring figure of the society and polity.

This spontaneous principle of life was respected by the age of growing intellectual culture. The Indian thinkers on society, economics and politics, Dharma Shastra and Artha Shastra, made it their business not to construct ideals and systems of society and government in the abstract intelligence, but to understand and regulate by the practical reason the institutions and ways of communal living already developed by the communal mind and life and to develop, fix and harmonise without destroying the original elements, and whatever new element or idea was needed was added or introduced as a superstructure or a modifying but not a revolutionary and destructive principle. It was in this way that the transition from the earlier stages to the fully developed monarchical polity was managed; it proceeded by an incorporation of the existing institutions under the supreme control of the king or the emperor. The character and status of many of them was modified by the superimposition of the monarchical or imperial system, but, as far as possible, they did not pass out of existence. As a result we do not find in India the element of intellectually idealistic political progress or revolutionary experiment which has been so marked a feature of ancient and of modern Europe. A profound respect for the creations of the past as the natural expression of the Indian mind and life, the sound manifestation of its Dharma or right law of being, was the strongest element in the mental attitude and this preservative instinct was not disturbed but rather yet more firmly settled and fixed by the great millennium of high intellectual culture. A slow evolution of custom and institution conservative of the principle of settled order, of social and political precedent, of established framework and structure was the one way of progress possible or admissible. On the other hand, Indian polity never arrived at that unwholesome substitution of the mechanical for the natural order of the life of the people which has been the disease of European civilisation now culminating in the monstrous artificial organisation of the bureaucratic and industrial State. The advantages of the idealising intellect were absent, but so also were the disadvantages of the mechanising rational intelligence.

The Indian mind has always been profoundly intuitive in habit even when it was the most occupied with the development of the reasoning intelligence, and its political and social thought has therefore been always an attempt to combine the intuitions of life and the intuitions of the spirit with the light of the reason acting as an intermediary and an ordering and regulating factor. It has tried to base itself strongly on the established and persistent actualities of life and to depend for its idealism not on the intellect but on the illuminations, inspirations, higher experiences of the spirit, and it has used the reason as a critical power testing and assuring the steps and aiding but not replacing the life and the spirit—always the true and sound constructors. The spiritual mind of India regarded life as a manifestation of the self: the community was the body of the creator Brahma, the people was a life body of Brahman in the *samaṣṭi,* the collectivity, it was the collective Narayana, as the individual was Brahman in the *vyaṣṭi,* the separate Jiva, the individual Narayana; the king was the living representative of the Divine and the other orders of the community the natural powers of the collective self, *prakṛtayaḥ*. The agreed conventions, institutes, customs, constitution of the body social and politic in all its parts had therefore not only a binding authority but a certain sacrosanct character.

The right order of human life as of the universe is preserved according to the ancient Indian idea by each individual being following faithfully his *svadharma,* the true law and norm of his nature and the nature of his kind and by the group being, the organic collective life, doing likewise. The family, clan, caste, class, social, religious, industrial or other community, nation, people are all organic group beings that evolve their own dharma and to follow it is the condition of their preservation, healthy continuity, sound action. There is also the dharma of the position, the function, the particular relation with others, as there is too the dharma imposed by the condition, environment, age, *yugadharma,* the universal religious or ethical dharma, and all these acting on the natural dharma, the action according to the *svabhāva,* create the body of the Law. The ancient theory supposed that in an entirely right and sound condition of man, individual and collective,—a condition typified by the legendary golden Age, Satya Yuga, Age of Truth,—there is no need of any political government or State or artificial construction of society, because all then live freely according to the truth of their enlightened self and God-inhabited being and therefore spontaneously according to the inner divine Dharma. The self-determining individual and self-determining community living according to the right and free law of his and its being is therefore the ideal. But in the actual condition of humanity, its ignorant and devious nature subject to perversions and violations of the true individual and the true social dharma, there has to be superimposed on the natural life of society a State, sovereign power, a king or governing body, whose business is not to interfere unduly with the life of the society, which must be allowed to function for the most part according to its natural law and custom and spontaneous development, but to superintend and assist its right process and see that the Dharma is observed and in vigour and, negatively, to punish and repress and, as far as may be, prevent offences against the Dharma. A more advanced stage of corruption of the Dharma is marked by the necessity of the appearance of the legislator and the formal government of the whole of life by external or written law and code and rule; but to determine it—apart from external administrative detail—was not the function of the political sovereign, who was only its administrator, but of the socio-religious creator, the Rishi, or the Brahminic recorder and interpreter. And the Law itself written or unwritten was always not a thing to be new created or fabricated by a political and legislative authority, but a thing already existent and only to be interpreted and stated as it was or as it grew naturally out of pre-existing law and principle in the communal life and consciousness. The last and worst state of the society growing out of this increasing artificiality and convention must be a period of anarchy and conflict and dissolution of the dharma,—Kali Yuga,—which must precede through a red-grey evening of cataclysm and struggle a recovery and a new self-expression of the spirit in the human being.

The main function of the political sovereign, the king and council and the other ruling members of the body politic, was therefore to serve and assist the maintenance of the sound law of life of the society: the sovereign was the guardian and administrator of the Dharma. The function of society itself included the right satisfaction of the vital, economic and other needs of the human being and of his hedonistic claim to pleasure and enjoyment, but according to their right law and measure of satisfaction and subject and subordinated to the ethical and social and religious dharma. All the members and groups of the socio-political body had their Dharma determined for them by their nature, their position, their relation to the whole body and must be assured and maintained in the free and right exercise of it, must be left to their own natural and self-determined functioning within their own bounds, but at the same time restrained from any transgression, encroachment or deviation from their right working and true limits. That was the office of the supreme political authority, the sovereign in his Council aided by the public assemblies. It was not the business of the state authority to interfere with or encroach upon the free functioning of the caste, religious community, guild, village, township or the organic custom of the region or province or to abrogate their rights, for these were inherent because necessary to the sound exercise of the social Dharma. All that it was called upon to do was to coordinate, to exercise a general and supreme control, to defend the life of the community against external attack or internal disruption, to repress crime and disorder, to assist, promote and regulate in its larger lines the economic and industrial welfare, to see to the provision of facilities, and to use for these purposes the powers that passed beyond the scope of the others.

Thus in effect the Indian polity was the system of a very complex communal freedom and self-determination, each group unit of the community having its own natural existence and administering its own proper life and business, set off from the rest by a natural demarcation of its field and limits, but connected with the whole by well-understood relations, each a copartner with the others in the powers and duties of the communal existence, executing its own laws and rules, administering within its own proper limits, joining with the others in the discussion and the regulation of matters of a mutual or common interest and represented in some way and to the degree of its importance in the general assemblies of the kingdom or empire. The State, sovereign or supreme political authority was an instrument of coordination and of a general control and efficiency and exercised a supreme but not an absolute authority; for in all its rights and powers it was limited by the Law and by the will of the people and in all its internal functions only a copartner with the other members of the socio-political body.

This was the theory and principle and the actual constitution of the Indian polity, a complex of communal freedom and self-determination with a supreme coordinating authority, a sovereign person and body, armed with efficient powers, position and prestige, but limited to its proper rights and functions, at once controlling and controlled by the rest, admitting them as its active copartners in all branches, sharing the regulation and administration of the communal existence, and all alike, the sovereign, the people and all its constituent communities, bound to the maintenance and restrained by the yoke of the Dharma. Moreover the economic and political aspects of the communal life were only a part of the Dharma and a part not at all separate but inextricably united with all the rest, the religious, the ethical, the higher cultural aim of the social existence. The ethical law coloured the political and economic and was imposed on every action of the king and his ministers, the council and assemblies, the individual, the constituent groups of the society; ethical and cultural considerations counted in the use of the vote and the qualifications for minister, official and councillor; a high character and training was expected from all who held authority in the affairs of the Aryan people. The religious spirit and the reminders of religion were the head and the background of the whole life of king and people. The life of the society was regarded not so much as an aim in itself in spite of the necessary specialisation of parts of its system, but in all its parts and the whole as a great framework and training ground for the education of the human mind and soul and its development through the natural to the spiritual existence.

A DEFENCE OF INDIAN CULTURE

CHAPTER XVII

INDIAN POLITY

THE socio-political evolution of Indian civilisation, as far as one can judge from the available records, passed through four historical stages, first the simple Aryan community, then a long period of transition in which the national life was proceeding through a considerable variety of experimental formations in political structure and synthesis, thirdly, the definite formation of the monarchical state coordinating all the complex elements of the communal life of the people into regional and imperial unities, and last the era of decline in which there was an internal arrest and stagnation and an imposition of new cultures and systems from western Asia and Europe. The distinguishing character of the first three periods is a remarkable solidity and stability in all the formations and a sound and vital and powerful evolution of the life of the people rendered slow and leisurely by this fundamental conservative stability of the system but all the more sure in its building and living and complete in its structure. And even in the decline this solidity opposes a strong resistance to the process of demolition. The structure breaks up at the top under foreign pressure, but preserves for a long time its basis, keeps, wherever it can maintain itself against invasion, much of its characteristic system and is even towards the end capable of attempts at revival of its form and its spirit. And now too though the whole political system has disappeared and its last surviving elements have been ground out of existence, the peculiar social mind and temperament which created it remains even in the present social stagnation, weakness, perversion and disintegration and may yet in spite of immediate tendencies and appearances, once it is free to work again at its own will and after its own manner, proceed not along the western line of evolution, but to a new creation out of its own spirit which may perhaps lead at the call of the demand now vaguely beginning to appear in the advanced thought of the race towards the inception of the third stage of communal living and a spiritual basis of human society. In any case the long stability of its constructions and the greatness of the life they sheltered is certainly no sign of incapacity, but rather of a remarkable political instinct and capacity in the cultural mind of India.

The one principle permanent at the base of construction throughout all the building and extension and rebuilding of the Indian polity was the principle of an organically self-determining communal life,—self-determining not only in the mass and by means of the machinery of the vote and a representative body erected on the surface, representative only of the political mind of a part of the nation, which is all that the modern system has been able to manage, but in every pulse of its life and in each separate member of its existence. A free synthetic communal order was its character, and the condition of liberty it aimed at was not so much an individual as a communal freedom. In the beginning the problem was simple enough as only two kinds of communal unit had to be considered, the village and the clan, tribe or small regional people. The free organic life of the first was founded on the system of the self-governing village community and it was done with such sufficiency and solidity that it lasted down almost to our own days resisting all the wear and tear of time and the inroad of other systems and was only recently steam-rollered out of existence by the ruthless and lifeless machinery of the British bureaucratic system. The whole people living in its villages mostly on agriculture formed in the total a single religious, social, military and political body governing itself in its assembly, *samiti,* under the leadership of the king, as yet without any clear separation of functions or class division of labour.

It was the inadequacy of this system for all but the simplest form of agricultural and pastoral life and all but the small people living within a very limited area that compelled the problem of the evolution of a more complex communal system and a modified and more intricate application of the fundamental Indian principle. The agricultural and pastoral life common at first to all the members of the Aryan community, *kṛṣṭayaḥ,* remained always the large basis, but it developed an increasingly rich superstructure of commerce and industry and numerous arts and crafts and a smaller superstructure of specialised military and political and religious and learned occupations and functions. The village community remained throughout the stable unit, the firm grain or indestructible atom of the social body, but there grew up a group life of tens and hundreds of villages, each under its head and needing its administrative organisation, and these, as the clan grew into a large people by conquest or coalition with others, became constituents of a kingdom or a confederated republican nation, and these again the circles, *maṇḍala,* of larger kingdoms and finally of one or more great empires. The test of the Indian genius for socio-political construction lay in the successful application of its principle of a communal self-determined freedom and order to suit this growing development and new order of circumstances.

The Indian mind evolved, to meet this necessity, the stable socio-religious system of the four orders. Outwardly this might seem to be only a more rigid form of the familiar social system developed naturally in most human peoples at one time or another, a priesthood, a military and political aristocracy, a class of artisans and free agriculturalists and traders and a proletariate of serfs or labourers. The resemblance however is only in the externals and the spirit of the system of Chaturvarna was different in India. In the later Vedic and the epic times the fourfold order was at once and inextricably the religious, social, political and economic framework of the society and within that framework each order had its natural portion and in none of the fundamental activities was the share or position of any of them exclusive. This characteristic is vital to an understanding of the ancient system, but has been obscured by false notions formed from a misunderstanding or an exaggeration of later phenomena and of conditions mostly belonging to the decline. The Brahmins, for example, had not a monopoly either of sacred learning or of the highest spiritual knowledge and opportunities. At first we see a kind of competition between the Brahmins and the Kshatriyas for the spiritual lead and the latter for a long time held their own against the pretensions of the learned and sacerdotal order. The Brahmins, however, as legists, teachers, priests, men who could give their whole time and energy to philosophy, scholarship, the study of the sacred writings, prevailed in the end and secured a settled and imposing predominance. The priestly and learned class became the religious authorities, the custodians of the sacred books and the tradition, the interpreters of the law and Shastra, the recognised teachers in all the departments of knowledge, the ordinary religious preceptors or gurus of the other classes and supplied the bulk, though never the totality of the philosophers, thinkers, literary men, scholars. The study of the Vedas and Upanishads passed mainly into their hands, although always open to the three higher orders; it was denied in theory to the Shudras. As a matter of fact, however, a series of religious movements kept up even in the later days the essential element of the old freedom, brought the highest spiritual knowledge and opportunity to all doors and, as in the beginning we find the Vedic and Vedantic Rishis born from all classes, we find too up to the end the yogins, saints, spiritual thinkers, innovators and restorers, religious poets and singers, the fountain-heads of a living spirituality and knowledge as distinguished from traditional authority and lore, derived from all the strata of the community down to the lowest Shudras and even the despised and oppressed outcastes.

The four orders grew into a fixed social hierarchy, but, leaving aside the status of the outcastes, each had attached to it a spiritual life and utility, a certain social dignity, an education, a principle of social and ethical honour and a place and duty and right in the communal body. The system served again as an automatic means of securing a fixed division of labour and a settled economic status, the hereditary principle at first prevailing, although here even the theory was more rigid than the practice, but none was denied the right or opportunity of amassing wealth and making some figure in society, administration and politics by means of influence or status in his own order. For, finally, the social hierarchy was not at the same time a political hierarchy: all the four orders had their part in the common political rights of the citizen and in the assemblies and administrative bodies their place and their share of influence. It may be noted too that in law and theory at least women in ancient India, contrary to the sentiment of other ancient peoples, were not denied civic rights, although in practice this equality was rendered nugatory for all but a few by their social subordination to the male and their domestic preoccupation; instances have yet survived in the existing records of women figuring, not only as queens and administrators and even in the battlefield, a common enough incident in Indian history, but as elected representatives on civic bodies.

The whole Indian system was founded upon a close participation of all the orders in the common life, each predominating in its own field, the Brahmin in religion, learning and letters, the Kshatriya in war, king-craft and interstate political action, the Vaishya in wealth-getting and productive economical function, but none, not even the Shudra, excluded from his share in the civic life and an effective place and voice in politics, administration, justice. As a consequence the old Indian polity at no time developed, or at least it did not maintain for long, those exclusive forms of class rule that have so long and powerfully marked the political history of other countries. A priestly theocracy, like that of Tibet, or the rule of a landed and military aristocracy that prevailed for centuries in France and England and other European countries or a mercantile oligarchy, as in Carthage and Venice, were forms of government foreign to the Indian spirit. A certain political predominance of the great Kshatriya families at a time of general war and strife and mobile expansion, when the clans and tribes were developing into nations and kingdoms and were still striving with each other for hegemony and overlordship, seems to be indicated in the traditions preserved in the Mahabharata and recurred in a cruder form in the return to the clan nation in mediaeval Rajputana: but in ancient India this was a passing phase and the predominance did not exclude the political and civic influence of men of the other orders or interfere with or exercise any oppressive control over the free life of the various communal units. The democratic republics of the intermediate times were in all probability polities which endeavoured to preserve in its fullness the old principle of the active participation of the whole body of the people in the assemblies and not democracies of the Greek type; the oligarchical republics were clan governments or were ruled by more limited senates drawn from the dignified elements of the society and this afterwards developed into councils or assemblies representing all the four orders as in the later royal councils and urban bodies. In any case the system finally evolved was a mixed polity in which none of the orders had an undue predominance. Accordingly we do not find in India either that struggle between the patrician and plebeian elements of the community, the oligarchic and the democratic idea, ending in the establishment of an absolute monarchical rule, which characterises the troubled history of Greece and Rome or that cycle of successive forms evolving by a strife of classes,—first a ruling aristocracy, then replacing it by encroachment or revolution the dominance of the moneyed and professional classes, the regime of the bourgeois industrialising the society and governing and exploiting it in the name of the commons or masses and, finally, the present turn towards a rule of the proletariate of Labour,—which we see in later Europe. The Indian mind and temperament less exclusively intellectual and vital, more intuitively synthetic and flexible than that of the occidental peoples arrived, not certainly at any ideal system of society and politics, but at least at a wise and stable synthesis—not a dangerously unstable equilibrium, not a compromise or balance—of all the natural powers and orders, an organic and vital coordination respectful of the free functioning of all the organs of the communal body and therefore ensured, although not against the decadence that overtakes all human systems, at any rate against any organic disturbance or disorder.

The summit of the political structure was occupied by three governing bodies, the King in his ministerial council, the metropolitan assembly and the general assembly of the kingdom. The members of the Council and the ministers were drawn from all orders. The Council included a fixed number of Brahmin, Kshatriya, Vaishya and Shudra representatives. The Vaishyas had indeed numerically a great preponderance, but this was a just proportion as it corresponded to their numerical preponderance in the body of the people: for in the early Aryan society the Vaishya order comprised not only the merchants and small traders but the craftsmen and artisans and the agriculturalists and formed therefore the bulk of the commons, *viśaḥ*, and the Brahmins, Kshatriyas, Shudras, however considerable the position and influence of the two higher orders, were later social growths and were comparatively very inferior in number. It was only after the confusion created by the Buddhist upheaval and the Brahminic reconstitution of the society in the age of cultural decadence that the mass of the cultivators and artisans and small traders sank in the greater part of India to the condition of Shudras with a small Brahmin mass at the top and in between a slight sprinkling of Kshatriyas and of Vaishyas. The Council, representing thus the whole community, was the supreme executive and administrative body and its assent and participation necessary to all the action and decrees of the sovereign in all more important matters of government, finance, policy, throughout the whole range of the communal interests. It was the King, the ministers and the council who aided by a system of boards of administration superintended and controlled all the various departments of the State action. The power of the king undoubtedly tended to grow with time and he was often tempted to act according to his own independent will and initiative; but still, as long as the system was in its vigour, he could not with impunity defy or ignore the opinion and will of the ministers and council. Even, it seems, so powerful and strong-willed a sovereign as the great emperor Asoka was eventually defeated in his conflict with his council and was forced practically to abdicate his power. The ministers in council could and did often proceed to the deposition of a recalcitrant or an incompetent monarch and replace him by another of his family or by a new dynasty and it was in this way that there came about several of the historic changes, as for example the dynastic revolution from the Mauryas to the Sungas and again the initiation of the Kanwa line of emperors. As a matter of constitutional theory and ordinary practice all the action of the king was in reality that of the king in his council with the aid of his ministers and all his personal action was only valid as depending on their assent and in so far as it was a just and faithful discharge of the functions assigned to him by the Dharma. And as the Council was, as it were, a quintessential power body or action centre taking up into itself in a manageable compass, concentrating and representing in its constitution the four orders, the main elements of the social organism, the king too could only be the active head of this power and not, as in an autocratic regime, himself the State or the owner of the country and the irresponsible personal ruler of a nation of obedient subjects. The obedience owed by the people was due to the Law, the Dharma, and to the edicts of the King in council only as an administrative means for the service and maintenance of the Dharma.

At the same time a small body like the Council subject to the immediate and constant influence of the sovereign and his ministers might, if it had been the sole governing body, have degenerated into an instrument of autocratic rule. But there were two other powerful bodies in the State which represented on a larger scale the social organism, were a nearer and closer expression of its mind, life and will independent of the immediate regal influence and exercising large and constant powers of administration and administrative legislation and capable at all times of acting as a check on the royal power, since in case of their displeasure they could either get rid of an unpopular or oppressive king or render his administration impossible until he made submission to the will of the people. These were the great metropolitan and general assemblies sitting separately for the exercise each of its separate powers and together for matters concerning the whole people.* The Paura or metropolitan civic assembly sat constantly in the capital town of the kingdom or empire—and under the imperial system there seem also to have been similar lesser bodies in the chief towns of the provinces, survivals of the assemblies that governed them when they were

* The facts about these bodies—I have selected only those that are significant for my purpose—are taken from the luminous and scrupulously documented contribution of Mr. Jayaswal to the subject.

themselves capitals of independent kingdoms—and was constituted of representatives of the city guilds and the various caste bodies belonging to all the orders of the society or at least to the three lower orders. The guilds and caste bodies were themselves organic self-governing constituents of the community both in the country and the city and the supreme assembly of the citizens was not an artificial but an organic representation of the collective totality of the whole organism as it existed within the limits of the metropolis. It governed all the life of the city, acting directly or through subordinate lesser assemblies and administrative boards or committees of five, ten or more members, and, both by regulations and decrees which the guilds were bound to obey and by direct administration, controlled and supervised the commercial, industrial, financial and municipal affairs of the civic community. But in addition it was a power that had to be consulted and could take action in the wider affairs of the kingdom, sometimes separately and sometimes in cooperation with the general assembly, and its constant presence and functioning at the capital made it a force that had always to be reckoned with by the king and his ministers and their council. In a case of conflict with the royal ministers or governors even the distant civic parliaments in the provinces could make their displeasure felt if offended in matters of their position or privileges or discontented with the king's administrators and could compel the withdrawal of the offending officer.

The general assembly was similarly an organic representation of the mind and will of the whole country outside the metropolis; for it was composed of the deputies, elective heads or chief men of the townships and villages. A certain plutocratic element seems to have entered into its composition, as it was principally recruited from the wealthier men of the represented communities, and it was therefore something of the nature of an assembly of the commons not of an entirely democratic type, —although unlike all but the most recent modern parliaments it included Shudras as well as Kshatriyas and Vaishyas,—but still a sufficiently faithful expression of the life and mind of the people. It was not however a supreme parliament: for it had ordinarily no fundamental legislative powers, any more than had the king and council or the metropolitan assembly, but only of decree and regulation. Its business was to serve as a direct instrument of the will of the people in the coordination of the various activities of the life of the nation, to see to the right direction of these and to the securing of the general order and welfare of the commerce, industry, agriculture, social and political life of the nation, to pass decrees and regulations to that purpose and secure privileges and facilities from the king and his council, to give or withhold the assent of the people to the actions of the sovereign and, if need be, to oppose him actively and prevent misgovernment or end it by the means open to the people's representatives. The joint session of the metropolitan and general assemblies was consulted in matters of succession, could depose the sovereign, alter the succession at his death, transfer the throne outside the reigning family, act sometimes as a supreme court of law in cases having a political tincture, cases of treason or of miscarriage of justice. The royal resolutions on any matter of State policy were promulgated to these assemblies and their assent had to be taken in all matters involving special taxation, war, sacrifice, large schemes of irrigation etc., and all questions of vital interest to the country. The two bodies seem to have sat constantly, for matters came up daily from them to the sovereign: their acts were registered by the king and had automatically the effect of law. It is clear indeed from a total review of their rights and activities that they were partners in the sovereignty and its powers were inherent in them and even those could be exercised by them on extraordinary occasions which were not normally within their purview. It is significant that Asoka in his attempt to alter the Dharma of the community, proceeded not merely by his royal decree but by discussion with the Assembly. The ancient description seems therefore to have been thoroughly justified which characterised the two bodies as executors of the kingdom's activities and at need the instruments of opposition to the king's government.

It is not clear when these great institutions went out of existence, whether before the Mahomedan invasion or as a result of the foreign conquest. Any collapse of the system at the top leaving a gulf between the royal government, which would grow more autocratic by its isolation and in sole control of the larger national affairs, and the other constituents of the socio-political body each carrying on its own internal affairs, as was to the end the case with the village communities, but not in any living relation with the higher State matters, would obviously be in an organisation of complex communal freedom where coordination of the life was imperatively needed, a great cause of weakness. In any case the invasion from Central Asia, bringing in a tradition of personal and autocratic rule unfamiliar with these restraints would immediately destroy such bodies, or their remnants or survivals wherever they still existed, and this happened throughout the whole of Northern India. The Indian political system was still maintained for many centuries in the south, but the public assemblies which went on existing there do not seem to have been of the same constitution as the ancient political bodies, but were rather some of the other communal organisations and assemblies of which these were a coordination and supreme instrument of control. These inferior assemblies included bodies originally of a political character, once the supreme governing institutions of the clan nation, *kula*, and the republic, *gaṇa*. Under the new dispensation they remained in existence, but lost their supreme powers and could only administer with a subordinate and restricted authority the affairs of their constituent communities. The *kula* or clan family persisted, even after it had lost its political character, as a socio-religious institution, especially among the Kshatriyas, and preserved the tradition of its social and religious law, *kula-dharma*, and in some cases its communal assembly, *kula-sangha*. The public assemblies that we find even in quite recent times filling the role of the old general assembly in Southern India, more than one coexisting and acting separately or in unison, appear to have been variations on this type of body. In Rajputana also the clan family, *kula*, recovered its political character and action, but in another form and without the ancient institutions and finer cultural temper, although they preserved in a high degree the Kshatriya dharma of courage, chivalry, magnanimity and honour.

A stronger permanent element in the Indian communal system, one that grew up in the frame of the four orders—in the end even replacing it—and acquired an extraordinary vitality, persistence and predominant importance was the historic and still tenacious though decadent institution of caste, *jāti*. Originally this rose from subdivisions of the four orders that grew up in each order under the stress of various forces. The subdivision of the Brahmin castes was mainly due to religious, socio-religious and ceremonial causes, but there were also regional and local divisions: the Kshatriyas remained for the most part one united order, though divided into Kulas. On the other hand the Vaishya and Shudra orders split up into innumerable castes under the necessity of a subdivision of economic functions on the basis of the hereditary principle. Apart from the increasingly rigid application of the hereditary principle, this settled subdivision of function could well enough have been secured, as in other countries, by a guild system and in towns we do find a vigorous and efficient guild system in existence. But the guild system afterwards fell into desuetude and the more general institution of caste became the one basis of economic function everywhere. The caste in town and village was a separate communal unit, at once religious, social and economic, and decided its religious social and other questions, carried on its caste affairs and exercised jurisdiction over its members in a perfect freedom from all outside interference: only on fundamental questions of the Dharma the Brahmins were referred to for an authoritative interpretation or decision as custodians of the Shastra. As with the *kula,* each caste had its caste law and rule of living and conduct, *jāti-dharma,* and its caste communal assembly, *jāti-saṅgha.* As the Indian polity in all its institutions was founded on a communal and not on an individual basis, the caste also counted in the political and administrative functioning of the kingdom. The guilds equally were self-functioning mercantile and industrial communal units, assembled for the discussion and administration of their affairs and had besides their united assemblies which seem at one time to have been the governing urban bodies. These guild governments, if they may so be called, —for they were more than municipalities,—disappeared afterwards into the more general urban body which represented an organic unity of both the guilds and the caste assemblies of all the orders. The castes as such were not directly represented in the general assembly of the kingdom, but they had their place in the administration of local affairs.

The village community and the township were the most tangibly stable basis of the whole system; but these, it must be noted, were not solely territorial units or a convenient mechanism for electoral, administrative or other useful social and political purposes, but always true communal unities with an organic life of their own that functioned in its own power and not merely as a subordinate part of the machinery of the State. The village community has been described as a little village republic, and the description is hardly an exaggeration: for each village was within its own limits autonomous and self-sufficient, governed by its own elected Panchayats and elected or hereditary officers, satisfying its own needs, providing for its own education, police, tribunals, all its economic necessities and functions, managing itself its own life as an independent and self-governing unit.

The villages carried on also their affairs with each other by combinations of various kinds and there were too groups of villages under elected or hereditary heads and forming therefore, though in a less closely organised fashion, a natural body. But the townships in India were also in a hardly less striking way autonomous and self-governing bodies, ruled by their own assembly and committees with an elective system and the use of the vote, managing their own affairs in their own right and sending like the villages their representative men to the general assembly of the kingdom. The administration of these urban governments included all works contributing to the material or other welfare of the citizens, police, judicial cases, public works and the charge of sacred and public places, registration, the collection of municipal taxes and all matters relating to trade, industry and commerce. If the village community can be described as a little village republic, the constitution of the township can equally be described as a larger urban republic. It is significant that the Naigama and Paura assemblies,—the guild governments and the metropolitan bodies,—had the privilege of striking coins of their own, a power otherwise exercised only by the monarchical heads of States and the republics.

Another kind of community must be noted, those which had no political existence, but were yet each in its own kind a self-governing body; for they illustrate the strong tendency of Indian life to throw itself in all its manifestations into a closely communal form of existence. One example is the joint family, prevalent everywhere in India and only now breaking down under the pressure of modern conditions, of which the two fundamental principles were first a communal holding of the property by the agnates and their families and, as far as possible, an undivided communal life under the management of the head of the family and, secondly, the claim of each male to an equal portion in the share of his father, a portion due to him in case of separation and division of the estate. This communal unity with the persistent separate right of the individual is an example of the synthetic turn of the Indian mind and life, its recognition of fundamental tendencies and its attempt to harmonise them even if they seemed in their norm of practice to be contradictory to each other. It is the same synthetic turn as that which in all parts of the Indian socio-political system tended to fuse together in different ways the theocratic, the monarchic and aristocratic, the plutocratic and the democratic tendencies in a whole which bore the characteristics of none of them nor was yet an accommodation of them or amalgamation whether by a system of checks and balances or by an intellectually constructed synthesis, but rather a natural outward form of the inborn tendencies and character of the complex social mind and temperament.

At the other end, forming the ascetic and purely spiritual extreme of the Indian life-mind, we find the religious community and, again, this too takes a communal shape. The original Vedic society had no place for any Church or religious community or ecclesiastical order, for in its system the body of the people formed a single socio-religious whole with no separation into religious and secular, layman and cleric, and in spite of later developments the Hindu religion has held, in the whole or at least as the basis, to this principle. On the other hand an increasing ascetic tendency that came in time to distinguish the religious from the mundane life and tended to create the separate religious community, was confirmed by the rise of the creeds and disciplines of the Buddhists and the Jains. The Buddhist monastic order was the first development of the complete figure of the organised religious community. Here we find that Buddha simply applied the known principles of the Indian society and polity to the ascetic life. The order he created was intended to be a *dharma-sangha*, and each monastery a religious commune living the life of a united communal body which existed as the expression and was based in all the rules, features, structure of its life on the maintenance of the Dharma as it was understood by the

Buddhists. This was, as we can at once see, precisely the principle and theory of the whole Hindu society, but given here the higher intensity possible to the spiritual life and a purely religious body. It managed its affairs too like the Indian social and political communal unities. An assembly of the order discussed debatable questions of the Dharma and its application and proceeded by vote as in the meeting-halls of the republics, but it was subject still to a limiting control intended to avoid the possible evils of a too purely democratic method. The monastic system once thus firmly established was taken over from Buddhism by the orthodox religion, but without its elaborate organisation. These religious communities tended, wherever they could prevail against the older Brahminic system, as in the order created by Shankaracharya, to become a sort of ecclesiastical head to the lay body of the community, but they arrogated to themselves no political position and the struggle between Church and State is absent from the political history of India.

It is clear therefore that the whole life of ancient India retained even in the time of the great kingdoms and empires its first principle and essential working and its social polity remained fundamentally a complex system of self-determined and self-governing communal bodies. The evolution of an organised State authority supervening on this system was necessitated in India as elsewhere partly by the demand of the practical reason for a more stringent and scientifically efficient coordination than was possible except in small areas to the looser natural coordination of life, and more imperatively by the need of a systematised military aggression and defence and international action concentrated in the hands of a single central authority. An extension of the free republican State might have sufficed to meet the former demand, for it had the potentiality and the necessary institutions, but the method of the monarchical State with its more constricted and easily tangible centrality presented a more ready and manageable device and a more facile and apparently efficient machinery. And for the external task, involving almost from the commencement the supremely difficult age-long problem of the political unification of India, then a continent rather than a country, the republican system, more suited to strength in defence than for aggression, proved in spite of its efficient military organisation to be inadequate. It was, therefore, in India as elsewhere, the strong form of the monarchical State that prevailed finally and swallowed up the others. At the same time the fidelity of the Indian mind to its fundamental institutions and ideals preserved the basis of communal self-government natural to the temperament of the people, prevented the monarchical State from developing into an autocracy or exceeding its proper functions and stood successfully in the way of its mechanising the life of the society. It is only in the long decline that we find the free institutions that stood between the royal government and the self-determining communal life of the people either tending to disappear or else to lose much of their ancient power and vigour and the evils of personal government, of a bureaucracy of scribes and officials and of a too preponderant centralised authority commencing to manifest in some sensible measure. As long as the ancient traditions of the Indian polity remained and in proportion as they continued to be vital and effective, these evils remained either sporadic and occasional or could not assume any serious proportions. It was the combination of foreign invasion and conquest with the slow decline and final decadence of the ancient Indian culture that brought about the collapse of considerable parts of the old structure and the degradation and disintegration, with no sufficient means for revival or new creation, of the socio-political life of the people.

At the height of its evolution and in the great days of Indian civilisation we find an admirable political system efficient in the highest degree and very perfectly combining communal self-government with stability and order. The State carried on its work administrative, judicial, financial and protective without destroying or encroaching on the rights and free activities of the people and its constituent bodies in the same departments. The royal courts in capital and country were the supreme judicial authority coordinating the administration of justice throughout the kingdom, but they did not unduly interfere with the judicial powers entrusted to their own courts by the village and urban communes and, even, the regal system associated with itself the guild, caste and family courts, working as an ample means of arbitration and only insisted on its own exclusive control of the more serious criminal offences. A similar respect was shown to the administrative and financial powers of the village and urban communes. The king's governors and officials in town and country existed side by side with the civic governors and officials and the communal heads and officers appointed by the people and its assemblies. The State did not interfere with the religious liberty or the established economic and social life of the nation; it confined itself to the maintenance of social order and the provision of a needed supervision, support, coordination and facilities for the rich and powerful functioning of all the national activities. It understood too always and magnificently fulfilled its opportunities as a source of splendid and munificent stimulation to the architecture, art, culture, scholarship, literature already created by the communal mind of India. In the person of the monarch it was the dignified and powerful head and in the system of his administration the supreme instrument—neither an arbitrary autocracy or bureaucracy, nor a machine oppressing or replacing life—of a great and stable civilisation and a free and living people.

A DEFENCE OF INDIAN CULTURE

CHAPTER XVIII

INDIAN POLITY

A RIGHT knowledge of the facts and a right understanding of the character and principle of the Indian socio-political system disposes at once of the contention of occidental critics that the Indian mind, even if remarkable in metaphysics, religion, art and literature was inapt for the organisation of life, inferior in the works of the practical intelligence and, especially, that it was sterile in political experiment and its record empty of sound political construction, thinking and action. On the contrary, Indian civilisation evolved an admirable political system, built solidly and with an enduring soundness, combined with a remarkable skill the monarchical, democratic and other principles and tendencies to which the mind of man has leaned in its efforts of civic construction and escaped at the same time the excess of the mechanising turn which is the defect of the modern European State. I shall consider afterwards the objections that can be made to it from the evolutionary standpoint of the West and its idea of progress.

But there is another side of politics on which it may be said that the Indian political mind has registered nothing but failure. The organisation it developed may have been admirable for stability and effective administration and the securing of communal order and liberties and the well-being of the people under ancient conditions, but even if its many peoples were each of them separately self-governed, well governed and prosperous and the country at large assured in the steady functioning of a highly developed civilisation and culture, yet that organisation failed to serve for the national and political unification of India and failed in the end to secure it against foreign invasion, the disruption of its institutions and an agelong servitude. The political system of a society has to be judged, no doubt first and foremost by the stability, prosperity, internal freedom and order it ensures to the people, but also it must be judged by the security it erects against other States, its unity and power of defence and aggression against external rivals and enemies. It is not perhaps altogether to the credit of humanity that it should be so and a nation or people that is inferior in this kind of political strength, as were the ancient Greeks and mediaeval Italians, may be spiritually and culturally far superior to its conquerors and may well have contributed more to a true human progress than successful military States, aggressive communities, predatory empires. But the life of man is still predominatingly vital and moved therefore by the tendencies of expansion, possession, aggression, mutual struggle for absorption and dominant survival which are the first law of life, and a collective mind and consciousness that gives a constant proof of incapacity for aggression and defence and does not organise the centralised and efficient unity necessary to its own safety, is clearly one that in the political field falls far short of the first order. India has never been nationally and politically one. India was for close on a thousand years swept by barbaric invasions and for almost another thousand years in servitude to successive foreign masters. It is clear therefore that judgment of political incapacity must be passed against the Indian people.

Here again the first necessity is to get rid of exaggerations, to form a clear idea of the actual facts and their significance and understand the tendencies and principles involved in the problem that admittedly throughout the long history of India escaped a right solution. And first, if the greatness of a people and a civilisation is to be reckoned by its military aggressiveness, its scale of foreign conquest, its success in warfare against other nations and the triumph of its organised acquisitive and predatory instincts, its irresistible push towards annexation and exploitation, it must be confessed that India ranks perhaps the lowest in the list of the world's great peoples. At no time does India seem to have been moved towards an aggressive military and political expansion beyond her own borders; no epic of world dominion, no great tale of far-borne invasion or expanding colonial empire has ever been written in the tale of Indian achievement. The sole great endeavour of expansion, of conquest, of invasion she attempted was the expansion of her culture, the invasion and conquest of the eastern world by the Buddhistic idea and the penetration of her spirituality, art and thought-forces. And this was an invasion of peace and not of war, for to spread a spiritual civilisation by force and physical conquest, the vaunt or the excuse of modern imperialism, would have been uncongenial to the ancient cast of her mind and temperament and the idea underlying her Dharma. A series of colonising expeditions carried indeed Indian blood and Indian culture to the islands of the archipelago, but the ships that set out from both the eastern and western coast were not fleets of invaders missioned to annex those outlying countries to an Indian empire but of exiles or adventurers carrying with them to yet uncultured peoples Indian religion, architecture, art, poetry, thought, life, manners. The idea of empire and even of world-empire was not absent from the Indian mind, but its world was the Indian world and the object the founding of the imperial unity of its peoples.

This idea, the sense of this necessity, a constant urge towards its realisation is evident throughout the whole course of Indian history from earlier Vedic times through the heroic period represented by the traditions of the Ramayana and Mahabharata and the effort of the imperial Mauryas and Guptas up to the Moghul unification and the last ambition of the Peshwas, until there came the final failure and the levelling of all the conflicting forces under a foreign yoke, a uniform subjection in place of the free unity of a free people. The question then is whether the tardiness, the difficulty, the fluctuating movements of the process and the collapse of the long effort were due to a fundamental incapacity in the civilisation or in the political consciousness and ability of the people or to other forces. A great deal has been said and written about the inability of Indians to unite, the want of a common patriotism—now only being created, it is said, by the influence of Western culture—and the divisions imposed by religion and caste. Admitting even in their full degree the force of these strictures,—all of them are not altogether true or rightly stated or vitally applicable to the matter,—they are only symptoms and we have still to seek for the deeper causes.

The reply made for the defence is usually that India is practically a continent almost as large as Europe containing a great number of peoples and the difficulties of the problem have been as great or at least almost as considerable. And if then it is no proof of the insufficiency of Western civilisation or of the political incapacity of the European peoples that the idea of European unity should still remain an ineffective phantasm on the ideal plane and to this day impossible to realise in practice, it is not just to apply a different system of values to the much more clear ideal of unity or at least of unification, the persistent attempt at its realisation and the frequent near approach to success that marked the history of the Indian peoples. There is some force in the contention, but it is not in the form entirely apposite, for the analogy is far from perfect and the conditions were not quite of the same order. The peoples of Europe are nations very sharply divided from each other in their collective personality, and their spiritual unity in the Christian religion or even their cultural unity in a common European civilisation, never so real and complete as the ancient spiritual and cultural unity of India, was also not the very centre of their life, not its basis or firm ground of existence, not its supporting earth but only its general air or circumambient atmosphere. Their base of existence lay in the political and economic life which was strongly separate in each country, and it was the very strength of the political consciousness in the western mind that kept Europe a mass of divided and constantly warring nations. It is only the increasing community of political movements and the now total economic interdependence of the whole of Europe that has at last created not any unity, but a nascent and still ineffective League of Nations struggling vainly to apply the mentality born of an agelong separatism to the common interests of the European peoples. But in India at a very early time the spiritual and cultural unity was made complete and became the very stuff of the life of all this great surge of humanity between the Himalayas and the two seas. The peoples of ancient India were never so much distinct nations sharply divided from each other by a separate political and economic life as sub-peoples of a great spiritual and cultural nation itself firmly separated, physically, from other countries by the seas and the mountains and from other nations by its strong sense of difference, its peculiar common religion and culture. The creation of a political unity, however vast the area and however many the practical difficulties, ought therefore to have been effected more easily than could possibly be the unity of Europe. The cause of the failure must be sought deeper down and we shall find that it lay in a dissidence between the manner in which the problem was or ought to have been envisaged and the actual turn given to the endeavour and in the latter a contradiction of the peculiar mentality of the people.

The whole basis of the Indian mind is its spiritual and inward turn, its propensity to seek the things of the spirit and the inner being first and foremost and to look at all else as secondary, dependent, to be handled and determined in the light of the higher knowledge and as an expression, a preliminary or field or aid or at least a pendent to the deeper spiritual aim,—a tendency therefore to create whatever it had to create first on the inner plane and afterwards in its other aspects. This mentality and this consequent tendency to create from within outwards being given, it was inevitable that the unity India first created for herself should be the spiritual and cultural oneness. It could not be, to begin with, a political unification effected by an external rule centralised, imposed or constructed, as was done in Rome or ancient Persia, by a conquering kingdom or the genius of a military and organising people. It cannot, I think, justly be said that this was a mistake or a proof of the unpractical turn of the Indian mind and that the single political body should have been created first and afterwards the spiritual unity could have securely grown up in the vast body of an Indian national empire. The problem that presented itself at the beginning was that of a huge area containing more than a hundred kingdoms, clans, peoples, tribes, races, in this respect another Greece, but a Greece on an enormous scale, almost as large as modern Europe. As in Greece a cultural Hellenic unity was necessary to create a fundamental feeling of oneness, here too and much more imperatively a conscious spiritual and cultural unity of all these peoples was the first, the indispensable condition without which no enduring unity could be possible. The instinct of the Indian mind and of its great Rishis and founders of its culture was sound in this matter. And even if we suppose that an outward imperial unity like that of the Roman world could have been founded among the peoples of early India by military and political means, we must not forget that the Roman unity did not endure, that even the unity of ancient Italy founded by the Roman conquest and organisation did not endure, and it is not likely that a similar attempt in the vast reaches of India without a previous spiritual and cultural basis would have been of an enduring character. It cannot be said either, even if the emphasis on spiritual and cultural unity be pronounced to have been too engrossing or excessive and the insistence of political and external unity too feeble, that the effect of this precedence has been merely disastrous and without any advantage. It is due to this original peculiarity, to this indelible spiritual stamp, to this underlying oneness amidst all diversities that if India is not yet a single organised political nation, she still survives and is still India.

After all, the spiritual and cultural is the only enduring unity and it is by a persistent mind and spirit much more than by an enduring physical body and outward organisation that the soul of a people survives. This is a truth the positive western mind may be unwilling to understand or concede, and yet its proofs are written across the whole story of the ages. The ancient nations, contemporaries of India, and many younger born than she are dead and only their monuments left behind them. Greece and Egypt exist only on the map and in name, for it is not the soul of Hellas or the deeper nation-soul that built Memphis which we now find at Athens or at Cairo. Rome imposed a political and a purely outward cultural unity on the Mediterranean peoples, but their living spiritual and cultural oneness she could not create, and therefore the east broke away from the west, Africa kept no impress of the Roman interlude, and even the western nations still called Latin could offer no living resistance to barbarian invaders and had to be reborn by the infusion of a foreign vitality to become modern Italy, Spain and France. But India still lives and keeps the continuity of her inner mind and soul and spirit with the India of the ages. Invasion and foreign rule, the Greek, the Parthian and the Hun, the robust vigour of Islam, the levelling steam-roller heaviness of the British occupation and the British system, the enormous pressure of the occident have not been able to drive or crush the ancient soul out of the body her Vedic Rishis made for her. At every step, under every calamity and attack and domination, she has been able to resist and survive either with an active or a passive resistance. And this she was able to do in her great days by her spiritual solidarity and power of assimilation and reaction, expelling all that would not be absorbed, absorbing all that could not be expelled, and even after the beginning of the decline she was still able to survive by the same force, abated but not slayable, retreating and maintaining for a time her ancient political system in the south, throwing up under the pressure of Islam, Rajput and Sikh and Mahratta to defend her ancient self and its idea, persisting passively where she could not resist actively, condemning to decay each empire that could not answer her riddle or make terms with her, awaiting always the day of her revival. And even now it is a similar phenomenon that we see in process before our eyes. And what shall we say then of the surpassing vitality of the civilisation that could accomplish this miracle and of the wisdom of those who built its foundation not on things external but on the spirit and the inner mind and made a spiritual and cultural oneness the root and stock of her existence and not solely its fragile flower, the eternal basis and not the perishable superstructure?

But spiritual unity is a large and flexible thing and does not insist like the political and external on centralisation and uniformity; rather it lives diffused in the system and permits readily a great diversity and freedom of life. Here we touch on the secret of the difficulty in the problem of unifying ancient India. It could not be done by the ordinary means of a centralised uniform imperial State crushing out all that made for free divergence, local autonomies, established communal liberties, and each time that an attempt was made in this direction, it has failed after however long a term of apparent success, and we might even say that the guardians of India's destiny wisely compelled it to fail that her inner spirit might not perish and her soul barter for an engine of temporary security the deep sources of its life.

The ancient mind of India had the intuition of its need; its idea of empire was a uniting rule that respected every existing regional and communal liberty, that unnecessarily crushed out no living autonomy, that effected a synthesis of her life and not a mechanical oneness. Afterwards the conditions under which such a solution might securely have evolved and found its true means and form and basis, disappeared and there was instead an attempt to establish a single administrative empire. That endeavour, dictated by the pressure of an immediate and external necessity, failed to achieve a complete success in spite of its greatness and splendour. It could not do so because it followed a trend that was not eventually compatible with the true turn of the Indian spirit. It has been seen that the underlying principle of the Indian politico-social system was a synthesis of communal autonomies, the autonomy of the village, of the town and capital city, of the caste, guild, family, *kula*, religious community, regional unit. The state or kingdom or confederated republic was a means of holding together and synthetising in a free and living organic system these autonomies. The imperial problem was to synthetise again these states, peoples, nations, effecting their unity but respecting their autonomy, into a larger free and living organism. A system had to be found that would maintain peace and oneness among its members, secure safety against external attack and totalise the free play and evolution, in its unity and diversity, in the uncoerced and active life of all its constituent communal and regional units, of the soul and body of Indian civilisation and culture, the functioning on a grand and total scale of the Dharma.

This was the sense in which the earlier mind of India understood the problem. The administrative empire of later times accepted it only partially, but its trend was, very slowly and almost subconsciously, what the centralising tendency must always be, if not actively to destroy, still to wear down and weaken the vigour of the subordinated autonomies. The consequence was that whenever the central authority was weak, the persistent principle of regional autonomy essential to the life of India reasserted itself to the detriment of the artificial unity established and not, as it should have done, for the harmonious intensification and freer but still united functioning of the total life. The imperial monarchy tended also to wear down the vigour of the free assemblies, and the result was that the communal units instead of being elements of a united strength became isolated and dividing factors. The village community preserved something of its vigour, but had no living connection with the supreme authority and, losing the larger national sense, was willing to accept any indigenous or foreign rule that respected its own self-sufficient narrow life. The religious communities came to be imbued with the same spirit. The castes, multiplying themselves without any true necessity or true relation to the spiritual or the economic need of the country, became mere sacrosanct conventional divisions, a power for isolation and not, as they originally were, factors of a harmonious functioning of the total life-synthesis. It is not true that the caste divisions were in ancient India an obstacle to the united life of the people or that they were even in later times an active power for political strife and disunion,—except indeed at the end, in the final decline, and especially during the later history of the Mahratta confederation; but they did become a passive force of social division and of a stagnant compartmentalism obstructive to the reconstitution of a free and actively united life.

The evils that attended the system did not all manifest themselves with any power before the Mahomedan invasions, but they must have been already there in their beginning and they increased rapidly under the conditions created by the Pathan and the Moghul empires. These later imperial systems however brilliant and powerful, suffered still more than their predecessors from the evils of centralisation owing to their autocratic character and were constantly breaking down from the same tendency of the regional life of India to assert itself against an artificial unitarian regime, while, because they had no true, living and free relation with the life of the people, they proved unable to create the common patriotism which would have effectively secured them against the foreign invader. And in the end there has come a mechanical western rule that has crushed out all the still existing communal or regional autonomies and substituted the dead unity of a machine. But again in the reaction against it we see the same ancient tendencies reviving, the tendency towards a reconstitution of the regional life of the Indian peoples, the demand for a provincial autonomy founded on true subdivisions of race and language, a harking back of the Indian mind to the ideal of the lost village community as a living unit necessary to the natural life of the national body and, not yet reborn but dimly beginning to dawn on the more advanced minds, a truer idea of the communal basis proper to Indian life and the renovation and reconstruction of Indian society and politics on a spiritual foundation.

The failure to achieve Indian unity of which the invasions and the final subjection to the foreigner were the consequence, arose therefore at once from the magnitude and from the peculiarity of the task, because the easy method of a centralised empire could not truly succeed in India, while yet it seemed the only device possible and was attempted again and again with a partial success that seemed for the time and a long time to justify it, but always with an eventual failure. I have suggested that the early mind of India better understood the essential character of the problem. The Vedic Rishis and their successors made it their chief work to found a spiritual basis of Indian life and to effect the spiritual and cultural unity of the many races and peoples of the peninsula. But they were not blind to the necessity of a political unification. Observing the constant tendency of the clan life of the Aryan peoples to consolidate under confederacies and hegemonies of varying proportions, *vairājya, sāmrājya,* they saw that to follow this line to its full conclusion was the right way and evolved therefore the ideal of the *cakravartin,* a uniting imperial rule, uniting without destroying the autonomy of India's many kingdoms and peoples, from sea to sea. This ideal they supported, like everything else in Indian life, with a spiritual and religious sanction, set up as its outward symbol the Aswamedha and Rajasuya sacrifices, and made it the dharma of a powerful King, his royal and religious duty, to attempt the fulfilment of the ideal. He was not allowed by the Dharma to destroy the liberties of the peoples who came under his sway nor to dethrone or annihilate their royal houses or replace their archons by his officials and governors. His function was to establish a suzerain power possessed of sufficient military strength to preserve internal peace and to combine at need the full forces of the country. And to this elementary function came to be added the ideal of the fulfilment and maintenance under a strong uniting hand of the Indian dharma, the right functioning of the spiritual, religious, ethical and social culture of India.

The full flowering of the ideal is seen in the great epics. The Mahabharata is the record of a legendary or, it may be, a historic attempt to establish such an empire a *dharmarājya* or kingdom of the Dharma. There the ideal is pictured as so imperative and widely acknowledged that even the turbulent Shishupala is represented as motiving his submission and attendance at the Rajasuya sacrifice on the ground that Yudhisthira was carrying out an action demanded by the Dharma. And in the Ramayana we have an idealised picture of such a Dharmarajya, a settled universal empire. Here too it is not an autocratic despotism but a universal monarchy supported by a free assembly of the city and provinces and of all the classes that is held up as the ideal, an enlargement of the monarchical state synthetising the communal autonomies of the Indian system and maintaining the law and constitution of the Dharma. The ideal of conquest held up is not a destructive and predatory invasion annihilating the organic freedom and the political and social institutions and exploiting the economic resources of the conquered peoples, but a sacrificial progression bringing with it a trial of military strength of which the result was easily accepted because defeat entailed neither humiliation nor servitude and suffering but merely a strengthening adhesion to a suzerain power concerned only with establishing the visible unity of the nation and the Dharma. The ideal of the ancient Rishis is clear and their political utility and necessity of a unification of the divided and warring peoples of the land, but they saw also that it ought not to be secured at the expense of the free life of the regional peoples or of the communal liberties and not therefore by a centralised monarchy or a rigidly unitarian imperial State. A hegemony or confederacy under an imperial head would be the nearest western analogy to the conception they sought to impose on the minds of the people.

There is no historical evidence that this ideal was ever successfully carried into execution, although the epic tradition speaks of several such empires preceding the Dharmarajya of Yudhishthira. At the time of Buddha and later when Chandragupta and Chanakya were building the first historic Indian empire, the country was still covered with free kingdoms and republics and there was no united empire to meet the great raid of Alexander. It is evident that if any hegemony had previously existed, it had failed to discover a means or system of enduring permanence. This might however have evolved if time had been given, but a serious change had meanwhile taken place which made it urgently necessary to find an immediate solution. The historic weakness of the Indian peninsula has always been until modern times its vulnerability through the north-western passes. This weakness did not exist so long as ancient India extended northward far beyond the Indus and the powerful kingdoms of Gandhara and Vahlika presented a firm bulwark against foreign invasion. But they had now gone down before the organised Persian empire and from this time forward the trans-Indus countries, ceasing to be part of India, ceased also to be its protection and became instead the secure base for every successive invader. The inroad of Alexander brought home the magnitude of the danger to the political mind of India and from this time we see poets, writers, political thinkers constantly upholding the imperial ideal or thinking out the means of its realisation. The immediate practical result was the rise of the empire founded with remarkable swiftness by the statesmanship of Chanakya and constantly maintained or restored through eight or nine centuries, in spite of periods of weakness and incipient disintegration, successively by the Maurya, Sunga, Kanwa, Andhra and Gupta dynasties. The history of this empire, its remarkable organisation, administration, public works, opulence, magnificent culture and the vigour, the brilliance, the splendid fruitfulness of the life of the peninsula under its shelter emerges only from scattered insufficient records, but even so it ranks among the greatest constructed and maintained by the genius of the earth's great peoples. India has no reason, from this point of view, to be anything but proud of her ancient achievement in empire-building or to submit to the hasty verdict that denies to her antique civilisation a strong practical genius or high political virtue.

At the same time this empire suffered by the inevitable haste, violence and artificiality of its first construction to meet a pressing need, because that prevented it from being the deliberate, natural and steady evolution in the old solid Indian manner of the truth of her deepest ideal. The attempt to establish a centralised imperial monarchy brought with it not a free synthesis but a breaking down of regional autonomies. Although according to the Indian principle their institutes and customs were respected and at first even their political institutions not wholly annulled, at any rate in many cases, but brought within the imperial system, these could not really flourish under the shadow of the imperial centralisation. The free peoples of the ancient Indian world began to disappear, their broken materials serving afterwards to create the now existing Indian races. And I think it can be concluded on the whole that although for a long time the great popular assemblies continued to remain in vigour, their function in the end tended to become more mechanical and their vitality to decline and suffer. The urban republics too tended to become more and more mere municipalities of the organised kingdom or empire. The habits of mind created by the imperial centralisation and the weakening or disappearance of the more dignified free popular institutions of the past created a sort of spiritual gap, on one side of which were the administered content with any government that gave them security and did not interfere too much with their religion, life and customs and on the other the imperial administration beneficent and splendid, no doubt, but no longer that living head of a free and living people contemplated by the earlier and the true political mind of India. These results became prominent and were final only with the decline, but they were there in seed and rendered almost inevitable by the adoption of a mechanical method of unification. The advantages gained were those of a stronger and more coherent military action and a more regularised and uniform administration, but these could not compensate in the end for the impairment of the free organic diversified life which was the true expression of the mind and temperament of the people.

A worse result was a certain fall from the high ideal of the Dharma. In the struggle of kingdom with kingdom for supremacy, a habit of Machiavellian statecraft replaced the nobler ethical ideals of the past, aggressive ambition was left without any sufficient spiritual or moral check and there was a coarsening of the national mind in the ethics of politics and government already evidenced in the draconic penal legislation of the

Maurya times and in Asoka's sanguinary conquest of Orissa. The deterioration, held in abeyance by a religious spirit and high intelligence, did not come to a head till more than a thousand years afterwards and we only see it in its full force in the worst period of the decline when unrestrained mutual aggression, the unbridled egoism of princes and leaders, a total lack of political principle and capacity for effective union, the want of a common patriotism and the traditional indifference of the common people to a change of rulers gave the whole of the vast peninsula into the grasp of a handful of merchants from across the seas. But however tardy the worst results in their coming and however redeemed and held in check at first by the political greatness of the empire and a splendid intellectual and artistic culture and by frequent spiritual revivals, India had already lost by the time of the later Guptas the chance of a natural and perfect flowering of her true mind and inmost spirit in the political life of her peoples.

Meanwhile the empire served well enough, although not perfectly, the end for which it was created, the saving of Indian soil and Indian civilisation from that immense flood of barbarian unrest which threatened all the ancient stabilised cultures and finally proved too strong for the highly developed Graeco-Roman civilisation and the vast and powerful Roman empire. That unrest throwing great masses of Teutons, Slavs, Huns and Scythians to west and east and south battered at the gates of India for many centuries, effected certain inroads, but, when it sank, left the great edifice of Indian civilisation standing and still firm, great and secure. The irruptions took place whenever the empire grew weak and this seems to have happened whenever the country was left for some time secure. The empire was weakened by the suspension of the need which created it, for then the regional spirit reawoke in separatist movements disintegrating its unity or breaking down its large extension over all the North. A fresh peril brought about the renewal of its strength under a new dynasty, but the phenomenon continued to repeat itself until, the peril ceasing for a considerable time, the empire called into existence to meet it passed away not to revive. It left behind it a certain number of great kingdoms in the east, south and centre and a more confused mass of peoples in the north-west, the weak point at which the Mussulmans broke in and in a brief period rebuilt in the North, but in another, a Central Asiatic type, the ancient empire.

These earlier foreign invasions and their effects have to be seen in their true proportions, which are often disturbed by the exaggerated theories of oriental scholars. The invasion of Alexander was an eastward impulsion of Hellenism that had a work to do in western and central Asia, but no future in India. Immediately ejected by Chandragupta, it left no traces. The entrance of the Graeco-Bactrians which took place during the weakness of the later Mauryas and was annulled by the reviving strength of the empire, was that of a Hellenised people already profoundly influenced by Indian culture. The later Parthian, Hun and Scythian invasions were of a more serious character and for a time seemed dangerous to the integrity of India. In the end however they affected powerfully only the Punjab, although they threw their waves farther south along the western coast and dynasties of a foreign extraction may have been established for a time far down towards the south. To what degree the racial character of these parts was affected, is far from certain. Oriental scholars and ethnologists have imagined that the Punjab was scythianised, that the Rajputs are of the same stock and that even farther south the race was changed by the intrusion. These speculations are founded upon scanty or no evidence and are contradicted by other theories, and it is highly doubtful whether the barbarian invaders could have come in such numbers as to produce so considerable a consequence. It is farther rendered improbable by the fact that in one or two or three generations the invaders were entirely Indianised, assumed completely the

Indian religion, manners, customs, culture and melted into the mass of the Indian peoples. No such phenomenon took place as in the countries of the Roman empire, of barbarian tribes imposing on a superior civilisation their laws, political system, barbaric customs, alien rule. This is the common significant fact of these irruptions and it must have been due to one or all of three factors. The invaders may have been armies rather than peoples: the occupation was not a continuous external rule which had time to stiffen in its foreign character, for each was followed by a revival of the strength of the Indian empire and its return upon the conquered provinces: and finally the powerfully vital and absorbing character of Indian culture was too strong to allow of any mental resistance to assimilation in the intruders. At any rate if these irruptions were of a very considerable character, Indian civilisation must be considered to have proved itself much more sound, more vital and more solid than the younger Graeco-Roman which went down before the Teuton and the Arab or survived only underneath and in a debased form heavily barbarised, broken and unrecognisable. And the Indian empire too must be pronounced to have proved after all more efficacious than was the Roman with all its vaunt of solidity and greatness, for it succeeded, even if pierced in the west, in preserving the security of the great mass of the peninsula.

It is a later downfall, the Mussulman conquest failing in the hands of the Arabs but successfully reattempted after a long interval, and all that followed it which serves to justify the doubt thrown on the capacity of the Indian peoples. But first let us put aside certain misconceptions which cloud the real issue. This conquest took place at a time when the vitality of ancient Indian life and culture after two thousand years of activity and creation was already exhausted for a time or very near exhaustion and needed a breathing space to rejuvenate itself by transference from the Sanskrit to the popular tongues and the newly forming regional peoples. The conquest was effected rapidly enough in the north, although not entirely complete there for several centuries, but the south long preserved its freedom as of old against the earlier indigenous empire and there was not so long a distance of time between the extinction of the kingdom of Vijayanagara and the rise of the Mahrattas. The Rajputs maintained their independence until the time of Akbar and his successors and it was in the end partly with the aid of Rajput princes acting as their generals and ministers that the Moghuls completed their sway over the east and the south. And this was again possible because—a fact too often forgotten—the Mussulman domination ceased very rapidly to be a foreign rule. The vast mass of the Mussulmans in the country were and are Indians by race, only a very small admixture of Pathan, Turkish and Moghul blood took place, and even the foreign kings and nobles became almost immediately wholly Indian in mind, life and interest. If the race had really like certain European countries remained for many centuries passive, acquiescent and impotent under an alien sway, that would indeed have been a proof of a great inherent weakness; but the British is the first really continuous foreign rule that has dominated India. The ancient civilisation underwent indeed an eclipse and decline under the weight of a Central Asiatic religion and culture with which it failed to coalesce, but it survived its pressure, put its impact on it in many directions and remained to our own day alive even in decadence and capable of recovery, thus giving a proof of strength and soundness rare in the history of human cultures. And in the political field it never ceased to throw up great rulers, statesmen, soldiers, administrators. Its political genius was not in the decadence sufficient, not coherent enough or swift in vision and action, to withstand the Pathan, Moghul and European, but it was strong to survive and await every opportunity of revival, made a bid for empire under Rana Sanga, created the great kingdom of Vijayanagara, held its own for centuries against Islam in the hills of Rajputana, and in its worst days still built and maintained against the whole power of the ablest of the Moghuls the kingdom of Shivaji, formed the Mahratta confederacy and the Sikh Khalsa, undermined the great Moghul structure and again made a last attempt at empire. On the brink of the final and almost fatal collapse in the midst of unspeakable darkness, disunion and confusion it could still produce Ranjit Singh and Nana Fadnavis and Madhoji Scindia and oppose the inevitable march of England's destiny. These facts do not diminish the weight of the charge that can be made of an incapacity to see and solve the central problem and answer the one persistent question of Fate, but considered as the phenomena of a decadence they make a sufficiently remarkable record not easily parallelled under similar circumstances and certainly put a different complexion on the total question than the crude statement that India has been always subject and politically incapable.

The real problem introduced by the Mussulman conquest was not that of subjection to a foreign rule and the ability to recover freedom, but the struggle between two civilisations, one ancient and indigenous, the other mediaeval and brought in from outside. That which rendered the problem insoluble was the attachment of each to a powerful religion, the one militant and aggressive, the other spiritually tolerant indeed and flexible, but obstinately faithful in its discipline to its own principle and standing on the defence behind a barrier of social forms. There were two conceivable solutions, the rise of a greater spiritual principle and formation which could reconcile the two or a political patriotism surmounting the religious struggle and uniting the two communities. The first was impossible in that age. Akbar attempted it on the Mussulman side, but his religion was an intellectual and political rather than a spiritual creation and had never any chance of assent from the strongly religious mind of the two communities. Nanak attempted it from the Hindu side, but his religion, universal in principle, became a sect in practice. Akbar attempted also to create a common political patriotism, but this endeavour too was foredoomed to failure. An autocratic empire built on the Central Asian principle could not create the desired spirit by calling in the administrative ability of the two communities in the person of great men and princes and nobles to a common service in the creation of a united imperial India: the living assent of the people was needed and that remained passive for want of awakening political ideals and institutions. The Mogul empire was a great and magnificent construction and an immense amount of political genius and talent was employed in its creation and maintenance. It was as splendid, powerful and beneficent and, it may be added, in spite of Aurangzeb's fanatical zeal, infinitely more liberal and tolerant in religion than any mediaeval or contemporary European kingdom or empire and India under its rule stood high in military and political strength, economic opulence and the brilliance of its art and culture. But it failed like the empires before it, more disastrously even, and in the same way, crumbling not by external attack but by internal disintegration. A military and administrative centralised empire could not effect India's living political unity. And although a new life seemed about to rise in the regional peoples, the chance was cut short by the intrusion of the European nations and their seizure of the opportunity created by the failure of the Peshwas and the desperate confusion of the succeeding anarchy and decadence.

Two remarkable creations embodied in the period of disintegration the last effort of the Indian political mind to form the foundations of a new life under the old conditions, but neither proved to be of a kind that could solve the problem. The Mahratta revival inspired by Ramdas's conception of the Maharashtra Dharma and cast into shape by Shivaji was an attempt to restore what could still be understood or remembered of the ancient form and spirit, but it failed, as all attempts to revive the past must fail, in spite of the spiritual impetus and the democratic forces that assisted its inception. The Peshwas for all their genius lacked the vision of the founder and could only establish a military and political confederacy. And their endeavour to found an empire could not succeed because it was inspired by a regional patriotism that failed to enlarge itself beyond its own limits and awaken to the living ideal of a united India. The Sikh Khalsa on the other hand was an astonishingly original and novel creation and its face was turned not to the past but the future. Apart and singular in its theocratic head and democratic soul and structure, its profound spiritual beginning, its first attempt to combine the deepest elements of Islam and Vedanta, it was a premature drive towards an entrance into the third or spiritual stage of human society, but it could not create between the spirit and the external life the transmitting medium of a rich creative thought and culture. And thus hampered and deficient it began and ended within narrow local limits, achieved intensity but no power of expansion. The conditions were not then in existence that could have made possible a successful endeavour.

Afterwards came the night and a temporary end of all political initiative and creation. The lifeless attempt of the last generation to imitate and reproduce with a servile fidelity the ideals and forms of the West has been no true indication of the political mind and genius of the Indian people. But again amid all the mist of confusion there is still the possibility of a new twilight, not of an evening but a morning *yuga-sandhyā*. India of the ages is not dead nor has she spoken her last creative word; she lives and has still something to do for herself and the human peoples. And that which must seek now to awake is not an Anglicised oriental people, docile pupil of the West and doomed to repeat the cycle of the occident's success and failure, but still the ancient immemorable Shakti recovering her deepest self, lifting her head higher towards the supreme source of light and strength and turning to discover the complete meaning and a vaster form of her Dharma.

APPENDIX

INDIAN CULTURE AND EXTERNAL INFLUENCE

In considering Indian civilisation and its renascence, I suggested that a powerful new creation in all fields was our great need, the meaning of the renascence and the one way of preserving the civilisation. Confronted with the huge rush of modern life and thought, invaded by another dominant civilisation almost her opposite or inspired at least with a very different spirit to her own, India can only survive by confronting this raw, new, aggressive, powerful world with fresh diviner creations of her own spirit, cast in the mould of her own spiritual ideals. She must meet it by solving its greater problems,—which she cannot avoid, even if such avoidance could be thought desirable,—in her own way, through solutions arising out of her own being and from her own deepest and largest knowledge. In that connection I spoke of the acceptance and assimilation from the West of whatever in its knowledge, ideas, powers was assimilable, compatible with her spirit, reconcilable with her ideals, valuable for a new statement of life. This question of external influence and new creation from within is of very considerable importance; it calls for more than a passing mention. Especially it is necessary to form some more precise idea of what we mean by acceptance and of the actual effect of assimilation; for this is a problem of pressing incidence in which we have to get our ideas clear and fix firmly and seeingly on our line of solution.

But it is possible to hold that while new creation—and not a motionless sticking to old forms—is our one way of life and salvation, no acceptance of anything western is called for, we can find in ourselves all that we need; no considerable acceptance is possible without creating a breach which will bring pouring in the rest of the occidental deluge. That, if I have not misread it, is the sense of a comment on these articles in a Bengali literary periodical* which holds up the ideal of a new creation to arise from within entirely on national lines and in the national spirit. The writer takes his stand on a position which is common ground, that humanity is one, but different peoples are variant soul-forms of the common humanity. When we find the oneness, the principle of variation is not destroyed but finds rather its justification; it is not by abolishing ourselves, our own special temperament and power, that we can get at the living oneness, but by following it out and raising it to its highest possibilities of freedom and action. That is a truth which I have myself insisted on repeatedly, with regard to the modern idea and attempt at some kind of political unification of humanity, as a very important part of the psychological sense of social development, and again in this question of a particular people's life and culture in all its parts and manifestations. I have insisted that uniformity is not a real but a dead unity: uniformity kills life while real unity, if well founded, becomes vigorous and fruitful by a rich energy of variation. But the writer adds that the idea of taking over what is best in occidental civilisation, is a false notion without a living meaning; to leave the bad and take the good sounds very well, but this bad and this good are not separable in that way: they are the inextricably mingled growth of one being, not separate blocks of a child's toy house set side by side and easily detachable,—and what is meant then by cutting out and taking one element and leaving the rest? If we take over a western ideal, we take it over from a living form which strikes us; we imitate that form, are subjugated by its spirit and natural tendencies, and the good and bad intertwined in the living growth come in upon us together and take united possession. In fact, we have been for a long time so imitating the West, trying to become like it or partly like it and have fortunately failed, for that would have meant creating a bastard or twy-natured culture; but twy-natured, as Tennyson makes his Lucretius say, is no-natured and a bastard culture is no sound, truth-living culture. An entire return upon ourselves is our only way of salvation.

There is much to be said here, it seems to me, both in the way of confirmation and of modification. But let us be clear about the

* *Narayan*, edited by Mr. C. R. Das

meaning of our terms. That the attempt in the last century which still in some directions continues,—to imitate European civilisation and to make ourselves a sort of brown Englishmen, to throw our ancient culture into the dust-bin and put on the livery or uniform of the West was a mistaken and illegitimate endeavour, I heartily agree. At the same time a certain amount of imitation, a great amount even, was, one might almost say, a biological necessity, at any rate a psychological necessity of the situation. Not only when a lesser meets a greater culture, but when a culture which has fallen into a state of comparative inactivity, sleep, contraction, is faced with, still more when it receives the direct shock of a waking, active, tremendously creative civilisation, finds thrown upon it novel and successful powers and functionings, sees an immense succession and development of new ideas and formations, it is impelled by the very instinct of life to take over these ideas and forms, to annex, to enrich itself, even to imitate and reproduce, and in one way or in another take large account and advantage of these new forces and opportunities. That is a phenomenon which has happened repeatedly in history, in a greater or a lesser degree, in part or in totality. But if there is only a mechanical imitation, if there is a subordination and servitude, the inactive or weaker culture perishes, it is swallowed up by the invading leviathan. And even short of that, in proportion as there is a leaning towards these undesirable things, it languishes, is unsuccessful in its attempt at annexation, loses besides the power of its own spirit. To recover its own centre, find its own base and do whatever it has to do in its own strength and genius is certainly the one way of salvation. But even then a certain amount of acceptance, of forms too,—some imitation, if all taking over of forms must be called imitation,—is inevitable. We have, for instance, taken over in literature the form of the novel, the short story, the critical essay among a number of other adoptions, in science not only the discoveries and inventions, but the method and instrumentation of inductive research, in politics the press, the platform, the forms and habits of agitation, the public association. I do not suppose that anyone seriously thinks of renouncing or exiling these modern additions to our life,—though they are not all of them by any means unmixed blessings,—on the ground that they are foreign importations. But the question is what we do with them and whether we can bring them to be instruments and by some characteristic modification moulds of our own spirit. If so, there has been an acceptance and an assimilation; if not there has been merely a helpless imitation.

But the taking over of forms is not the heart of the question. When I speak of acceptance and assimilation, I am thinking of certain influences, ideas, energies brought forward with a great living force by Europe, which can awaken and enrich our own cultural activities and cultural being if we succeed in dealing with them with a victorious power and originality, if we can bring them into our characteristic way of being and transform them by its shaping action. That was in fact what our own ancestors did, never losing their originality, never effacing their uniqueness, because always vigorously creating from within, with whatever knowledge or artistic suggestion from outside they thought worthy of acceptance or capable of an Indian treatment. But I would certainly repel the formula of taking the good and leaving the bad as a crudity, one of those facile formulas which catch the superficial mind but are unsound in conception. Obviously, if we "take over" anything, the good and the bad in it will come in together pell-mell. If we take over for instance that terrible, monstrous and compelling thing, that giant Asuric creation, European industrialism,—unfortunately we are being forced by circumstances to do it,—whether we take it in its form or its principle, we may under more favourable conditions develop by it our wealth and economic resources, but assuredly we shall get too its social discords and moral plagues and cruel problems, and I do not see how we shall avoid becoming the slaves of the economic aim in life and losing the spiritual principle of our culture.

But, besides, these terms good and bad in this connection mean nothing definite, give us no help. If I must use them, where they can have only a relative significance, in a matter not of ethics, but of an interchange between life and life, I must first give them this general significance that whatever helps me to find myself more intimately, nobly, with a greater and sounder possibility of self-expressive creation, is good; whatever carries me out of my orientation, whatever weakens and belittles my power, richness, breadth and height of self-being, is bad for me. If the distinction is so understood, it will be evident, I think, to any serious and critical mind which tries to fathom things, that the real point is not the taking over of this or that formal detail, which has only a sign value, for example, widow remarriage, but a dealing with great effective ideas, such as are the ideas, in the external field of life, of social and political liberty, equality, democracy. If I accept any of these ideas it is not because they are modern or European, which is in itself no recommendation, but because they are human, because they present fruitful view-points to the spirit, because they are things of the greatest importance in the future development of the life of man. What I mean by acceptance of the effective idea of democracy,–the thing itself, never fully worked out, was present as an element in ancient Indian as in ancient European polity and society,–is that I find its inclusion in our future way of living, in some shape, to be a necessity of our growth. What I mean by assimilation, is that we must not take it crudely in the European forms, but must go back to whatever corresponds to it, illumines its sense, justifies its highest purport in our own spiritual conception of life and existence, and in that light work out its extent, degree, form, relation to other ideas, application. To everything I would apply the same principle, to each in its own kind, after its proper dharma, in its right measure of importance, its spiritual, intellectual, ethical, aesthetic, dynamic utility.

I take it as a self-evident law of individual being applicable to group-individuality, that it is neither desirable nor possible to exclude everything that comes in to us from outside. I take it as an equally self-evident law that a living organism, which grows not by accretion, but by self-development and assimilation, must recast the things it takes in to suit the law and form and characteristic action of its biological or psychological body, reject what would be deleterious or poisonous to it,–and what is that but the non-assimilable?–take only what can be turned into useful stuff of self-expression. It is, to use an apt Sanskritic phrase employed in the Bengali tongue, *ātmasātkaraṇa,* an assimilative appropriation, a making the thing settle into oneself and turn into characteristic form of our self-being. The impossibility of entire rejection arises from the very fact of our being a term of diversity in a unity, not really separate from all other existence, but in relation with all that surrounds us, because in life this relation expresses itself very largely by a process of interchange. The undesirability of total rejection, even if it were entirely possible, arises from the fact that interchange with the environment is necessary to a healthy persistence and growth; the living organism which rejects all such interchange, would speedily languish and die of lethargy and inanition.

Mentally, vitally and physically I do not grow by a pure self-development from within in a virgin isolation; I am not a separate self-existent being proceeding from a past to a new becoming in a world of its own where no one is but itself, nothing works but its own inner powers and musings. There is in every individualised existence a double action, a self-development from within which is its greatest intimate power of being and by which it is itself, and a reception of impacts from outside which it has to accommodate to its own individuality and make into material of self-growth and self-power. The two operations are not mutually exclusive, nor is the second harmful to the first except when the inner genius is too weak to deal victoriously with its environmental world; on the contrary the reception of impacts stimulates in a vigorous and healthy being its force for self-development and is an aid to a greater and more pronouncedly characteristic self-determination. As we rise in the scale we find that the power of original development from within, of conscious self-determination increases more and more, while in those who live most powerfully in themselves it reaches striking, sometimes almost divine proportions. But at the same time we see that the allied power of seizing upon the impacts and suggestions of the outside world grows in proportion; those who live most powerfully in themselves, can also most largely use the world and all its material for the Self,—and, it must be added, most successfully help the world and enrich it out of their own being. The man who most finds and lives from the inner self, can most embrace the universal and become one with it; the *Svarāṭ*, independent, self-possessed and self-ruler, can most be the *Samrāṭ*, possessor and shaper of the world in which he lives, can most too grow one with all in the Atman. That is the truth this developing existence teaches us, and it is one of the greatest secrets of the old Indian spiritual knowledge.

Therefore to live in one's self, determining one's self-expression from one's own centre of being in accordance with one's own law of being, *svadharma*, is the first necessity. Not to be able to do that means disintegration of the life; not to do it sufficiently means languor, weakness, inefficiency, the danger of being oppressed by the environing forces and overborne; not to be able to do it wisely, intuitively, with a strong use of one's inner material and inner powers, means confusion, disorder and finally decline and loss of vitality. But also not to be able to use the material that the life around offers us, not to lay hold on it with an intuitive selection and a strong mastering assimilation is a serious deficiency and a danger to the existence. To a healthy individuality the external impact or entering energy, idea, influence may act as an irritant awakening the inner being to a sense of discord, incompatibility or peril, and then there is a struggle, an impulse and process of rejection; but even in this struggle, in this process of rejection there is some resultant of change and growth, some increment of the power and material of life; the energies of the being are stimulated and helped by the attack. It may act as a stimulus, awakening a new action of the self-consciousness and a sense of fresh possibility,—by comparison, by suggestion, by knocking at locked doors and arousing slumbering energies. It may come in as a possible material which has then to be reshaped to a form of the inner energy, harmonised with the inner being, reinterpreted in the light of its own characteristic self-consciousness. In a great change of environment or a close meeting with a mass of invading influences all these processes work together and there is possibly much temporary perplexity and difficulty, many doubtful and perilous movements, but also the opportunity of a great self-developing transformation or an immense and vigorous renascence.

The group-soul differs from the individual only in being more self-sufficient by reason of its being an assemblage of many individual selves and capable within of many group variations. There is a constant inner interchange which may for a long time suffice to maintain the vitality, growth, power of developing activity, even when there is a restricted interchange with the rest of humanity. Greek civilisation,—after growing under the influence of Egyptian, Phoenician and other Oriental influences,—separated itself sharply from the non-Hellenic "barbarian" cultures and was able for some centuries to live within itself by a rich variation and internal interchange. There was the same phenomenon in ancient India of a culture living intensely from within in a profound differentiation from all surrounding cultures, its vitality rendered possible by an even greater richness of internal interchange and variation. Chinese civilisation offers a third instance. But at no time did Indian culture exclude altogether external influences; on the contrary a very great power of selective assimilation, subordination and transformation of external elements was a characteristic of its processes; it protected itself from any considerable or overwhelming invasion, but laid hands on and included whatever struck or impressed it and in the act of inclusion subjected it to a characteristic change which harmonised the new element with the spirit of its own culture. But nowadays any such strong separative aloofness as distinguished the ancient civilisations, is no longer possible; the races of mankind have come too close to each other, are being thrown together in a certain unavoidable life unity. We are confronted with the more difficult problem of living in the full stress of this greater interaction and imposing on its impacts the law of our being.

Any attempt to remain exactly what we were before the European invasion or to ignore in future the claims of a modern environment and necessity is foredoomed to an obvious failure. However much we may deplore some of the characteristics of that intervening period in which we were dominated by the Western standpoint or move away from the standpoint back to our own characteristic way of seeing existence, we cannot get rid of a certain element of inevitable change it has produced upon us, any more than a man can go back in life to what he was some years ago and recover entire and unaffected a past mentality. Time and its influences have not only passed over him, but carried him forward in their stream. We cannot go backward to a past form of our being, but we can go forward to a large repossession of ourselves in which we shall make a better, more living, more real, more self-possessed use of the intervening experience. We can still think in the essential sense of the great spirit and ideals of our past, but the form of our thinking, our speaking, our development of them has changed by the very fact of new thought and experience; we see them not only in the old, but in new lights, we support them by the added strength of new view-points, even the old words we use acquire for us a modified, more extended and richer significance. Again, we cannot be "ourselves alone" in any narrow formal sense, because we must necessarily take account of the modern world around us and get full knowledge of it, otherwise we cannot live. But all such taking account of things, all added knowledge modifies our subjective being. My mind, with all that depends on it, is modified by what it observes and works upon, modified when it takes in from it fresh materials of thought, modified when it is wakened by its stimulus to new activities, modified even when it denies and rejects; for even an old thought or truth which I affirm against an opposing idea, becomes a new thought to me in the effort of affirmation and rejection, clothes itself with new aspects and issues. My life is modified in the same way by the life influences it has to encounter and confront. Finally, we cannot avoid dealing with the great governing ideas and problems of the modern world. The modern world is still mainly European, a world dominated by the European mind and western civilisation. We claim to set right this undue preponderance, to reassert the Asiatic and, for ourselves, the Indian mind and to preserve and develop the great values of Asiatic and of Indian civilisation. But the Asiatic or the Indian mind can only assert itself successfully by meeting these problems and by giving them a solution which will justify its own ideals and spirit.

The principle I have affirmed results both from the necessity of our nature and the necessity of things, of life,—fidelity to our own spirit, nature, ideals, the creation of our own characteristic forms in the new age and the new environment, but also a strong and masterful dealing with external influences which need not be and in the nature of the situation cannot be a total rejection; therefore there must be an element of successful assimilation. There remains the very difficult question of the application of the principle,—the degree, the way, the guiding perceptions. To think that out we must look at each province of culture and, keeping always firm hold on a perception of what the Indian spirit is and the Indian ideal is, see how they can work upon the present situation and possibilities in each of these provinces and lead to a new victorious creation. In such thinking it will not do to be too dogmatic. Each capable Indian mind must think it out or, better, work it out in its own light and power,—as the Bengal artists are working it out in their own sphere,—and contribute some illumination or effectuation. The spirit of the Indian renascence will take care of the rest, that power of the universal Time-Spirit which has begun to move in our midst for the creation of a new and greater India.